MEDIEVALISM AND THE IDEOLOGIES
OF THE ENLIGHTENMENT

The World and Work of La Curne de Sainte-Palaye

MEDIEVALISM AND THE IDEOLOGIES OF THE ENLIGHTENMENT

The World and Work of La Curne de Sainte-Palaye

BY

Lionel Gossman

THE JOHNS HOPKINS PRESS
BALTIMORE, MARYLAND

In Memory of
Ludwig Edelstein

INTRODUCTION

Increasingly in recent years the attention of historians has shifted from the history of ideas to social history. Present-day historians are likely to be less concerned with what the British scholar Kitson Clark has called "that self-conscious, self-confident minority who seem to have made history, whose voices, unless we are careful, are the only ones we are likely to hear from the past" than with ephemeral sources of opinion, documents of popular life and culture, not to say social and economic statistics. Those of us who are interested in the eighteenth century are now keenly aware that the movement of ideas loosely described as the Enlightenment concerned only a small fraction of the population even of the advanced countries of Europe. The peasants, the humblest laborers, the poor, that vast majority which in France was referred to contemptuously, particularly by a bourgeoisie eager to distinguish itself from it, as *le peuple*, made almost no direct contribution to the ideologies of the Enlightenment. Indeed the Enlightenment seems, in some respects, to have been carried through *against* it. Now, in our own day, this vast *terra incognita of* eighteenth-century popular culture has begun to be explored.

But even in the limited spheres of the influential, the educated and the well-to-do, the Enlightenment was infinitely varied and no one can possibly see it as an unbroken thread leading from the ideas of some outstanding thinkers at the beginning of the century to the French Revolution at the end. In each country—and there was Enlightenment not only in England, France, and Germany, but in Italy, in Spain, in Poland, in Russia, in the Austrian Empire, in the Scandinavian countries, in the Americas—it assumed a particular form and developed a particular history, and within each country different groups in the upper strata of society elaborated often conflicting theories and programs, most of which are nonetheless recognizably part of Enlightenment and contribute to an extremely complex whole. The Enlightenment as we can now envisage it is more like a language than a single idea, imposing by its very nature certain modes of thought on those who use it, while remaining always at the same time the expression, in any actual usage, of particular desires and meanings and a response to particular conditions. Thus, in France there occurred an adaptation and adjustment of almost all the leading political traditions and ideologies to the language and modes of thought of the Enlightenment, the latter being themselves, no doubt, predominantly "bourgeois" in their emphasis on the here and now and on the rational analysis and organization of the human environment. There seems, indeed, to have been an enlightened "parlementarism," as there was an "enlightened despotism" in the century of the *Encyclopédie*.

The present study of medieval scholarship in eighteenth-century France and of its leading practitioner, La Curne de Sainte-Palaye, will, I hope, contribute to a varied program of investigation which is already disclosing, even on the limited level of the history of ideas, a much richer pattern than was suspected by many earlier historians. The research was begun over a decade ago in preparation for a Doctor of Philosophy dissertation at Oxford under the direction of Professor Jean Seznec. From the original presentation, I have retained the basic idea of combining history of ideas with biography and social history but, instead of treating these as adjacent areas of study in the traditional "Life and Work" manner, I have tried to work them out in their interrelations. This approach brings with it a number of difficulties. The attempt to interpret the ideas of the Enlightenment in their social context raises the thorny problem of how the social groups in the *ancien régime* are to be defined and what terms are to be applied to them. Anyone who has not been trained as a social historian can expect to encounter pitfalls as he ventures on to a terrain, the chart of which is only now being drawn—and constantly redrawn—by returning travelers. I too have undoubtedly stumbled, but I have sought to use common terms as clearly and consistently as I could.

It was already suggested at the end of the eighteenth century and is now widely accepted that the traditional categories of nobility, clergy, and third estate are virtually useless as tools of social analysis. In the following pages I do not consider the clergy at all as a separate social group. It was, in fact, divided by the same class differences as the rest of society. The bishops were mostly from noble families—increasingly so in the eighteenth century—and their outlook was often that of the social class from which they sprang and with which they remained associated; the differences in theology and ecclesiastical policy which still divided them in the first decades of the century were all but forgotten as their ranks became more and more exclusively noble. The lower clergy, and notably the parish priests, were of humbler origin, lived in close proximity to the peasantry and to the poor, and shared to a considerable degree the anxieties and the aspirations of those whom they served. In interest and outlook the princes of the Church were often as far from its humbler ministers as the Court and the aristocracy were from the *peuple*.

The nobility is a vague term, but it is hard to do without it. Historians sometimes draw or imply a distinction between nobility and aristocracy, the former serving to define the *noblesse d'épée*, those entitled to the *honneurs de la cour* on genealogical grounds, for instance, while the latter refers to the totality of the wealthy, privileged classes, including the *robe* and the large group of *anoblis*, ex-members of the bourgeoisie, whose titles had been recently acquired by one form or another of purchase or, on occasion, as a reward for services to the Crown (themselves usually of a pecuniary nature). I have, on the whole, followed this usage; I should add, however, that I would include among the nobility those whose elevation from the bourgeoisie occurred in a relatively remote past (it seems that very few nobles in France were "de noblesse immémoriale ou de race"), while I do not usually mean to refer to the impoverished nobility of certain provinces, the *hoberaux*. A few die-hards still thought of the *robe* as bourgeois in the eighteenth century, but it seems on the whole appropriate to distinguish at least the *grande robe*—the magistracy and urban patriciate—from the bourgeoisie. In what follows I mean by *robe* and *robin* the holders and possessors—or their heirs—of charges or offices in the so-called sovereign courts (*parlements, cours des aides, chambres des comptes, chambres des requêtes,* etc.), although I also use the term to describe the *petite robe* or holders of minor legal and administrative offices (*receveurs des tailles, lieutenants civils* and *criminels,* etc.), who are admittedly part of the bourgeoisie.

Likewise the *tiers* must be abandoned as a useful social category.

I prefer to use the term bourgeois, which, although still fairly indeterminate, has at least the merit of sharply distinguishing the relatively small, more or less cultured and well-to-do upper layer of the so-called *tiers*—those engaged in banking, commerce, trade, and the professions, or living off income from bonds and investments—from the *peuple*—the peasants and working people who made up about 90 per cent of the French population. I also use the term bourgeois to refer to the mentality or *Weltanschauung* which has been associated with this class in the works of Sombart, Weber, and Groethuysen, among others. I am well aware, however, that between the "aristocracy" and a certain fraction of the "bourgeoisie" in the last century of the *ancien régime*, it is almost impossible to draw a clear line.

The approach I have followed also raises problems of presentation which are not easy to resolve and which make it difficult to achieve formal elegance and limpidity. They were aggravated in this instance by the fact that Sainte-Palaye's life is relatively uneventful and that as an individual, although he mixed in the same world as Madame du Deffand and Horace Walpole, he seems not to have been particularly interesting; at least he has left no record of an interesting personality, his letters, while pleasant and human enough, being mostly communications with other scholars. It is thus less his individual significance than his social significance that is of interest to us today and that I have attempted to define.

In the first part of the book, therefore, I have tried to set Sainte-Palaye in his milieu and to establish the character of this milieu by examining his family background, social position, education and travels, by showing who were his early mentors, who the friends and colleagues of his maturity, and by determining what clusters of ideas were dominant in the circles he frequented, what points of tension and contention might have disturbed them and in particular where they stood in relation to the *philosophes*. In this way I hoped to indicate the framework of ideas, attitudes, prejudices, commitments, conflicts, and interests in which Sainte-Palaye's work was carried out. Sainte-Palaye himself has thus been approached indirectly by a series of forays into the territories where he passed, and it is a certain world rather than an individual which is in many ways the principal subject of this part of the book—the world of the eighteenth-century scholars, the majority of whom, like Sainte-Palaye himself, were members or children of robe families.

In the second part of the book I have outlined the nature of the evolving historiographical tradition in which Sainte-Palaye was trained and to which he later contributed. In particular, I have tried to show that both he himself and the Académie des Inscriptions, at which he played an important part, were fully alive to the latest critical methods, eager to carry them forward, and determined to renovate historical scholarship along the lines accepted by most Enlightenment thinkers. I have also tried to indicate that Sainte-Palaye's interest in the Middle Ages was neither unusual nor precocious but was shared by many other persons of his social class and upbringing in particular and reflects their concern with current political problems and their acceptance of the outlook of the early Enlighteners.

The third part of the book deals with the main areas of Sainte-Palaye's activity and with his principal works. The encyclopaedic tradition of the Renaissance was still strong in the eighteenth century, especially in the magistracy with its proud Renaissance associations, and the humanist man of letters, active in many fields, had not yet been supplanted by the specialist scholar. In the vast and still fairly intact territory of medieval studies the encyclopaedic scholar was particularly at home, for the investigation of any single field required not only that the scholar be ready to branch out into many related fields, but that he be able to forge his own instruments of research. The development of the techniques and the tools of research was at this stage virtually identical with the research itself. Indeed, what is most impressive about Sainte-Palaye's work, and what most impressed his own contemporaries, is its sheer scope. He was not alone in studying the Middle Ages, but no one in the eighteenth century in France had covered the ground that he had covered. Inevitably a good deal of this third part of the book is taken up with following him into numerous territories, each of which is now ruled over by specialists and sub-specialists: the various branches of language study, the study of Old French and of Provençal literature, criticism of manuscripts and the establishment of sound texts, the collection and evaluation of the sources—manuscript and printed, chronicle and documentary—of medieval history, the drawing up of catalogues of the principal depots of manuscripts and printed works, the study of antiquities and of institutions, of the material and the mental products of men in the past.

Two problems were raised by the great extent of the material which had to be dealt with in this part of the book. The first was one of selection. While some readers would want to know as much as possible about Sainte-Palaye's methods of editing early texts or about his lexicographical work, for instance, and would desire the references to be as complete and as exact as I could make them, others would doubtless be thankful to be spared these details and to be informed as briefly as possible of what had been achieved in each field, judging that the important thing was to determine the governing ideas or modes of thought which gave unity to so many different activities. I have tried, as far as possible, to satisfy the first category of readers, since I consider that in a case such as this, where not much is known, the presentation of the material is as important as the interpretation put upon it. At the same time I could not and did not wish to abdicate the responsibility of interpretation, and this was the source of the second problem. For if it is by no means easy to present material in so many different fields, being a specialist in none of them, it is even less easy to interpret it. I do not imagine I shall have avoided the traps that await the temerarious. I can only hope that my lapses have not been too frequent.

The last two chapters of this part of the book, and in particular the chapter devoted to the *Mémoires sur l'ancienne chevalerie*, tie together a good deal of what is contained in Parts I and II as well as in the preceding chapters of Part III for, as they are not a work of compilation, however intelligently pursued, but a work of synthesis and interpretation, the *Mémoires* reveal in their form as well as in their content, in their method as well as in their subject matter, more clearly than anything else that Sainte-Palaye did, his most fundamental attitudes, assumptions, and aims, and it is these that I have tried to lay bare by a close analysis of this book.

Sainte-Palaye's work must be looked at not only in terms of the ideas about society and institutions which underlie it, but also as part of a wider cultural context in which its meaning and influence were constantly shifting according to the needs and interests of readers. This we have done in the first of two concluding chapters.

Sainte-Palaye turns out to have been at the center of an extremely varied literature on medieval themes in France in the eighteenth century and to have been a leading source for late eighteenth- and nineteenth-century scholars and historians concerned with the Middle Ages and, indeed, with earlier cultures in general, not only in France but in England and to some degree in Germany. His picture of chivalry, in particular, became common coin in the early nineteenth century and was taken over by many novelists and poets. Even the brief outline given in this chapter reveals that Sainte-Palaye's work underwent successive transformations as it was brought within the framework of ideas and feelings of post-Revolutionary and early industrial Europe: medievalism and the Middle Ages turn out to have been quite different things at different times and in different places, because they were in each case part of a particular structure of meanings. It seemed appropriate, therefore, to conclude this chapter with a discussion of Sainte-Palaye's own medievalism and of eighteenth-century medievalism in general in relation to the admittedly complex and shifting framework of ideas and feelings of which they were part.

The final chapter recalls that not only Sainte-Palaye's medievalism but every aspect of his work as a scholar and historian remains bound to the general problems and ways of thinking of the Enlightenment. It is possible to see with Meinecke how historicism is foreshadowed in it, just as it is possible to see how positivist historiography and scholarship are foreshadowed in it, but it did not give rise to either or have to be "perfected" by either. What it became is doubtless part of its reality. In what it was originally, however, it belongs to the Enlightenment.

TABLE OF CONTENTS

PART IV: CONCLUSION: MEDIEVALISM AND ENLIGHTENMENT

ABBREVIATIONS FREQUENTLY USED IN NOTES

Arsenal:	Paris, Bibliothèque de l'Arsenal. Manuscripts.
Besterman:	*Voltaire's Correspondence*, ed. Theodore Besterman. 107 vols. (Geneva, 1953–65).
B.N. Français:	Paris, Bibliothèque Nationale. Manuscripts. Fonds français.
B.N. Nouv. Acq. Fr.:	Paris, Bibliothèque Nationale. Manuscripts. Nouvelles acquisitions françaises.
Bréquigny:	Paris, Bibliothèque Nationale. Manuscripts. Collection Bréquigny.
Br. Mus.:	British Museum.
Corr. litt.:	*Correspondance littéraire de Grimm, Diderot, Raynal, Meister, etc.*, ed. Tourneux. 16 vols. (Paris, 1877–82).
Corr. Pol. Pologne:	Paris, Archives des Affaires Etrangères. Correspondance politique: Pologne.
Hist. litt. troub.:	*Histoire littéraire des troubadours*, 3 vols. Paris, 1774.
MAI:	*Mémoires de l'Académie des Inscriptions.*
MAI*:	*Mémoires de l'Académie des Inscriptions*, partie historique (a volume or part of a volume of the *Mémoires* in which those papers not published in full were summarized).
Moreau:	Paris, Bibliothèque Nationale. Manuscripts. Collection Moreau.
RHLF:	*Revue d'histoire littéraire de la France.*

PART I

AN EIGHTEENTH-CENTURY SCHOLAR
AND HIS WORLD

CHAPTER 1

BACKGROUND AND EDUCATION

Jean-Baptiste de La Curne de Sainte-Palaye, the foremost medievalist in eighteenth-century France, was born at Auxerre in Burgundy
in 1697. His family had followed the classical path by which the
bourgeoisie of the *ancien régime* entered the ranks of the aristocracy. Successful artisans and merchants in the fifteenth and sixteenth
centuries, the Lacurnes or Lacornes of Beaune and Arnay-le-Duc
had begun to raise themselves socially in the late sixteenth and
seventeenth centuries by the acquisition of lands and of royal offices,
especially in the judiciary.[1] They became thereby the most prominent persons in their communities, the most likely to receive royal
favors and excellently placed to usurp titles without risk of contra-

[1] A Lacurne may have been mayor of Beaune in the thirteenth century. (Charles
Bigarne, *Tombes et inscriptions de la Collégiale de Beaune* [Beaune, 1878–79], p.
243, n. 2.) Certainly, by the fifteenth century the Lacurnes were bourgeois and
merchants, according to local tombstone inscriptions. (*Ibid.;* also Charles Bigarne,
'Annales de Vignolles,' *Mémoires de la Société d'histoire, d'archéologie et de lit-
térature de Beaune* [1876], p. 37, n. 1.) A marriage contract of 1609 between an
Étienne Lacurne and an Antoinette Forneret was witnessed by a cousin of the
groom, described as "noble maître Jean Lacurne, receveur des deniers royaux"
(Archives de la Côte d'Or, contrat du 13.10.1609, Lebreth, notaire à Beaune). This
Jean Lacurne, who turns up again as "lieutenant criminel au baillage d'Arnay," left
money to found a college in the town. (P. Papillon, *Bibliothèque des Autheurs de
Bourgogne* [Dijon, 1742], 1:364; and 'Additions et corrections,' p. 9.) He was a
friend of Saumaise, who praised him highly. (Bénigne Saumaise, *Trad. et Comm.
Denys Alexandrin, de la Situation du Monde* [Paris, 1597], p. 121v.) At Arnay, a
Simon Lacurne is described as "honorable homme" (i.e., a lesser bourgeois or
merchant) in a title deed of 1568 and is an alderman of the town in 1566 and 1570.
(Albert Albrier, *Les Maires d'Arnay-le-Duc, 1596–1867* [Dijon, 1868], p. 27.) An
Abraham Lacurne, eleventh mayor of Arnay in 1623, is found in 1625 to be holding
the office of "receveur des impositions au baillage d'Arnay." (*Ibid.*) His children
already have lands and *seigneuries*. One of them, Jean-Baptiste, *écuyer* and *seigneur*
of La Tour and of Thielloy in 1665, was a lieutenant colonel in the infantry; his
son, Henri-Louis, was a sub-lieutenant in the Listenois regiment, in which Sainte-
Palaye's father also saw service. Another son of Abraham Lacurne—Simon—
followed the parliamentary rather than the military road; he had purchased lands,
was an *avocat au parlement*, and was probably Sainte-Palaye's grandfather. (*Ibid.;*
also 'Notes généalogiques' at the Château de Sainte-Palaye, copied from an unsigned article.)

3

diction.[2] Generally the ascending *officier* next had to pass by way of the local *parlement*. But some, especially in the Eastern or frontier provinces, managed to avoid this stage by serving as officers in the army.[3] Service in the royal household was another road to nobility. Sainte-Palaye's father, Edme, who improved the family name to *de La Curne*,[4] was in effect a dragoons officer and then a gentleman-in-waiting to the Duke of Orleans. He was thus certainly in possession of titles of nobility by the time he retired to Auxerre, where the Duke had pensioned him with the modest but comfortable office of *receveur* at the *grenier à sel*, and married Jeanne Brunet, the daughter of a well-to-do family of Beaune,[5] which had already been allied to the Lacurnes.[6] He had by her three daughters and three sons and then, about the turn of the century, he died, leaving Madame Lacurne to bring up the children.[7] Two of the daughters entered the Convent of the Visitation at Auxerre, in 1709 and in 1711,[8] the third married Jacques de Ganay, Chevalier d'honneur of the Chambre des Comptes de Dijon, Bourgogne et Bresse and seigneur de Marault.[9] Of the boys, one—Philibert—seems to have died young.[10] The other two, the twins Jean-Baptiste and Edme—

[2] Cf. Roland Mousnier, *La Vénalité des offices sous Henri IV et Louis XIII* (Rouen, n.d. [1945?]), p. 511.

[3] *Ibid.*, p. 528; also Philippe Sagnac, *La Formation de la société française moderne* (Paris, 1945–46), 1:40.

[4] So it appears, apparently for the first time, on the certificate of baptism of the twins Edme-Germain and Jean-Baptiste. (Archives de l'Yonne, Registres des Baptêmes, Mariages, Enterrements, etc., de la Paroisse de Notre-Dame Là d'Hors d'Auxerre, 6.6.1697.)

[5] The Brunets were mayors of Beaune in the early seventeenth century, and began to acquire offices about the same time as the Lacurnes. ('Remarques sur l'origine et l'ancienneté de la ville de Beaune, par M. de Lacurne,' *Mémoires de la Société d'histoire, d'archéologie et de littérature de Beaune* [1892], pp. 182–84.)

[6] At least once before, in 1657. (H. Forestier, *Répertoires et inventaires de fonds déposés par les notaires de l'Yonne, études de Sampic et Jouvin* [Auxerre, 1942], p. 191.)

[7] A testament of Jean-Baptiste La Curne, chanoine de Notre-Dame de Beaune, drawn up on 17.3.1700, includes legacies to the children of "feu Edme Lacurne, gentilhomme ordinaire de Monsieur." (Archives de l'Yonne, Minutes Guimard, vol. 155, année 1700, pièce 41.)

[8] Archives de l'Yonne, Minutes Jouvin, vol. 109, nos. 132, 136. Probably they had received their education there. The daughters of patrician families were usually educated in convent schools and many remained to take the veil. (François Bluche, *Les Magistrats du Parlement de Paris au XVIIIᵉ siècle, 1715–1771* [Paris, 1960], p. 245. Annales littéraires de l'Université de Besançon, 35).

[9] Archives de l'Yonne, dossier II B. 348.

[10] The testament mentioned above (n. 7) includes a Philibert among the children of Edme Lacurne. He does not, however, figure in the division of the estate of Sainte-Palaye's mother in 1737. (Information on this in papers at Château de Sainte-

baptized in the church of Notre-Dame Là d'Hors at Auxerre on June 6, 1697—remained together for seventy-six years and were separated only by the death of Edme. Their affection was celebrated in an age which regarded fraternal love and friendship as sweeter and more lasting than love between men and women. "Combien de fois," Chamfort recalled in his *Éloge*, "a-t-on vu les deux frères surtout dans leur vieillesse, paraissant aux assemblées publiques, aux promenades, aux concerts, attirer tous les regards, l'attention du respect, quelquefois même les applaudissements!"[11] De Brosses assured Sainte-Palaye that he and his wife were "de vrais Philadelphes," while Voltaire is said to have exclaimed in admiration: "O fratres Helenae lucida sidera."[12]

The education of young patricians was usually entrusted in their earliest years to a tutor, who was carefully briefed and supervised by the child's parents. When the young man was old enough, he was sent to one of the better schools; he was also instructed in the social accomplishments befitting a gentleman. A period of foreign travel often completed this education.[13] Sainte-Palaye's successors at the Académie des Inscriptions and at the Académie Française, tracing his biography in their *Éloges*, emphasized the role of Madame Lacurne in the education of her children, but it is unlikely that she herself was in charge of it. More probably she entrusted it, as was customary, to a tutor, while guiding it with care. At any rate, Sainte-Palaye's education from the age of eight on was that of most members of his social class.

In 1705 he entered the Collège de Juilly, where Richard Simon had taught and Boulainviller had been a student. Montesquieu had just preceded him.[14] The Oratorian Fathers of Juilly were modern-minded men, faithful to the early association of their founder with Descartes and to the rationalism of their own great son and teacher,

---

Palaye, by courtesy of the present proprietor M. le Colonel de Montaudouin.) Nor is he ever mentioned in any of Sainte-Palaye's papers or correspondence.

[11] *Recueil des harangues prononcées par MM. de l'Académie Françoise dans leurs Réceptions* (Paris, 1787), 8:380.

[12] B. N. Moreau, 1567, fol. 9, de Brosses to Sainte-Palaye, 17.6, n.d.; Chamfort, 'Éloge,' p. 378.

[13] Bluche, *Les Magistrats*, pp. 243–46.

[14] On Juilly, see C. Hamel, *Histoire de l'abbaye et du collège de Juilly* (3d ed.; Paris, 1888); also Renée Simon, *Henry de Boulainviller, historien politique, philosophe, astrologue, 1658–1722* (Paris, n.d. [1942]), pp. 23–28, and H. Roddier, 'De la Composition de "L'Esprit des Lois": Montesquieu et les Oratoriens de l'Académie de Juilly,' *Revue d'histoire littéraire de la France* (1952), 52:439–50.

Malebranche. Here Sainte-Palaye received a sound historical training, and here he was initiated into the latest methods of critical
scholarship. The professors at Juilly—Rollin, Des Molets, Collard,
Thomassin—had one ear cocked to catch the latest news and views
coming in from Holland, and it is no surprise that all their students
were deeply marked by the critical movement of which Bayle and
Le Clerc were the leaders. Many of Sainte-Palaye's future friends
and associates at the Académie des Inscriptions were products of
Juilly. Montesquieu was the most eminent, but Fréret, the pupil of
Rollin and intimate friend of Des Molets, and Secousse, whom
Rollin counted among his prize students, are not insignificant
names.[15] Foncemagne was an Oratorian for a time, as was the Abbé
Bignon. At the Académie Française, Hénault reported that he was
happy, on being elected, to discover "sept ou huit confrères qui
avaient été de l'Oratoire" like himself.[16] They included the Abbé
Terrasson, the ally of Fontenelle and La Motte in the Querelle des
Anciens et des Modernes, the Abbé Houteville, the author of *La
Religion chrétienne prouvée par les faits*, in which there is evidence
of a wide reading of Spinoza's historical works,[17] and J. B. Mirabaud, to whom several free-thinking tracts have been attributed. In
ecclesiastical matters the Oratory was staunchly Gallican with
strong Jansenist sympathies. Many Oratorians were Appellants from
the bull *Unigenitus*. As late as 1739, when the University of Paris
finally submitted to the bull, it did so over the head of Rollin who
was then Rector.[18] The historical scholarship of the Oratorian
Fathers and their pupils was often placed at the service of ecclesiastical reform movements. Gaspard Terrasson, for instance, an Oratorian who was in the inner councils of Monsieur de Caylus, Bishop
of Auxerre, demonstrated in his *Lettres d'un ecclésiastique sur la
justice chrétienne* (1733) that the confession and absolution of
venial sins was a practice unknown in the first two centuries of
Christianity, and argued that it could not therefore be a necessary

[15] Renée Simon, *Nicolas Fréret Académicien*, Studies on Voltaire and the Eighteenth Century (Geneva, 1961), 17:15, 57n, 133; Robert Shackleton, *Montesquieu,
a Critical Biography* (Oxford, 1961), p. 9; Bougainville, 'Éloge de Secousse,' *MAI**
25:289–302.

[16] *Mémoires du Président Hénault* (Paris, 1911), p. 69.

[17] On Houteville, see Paul Vernière, *Spinoza et la pensée française avant la
Révolution* (Paris, 1954), pp. 417–21; R. R. Palmer, *Catholics and Unbelievers in
Eighteenth Century France* (Princeton, 1939), pp. 80–81 *et passim*.

[18] E. Préclin and E. Jarry, *Les Luttes politiques et doctrinales aux XVIIe et
XVIIIe siècles*, 2 vols. (Paris, 1955–56), 1:248. Histoire de l'Eglise depuis les origines
jusqu'à nos jours, 19.

condition for taking Holy Communion—an argument favorable to the Jansenists of the time. Terrasson's work was continued in a radical direction by Nicolas Travers, another Oratorian and pupil of Oratorians, and a good friend of Des Molets. Looking backward beyond the Council of Trent to the early and medieval Church, Travers sought to establish that in the true historical tradition of the Church the power of the priest to confess and to give absolution is not dependent on the authority of his bishop but is equal to it,[19] and that "le nom d'évêque n'avait rien d'honorable dans l'antiquité et ne doit pas, aujourd'hui qu'il est plus respectable, nous empêcher de reconnaître que Saint Pierre l'a donné aux prêtres."[20] There is doubtless exaggeration in the remark of Travers' biographer that "dans le théologien de la confession, on sent que fermentent les droits de l'homme."[21] Nevertheless, Travers' use of historical research to probe and question established practices contributed to the ferment of ideas and to the atmosphere of speculation and criticism that was an essential part of the Enlightenment. History, as the Oratorian Fathers presented it to their students, was obviously a potent weapon and not a curiosity, and it is understandable that the Oratory was highly suspect to orthodox clergymen and champions of absolutism. The Jesuit Tellier, Louis XIV's confessor in his last years and a bitter enemy of the Jansenists, considered it "comme l'âme, le centre et la forteresse du Jansénisme et comme une république fondée au milieu d'un État monarchique."[22]

In November, 1714, Sainte-Palaye left Juilly and entered the law faculty of the University of Paris, and in July, 1717, he graduated[23] —probably without having learned very much.[24] The syllabus was narrow and the instruction uninspired.[25] Nevertheless, a few of the

---

[19] Consultation sur la jurisdiction, 1734; La Consultation défendue, 1736; Pouvoirs légitimes du second ordre dans l'administration des Sacrements et le gouvernement de l'Église, 1744; cf. E. Préclin, Les Jansénistes du XVIIIᵉ siècle et la constitution civile du clergé: le richérisme et sa propagation dans le bas clergé, 1713–1791 (Paris, 1928), pp. 153–59, 228–31 et passim.

[20] La Consultation défendue, p. 72, quoted by Préclin, p. 154.

[21] Dugast Matifeux, Nicolas Travers, historien de Nantes (1857), p. 28, quoted by Préclin, p. 231.

[22] Quoted by L. Séché, Les derniers Jansénistes, 3 vols. (Paris, 1890–91), 1:20, 30.

[23] The original parchments granted by the University of Paris and the admission to the Parlement de Paris are in Bréquigny 95, fols. 110–15.

[24] One student described the thesis that was supposed to be handed in at the end of the third year as "plutôt une formalité à remplir qu'une réelle occupation." ('Un étudiant à Paris au XVIIIᵉ siècle,' Revue des Deux Mondes [1902], 10:438.)

[25] Baron Francis Delbecke, L'Action politique et sociale des avocats au XVIIIᵉ siècle (Louvain and Paris, 1927).

Regents continued to be interested in the relation of laws and institutions to political and social history, and Sainte-Palaye might have learned something from them.[26] He was immediately received as an *avocat* at the parlement of Paris.[27] But the precise nature of his career had not yet been decided. It was considered good experience for future *Conseillers* and *Présidents* of the sovereign courts to spend a short time as *avocats*, and Madame de La Curne may have had in mind some such office for her sons. A year later she purchased an office of *Conseiller* at the Cour des Aides in Paris for Edme.[28] Sainte-Palaye, however, seems not to have wanted to follow this course. For several years he lived "noblement," traveling, studying, pursuing pleasure, and waiting for events to determine his future.

Some time before 1713, Jeanne de La Curne had settled in Paris where she lived with her two sons until her death in 1737.[29] The links with Burgundy were not severed by this change, however, for between 1713 and 1725 Sainte-Palaye paid frequent visits to Auxerre and to Dijon where he took part in the social life of the province and helped to look after his mother's affairs.[30] In both places he encountered men whose critical and oppositional cast of mind was similar to that of his teachers at Juilly.

The rather stagnant society of seventeenth- and eighteenth-century Burgundy has been well described by several historians, in particular by Gaston Roupnel in his influential study of 1922, *La Ville et la campagne au XVIIᵉ siècle, étude sur les populations du pays dijonnais*.[31] Against those who have held that the opposition of the provincial parlement to the absolute power of the monarchy

[26] Delbecke, p. 49.   [27] See n. 23 above.

[28] The *Almanach Royal* for 1732 lists a La Curne as counsellor in the third Chamber of the Cour des Aides since 26.11.1718. This was Edme, not Jean-Baptiste, for the former is referred to as "conseiller à la Cour des Aydes" in a legal document in the Archives de l'Yonne, 9 B 802, Baillage de Saint-Bris, 1738–58.

[29] The division of the estate occurred in 1737. She may have died earlier, however. The last mention of her in Sainte-Palaye's correspondence is in 1732.

[30] As late as 1731 Madame La Curne was still acquiring property in her native province, for in that year she came into possession of the lands of Sainte-Palaye, Prégilbert, and Fontenoy, according to a copy of the deed of sale by which the Château de Sainte-Palaye passed to a Monsieur de Boissy on 9.3.1760. This copy is at the Château de Sainte-Palaye.

[31] In addition to Roupnel, the following works are also worth consulting: Marcel Bouchard, *De l'Humanisme à l'Encyclopédie, essai sur l'évolution des esprits dans la bourgeoisie bourguignonne sous les règnes de Louis XIV et Louis XV* (Paris, 1929); A. Colombet, *Les Parlementaires bourguignons à la fin du XVIIIᵉ siècle* (Lyon, 1936); A. Thomas, *Une Province sous Louis XIV, situation politique et administrative de la Bourgogne de 1661 à 1715* (Paris and Dijon, 1844).

was a feeble continuation of the *Fronde*, Roupnel argues that the Burgundian magistracy stood, on the whole, firmly behind the King. Only after 1690, he claims, when the endless military adventures of Louis XIV were eating away the resources of the province, did the parlement grow more obdurate, though by that time it was too late for any effective opposition.[32] More recently the Russian historian Boris Porchnev has argued that the end of the "bourgeois" *Fronde* in 1648 marked in effect the capitulation of the bourgeoisie and the magistracy, terrified by the specter of the popular revolution they had almost unleashed, to the King. Henceforth—Porchnev claims—the bourgeoisie was tied to the monarchy, however unwelcome many of the policies of the monarchy may have been to it.[33] In return, the royal authority enabled it to concentrate in its hands all the dignities and much of the landed wealth of the province,[34] and this was a further bond between the patriciate and the monarchy. A combination of laborious submission with private, inward resistance which can on no account be allowed to assume serious proportions is thus typical of the patriciate class, reflecting its political and economic position in the feudal-absolutist state and informing its intellectual and literary labors in the latter part of the century as well as its social and political attitudes. "Les Dijonnais lettrés de la fin du XVIIe siecle," Roupnel writes, "sont d'élégants humanistes ou des disciples plus laborieux que doués. Et s'ils se reposent de l'érudition, c'est pour écrire en patois et penser en 'barozais.' Ils ne quittent le Forum ou Catulle que pour entrer dans les 'escraignes.' Ils hésitent entre l'Athènes antique et la rue Saint-Philibert. Jamais ils ne sont ni eux, ni leur temps. . . L'esprit publique s'est réfugié dans le fatras pédantesque ou affaissé vers le terre-à-terre."[35]

Jean Bouhier can be taken as an example of the flower of the

---

[32] Roupnel, p. 7.

[33] B. Porchnev, *Les Soulèvements populaires en France de 1623 à 1648* (Paris, 1963), pp. 520–30. (Russian edition, 1948.)

[34] Roupnel, pp. 155–57, 182–83; Colombet, pp. 106–8. On the expansion of the rural patrimony of the robe, see also H. Carré, *La Fin des parlements* (Paris, 1912), pp. 1–6. The magistrates were interested above all in land. They resisted Colbert's efforts to encourage industry (Roupnel, p. 215 *et passim*) and they were not attracted by trade, the most rewarding field of enterprise at the time. They were also suspicious of speculation. De Brosses, according to Colombet (p. 75) was the only member of the Burgundian magistracy to take out shares in the Compagnie des Indes. On the similar outlook of the patriciate at Toulouse, see Robert Forster, *The Nobility of Toulouse in the Eighteenth Century: a Social and Economic Study* (Baltimore, 1960).

[35] Roupnel, pp. 8–13.

Burgundian patriciate in the last decades of the seventeenth century and the early years of the eighteenth. Possessor of one of the finest estates in the province,[36] president of the parlement, heir to a notable collection of printed books and manuscripts, Bouhier was well versed in both classical letters and the history and customs of his native province, as a glance at his printed works will show. From his stronghold at Dijon, he conducted an extensive and international correspondence with the most eminent figures in the world of learning. Claude Saumaise, Nicolas Heinsius, Isaac Vossius, Montfaucon, and Le Clerc were among the many scholars with whom he exchanged letters.[37] His prestige was enormous. The Académie Française, having elected him a member in 1727, overlooked the fact that he failed to take up residence in the Capital as he had promised to do and as the statutes required.[38] Although he was not a member of the Inscriptions, any notes or essays he submitted to it were discussed at length and reported in full in the Registers.[39]

The young Burgundians of talent to whom Bouhier played host at his home in Dijon—La Monnoye, Lantin le Jeune, Oudin—all concentrated like Bouhier on textual criticism or compilation, turning occasionally perhaps for light relief to poetry in *patois*. Bouhier himself wrote poetry in odd moments. Sending a copy of a collection of his poems to Sainte-Palaye, he remarked that he hoped "qu'elles puissent vous amuser quelques momens et vous distraire du travail fatigant de vos Poëtes Provençaux."[40]

Just as he liked to contemplate his extensive domain, Bouhier liked to contemplate his library which reminded him of his eminently respectable place in society. "Je trouve quelque plaisir," he confessed with naive pride, "à penser que depuis plus de deux siècles, il n'y a eu aucun de mes Ancêtres qui n'ait aimé les sciences et les livres."[41] A patrician in his hôtel, on his lands, and in his parlement, Bouhier was also a patrician in his library. Conscious of his dignity, he did not like it to be attacked. When Bimard de La Bastie questioned some observations he had made on the powers of

[36] *Ibid.*, p. 247.   [37] Bouhier's correspondence is preserved at the B.N.

[38] Tyrtée Tastet, *Histoire des quarante fauteuils de l'Académie Française, 1624–1844* (Paris, 1844), 4:287–92, and D'Alembert, *Oeuvres* (Paris ed., an XIII), 10:370.

[39] Institut de France, Registres de l'Académie des Inscriptions, *passim*.

[40] Bréquigy 66, fol. 15, Bouhier to Sainte-Palaye, 27.7.1742.

[41] "Commentarius de vita et scriptis Johannis Buherii," p. 44, in Jean Bouhier, *Recherches et Dissertations sur Hérodote* (Dijon, 1746).

the Roman *pontifices maximi*, the doyen of Burgundian letters wrote sneeringly to Sainte-Palaye of "votre confrère M. de la Bâtie" and of his "critique impertinente" and tried to have La Bastie censured by the Académie des Inscriptions.[42] He immediately composed a reply to the young scholar and dispatched it to eminent antiquarians in the Capital. Probably Mazaugues tried to restrain Bouhier, for La Bastie was gravely ill at the time.[43] But nothing could hold back the patrician who felt himself attacked in his honor and his prestige. A month later La Bastie was dead. Sainte-Palaye appears to have grasped the necessity of humoring this powerful patron whose library and literary connections were invaluable to him, and though he felt the loss of the young man who had been his friend and colleague, he prudently flattered the vanity of the *Premier Président*. Bouhier was pleased. "Vous avez très bien jugé du Baron ci-devant votre confrère," he wrote. "Quoi qu'il eût quelques connoissances elles étoient fort au-dessous de celles qu'il croyoit avoir et que son ton décisif faisoit croire à bien des gens qu'il avoit en effet."[44] This mean opinion was not shared by Fréret, by Muratori, or by Mazaugues. Such was the atmosphere of the literary circles of Burgundy: masters of the soil and of the dignities of the province, the patricians intended to be masters of its literature too.

The Burgundian patriciate, however, was vaguely disturbed by the thought that all was not quite well with literature and learning at Dijon. Bouhier himself complained to Sainte-Palaye of "la stérilité de notre littérature,"[45] while the President's indefatigable correspondent, the *avocat* Michault, commented: "Ce n'est pas qu'aujourd'hui les sciences soient fort cultivées (at Dijon), il faut l'avouer ingénuement; on y voit principalement régner le goût d'une littérature aisée et superficielle; on s'y amuse bien plus à voltiger sur les fleurs du bel esprit qu'on ne s'y occupe à recueillir les fruits d'une étude sérieuse; on y chérit les lectures où le divertissement a plus de part que l'instruction, et nos curieux rassemblent beaucoup plus de

---

[42] Bréquigny 66, fol. 16, Bouhier to Sainte-Palaye, 6.10.1742. For a full account of the quarrel, see Nicolas Fréret's *Éloge* of Bimard de La Bastie, *MAI** 16:335–47.

[43] Bréquigny 65, fol. 155, Mazaugues to Sainte-Palaye, 19.10.1742. Mazaugues shared Sainte-Palaye's regard for La Bastie and expresses regret that Bouhier was in such haste to publish his reply.

[44] Bréquigny 66, fol. 17, Bouhier to Sainte-Palaye, 2.11.1742.

[45] Bréquigny 66, fol. 15, Bouhier to Sainte-Palaye, 27.7.1742.

livres que nos vrais savants qui se bornent ordinairement à une petite quantité de volumes bien choisis, et dont ils font un utile et excellent usage."[46] The Burgundian magistracy was inclined to look back nostalgically upon the great period of the learned commentators, many of whom, like the incomparable and unforgotten Saumaise, came from its own ranks. Literature was part of a general movement —social, economic, and political as well as intellectual—that was leading away from the old magistracy and leaving it behind. The magistrates—the more conservative provincial ones particularly— sensed this, and they expressed their concern by lamenting the decadence of taste and of manners, and pointing backward—as they did also in political and religious matters—to the pure sources which, they proclaimed, should never have been abandoned and in which the true genius of France was enshrined. Father Oudin, one of the luminaries of the Dijon circle, gave a simple definition of this conservatism as it affected literature. "En fait de poètes," he said, "comme en tout autre genre littéraire, il en est comme du vin: vetus melius est. . . Qui a Térence, Virgile, Horace, Racine, Boileau. . . a tout ce qui est nécessaire, et au-delà."[47]

The older members of the magistracy kept a watchful eye on their protégés so that they might be preserved from the temptations and corruptions of the age. When Leblanc sent Bouhier some verses in which he undertook "d'entremêler quelques vers mesurés à l'Angloise," the *Premier Président* expressed pedantic disapproval: "Dans le temps de l'enfance de notre langue et dans nos vieux romans en vers, on trouve des variations à-peu-près pareilles. On les a bannies peu à peu à mesure que notre langue s'est polie et que notre poésie a pris une forme régulière. Voudrions-nous donc retomber dans la barbarie des temps passés, parce que cette irrégularité bizarre plaît à nos voisins, dont vous convenez que le goût n'est encore nullement formé?" One may take liberties with strict verse forms, Bouhier warned, only "pour de petites pièces."[48] Clearly, all progress had not been bad, since there had been a time— no doubt preceding the magistracy's own social ascension—when the ideal had not yet been achieved. But any attempt to move for-

---

[46] Quoted by E. Deberre, *La Vie littéraire à Dijon au XVIIIe siècle* (Paris, 1902), pp. 291–93.

[47] *Ibid.*, pp. 82–83.

[48] Hélène Monod Cassidy, *Un Voyageur-Philosophe au XVIIIe siècle, l'abbé Jean-Bernard Le Blanc* (Cambridge, Mass., 1941), pp. 304, 515–16.

ward from the position of classicism was judged dangerous; the magistrates had no sympathy with experimental and individualist trends in literature. This does not mean that in private they did not nourish independent and sometimes highly speculative ideas. The magistracy's Ludovician aesthetics, politics, and religion were never as orthodox as they sometimes appeared. It has been said that the magistrates paid their respects to Racine and Boileau as they did to the King and the Church, dutifully but without enthusiasm, while privately they continued to read and enjoy the humanist writers of the sixteenth century.[49] Their own literary labors were devoted to editing and translating the poets of the Renaissance and the ancient singers of the life of withdrawal and pleasure. Horace and Ovid, Catullus and Anacreon were their favorites.[50] In addition many of them liked to collect or compose light satirical verse in French, Latin, or *patois*.

Their private unorthodoxy was not confined to literary matters. Bouhier was interested in Locke some time before his philosophy was popularized by Voltaire and others,[51] and he is known to have possessed one of the manuscripts of the notorious *Testament de Jean Meslier* as well as other examples of clandestine literature.[52] La Monnoye made collections of the poems of Charles d'Orléans, of François Ier, of Marguerite de Navarre, and he prepared an edition of the works of Melin de Saint-Gelais; but his library shows that his unorthodoxy went further than a slight divergence from classical literary taste. "Ce vieil athée"—as Mathieu Marais called him[53]— had in his possession works by Spinoza, Vanini, Herbert of Cherbury, and Campanella, and he was active in procuring "dangerous" literature for his friends.[54] Bayle was acclaimed enthusiastically at Dijon, La Monnoye in particular finding no praise too high for him.[55] At the gatherings in Jean Bouhier's hôtel in the rue Saint-Fiacre, Sainte-Palaye thus imbibed more than a love for classical learning and a curiosity about native French antiquities. The traditions of humanist criticism and free thought, to which the magis-

---

[49] Bouchard, p. 125. The magistrates enjoyed Rabelais, Montaigne, des Périers more than they enjoyed Bossuet, according to Bouchard, pp. 423–24.

[50] *Ibid.*, pp. 222–27, 353–54 *et passim*.   [51] *Ibid.*, pp. 162, 430.

[52] Ira O. Wade, *The Clandestine Organization and Diffusion of Philosophic Ideas in France from 1700 to 1750* (Princeton, 1938), pp. 17, 18, 26.

[53] Mathieu Marais, *Journal et Mémoires,* ed. Lescure (Paris, 1863–68). 2:444.

[54] Vernière, p. 388, and Wade, pp. 24–25.   [55] Deberre, pp. 119–20.

trates had contributed so much earlier in the century, were by no means extinct at Dijon. Sainte-Palaye was well aware of them, and in later years he himself showed special interest in one of his forebears, that Jean Lacurne, founder of the College of Arnay, who had been a friend of the great Saumaise.[56]

In Sainte-Palaye's own home town of Auxerre there was ferment of a different sort. The Bishop of Auxerre, unlike the magistrates, refused to bow to the absolutism of Rome and Versailles. Monsieur de Caylus, brother-in-law of the celebrated wit and beauty, Madame de Caylus, and uncle of the antiquarian, came of an ancient and distinguished noble family. He rose to high office through the patronage of Madame de Maintenon, but he turned out to be less docile than those who got on in such ways were expected to be. Consecrated Bishop of Auxerre in 1705, he at first accepted the bull *Unigenitus*, but in 1718 he joined Cardinal de Noailles in the appeal to Rome. Two years later he was one of seven bishops who refused the compromise which Noailles himself accepted, and he became thereafter an ardent and distinguished opponent of the bull. Against the Jesuits, against Rome, against Royal authority, he extolled the rights of the bishops as leaders of their flocks, and in defense of his position he looked back to and drew inspiration from the early Church, much as magistrates and nobles looked back for inspiration —each in his own way—to the ancient usages of the nation. He was among the few bishops who joined their voices with some 2,000 ecclesiastics of all kinds—138 of them from his own diocese of Auxerre—in protesting against the deposition of Jean Soanen, Bishop of Senez.[57] In 1729 Caylus again voiced his opposition to

---

[56] He proposed additions and corrections to the information on his family in Papillon's *Bibliothèque des Autheurs de Bourgogne;* cf. letters to Bouhier of 24.4.1741 and 26.6.1742 in B.N. Français 24418, fols. 362, 378.

[57] Préclin, p. 123. Soanen, together with the Bishop of Bayeux, de Lorraine, and the Bishop of Montpellier, Colbert, had appealed from the bull again in 1720, despite a royal decree prohibiting further appeals. The government had hesitated to mobilize the bishops, a majority of whom were opposed to the appellants, against Soanen's colleagues, on account of their family connections, but it gave the green light to the enemies of Soanen himself, a man of lowly birth. The pretext was a pastoral letter issued by Soanen in August, 1726, in which the elderly prelate criticized the King, the Popes, and "bad shepherds" in general, defended Quesnel, and praised the appellant bishops, "seuls défenseurs de la vérité" (Préclin and Jarry, p. 246). In September, 1726, Soanen was suspended by the provincial council of Embrun and relegated to the monastery of La Chaise-Dieu. According to Préclin, the suspension of Soanen marked the capitulation of the bishops and the end of episcopal Jansenism. Only the Bishops of Montpellier and Troyes continued with Caylus to oppose the *Unigenitus* bull.

Papal policies and to the absolutist pretensions of Rome. In a new edition of the Breviary, Benedict XIII praised Gregory VII for having excommunicated the Emperor Henry IV and released his subjects from their oaths of fealty. Prayers were to be offered so that future Popes might be granted the same courage. On July 20, 1729, and again on February 23, 1730, the Parlement of Paris condemned the Papal Brief, while from Auxerre, Caylus issued a pastoral letter "qui défend de suivre l'office imprimé dans une feuille volante qui commence par ces mots: Die XXV maii, in festo S. Gregorii VII." The parlement was defending the State—which the Church, in its view, was meant to uphold—against the claims of a rival power, the Holy See. The intention of Caylus and of the five bishops—a small proportion of the total number of bishops—who joined him in rejecting the Brief was ostensibly to preserve the Church from the corruption of temporal ambitions and power politics; but it is difficult not to discern in their action the same tendencies as were manifest in the political sphere at the end of the reign of Louis XIV, when the aristocracy tried to reduce the power of the centralized monarchy. In both cases the great, while acting and speaking for themselves, seemed to represent a new democratic force and did, in some measure, succeed in winning the support of the lower orders.

Caylus's interest in the spiritual reform of the Church is manifested most concretely in the liturgy he composed for his diocesans. Of eighteenth-century missals, those of Auxerre and of Troyes are —in Professor Préclin's opinion—the two that show deepest marks of Jansenist and Richerist inspiration;[58] on account of them both Caylus and Bossuet, Bishop of Troyes, incurred the wrath of their metropolitan, Archbishop Languet of Sens. The Troyes liturgy, the Archbishop charged, reduced "les cérémonies de la sainte administration de l'Eucharistie à la manière sèche et grossière dont la cène se distribue dans les prêches des Huguenots"; it was scandalous, full of errors, denuded the altar of ornaments—even to the crucifix— and did not pay proper respect to the Holy Virgin or to Saint Peter.[59] About the same time (1733) Cardinal Fleury reproached Caylus with having insinuated in the *Rituel d'Auxerre* "des mots qui semblent dénoter que le peuple sacrifie avec le prêtre, ainsi qu'on

---

[58] On Edmond Richer and his ideas, see Préclin, pp. 1–12.
[59] *Ibid.*, pp. 187–88.

l'avance dans quelques libelles." Caylus replied that "le peuple n'offre pas le sacrifice *comme* le prêtre, mais il l'offre *avec* le prêtre; c'est l'esprit et la doctrine de l'Église."[60] So too Bossuet, answering Languet, formulated one of the essential principles of the dissident bishops: "Le sacrifice de la messe est une action commune du prêtre et du peuple, bien qu'ils y coopèrent d'une manière bien différente."[61] The political implications of this theology were not lost on those whose task it was to preserve and promote absolutism.

In his own diocese Caylus was respected and beloved. Sainte-Palaye must have been constantly informed of his independence of spirit in political and religious matters. The fact that he himself was sent to school with the Oratorian fathers at Juilly instead of to the Molinist Collège Louis-le-Grand (*olim* de Clermont) favored by the majority of robe families[62] suggests that his own family was in sympathy with the views of Monsieur de Caylus. In later years Sainte-Palaye was to encounter among his scholarly colleagues in France and in Italy many men by whom the Bishop of Auxerre was held in high regard.

Monsieur de Caylus was a great nobleman and he had the sympathy of the men of his class, who had themselves mounted a vigorous campaign for the reform of the absolutist state. Saint-Simon spoke highly of him and contrasted him favorably with his opponent, Languet of Sens, "sujet . . . infâme" and, incidentally, a man of far lower birth.[63] Like many other independent noblemen of the time—Boulainviller, for instance, or the dashing Comte de Plélo—Monsieur de Caylus had a speculative bent; adventurous thinking was for him one of the ways in which a nobleman might prove his valor, his initiative and his honor. It was not at all inconsistent with his religious convictions that Caylus was a client of those whose business it was to procure forbidden deistic and other speculative tracts, which were copied and circulated in manuscript form.[64]

There is no evidence that Sainte-Palaye was personally known to the Bishop of Auxerre. He was closely associated, however, with the man Caylus called to Auxerre to be succentor of the cathedral. Jean Le Beuf was a scholarly churchman whose theological views were similar to those of his bishop. He already had some published

[60] *Ibid.*, p. 187.   [61] *Ibid.*, p. 190.   [62] Bluche, p. 245.
[63] *Mémoires*, ed. Les Grands Écrivains de France, 37:68–70.
[64] Wade, pp. 3–4.

essays to his credit when he began discussing questions of erudition with Sainte-Palaye around 1722.[65] The friendship of the two men lasted many years, and their correspondence covers a wide range of subjects in French history and antiquities. Le Beuf was Sainte-Palaye's guest at his country house not far from Auxerre, and when he was elected to the Académie des Inscriptions in 1740, Sainte-Palaye had prepared the ground for him. On his side, Le Beuf introduced Sainte-Palaye in 1724 to Father Des Molets' little Academy, where every Tuesday outstanding men of letters such as Montesquieu and Fréret mingled with scholarly ecclesiastics.[66] We have already mentioned some of the Oratorian Fathers who were connected with Des Molets and whose erudition was at the service of their reforming aspirations. Le Beuf himself was such a man. His earliest large-scale work, *La Prise d'Auxerre par les Huguenots* (1723), which dealt with the period of the Wars of Religion, had included at one point a sixteenth-century prayer invoking God's help for the Pope as an "homme qui peut errer et faillir comme les autres." The allusion to contemporary political and theological disputes, and the Gallican tone of the whole passage were so patent that Le Beuf's printer was afraid to print it.[67] Le Beuf was also closely associated with Jacques Jubé, the celebrated Curé of Asnières, whose liturgical reforms excited the wrathful indignation of conservatives. An appellant and reappellant from the bull, Jubé dreamed of restoring the ancient disciplines and rites, as he understood them, of the primitive Christian communities. In his new church at Asnières the walls were decorated, not with the customary paintings representing the lives of the saints but with engravings of Biblical scenes. In flagrant defiance of the *Unigenitus*, a copy of Baillet's *Vie des Saints* and of the French Bible of Le Maistre de Sacy was prominently displayed for consultation. The altar in Jubé's church was stark; there was neither cross nor candelabra.

[65] Bréquigny 62, fol. 181, Le Beuf to Sainte-Palaye, 13.12.1723. Cf. also a letter from Le Beuf to Prévost in *Lettres de l'abbé Le Beuf*, ed. Quantin and Cherest (Auxerre, 1866–67), 1:301–2.

[66] The correspondence is in part in *Lettres de l'abbé Le Beuf* (see note above), in part also in 'Correspondance de l'abbé Le Beuf avec La Curne de Sainte-Palaye,' ed. E. Petit, *Annuaire historique du département de l'Yonne* (1884), 48:244–69, and there is additional material in Bréquigny 62, where the references to Des Molets are found (fols. 178–79, 182).

[67] See the article by H. Leclercq on Le Beuf in *Dictionnaire d'archéologie chrétienne et de liturgie*.

Likewise, the celebration of the Mass included a number of innovations designed to reduce the gap between the celebrant and the faithful. In this part of his reform Jubé's guide was Jean Le Beuf himself.[68] Although Jubé had to flee to Holland in 1724, Le Beuf carried on his work of liturgical reform, and turned out pupils—the most eminent being Jean Mignot—who continued the work after Le Beuf's own death. The intentions of Le Beuf and Jubé were sufficiently close to those of Caylus and the bishops to make collaboration among them possible, even though the defection of most of the bishops from the appellant movement indicates that there were significant differences between their aims and ideals and those of Le Beuf and Jubé. At all events it is impossible to separate the scholarship of Le Beuf and Jubé from the deep intellectual, spiritual, and social currents on which it was borne. "L'historien," Préclin declares, "trouve dans le *Cérémonial* (i.e., of Asnières) autre chose qu'une oeuvre d'archéologue ou de liturgiste. Les innovations de la seconde partie de la messe, qui ne ressemblent que d'assez loin aux usages de la primitive Église, présentent avec les doctrines richéristes des coincidences qui ne sont vraisemblablement pas fortuites."[69] Le Beuf's interest in the early Church and in Gothic architecture is part of a deep nostalgia for what he took to be the pre-Tridentine spirit of the Church, and it is misleading to say—as a recent writer did—that "it was an eccentric love of things medieval that made him dislike the modern style."[70]

Though unusually learned, Jean Le Beuf was probably quite typical of the kind of churchman with whom Sainte-Palaye associated in his native Auxerre, for the history of the city in the eighteenth century indicates that the ideas of Richer and his eighteenth century interpreters—Vivien de La Borde, Nicholas Le Gros, Nicolas Travers, P. F. Le Courayer—had taken firm root among the local clergy.[71]

[68] Préclin, p. 183.   [69] *Ibid.*, p. 185.

[70] W. Herrmann, *Laugier and Eighteenth Century French Theory* (London, 1962), p. 79.

[71] Caylus himself should probably be judged a moderate, compared to the most ardent disciples of Richer. But the appeal which the latter's ideas must have had for noblemen like Caylus is suggested by Roland Mousnier's summary of them: "Richer . . . soutenait (1611) que le Christ a donné sa puissance, non au seul saint-Pierre, mais à tous les évêques qui succèdent aux douze apôtres, ils sont donc comme le Pape de droit divin et doivent être indépendants de lui. De même les prêtres succèdent aux soixante-douze disciples. L'église n'est donc pas une monarchie universelle mais une aristocratie nationale. Richelieu fut hostile au riché-

At Auxerre, therefore, Sainte-Palaye was in the midst of one of the most restless and learned ecclesiastical bodies in the country. He could have heard many issues discussed there which he was to hear discussed again in Paris among the friends to whom he was introduced by his Auxerre associates, among his colleagues at the Académie des Inscriptions, and even in the salons which he frequented. His friendship with Le Beuf is in no way surprising. Like the clergy, and for similar reasons, the aristocracy was deeply interested in history, and historical erudition stood at the center of the occupations of churchmen, nobles, and *parlementaires* alike. At Auxerre, at Dijon, at Juilly, and in the academies of Paris and the provinces it was in the forefront of contemporary conflicts, political, intellectual, and spiritual.

The influence of Auxerre and of his patrician background was felt socially as well as intellectually by Sainte-Palaye. His family was not, as we have seen, of ancient nobility but it had begun its ascent of the social ladder fairly early, and Sainte-Palaye's father had been a courtier. One can imagine that all the doors of the local gentry were open to him, the more so as the social barrier between robe and sword was falling rapidly. Indeed, as the eighteenth century progressed, robe and sword came more and more to be regarded and to regard themselves as distinguished by *état* or profession rather than by social class.[72] In the upper ranks of the robe, moreover, there had already been a great deal of intermarriage with the sword and, just as many robe families had withdrawn completely from the exercise of the law to live as landed gentlemen, some families of the sword had entered the robe.[73] Doubtless there was still distrust and hostility especially between the lesser robins

---

risme: Tout se tient, celui qui veut introduire l'aristocratie dans l'Église ne peut en être l'adversaire dans l'État." (*Les XVIe et XVIIe siècles* [Paris, 1954], p. 264. Histoire generale des Civilisations, 4.) Whatever Caylus's own attitude to Richerism may have been, it was during the long years of the bishop's rule that Richerist ideas took root and flourished in Auxerre (cf. Préclin, pp. 214–15 and the map opposite p. 84), extending downward and outward till they took on an almost democratic turn. How deeply they had penetrated the ranks of the clergy became apparent on Caylus's death when the Cathedral Chapter rose up in opposition to the new bishop, the anti-Jansenist Caritat de Condorcet, invoking Richerist arguments in support of the rights it claimed for itself. It has also been held that the ready acceptance at Auxerre of the Civil Constitution of the Clergy can be traced in part to the deep mark left by Caylus on his diocese. (Préclin, pp. 502–3, 510–11.)

[72] Bluche, *Les Magistrats*, pp. 303–6 et passim.
[73] Roland Mousnier, *Vénalité des charges*, pp. 522–26.

and the aristocracy, and this hostility was to be a significant factor in the *Querelle* of the *Anciens* and the *Modernes*, but the history of the first half of the century is largely the history of the rapprochement of the two segments of the aristocracy,[74] and it is this rapprochement that was the condition of certain parts of Sainte-Palaye's work, notably the *Mémoires sur l'ancienne chevalerie*. At any rate, by the early years of the century all the upper strata of society mixed freely in provincial centers and parliamentary seats. At Dijon, Rennes, Strasbourg, Montpellier, Aix, Poitiers, Toulouse landed nobility, intendants, bishops, regimental officers, and magistrates frequented each other regularly.[75] Even the smaller cities came to life. Louis Ducros quotes the superintendent of the tobacco warehouse at Autun, not far from Auxerre: "Our one occupation was to divert ourselves, our one care to vary our amusements. Thus, every day saw a succession of dinner parties, suppers, concerts, balls, card parties, excursions, and entertainments of all kinds."[76]

Sainte-Palaye was one of the lions of the provincial society of Auxerre. "Vous ne me parlez que de plaisirs, de tendresses," his boyhood friend de Croisoeil wrote in 1715. "Quinze ou vingt plats morbleu, passer les nuits à danser, faire l'amour tout le reste du temps ce n'est pas trop mal débuter."[77] Affable and urbane, Sainte-Palaye never lost his taste for polite society. At the age of eighteen he was writing little rococo verses to the young ladies of Auxerre, and at eighty he was still eager to turn a pretty compliment in verse, as La Harpe records in his *Correspondance littéraire*.[78] Hunting must have been one of the favorite occupations of the gentlefolk of Auxerre and the surrounding country, and Sainte-Palaye never lost his taste for it. Later, when he was in the service of Stanislas of Poland, he often went hunting with his royal master in the great park at Chambord,[79] and between 1752 and 1758 he presented a

---

[74] Cf. especially Franklin H. Ford, *Robe and Sword: The Regrouping of the French Aristocracy after Louis XIV* (Cambridge, Mass., 1953).

[75] H. Carré, *La Noblesse de France devant l'opinion publique au XVIII᷎ siècle* (Paris, 1920), p. 96.

[76] Louis Ducros, *French Society in the Eighteenth Century* (London, 1926), p. 219; also Carré, *Noblesse*, p. 99.

[77] Bréquigny 66, fol. 67. The letter is undated, but Bréquigny has written in the year 1715.

[78] La Harpe, *Correspondence littéraire* (Paris, 1801), 1:220.

[79] Bréquigny 66, fol. 5, Stanislas to Sainte-Palaye, 25.5.1726.

series of learned *Mémoires historiques sur la chasse* to the Académie des Inscriptions. The best example of the gaiety and sociability of the new generation of the robe is also the most famous. In 1739 Sainte-Palaye went on a tour of Italy with his brother Edme, de Brosses, and some other Burgundian friends. The historian of the Académie des Inscriptions, L. F. Maury, was to describe this journey as "un véritable événement scientifique,"[80] on account of Sainte-Palaye's assiduous tracking down of manuscripts relative to French history and literature in the Italian libraries. In his *Lettres familières*, however, de Brosses took care to preserve another, lighter side of the trip. A series of delightful cameos bring the adventures of the little band alive before our eyes—Sainte-Palaye and Migieu making themselves sick on nougat, Edme unsuccessfully pursuing the dark-eyed Madame de Bentivoglio, Sainte-Palaye's evening rendezvous with Mlle Grognet, the dancer, who went about *vestita da uomo*—an encounter which provoked some sly comments from de Brosses—and the merry escapade in the gardens of the Borghese villa at Frascati, when all six companions played practical jokes on each other round the fountains and returned to their inn soaked to the skin.

Sainte-Palaye did not forget the friends of these early years. De Croisoeil emigrated to Santo Domingo, settling at Fort Dauphin, about forty miles from Le Cap Français, but the War of the Austrian Succession disrupted the economic life of the colony, and in 1747 he returned to France, ill and destitute.[81] Sainte-Palaye immediately came to his assistance.[82] With those of his early friends who shared his own interests, Sainte-Palaye's relations were naturally

[80] L. F. Maury, *L'ancienne Académie des Inscriptions et Belles-Lettres* (Paris, 1864), p. 286. On this journey, see also T. Foisset, 'Un chapitre de l'histoire du Président de Brosses,' *Mémoires de l'Académie de Dijon* (1835), pp. 133–48. Above all, Charles de Brosses, *Lettres familières écrites d'Italie en 1739 et 1740*, ed. M. R. Colomb (Paris, 1861); a more modern edition of the *Lettres* was prepared by Y. Bézard, 2 vols. (Paris, 1931).

[81] Cf. Moreau de Saint-Méry, *Description topographique, physique, civile, politique et historique de la partie française de l'isle Saint-Domingue*, ed. Blanche Maurel and Étienne Taillemite, 3 vols. (Paris, 1958), Appendix, 3:1471. On the movement of impoverished noblemen to the West Indies in the eighteenth century, see Carré, *Noblesse*, pp. 124, 140, Pierre de Vaissière, *Saint-Domingue, la Société et la vie des Créoles sous l'ancien régime, 1628–1789* (Paris, 1909), pp. 97–99, and Georges Hardy, *Histoire sociale de la colonisation française* (Paris, 1953).

[82] Bréquigny 66, fols. 83–89, letters from de Croisoeuil to Sainte-Palaye from Fort Dauphin and Toulouse.

closer still. He corresponded regularly with Bouhier and with de Brosses, and seems to have acted as a sort of literary agent in Paris for them both.[83] During the recesses of the Académie des Inscriptions he often returned to the estate at Sainte-Palaye, not far from Auxerre, from which he took his name. Here he worked on his literary projects, went hunting, and visited the local gentry— Bouhier at Dijon, Buffon at Montbard,[84] or his old friend de Brosses in his magnificent château of Neuville-les-Comtesse, the scene of many a lavish reception.[85] He had considerable improvements made to his own château and to the grounds in order to bring them into line with the taste of the age.[86] Gradually he did detach himself somewhat from his Burgundian roots. Unmarried, childless, caught up in the intellectual and social life of the Capital, he was less concerned than families of his kind usually were with the maintenance of his landed interests and, after vainly trying to rent his château at Sainte-Palaye to Voltaire and Madame Denis in 1753,[87] he ended by selling the whole estate in 1760. Nevertheless, despite his relative alienation from his origins, Sainte-Palaye continued throughout his life to move in magisterial and aristocratic circles. His will shows how closely tied to the robe he remained. It included bequests to the families of two presidents of the Parlement of Paris, Bourrée de Corberon and Le Couturier de Mauregard, while the principal legatees were two members of the distinguished Thiroux family, Thiroux d'Arçonville, another president of the Parlement of Paris, and Thiroux d'Ouarville, a *conseiller* at the Parlement and later *maître des requêtes*.

---

[83] Of Sainte-Palaye's letters to Bouhier, fourteen have been preserved covering the years 1739–45 (B.N. Français 24418, fols. 358–84). Of Bouhier's letters to Sainte-Palaye there are eight written in 1741 and 1742, in Bréquigny 66, fols. 11–20. All of these letters contain mention of other Burgundians, in particular de Brosses whom the two correspondents obviously saw often. Only one letter from de Brosses to Sainte-Palaye survives in Moreau 1567, fol. 9. It is undated, but was written after de Brosses' quarrel with Voltaire. I have found no letters from Sainte-Palaye to de Brosses.

[84] Bouhier speaks of a visit made to him by Sainte-Palaye and Buffon together in a letter to Le Blanc of 4.7.1737 ('Lettres de Bouhier à l'abbé Le Blanc,' ed. Marquis de Chateaugiron, *Mélanges de la Société des Bibliophiles français* [Paris, 1827], letter 8.)

[85] Carré, *Noblesse*, pp. 99–100.

[86] Bluche (*Les Magistrats*, pp. 198–201) relates that robin families took great care of their properties and spent large sums on embellishing them.

[87] *Voltaire's Correspondence*, ed. T. Besterman, 4903, 4907, 4912, 4928, 4980, 4982, 4984, 4993, 5012, 5052, 5071.

In May, 1719, Sainte-Palaye set off with his brother Edme on a tour of the Low Countries.[88] Their itinerary took them by way of Rheims to Aix-la-Chapelle, Rotterdam, Delft, The Hague, Leiden, Amsterdam, Utrecht, Antwerp, Brussels, and Louvain. Altogether, they were away three months.

Travel in foreign countries had not normally been part of a young man's education, but it was increasingly so, especially in the circles of the well-to-do patriciate.[89] Some voices were even being raised in protest at the custom.[90] The reason for the increased popularity of travel may have been in part a desire to complete the education of young men by bringing them into contact with the great models of culture and the arts at the time, which were to be found principally in Italy, but to a lesser extent, since de Piles' successful campaign in favor of Rubens, also in the Low Countries. The aim of travel was thus, in a sense, to consolidate a culture. But there was another side to travel, which both Montaigne and Descartes had emphasized and which had motivated the free-thinking scholars of the early seventeenth-century magistracy, those "libertins érudits," who still dominated the intellectual world of their successors.[91] To them travel was, among other things, a means of broadening the mind and freeing it of myths and prejudices by revealing to it the variety of human beliefs and activities. Amid the questioning and speculation which marked the end of the seventeenth and the beginning of the eighteenth centuries, this aspect of travel must have loomed large. The principal motive for visiting Holland, in particular, must have been less to consolidate an established culture than to discover a different social world. Entirely governed by a patrician oligarchy of "deftige Burger,"[92] Holland enjoyed a nice degree of intellectual, religious, and political liberty,

---

[88] There is a complete account of this journey in B.N. Bréquigny 131, fols. 24–34. Quotations are taken from there.

[89] Bluche, Les Magistrats, pp. 246–47.

[90] Muralt himself, Lettres sur les Anglois, les François et les Voyages (Cologne ed., 1727), p. 269. Cf. also Paul Lacroix, Institutions, usages, coutumes: 1700–1789 (Paris, 1875), p. 455.

[91] On the travels of the libertins érudits and their predilection for Holland, see René Pintard, Le Libertinage érudit dans la première moitié du XVIIᵉ siècle (Paris, 1943), 1:101–4.

[92] Bernard H. M. Vlekke, Evolution of the Dutch Nation (New York, 1945), pp. 205–10, 237–38, 265–66 et passim. Cf. also Gustave Cohen, 'Le séjour de Saint-Evremond en Hollande, 1665–1670,' Revue de littérature comparée (1925), 5:431–54; (1926), 6:28–78, 402–23.

which the French magistracy could well have looked upon with envy and approval. It had been from Amsterdam and Rotterdam, moreover, that had come those Protestant-inspired revivals of the antimonarchical political theses of the sixteenth century with which the magistrates were certainly familiar—the famous *Soupirs de la France esclave* or the writings of Jurieu. Then again it was to Utrecht that many a French Jansenist, weary of the persecution to which he was subject in his own land, most naturally betook himself. The journey to Holland thus seems to have been intended as much to relax as to consolidate established opinions and values.

Some of the guidebooks of the time, moreover, were highly unorthodox. Misson, for instance, whom Sainte-Palaye consulted on a later journey to Italy with de Brosses, was not only an avowed partisan of the *Modernes* against the *Anciens*, but a free-thinking spirit schooled in the ideas of Bayle and Fontenelle.[93] The tourist of the early eighteenth century freed himself from the bonds of the familiar in more ways than one. Sainte-Palaye seems to have acquired a taste for this freedom, for on his return from Holland he made shorter trips through France and into Switzerland[94] and in 1766, after two trips to Italy, he returned once more to Holland and Flanders.[95]

His travel notes, though less extensive than those of Montesquieu a decade later, reveal interests and attitudes similar to those of his great contemporary. The encyclopaedic curiosity of Montesquieu, which is manifested throughout his travel notebooks, was shared by Sainte-Palaye, as indeed it was by many magistrates or children of magistrates in this period. In this way they were perhaps continuing an old tradition more than they were opening up a new one.[96] Like Montesquieu, he was interested in everything: sugar refineries and

[93] P. Lambriet, 'Les Guides de voyages au début du XVIIIᵉ siècle et la propagande philosophique,' *Studies on Voltaire and the Eighteenth Century*, ed. Besterman (1965), 32:269–326. R. Michéa, 'Le Président de Brosses en Italie,' *Revue de littérature comparée* (1934), 14:424–53, shows that de Brosses was guided by Misson in writing his own *Lettres d'Italie*. Three decades later P. J. Grosley, another friend of Sainte-Palaye's, was still using Misson, to whom he refers often in his *Nouveaux Mémoires, ou Observations sur l'Italie et les Italiens*, 3 vols. (London, 1764).

[94] His diary of these journeys is in Bréquigny 132, fols. 35–40.

[95] Bréquigny 66, fols. 130–153: 'Détail de tout ce que nous avons observé et éprouvé dans notre voyage de Hollande' (written up by Laugier).

[96] Cf. Alphonse Dupront, 'Livre et culture dans la société française du XVIIIᵉ siècle,' *Annales* (1965), 20:867–98.

tobacco factories at Dieppe,[97] commercial and maritime establishments in Rotterdam and Amsterdam, natural history collections and cabinets of curios, botanical and zoological gardens, the way of life and religious ceremonial of Quakers and Jews (Sephardi and Ashkenazi), the principles of government in foreign lands, buildings, paintings, people, and the customs and manners that give life to organizations and institutions. A letter of introduction to the Burgomeister of Rotterdam—Vandermal—procured him entry into the house of a leading Dutch burgher. He found the ladies of the household polite and well-educated and noted the fact with characteristic gallantry. The combination of refinement and sobriety seemed to him the most striking feature of Dutch life—and it was one that many of the older generation of the robe in particular would have admired.[98] The burgesses' homes are clean but simple, he noted, and they themselves are industrious, prudent to the point of frugality, and unconcerned to make a lavish display of their wealth. "On me dit"—he observed simply, but with a care for accuracy, of Vandermal—"que le mary qui est dans une place distinguée jouissoit de plus de 200,000 florins de Hollande, ce qui fait près de 3,000,000 d'argent de France, ce qui ne l'empesche pas de continuer le commerce et de vivre avec une grande économie." On the 1766 journey to Holland, he again commented on the sobriety and good husbandry of the Dutch people and on their relative social equality, which contrasted strikingly with France. "Le peuple est tranquille et honnête, les moeurs en général sont simples et pures, on voit l'aisance et la frugalité régner dans tout le païs; chaque paysan a son Cabriolet et est vêtu d'un habit de drap. Il n'y a presque point d'inégalité dans les conditions, quoiqu'il y en ait beaucoup dans les fortunes." France did not come out well from a comparison with Holland or with the Austrian Netherlands, then under a relatively enlightened administration. "Le beau païs de la Flandre avoit disparu," Sainte-Palaye and his companions lamented. "Tout paroissoit s'enlaidir et s'appauvrir en avançant dans le sein de la France."

[97] He visited Dieppe, then engaged actively in trade with the West Indies, in 1725, (cf. Régine Pernoud, *Histoire de la bourgeoisie en France* [Paris, 1962], 2:230) and wrote a detailed account in his journal of the manufacturing processes used in both the sugar and the tobacco factories there. This journal is in Bréquigny 131, fols. 47–50.

[98] Cf. Jean Ehrard, *L'Idée de nature en France dans la première moitié du XVIIIe siècle*, 2 vols. (Paris, 1963), 2:583–95.

Nevertheless, Sainte-Palaye did observe in Holland what Montesquieu had predicted—the growing power of the Stadhouder and the decline of the republican spirit.

Sainte-Palaye's comments reveal a mixture of ironical detachment and open-mindedness that is probably characteristic of his age and his social milieu. He is obviously not unsympathetic to the Dutch, though this does not mean that he wished to see his own countrymen follow their example.[99] But most strikingly he is interested in the coherency of all the aspects of Dutch life and, in particular, in the relation between certain modes of behavior and corresponding economic activities and political institutions. In later years this interest was to lead him to a line of thought and investigation of which Montesquieu was the master.

The esthetic interests revealed in these early travel notes also point to the future. Sainte-Palaye shared with Montesquieu and the rest of his generation a keen interest in town planning, that is to say in the social aspect of architecture. Like Montesquieu, he appre-

---

[99] At first sight, it might seem that Sainte-Palaye admired the commercial spirit of the Dutch and wished to introduce it into France. One might be tempted to range him alongside Buffon, who preferred the enterprise of Nantes to the genteel decadence of Dijon and Angers (*Correspondance inédite*, ed. Henri Nadault de Buffon [Paris, 1860], 1:4, Buffon to Ruffey, 5.11.1730) and to contrast his broadmindedness with de Brosses' contempt for the Genoese because they had no learned societies. (*Lettres familières*, ed. M. R. Colomb [Paris, 1861], 1:64.) Sainte-Palaye's attitude was probably similar in fact to that of Montesquieu. It is clear from the *Esprit des Lois* (bk. 20) and from his travel notes that Montesquieu did not underestimate the significance of commerce and that he was by no means opposed to it. On the contrary, he everywhere associates the absence of commerce with poverty and backwardness. (*Pensées* no. 1995. Notes on Rome and Holland, *Oeuvres complètes*, ed. Daniel Oster [Paris, 1964], pp. 256, 326–27.) Montesquieu was anxious, however, to preserve the monarchy and the different *états*. Since the principle which maintains the monarchy is that of honor, he feared any penetration of the commercial spirit into the nobility, as he observed it in England, for instance, and he resolutely opposed according noblemen the right to engage in commerce (*EL*, 20, 21, 22). Each estate in the nation has its function to fulfill and should fulfill it, he believes. Thus, he deplores the growing taste for luxury among the Dutch merchants as much as he deplores the greed of the English nobility and the stinginess of the Genoese. In keeping with his conservatism, Montesquieu is, on the whole, mercantilist. Commerce for him is a weapon of the feudal-absolutist state; it must, therefore, be both kept in existence and kept in control, so that it does not overwhelm the state (above all *EL*, 20:x). How to achieve this goal had indeed been once of the headaches of Colbert. Colbert wished to encourage commerce, the source of wealth of the King and the treasury as well as of the merchants themselves, but the very economic and fiscal structure of the ancien régime, as well as its social pressures and values, encouraged the bourgeois, as soon as he had amassed capital, to withdraw it from commerce and invest it in offices and titles carrying exemptions, in land, or in interest-bearing loans to the King and the nobility.

ciates light, air, open spaces, public promenades, good water sup-
plies, cleanliness, and the harmonious arrangement of individual
dwellings in the interests of the city as a whole; the success of the
Dutch in providing these advantages impressed him as it had impressed others before him[100] and as it was to impress Montesquieu a
decade later. Doubtless he remembered these impressions of the
Dutch cities when, in the forties and fifties of the century, he joined
in a campaign to improve the city of Paris.

In painting, his taste is abreast of the times but not adventurous.
Again there is a striking resemblance to Montesquieu. Rubens is the
king of painters, and the two brothers sought out and listed as many
canvasses as they could set eyes on in Brussels and Antwerp. In
Italy, Montesquieu likewise added to his reverence for Raphael, the
idol of Le Brun, a fondness for the Venetians whom de Piles had
rehabilitated along with Rubens. Sainte-Palaye never went back on
this eclecticism, which was perfectly compatible with the relaxed
neo-academicism characteristic of his circle.

These notebooks also provide the first comments on things medieval by the man who was later to do so much for medieval studies in
France. Partly, of course, they can be accounted for by supposing
that he was using a guidebook. The guidebooks of the seventeenth
and eighteenth centuries, particularly the series known as the
Délices, dealt indiscriminately with all the notable features of each
city or country, and carefully executed plans often accompanied
the description of cathedrals and churches.[101] Sainte-Palaye's comments do, however, appear to indicate a moderate receptiveness to
medieval art. Rheims cathedral, he described as "de la dernière
magnificence Gothique." The town hall of Louvain surpassed, in
his eyes, even that of Brussels "par la perfection de l'ouvrage
Gothique."[102] The diary he kept of later journeys in France and to
Switzerland in the fall of 1720 confirms the impression given by the

---

[100] Cf. *Pennant's Tour on the Continent, 1765*, ed. G. R. de Beer (London,
1948), pp. 151–52.

[101] On the early guide-books, see R. D. Middleton, "The Abbé de Cordemoy
and the Graeco-Gothic Ideal,' *Journal of the Warburg and Courtauld Institutes*
(1962), 25:278–320 and (1963), 26:90–123, esp. 25:294–96, 317.

[102] Although *Gothique* is used here as a descriptive—not an abusive—term, it is
not used very precisely. In the account of a later journey to Holland in 1766, care
was taken to distinguish three periods of Gothic, and the discussion was more
knowledgeable than that in the 1719 journal, thanks no doubt to Laugier who was
the Sainte-Palaye brothers' companion on this second journey.

Dutch journal. He admired the thirteenth-century portal of Notre Dame at Dijon, which Soufflot later selected to illustrate the brilliance of Gothic construction techniques, and the Chartreux of Champmol, close to Dijon. In the latter's "antiques bastimens . . . beaux et vastes . . . les deux magnifiques tombeaux" of the Dukes of Burgundy impressed him as a "chef d'oeuvre de la sculpture de ce tems."

What is the extent and the significance of this interest in medieval art? Thanks to Nathan Edelman's study of the attitudes of the seventeenth century to the Middle Ages,[103] it is no longer necessary to suppose that it was a product or an accompaniment of mysticism or romanticism, neither of which is remotely relevant to Sainte-Palaye, his friends, or their seventeenth-century predecessors. In fact, curiosity about medieval art as about medieval literature and a taste for both were by no means uncommon in the circles both of the robe and of the sword. Boileau himself, it will be remembered, had some kind things to say of Villon. This curiosity had been somewhat muted in the reign of the Sun King, especially perhaps during the sixties and seventies, but it had by no means died out.

To some degree it was connected with the *Modernes*. The circles in which "modernisme" flourished looked back with pride on a past that had been their own peculiar contribution to civilization, owing little or nothing to Greece and Rome. It was among the *Modernes* likewise that the "merveilleux chrétien" found its earliest champions. The *Modernes* could also admire the technical originality of the Gothic architects and invoke their successes to justify their own departures from strict classical canon. The architect Pierre de Vigny, for instance, who made a spirited defense of Gothic in an attempt to question classical dogma, was also an admirer of Borromini and a champion of the rococo.[104] Similarly Frémin's

[103] Nathan Edelman, *Attitudes of Seventeenth Century France toward the Middle Ages* (New York, 1946). Also Louis Hautecoeur, *Histoire de l'architecture classique en France* (Paris, 1950), 3:347–52; W. Herrmann, pp. 71–73, 92–95, 245–46. For a bibliography of the many studies devoted to the survival of medieval architectural traditions in France, see R. D. Middleton, cited n. 101 above. In a related study on England, 'Ancient History and the Antiquarian,' *Journal of the Warburg and Courtauld Institutes* (1949), 12:285. A. Momigliano attributes the curiosity about local antiquities in the eighteenth century to the landed gentry's love of and curiosity about its own traditions. Similarly, H. Ross Steeves, *Learned Societies and English Scholarship in Great Britain and the United States* (New York, 1913), pp. 66–71.

[104] Cf. Herrmann, pp. 64–65, 86–87.

praise of Gothic in his *Mémoires critiques d'architecture* (1702) was accompanied by a rejection of rules and the choice of a functional criterion of beauty in place of the classical aesthetic canon. Throughout the century praise of Gothic architecture was often directed at its structural brilliance. The characteristically *moderne* preference for *cose* rather than *parole* is plainly visible here. "L'architecture est an art de bâtir selon l'objet, selon le sujet et selon le lieu," Frémin observed in words that foreshadow Marivaux's defense of his style and vocabulary, against the attacks of the *Anciens* and the classicists. In literature, too, an interest in things medieval was usually the sign of a tolerant and emancipated *moderne* taste.

But interest in medieval things was not confined to the circles of the *Modernes*. Sainte-Palaye's curiosity, indeed, received powerful encouragement from learned ecclesiastics in his own home town of Auxerre, notably from Jean Le Beuf. It was Le Beuf who directed him to the medieval French manuscripts in the libraries of neighboring religious houses and who obtained his admittance to them.[105] Le Beuf's interest in the Middle Ages was somewhat different from that of a sophisticated architect such as Pierre de Vigny. It arose out of an ideal of purity and simplicity in spiritual matters which caused him to look backward beyond the Council of Trent to the medieval Church and which itself sprang from the reforming and purifying labors of the great scholars of the classical period. It was his theology rather than admiration for the technical inventiveness of the medieval architects that made Le Beuf into a passionate student and admirer of the Gothic, which, he tells, he found infinitely more delicate and touching than the classical style of the later seventeenth century. The latter was more appropriate to triumphal arches and palaces, the monuments and dwelling places of temporal power, than to churches and holy places. Le Beuf, in his very appreciation of Gothic architecture, is thus in agreement with Boileau and the *Anciens* on the matter of the separation of the genres and styles. The sacred and the profane each has its domain and its appropriate style in his view, and they should not be confused.

Of course, the attempt to scrape away the accretions of the ages and to rediscover the pristine form of Church or State implied a degree of detachment and criticism that placed the apologists of the

---

[105] Letters from Le Beuf to Sainte-Palaye in Bréquigny 62, fols. 161–92.

primitive church or the antique "constitution" remarkably close to rationalists and demystifiers such as Fontenelle or La Motte. But to see this is only to recognize that certain positions, certain attitudes were common to ancients and moderns, to reforming churchmen, noblemen, and magistrates alike. The very men who scolded modern fashions (rococo, Italian music, the *merveilleux chrétien*, the abominable style of Marivaux, etc.), were also moved, as we have seen, by their particularism, by their family pride, and by their strong spirit of independence to cultivate the poetic traditions of their provinces, the old "libertine" writers, even local *patois*.

Few of Sainte-Palaye's early mentors, however, despite their interest in pre-Ludovician literature and thought, actually favored the movements that were undermining the precarious compromise of Ludovician classicism. Like Boileau himself in the last two decades of the century, Bouhier and his friends in Dijon became increasingly disillusioned with and even critical of the King and his reign. Boileau's suspicion of the *Modernes*, indeed, his rejection of an art of flattery and pomp, his growing commitment to the cause of the *Anciens*, expresses not conformism but the increasingly critical attitude he and the men of his class were assuming toward the King. Yet just as Boileau, reflecting the political dilemma of the entire magistracy, could not develop a coherent and original aesthetic in opposition to the *Modernes*[106] but could only point backward to the humanist tradition, so too Bouhier and his friends wanted no revolutions. The classical canon was not to be overthrown, it was to be criticized, eased, and improved by a return to the purer sources of Greek and Latin. Similarly, the critical and free-thinking spirit of the Dijon magistracy was tempered by prudent distrust of the "superstitious" populace, which they feared even more than they resented the King. They had their speculative moments, therefore, but they intended them to be private and exclusive. Theirs was to be the spirit of the sage, not that of the reformer or the adventurer. The adventurism of the aristocratic champions of new styles and new ideas, the *éclat* of aristocratic libertinism, alarmed them. Mathieu Marais, the lawyer and Bouhier's close friend in Paris, knew and loved the Renaissance poets of his own country and of Italy but, like the *Président*, he was against the *Modernes* of his own generation—against Fontenelle, La Motte, and Moncrif. He com-

---

[106] *Cf.* René Bray, *Boileau: l'homme et l'oeuvre* (Paris, 1942), p. 120.

plained of the newfangled taste for Italian music that Madame de Prie was encouraging. "Elle protège déjà les La Motte et tous les autres censeurs d'Homère; il ne lui reste plus qu'à nous dégoûter de Molière et de Lulli . . ."[107] In his letters to the Marquis de Caumont —one of Sainte-Palaye's associates in the South of France—Dubuisson primly lamented the decadence of taste while, characteristically, he sent the Marquis copies of every piece of subversive, satirical, or erotic writing he could lay hands on.[108] Austere churchmen like Le Beuf were not likely to be more sympathetic to the *Modernes.* The Jansenists condemned the Epicureanism and libertinism of the Regency and the literature that went with it, and they had set their faces against the financiers who were increasingly influential patrons on the contemporary literary, artistic, and musical scene.

Sainte-Palaye, we can assume, was not indifferent to the views of patrons, mentors, and friends in the patriciate, in the Church, in the provincial nobility. But he was younger than Bouhier and Marais and, if the sons of high-placed officers of the parlements could not resist the new aristocratic and opportunistic spirit,[109] how much less could he whose father had been in the service of a Prince. Above all, he had his career to think of and ambitions to satisfy in a world that seemed to offer more and better opportunities for pleasure, advancement, and wealth than had been available for a long time. It is natural that his tastes and pursuits at this time were more adventurous than those of his mentors, for in the years between 1720 and 1725 Sainte-Palaye was making himself known in influential circles in Paris and at court.

[107] Mathieu Marais, 2:369; cf. also W. Krauss, *Cartaud de la Villate, ein Beitrag zur Entstehung des geschichtlichen Weltbildes in der französischen Frühaufklärung,* 2 vols. (Berlin, 1960), 2:112.

[108] *Lettres du Commissaire Dubuisson au Marquis de Caumont, 1735–1741,* ed. A. Rouxel (Paris, 1882).

[109] The *petits-maîtres*—Montesquieu wrote—"inspirent aux jeunes gens, choqués du sérieux de la robe de leurs pères, de répandre leur sang pour le service de la Patrie et de s'approcher du Prince." (*Pensées,* no. 1404.)

CHAPTER 2

A DIPLOMATIC CAREER

The period of the Regency and the administration of Monsieur le Duc marked in some respects the opening of a new era. In many fields the men and ideas associated with the Versailles monarchy lost ground as new men and ideas took over. Those who had surrounded the old King were dismissed, as de Croisoeil wrote Sainte-Palaye in 1715,[1] to make room for the favorites and supporters—first of Orléans, then of Bourbon. In the arts, too, it was the end of an era. As its energy waned, the old court had come to side with the *Anciens*,[2] but with the Regent the *Modernes* in literature and the partisans of the Italian style in music came back into favor.[3] J. B. Rousseau, the champion of Louis XIV, Boileau, and classicism in general, sulked and finally went into exile[4] as new protectors—noblemen and financiers—took over from the monolithic official patronage of Versailles. It was the heyday of the salon of Madame de Lambert where the tone was one of smiling skepticism, and of the less decorous gatherings at the Café Procope. It was a good time for financial, political, intellectual, and artistic speculation, and for ambitious young men who—like Sainte-Palaye—wanted to get on.

On the whole, the men of Sainte-Palaye's class stood back from speculative activities. Naturally, they were distressed to see that their reliance on traditional investments—in land, in offices, in state and local loans—was causing them to lose ground in relation to the other leading classes of society. The relative value of their offices,

---

[1] Bréquigny 66, fol. 69, 6.10.1715.
[2] Cf. *Correspondance de J. B. Rousseau et de Brossette*, ed. P. Bonnefon (Paris, 1910–11), 1:19, Brossette to Rousseau, 28.8.1715.
[3] On the Regent's musical education, at the hands of M. A. Charpentier, who had been trained in Italy and was opposed by the "classical" Lulli, and on his musical compositions, see P. M. Masson, *L'Opéra de Rameau* (Paris, 1930), p. 28, n. 4.
[4] Henry A. Grubbs, *J. B. Rousseau, His Life and Works* (Princeton, 1941), pp. 130–31, 136–37.

for instance, seems to have declined in the course of the century,[5] while the effect of the speculative boom of 1720 made itself felt on their *rentes*.[6] The robins expressed their discontent, as they had already done in the previous century, by despising and publicly condemning the financiers and those noblemen who had disgraced themselves by speculating, and by representing themselves as models of virtue and restraint in a world dizzy with greed and corruption.[7] In large measure they did win respect for their probity.[8] Yet there was something hypocritical about it, like the virtue of Molière's prudes, blaming loudly "non point par charité, mais par un trait d'envie."

In private, in fact, many magistrates were less grave and moral than they were in public. Epicurean tendencies at Dijon, for instance, are revealed in the work of La Monnoye. In Paris, especially, it was difficult not to swim with the tide.[9] Many magistrates compromised their virtue by marrying their sons to "filles de finance." Young men especially were restless, and the magistracy no longer appealed to them. Pont de Veyle, the elder son of the Ferriols, found the prospect of office so distasteful that he contrived to have himself disqualified by showing immoderate frivolity in public. As for his brother, d'Argental, whom his family expected to assume the career abandoned by Pont de Veyle, he developed a passion for the theatre and was so infatuated with the actress Adrienne Lecouvreur that his parents thought for a time of packing him off to Santo Domingo. This predilection for actresses never left him. "C'est un furieux ridicule à un homme sage et en charge," Mlle Aïssé commented later, "que d'être toujours attaché à une comédienne."[10] In the South of France another friend of Sainte-Palaye, the Marquis d'Eguilles, youngest son of a long line of magistrates at the Parle-

---

[5] Carré, *La Fin des Parlements*, pp. 1–8, and Forster, pp. 102–6.

[6] Cf. Mathieu Marais, 2:58–59.

[7] Cf. Duclos' description of the magistrate in his novel *Confessions du Comte de ****, ed. Uzanne (Paris, 1880), pp. 57–59.

[8] Duclos, *ibid.*; Marcel Marion, *Histoire financière de la France depuis 1715* (Paris, 1927), 1:107; Barbier, *Journal*, Jan., 1721.

[9] Cf. Bluche, *Les Magistrats*, pp. 307–8, 334–35, 369–70 *et passim*. Toward the end of the seventeenth century La Bruyère was already lamenting that "il y a un certain nombre de jeunes magistrats que les grands bien et les plaisirs ont associés à quelques-uns de ceux qu'on nomme à la cour de *petits-maîtres;* ils les imitent, ils se tiennent fort au-dessus de la gravité de la robe, et se croient dispensés par leur âge et par leur fortune d'être sages et modérés." ('De la Ville' in *Caractères*.)

[10] *Lettres portugaises; lettres de Mlle Aïssé*, ed. Eugène Asse (Paris, n.d.), p. 337. This letter was brought to my notice by Mrs. Maja May.

ment of Aix, took a commission in the navy rather than assume a
legal charge. Later, he was sent by d'Argenson on an adventurous
mission with Charles Stuart, the Young Pretender. His diplomatic
career ended with the defeat of the Pretender, for the French government, of necessity, virtually disowned him. Yet the thought of
returning to Aix, where his father had bought him an office of
Président à mortier, filled him with dismay. At best he viewed the
office as a useful source of income: "C'est un furieux changement
d'état," he wrote to his friend and protector Bachaumont. "Passer
de la conduite d'un bâtiment à la Présidence d'un parlement! Je
conviens que, quand même je ne voudrais pas l'exercer, ce me seroit
toujours un moyen d'être employé honorablement à autre chose."[11]

Sainte-Palaye, for his part, was also anxious to try his fortune. He
found his way into the circle of Bourbon and Madame de Prie[12] and
it was their favorite, the great financier Duverney—most opulent
and successful of the four Pâris brothers, and the true ruler of
France under M. le Duc, according to Président Hénault[13]—who
acted as his protector at Court.[14] Early in 1725 he received word
that he was to be employed in the foreign service at a salary of
6,000 livres.[15]

The mission on which he had been chosen to serve was the marriage of Louis XV to Marie Leszczinska, daughter of the exiled
Stanislas of Poland.[16] Sainte-Palaye's duties were to handle the
correspondence concerning the marriage. It was a post of confidence and honor rather than one of great responsibility. As the
person in charge of the negotiations, an old comrade of Stanislas
and a protégé of Madame de Prie called Vauchoux, was scarcely

---

[11] *Revue Rétrospective* (1886), 3:225–26.
[12] There are references to Mme de Prie among his papers; and in 1726 he was a
guest of Condé at Chantilly (Bréquigny 131, fol. 36). Condé's court was still lively
enough, despite his disgrace.
[13] *Mémoires*, pp. 71, 81, 85.
[14] Frequent allusions to him as his benefactor occur in Sainte-Palaye's correspondence with his brother Edme between May, 1725, and January, 1726 (Bréquigny 66, fols. 40–64).
[15] Bréquigny 66, fol. 115.
[16] On the negotiations for the marriage and the circumstances leading to it, see
Henry Gauthier-Villars, *Le Mariage de Louis XV* (Paris, 1900), esp. pp. 166–80;
also Pierre Boye, *Stanislas Leszczynski et le troisième traité de Vienne* (Nancy,
1898), pp. 37–53, 68–69; Gaston May, 'La Curne de Sainte-Palaye et ses relations
avec Stanislas,' *Mémoires de l'Académie de Stanislas*, 6ᵉ série (1921), 18:22–25;
Recueil des instructions données aux ambassadeurs et ministres de France: Pologne,
ed. L. Farges (Paris, 1898), 1:299 *et seq.*

more competent or experienced than Sainte-Palaye,[17] it is clear that not much importance was attached to either appointment. No one expected that the mission would encounter difficulties from Stanislas. The picture of the Court of Wissembourg given in Vauchoux's dispatches is a far cry from the brilliant Court at Lunéville, where Stanislas was later to play host to Voltaire, Saint Lambert, Madame du Châtelet, Montesquieu, and other outstanding figures.[18] At its head stood a saddened, impoverished exile, whose family spent most of their time in prayer and devotion, and whose future outlook was bleak until the unexpected stroke of luck which elevated his daughter to the throne of the most powerful monarchy in Europe. Stanislas was ready to make any sacrifice to ensure the successful conclusion of the negotiations. He took upon himself the humiliating role of the poor relation, promising to remain "toujours incognito, et sans jamais aller à la Cour publiquement."[19]

Stanislas was a man of wit, humour, intelligence, and a sort of accommodating piety which got in nobody's way.[20] The melancholy and monotony of his impoverished little court at Wissembourg must have weighed heavily on him, and one can surmise that he was delighted by the attentions of the promising young gentleman fortune had sent him. When he was offered Sainte-Palaye's services as private secretary he accepted with alacrity.[21]

Sainte-Palaye, for his part, was equally pleased. This was the opportunity he had hoped for, and he asked his brother to thank Duverney for following up his earlier favors.[22]

What did Sainte-Palaye expect from the post Duverney had obtained for him? He claimed that he was interested above all in an honorable employment. "Je vous prie . . . d'inspirer à Monsᵣ de Vernay que ce que je désire le plus est d'avoir un poste et un titre

[17] Archives des Affaires Étrangères, correspondance politique Pologne, vol. 173, fol. 36: "Trente-cinq années dans les troupes ne m'ont pas donné l'usage des négociations . . ."

[18] On the later career of Stanislas, see Gaston Maugras, *La Cour de Lunéville au XVIIIᵉ siècle* (Paris, 1904).

[19] Corr. Pol. Pologne, vol. 173, fol. 38.

[20] Corr. Pol. Pologne, vol. 173, fol. 288, Chaillon de Jonville's description.

[21] In a questionnaire sent to Vauchoux in April, 1725, the envoy was asked if Stanislas had a secretary who was also a gentleman of quality. The answer was *no* (Corr. Pol. Pologne, vol. 173, fol. 39). Duverney suggested Sainte-Palaye for the post (Bréquigny 66, fol. 44, Sainte-Palaye to Édme 3.6.1725), and Stanislas accepted eagerly. (*Ibid.*, fol. 49, Sainte-Palaye to Edme, 8.6.1725, and fols. 54–55, Sainte-Palaye to Edme, 22.6.1725.)

[22] Bréquigny 66, fols. 47–48, to Edme, 8.6.1725.

honorable," he wrote to his brother Edme, "les autres avantages ne me sont rien au prix de celuy là."[23] Not for him the career of a fawning courtier. Was he not, after all, as he wrote to Edme, a *philosophe?*[24]—and did he not profess, like many members of his class, that desire for independence that in some cases took the form of skepticism and in others of Jansenism? "Plus je suis à portée de ce qui flatte les autres," he wrote, "et plus je me confirme dans l'indifférence que j'ay depuis longtemps là dessus. Je croirois mesme vous avoir plus d'obligation que vous ne m'en auriez si vous cédant tous les avantages d'une espèce de fortune je me déchargeois en mesme tems sur vous des soins qu'elle me demande."[25]

Yet there is no doubt that Sainte-Palaye expected much from the position Duverney had given him. "Le poste dont vous me parlez," he wrote Edme, "est un poste de faveur que bien des gens voudroient, je crois, avoir . . . on y peut faire sa cour et se rendre agréable à tout ce qu'il y a de plus grand dans le Royaume. Je n'imagine rien de plus avantageux que cela."[26] In another letter he admitted that he hoped to be in a position to further Edme's career too,[27] and he reminded his brother that Madame de Prie had to be courted assiduously.[28] An observer in Stanislas' household commented that Sainte-Palaye had made himself a favorite of the King "à qui il fait très bien sa cour," adding in a manner which removes all suspicion of gaucherie in Sainte-Palaye—"C'est un garçon d'esprit."[29] Even before his brother, however, Sainte-Palaye felt the need to cover up what might be taken as a degrading opportunism. "Je suis ravi," he wrote him, "que vous entriez dans ma façon de penser Philosophique. Je tâcheray de ne m'en départir jamais."[30] In general, he tried to convince himself and his brother that by accepting the post with Stanislas he could further his ambitions without compromising his integrity or his freedom. "Je pense toujours de mesme sur ma fortune," he wrote, "et sur mon goust pour mes estudes ordinaires, mais je vous avoueray que l'engagement que je prendrois me feroit grand plaisir. Je ne ferois que changer un peu l'objet de mes estudes et je pourrois d'un autre costé faire un chemin

---

[23] *Ibid.*, fol. 44, to Edme, 3.6.1725.   [24] *Ibid.*
[25] *Ibid.*, fol. 50, to Edme, n.d. (probably June, 1725).
[26] *Ibid.*, fol. 47, 8.6.1725.   [27] *Ibid.*, fol. 50, to Edme, June, 1725.
[28] *Ibid.*, fol. 54, to Edme, 22.6.1725.
[29] Chaillon de Jonville in Corr. Pol. Pologne, vol. 174, fol. 289, dispatch of 17.9.1725.
[30] Bréquigny 66, fol. 54, 22.6.1725.

assez gratieux sans beaucoup de peine."[31] Nevertheless he admits to
having at least one "scrupule." What will his mother think? "Je
voudrois bien scavoir . . . si ses allarmes ordinaires, un éloignement
auquel elle n'est point accoutumée et mille autres choses ne trou-
blent pas un peu la satisfaction qu'elle doit avoir."[32] The contempt
with which the robins observed many members of the old aristocracy dishonor themselves in the scramble for wealth during the
Regency is well known. Religious convictions of a Jansenist tint
frequently deepened their disgust. Jeanne de La Curne's background was such that some aspects of the path on which her son was
embarking might have appeared distasteful to her. Sainte-Palaye
himself after Boileau, La Bruyère, and so many others of his class
who had tried to combine the pursuit of fortune with the profession
of indifference to it felt the need constantly to protest that there
was to be no sacrifice of honor or independence. "Je suis assez
heureux de trouver une Cour qui n'est pas incompatible à mon
goust," he insisted, "en sorte que je pourray m'y livrer du moins
autant qu'à Paris, en faisant mes affaires par-dessus le marché."[33]
But he knew the truth in his heart when he thanked Edme for
buying him a handsome suit of clothes appropriate to his courtly
duties: "L'habit de couleur rose vif dont vous me parlez m'effraye
furieusement. Quelle couleur pour un homme de mon âge et pour
un Philosophe."[34] He was pleased by—and at the same time
ashamed of—his success as a courtier. "Je fus dernièrement à portée
de remercier le Roy de la bonté qu'il avoit de m'agréer pour rester
auprès de sa personne," he related in one letter. "Il y répondit avec
sa gratieuseté ordinaire, mais, dit-il sçavez-vous bien que quand on
est auprès de moy je ne laisse pas volontiers aller les gens. Je souhaite, luy dis-je, Sire, que ce soit toutte ma vie. Mais il faudra
renoncer à l'Académie. Je luy répondis que je ne perdrois assurément au change." Sainte-Palaye ended the anecdote with a request
to Edme to say nothing of the incident to "nos Philosophes."[35]

He was soon to learn how slippery the path of fortune is. In
October 1725, the marriage ceremony over, Sainte-Palaye followed
his master to Chambord.[36] Stanislas remains at this time an impover-

---

[31] *Ibid.*, fol. 48, 8.6.1725.   [32] *Ibid.*
[33] *Ibid.*, fol. 54, to Edme, 22.6.1725.   [34] *Ibid.*, fol. 44, to Edme, 3.6.1725.
[35] *Ibid.*, fol. 54, 22.6.1725.
[36] His name heads the list of 'Gentil'hommes du Roy de Pologne' in a statement
of Stanislas's household drawn up in October, 1725. (Corr. Pol. Pologne, vol. 174,
fol. 316.)

ished gentleman, unsettled, dissatisfied, lonely and uneasy in the drafty apartments of his grandiose palace, and painfully aware that he is an irritating liability to his royal son-in-law. A letter to Sainte-Palaye from a friend at Chambord some twelve months later evokes an atmosphere of futility and boredom: "Les maladies continuent toujours. Le jésuite a la fièvre, celle de la Comtesse subsiste, Bouchinski se croit obligé de l'avoir aussy. Les poulmons de Chabannes se détachent de luy . . . l'abé Vau recomence à dire la messe, les capucins puent, madame royale joue, la reine cause, le roy fume, le comte Tarlo médite, l'évesque sue, Diesbac se porte bien . . . voilà toutes les nouvelles."[37]

Sainte-Palaye claimed that he was not dismayed by the isolation of Chambord. "Je vois tout le monde désolé de notre solitude . . . Moy je ris au milieu de tout cela, et j'en suis enchanté."[38] He pressed on with a memoir on Plutarch's Life of Romulus which he had promised his friend Secousse for the Académie des Inscriptions[39] and busied himself with Polish history as well as with classical literature and history, for he had undertaken to write a life of Stanislas.[40] From his royal employer he received many marks of favor and in the King's entourage he was referred to jokingly as "mon chancelier."[41] The King particularly enjoyed hunting with him, and he bore his secretary's occasional absences ill. "Je vous attends avec impatience," he wrote on one occasion. "Il n'y aura plus de sangliers dans le parc si vous tardez plus long temps."[42]

Gradually, however, Sainte-Palaye began to have doubts about the post he had accepted so eagerly and to sense that his prospects of advancement were not good. "Tant que je suis resté dans l'obscurité," he wrote his brother, "on a pu attribuer mon inaction

[37] Bréquigny 66, fol. 112 (dated September, 1726), probably from de Merzck.

[38] *Ibid.*, fol. 59, to Edme, Blois, 30.10.1725.

[39] *Ibid.*, fol. 63, to Edme, 25.12.1725, and Registres Ac. Insc., 1726, pp. 81 and 109–26.

[40] The Alsatian scholar Schoepflin was procuring for him books on Polish history and editions of Latin and Greek authors (Bréquigny 66, fols. 106–9, two letters from Schoepflin to Sainte-Palaye, March and August, 1726). As for the biography of Stanislas, it was Sainte-Palaye's suggestion. (Bréquigny 66, fol. 45, to Edme, 3.6.1725.) In the spring of 1726 Tournemine wrote Sainte-Palaye: "J'attends de vous l'histoire du héros que dieu vous a donné pour maître." (Bréquigny 66, fols. 103–4.) Sainte-Palaye also seems to have been the real author of Stanislas's *Avis salutaires du Roi Stanislas à la Reine de France au mois d'août, 1725* (Gaston May, "La Curne de Sainte-Palaye," p. 52, n. 1, cited in n. 16 above).

[41] Bréquigny 66, fol. 110, to Sainte-Palaye from an unidentified correspondent.

[42] *Ibid.*, fol. 3, Stanislas to Sainte-Palaye, 25.5.1726.

à mon indifférence et mon mépris pour les affaires, et on auroit à l'heure qu'il est raison de l'attribuer à mon incapacité et au peu de confiance qu'on a en moy; d'ailleurs je ne dois point m'éloigner gratis de l'estat tranquil où je vivois content et si je puis espérer des grâces je dois chercher des occasions de les mériter, autrement elles me déshonoreroient."[43] The attempt to combine fortune and *philosophie*, ambition and independence, was on the point of failing; and the *philosophes*, after all, began to seem justified in their suspicion and rejection of courtly ambition. In the same letter he told Edme that he intended to write to Duverney, asking him to clarify his position; but Duverney had his own troubles at this time. The clergy, the nobles, and the parlements were obstructing his new *cinquantième* tax, the price of wheat had soared, and there were bread riots in the streets.

The end, for Sainte-Palaye, came in mid-1726 when Bourbon was ousted from power, and Fleury took over the government. Duverney was exiled and then imprisoned. All those who had placed their hopes in the Duke and his mistress found themselves out of favor; even the Queen herself was disliked by Fleury on account of her connections with Bourbon. "Cet événement," Hénault recounts, ". . . détruisait, pour toujours, toutes mes espérances . . . Le Cardinal ne m'aimait pas, à cause de mes liaisons avec Mme de Prie, qu'il ne me pardonna jamais."[44] Sainte-Palaye's salary was stopped, and in August, 1726, he returned to Paris with a broken career behind him and the desire, reinforced by disappointment, to live "philosophically."

What this meant and what he referred to when he used the words *philosophe* and *philosophie* can be determined from a letter he received in 1722 from Secousse, one of those friends whom he had designated in his own letter to his brother as "nos Philosophes." Discussing Diodorus Siculus, Secousse declared that he respected him because of his "caractère d'honnête homme et de Philosophe." "Car vous sçavez," he explained, "qu'il estoit disciple du fameux Epictète Philosophe stoicien qui vivoit sous Néron."[45] *Philosophe*— for Secousse and for Sainte-Palaye—still meant, among other things, something of what it had meant to the earliest French translators of

[43] *Ibid.*, fol. 63, Chambord, 25.12.1725.
[44] *Mémoires*, pp. 86–162. Hénault had been in line for the Swiss Embassy. Cf. also *Mémoires et Lettres du Cardinal de Bernis*, ed. Masson (Paris, 1878), 1:52.
[45] Bréquigny 66, fol. 91, 20.8.1722.

Epictetus, Guillaume du Vair, and André Rivandeau.[46] In the preface to his edition of the *Manuel*, addressed to Honorast Prevost, a Protestant nobleman, Rivandeau declared: "Je veus aussi ramentevoir les fréquentes exhortations que vous me faisiés, pour m'avancer, ayant conceu une telle espérance de moy, que si la fortune . . . y eust satisfait, j'ay opinion, et ne me glorifie qu'en la grâce de Dieu, que le reste n'eust point manqué. Mais la mort du Treschrétien Roy Henry, de qui nous espérions beaucoup, et les troubles qui sont surveneus depuis m'ont fait embrasser la sentence: *qui a esté bien caché, a bien vescu.*" *Bene vixit qui bene latuit*—was not Ovid's dictum in Sainte-Palaye's mind when he expressed his bitterness in the words just quoted: "Tant que je suis resté dans l'obscurité . . ."? And how often, ruminating his disappointment in the drafty halls of Chambord, did he recall the admonitions of Epictetus concerning fortune, honors, and worldly success? His earnest attempts to justify his career in the letters to Edme are more urgent in the light of certain phrases of the *Manuel*.

Yet it would be misleading to interpret narrowly the Stoic strain in the notion of the *philosophe* as it was held by Sainte-Palaye and his friends. Stoicism, in the strict sense, had been so severely debunked by both Christians and skeptics in the seventeenth century that it was not acceptable either to the *Anciens* or to the *Modernes*. Although they sympathized with the Stoics' contempt for the things of the world, many of the *Anciens* could not tolerate the pagan philosophers' contention that it was possible for man to rise unaided above the values and desires of the world and to recover his pristine nature. For those of them who had Augustinian leanings in particular, there was only one road to salvation and one means of redemption; they delighted in belittling human reason and *unmasking* the pagan moralists.

Likewise, the *Modernes* did not accept the unworldliness of the Stoics. But whereas the *Anciens* questioned whether the Stoics really had succeeded in transcending social values and social ambitions, the *Modernes* questioned whether it was ever possible—or, above all, desirable—for men to do so. What they did prize in the

---

[46] Paul Hazard, *La Crise de la conscience européenne, 1680–1715* (Paris, 1935), p. 345, cites the definition of *philosophe* in the *Dictionnaire de l'Académie* of 1694: ". . . on appelle philosophe un homme sage qui mène une vie tranquille et retirée . . ."

teachings of the Stoa was the support the latter appeared to give to
that independent natural morality which they wished to substitute
for Christianity. "Il semble," Boulainviller observed, "que les vertus
humaines n'ont jamais été si bien pratiquées que par Cicéron, Caton,
Mécène, Sénèque, Festus, Traseus, Tite, Trajan, Marc-Aurèle et
tant d'autres, qui très certainement ne croyoient pas l'âme immor-
telle et n'attendoient après la mort ni récompenses ni châtiments."[47]
So too Voltaire declared in one of his Dialogues that the virtuous
man is not rewarded by the promise of paradise, but "pendant sa
vie, par le sentiment intérieur d'avoir fait son devoir; par la paix du
coeur, par l'applaudissement des peuples, l'amitié des gens de bien.
C'est l'opinion de Cicéron, c'est celle de Caton, de Marc-Aurèle,
d'Epictète; c'est le mien."[48]

In general the *Modernes* took from Stoicism what they wanted—
its natural morality and its rationalism—and combined it freely with
other doctrines to constitute a kind of united front against Christianity. The name of Epictetus was spoken in the same breath with
that of Socrates, Plato, Confucius, and even Spinoza.[49] In Voltaire
the difference between Epicureanism and Stoicism appears slight
compared with the respect for human nature he considered common
to both.[50] Boulainviller, like Voltaire and later Diderot, liked to
bring together as many philosophical systems as he could—from
antiquity, from the Renaissance, from China, India, Egypt, if
necessary—in order to confront the law of revelation with the law
of nature and to oppose to Christianity with its handful of unre-
liable witnesses the testimony of wise men in all places and in all
ages. The truly universal doctrine would then appear to be not that
of the Church but that of generations of humanists, naturalists, and
rationalists.

By the early eighteenth century the *Anciens* and their descend-
ants had themselves moved closer to this conception of *philosophie*.
Religious Jansenism had lost ground as the chief ideology of the
magistracy, even though political Jansenism remained strong, and
the old skeptical tradition of the seventeenth century *libertins*

---

[47] 'Extraits de ses lectures,' MS. quoted by Renée Simon, *Boulainviller*, p. 552.
[48] 'Sophronime et Adelos, traduit de Maxime de Madaure,' *Mélanges*, ed. Pléiade,
p. 1319.
[49] Cf. for instance, Voltaire, 'Homélie sur l'athéisme,' *Mélanges*, p. 1133.
[50] 'Le Philosophe Ignorant,' *ibid.*, p. 923.

érudits provided a certain common ground in which *Anciens* and *Modernes* alike could feel at home. Differences remained, of course. The skepticism of the magistracy could still be a means of devaluing all human and social institutions, on the ground that they were arbitrary, and thus justifying paradoxically the most extreme conservatism; the *Modernes,* on the other hand, looked more positively on human and social institutions, even though they were sanctified neither by God nor by reason, and they tried to understand them for what they were—a response to particular human needs. On the whole, however, there was much that was shared by both groups. Both set themselves off from the "superstitious" populace and its blindly accepted traditions, both were eclectic in their philosophical interests. Cicero, in particular, was much favored by the philosophically minded among *Anciens* and *Modernes* alike. Madame de Lambert's *Traité de la vieillesse* was inspired by the elegantly skeptical Academic whom the young Montesquieu considered the very model of a philosopher[51] and who was likewise the delight of the conservative Abbé d'Olivet and his friends in the Burgundian magistracy.

In their way of life too, the two groups were no longer far apart. Some *Anciens* as well as many *Modernes* might have recognized themselves in Cartaud de la Villate's portrait of the Athenians. Contrasting them with the Spartans who were entirely given over to the public life, Cartaud wrote admiringly of them that "leur sagesse subordonnoit les intérêts brillants de l'État au goût d'une vie délicieuse. Ils étoient Philosophes, ainsi la Gloire ne les éblouissoit pas. Peu de religion, rien d'imposant de la part du Trône, toujours libres et réfléchis au milieu des richesses et de l'oisiveté, ils étudièrent dans leurs discours la coquéterie des grâces."[52]

Sainte-Palaye's outlook appears to have been that of many young people of his generation and of his class in the early decades of the eighteenth century. He had little or no religion and little or no

[51] 'Discours sur Cicéron,' *Oeuvres complètes,* ed. D. Oster (Paris, 1964), pp. 34–36. Cf. also Günter Gawlick, 'Cicero and the Enlightenment,' *Studies on Voltaire and the Eighteenth Century* (1963), 25:657–82; and Renée Simon, *Boulainviller,* pp. 547, 550–51.

[52] *Essai historique et Philosophique sur le goût,* 1736, in W. Krauss, 1:215. In fact, Cartaud's description of the Athenians sums up several of the attitudes which Groethuysen characterizes as 'bourgeois' (*Die Entstehung der bürgerlichen Welt- und Lebensanschauung in Frankreich* [Halle, 1927–30]), and which were found alike among *Anciens* and *Modernes.*

political ambition.[53] He desired most of all a pleasurable and interesting life. His brief diplomatic career had only confirmed him in
that pursuit. It had served to bring him closer to the Court and he
maintained the association. In 1750, for instance, Stanislas consulted
his old secretary and companion on the setting up of an academy at
Nancy;[54] a few years later the Queen supported his candicacy for
a place at the Académie Française.[55] Yet his worldliness did not
seriously weaken his affiliation with the men of his class, for the
magistracy itself was changing and, despite disputes and jealousies,
becoming less and less distinguishable from other groups in the
aristocracy. In 1726 Sainte-Palaye's decision to live philosophically
no longer involved either withdrawal from society or the kind of
grudging and unhappy acceptance of it that had been characteristic
of an earlier generation of robins.

[53] "Je ne vais guères aux dévotions d'après dîner attendu qu'elles sont bien
fatigantes pour gens qui n'ont pas autant de zèle que nos Maistres," he admitted in
a letter to Edme from Wissembourg. (Bréquigny 66, fol. 51, 16.6.1725.) Years later,
in a letter to Mme Doublet telling her of a meeting he had with the Pope at
Castel Gondolfo he observed slyly that "les propos du St.-Père adressez à nous ont
été d'une affabilité paternelle à faire revenir les hérétiques les plus endurcis."
(Arsenal 4900, fol. 308, 24.6.1749.)

[54] Bréquigny 66, fol. 5, Stanislas to Sainte-Palaye from Lunéville, 4.11.1750, and
Bréquigny 62, fols. 193–201, a memorandum drawn up by Sainte-Palaye for Stanislas on the subject of the proposed Academy at Nancy. Sainte-Palaye was elected
to the new Academy in 1751. (Bréquigny 68, fol. 60, Stanislas to Sainte-Palaye,
24.5.1751.)

[55] On Sainte-Palaye's election to the Académie Française, see ch. 4 below.
Laugier recounts that in 1766 the Queen, seeing Sainte-Palaye at Compiègne, "lui
parla avec bonté." (Bréquigny 66, fol. 155, account of a 'Voyage autour de Paris.')

CHAPTER 3

INTELLECTUAL SOCIETIES, SALONS, AND FRIENDS

Back in Paris in 1726 Sainte-Palaye renewed old associations and established new ones. In general he lived well, in a style befitting an educated young gentleman. He had a house in the rue du Grand Chantier in the Marais, a valet, a cook, a coachman, various other servants, and two coaches.[1] Obviously he was—as one of his friends observed—"fort à son aise."[2] Being so, he took advantage of much that Paris had to offer in the way of society, amusement, and instruction.

"Paris et notre siècle sont féconds en . . . penseurs libres," Dubuisson complained to the Marquis de Caumont in 1737; "Ils forment des sociétés que la liberté dans laquelle on les laisse vivre leur donne lieu d'accroître tous les jours. Ce que nous avons de plus brillant dans la jeunesse par l'esprit et les sciences les compose, et vous ne sauriez croire combien ce germe pullule."[3] Sainte-Palaye was among the young men of promise from noble and robe families who frequented these societies. Some were pleasure-loving and gay; others, more serious, concerned themselves with politics and religion. All were *frondeur*, free-thinking, or subversive, in one way or another.

Dubuisson would probably not have included the Académie des Inscriptions et des Belles-Lettres among the groups he described to Caumont, yet it was as subversive in its way as any. In 1724, when

---

[1] According to his will (Archives de la Seine, DC⁶ 260, fol. 9). This was an average household staff for fairly well-to-do members of the robe. (Cf. Ford, p. 158.)

[2] Bimard de la Bastie in a letter to Mazaugues, in J. Bauquier, 'Les Provençalistes du XVIIIᵉ siècle,' *Revue des langues romanes*, 3ème série (1880), 4:65–83. F. Bluche, *Les Magistrats*, pp. 331–32 gives an interesting description of the hôtel of Pierre Augustin Chaillon, a robin of moderate means, in the rue du Grand Chantier. The hôtel of Chaillon compares poorly—according to Bluche—with outstanding robin residences like the hôtel de Lamoignon, but it is far above a bourgeois home.

[3] *Lettres du Commissaire Dubuisson*, p. 333.

Sainte-Palaye was elected to it, the Académie des Inscriptions was a very different body indeed from the one formed in 1663 to work on the inscriptions and medals that were to perpetuate the glory of the Sun King. That "petite Académie," as it was called, had at first been composed of only four members, and it was in no sense a learned Academy, except in so far as a certain talent was required to sing the monarch's praises in suitable Latin. None of the most eminent scholars of the time was a member. In 1683 Louvois raised the number of members to eight, but effected no real change in their activities. The increased membership reflected only an extension of the court duties of the "petite Académie."[4]

The slowness of the monarchs of the seventeenth century to aid scholars by setting up academies for them—they were ready to help individual scholars who placed their erudition at the disposal of royal authority[5]—contrasts with their willingness to encourage scientists, but it is understandable.[6] As early as 1614-17 an attempt by Spelman in England to revive the sixteenth century Society of Antiquaries met with the opposition of the King, who viewed the projected association of gentlemen with suspicion[7] and, in fact, Spelman's views indicate that the royal judgment was not mistaken. Colbert's great plan for an Encyclopaedic Academy under royal supervision was allowed to lapse, possibly for similar reasons.[8] In 1701, however, the new Chancellor Pontchartrain was persuaded by his nephew, the Abbé Bignon, to enlarge the Academy's compe-

---

[4] L'Académie des Inscriptions et Belles-Lettres (Paris, 1924), pp. 1-2.

[5] Baluze and the Dupuys, for instance, were both employed by the King. C. Godard in his study of the former (De Stephano Baluzio Tutelensi libertatum ecclesiae gallicanae propugnatore [Paris, 1901], p. 61) declares him "non historiarum scriptoris sed causidici regii more scripsisse historiam"; a similar judgment of Pierre Dupuy in G. Demante, 'Histoire de la publication des livres de Pierre Dupuy sur les libertés de l'église gallicane,' Bibliothèque de l'École des Chartes (1843-44), 5:585.

[6] Erudition was largely in the hands of monks who wrote in support of their order (see, on Mabillon, L. Traube, Vorlesungen und Abhandlungen zur Paläographie und Handschriftenkunde [Munich, 1909], 1:20; on Sirmond and Petau, A. de Meyer, Les premières controverses jansénistes en France, 1640-1649 [Louvain, 1919], pp. 149-51, 152-61, 252-64, 462-64) or of men of the robe who might write in defense of their own interests against those of the crown. (See M. Lecomte, Les Bénédictins et l'histoire des provinces aux XVIIe et XVIIIe siècles [Paris, 1928], p. 70.) In England the situation was similar, historical scholarship being one of the keenest interests of the gentry. (See D. C. Douglas, English Scholars [London, 1939], pp. 130-31.)

[7] Joan Evans, History of the Society of Antiquaries (Oxford, 1956), pp. 13, 14.

[8] J. B. Du Hamel, Regiae Scientiarum Academiae Historia (Leipzig, 1700), p. 3.

tence and alter its character. As a result of the new establishment, signed by the King in 1701 and confirmed by Letters Patent in 1713, the membership was brought up to forty, and the Academy was recognized as no longer a select committee of the Académie Française, but as an Academy of learning in its own right. Among the objects to which it was to devote itself were included the history and antiquities of France.

Noblemen and members of the robe had always had a special interest in this field which, in the sixteenth century in particular, had been a battleground of conflicting political factions.[9] At the end of the seventeenth century, as dissatisfaction with the administration of Louis XIV increased or became more manifest, nobles and *parlementaires* again turned to the arsenal of the past. By persuading his uncle to include French history within the purview of the new Academy and by securing the election to it of historians such as Rollin, Vertot, and later Fréret, Bignon transformed the Académie des Inscriptions into the most prominent of a whole series of meeting places for the intellectual leaders of robe and sword, and especially of the former; for nearly all the provincial academies were also founded and dominated by members of the robe.[10] In some cases indeed, as at Dijon, provision was made in their charters to ensure their continued control by the magistracy. They were almost always prudent in their choice of publications or papers to be given a public reading, and signs of unorthodoxy were visible only on rare occasions—as in 1714, for instance, when Fréret was sent to the Bastille for having read a paper at the Académie des Inscriptions in which he dealt with the origins of the monarchy in a manner unsatisfactory to the King.[11] In fact, however, questing

[9] On the theoretical side of these disputes, see W. F. Church, *Constitutional Thought in Sixteenth Century France* (Cambridge, Mass., 1941).

[10] See the excellent pages in Ford, pp. 234–38. Ford does not list those academies founded in the late seventeenth century, on the model of the Académie Française—Nîmes [1682], Angers [1685], Arles [1689], the revived Jeux Floraux of Toulouse [1694], Soissons [1699]—doubtless because their activities were limited in those early years to literature. Cf. also Pierre Jourda in Grente, *Dictionnaire des lettres françaises, Dix-huitième siècle* (Paris, 1960), art. 'Académies de province'; Mornet, *Origines intellectuelles de la Révolution française* (Paris, 1933), pp. 145–52, 301, and, most recently, Alphonse Dupront, 'Livre et culture dans la société française du XVIII⁰ siècle: Réflexions sur une enquête,' *Annales* (1965), 20:867–98.

[11] On the episode, see R. Simon, *Fréret*, pp. 16–19, 131–32, and Sabathier de Castres, *Les trois Siècles de la littérature* (Paris and Amsterdam, 1772), 2:195.

spirits in the robe and the nobility were critical of much that was associated with absolutism—religious as well as political. The Académie des Inscriptions was by no means a gathering of timorous and blinkered pedants.[12] J. R. Carré relates that Fontenelle saw it as "une excellente pépinière d'incrédulité,"[13] while P. Vernière comments that men with new and radical ideas infiltrated the Académie des Inscriptions long before the *philosophes* took over the Académie Française: "Non que les assemblées du mardi et du vendredi au Vieux Louvre aient été consacrées à la philosophie libertine, mais elles permettaient des contacts réguliers et discrets; la cooptation n'est guère discutée par le pouvoir royal qui ne s'inquiète pas de paisibles érudits."[14]

Among the *beaux esprits* patronized by the noblemen and parle-mentaires of the early years of the century, there were many who were not noted for their piety or orthodoxy. Thanks probably to Bignon, quite a number of these persons regularly attended the meetings in the Louvre. Fontenelle, for instance, whom Bignon had already brought to the Académie des Sciences, was elected to the Académie des Inscriptions in 1701. Of the works he had written or was credited with in 1701—other than his pastorals, plays, and essays in scientific vulgarization—the *Histoire des Oracles*, published in 1686, seems to be the most likely title to a place at the Inscriptions. The skeptical tendencies of this work were so transparent, however, that Fontenelle had seen fit to have it appear anonymously. In all probability, Bignon also secured the election in 1701 of J. B. Rousseau, a wild spirit at that time and one of a circle of wits which included La Motte, Fontenelle, Boindin, Saurin, the Abbé Terrasson, and the Président Hénault.[15] The Abbés Fraguier, elected in 1705, and Gédoyn, elected in 1716, were also well known in libertine circles.[16] Nicolas Boindin, elected in 1706, was an habitué of the Café Procope where he could be heard holding forth

---

[12] As Albert Cherel, for instance, seems to have believed (*Histoire de la littérature française*, sous la direction de J. Calvet [Paris, 1933], 6:45).

[13] J. R. Carré, *La Philosophie de Fontenelle; ou le sourire de la raison* (Paris, 1932), p. 516.

[14] P. Vernière, p. 396.

[15] *Mémoires du Président Hénault*, pp. 29–30; Grubbs, p. 51.

[16] Gustave Lanson, 'Origines et premières manifestations de l'esprit philosophique dans la littérature française de 1675 à 1748,' *Revue des Cours et Conférences*, May, 1908, pp. 409–22; also Étienne Colombey (ed.), *Correspondance authentique de Ninon de Lenclos* (Paris, 1886), pp. 54–55, 209–11, 229.

on "Monsieur de L'Être"; his atheist views were so notorious that
Fleury later barred him from the Académie Française. In 1714
Nicolas Fréret was elected, though he was still a young man and had
written nothing, thanks to the influence of Bignon and Rollin.

Bignon himself, the King's librarian, was a man of adventurous
and inquiring mind. He was one of a special group of academicians,
who, as of 1707, began to gather for still freer discussion with extra-
academic friends at the house of "un haut personnage," as Bougainville later related in his *Éloge* of Fréret, in order to "discuter
les points les plus difficiles de l'histoire ecclésiastique et civile, de la
chronologie et de la géographie." The "haut personnage" was probably the Maréchal Duc de Noailles,[17] a great friend of Boulainviller,
and the "difficult points" which were discussed more freely in this
intimate group than at the Académie des Inscriptions itself were:
first, historical questions which, for political reasons, it would have
been dangerous to debate openly; and second, questions of chronology and Biblical criticism. The members of the group included,
besides Noailles and Bignon, Boulainviller, Fréret, and the Abbé
Sevin, keeper of the King's manuscripts. Gradually it was enlarged
to take in the grammarian Du Marsais—like Fréret, Montesquieu,
Sainte-Palaye, Secousse, and so many other scholars of the Enlightenment, a product of Juilly, and usually assumed to be the author
of several anti-Christian and materialist treatises;[18] J. B. Mirabaud,
a former member of the Oratory, the director of the education of
the Regent's daughters, the author of a popular translation of Tasso,
and later Permanent Secretary of the Académie Française, but best
known now for the antireligious tracts with which he is credited;[19]
Lévesque de Burigny, author of a skeptical *Examen critique des
apologistes de la religion chrétienne* and of an *Histoire de la
philosophie paienne* in which he examined at great length and with
much hypocritically pious amazement at their large number the
pagan philosophers who had held pantheistic views similar to those
attributed to Spinoza. Boulainviller, who was in many respects the
animating spirit of the group, and whose Spinozist sympathies were

[17] But cf. R. Simon, *Boulainviller*, pp. 87–88, who questions this.
[18] Cf., however, H. Dieckmann, *Le Philosophe: Texts and Interpretation* (St.
Louis, 1948), pp. 17–26, where the attribution of 'philosophic' texts to Du Marsais
is subjected to serious question.
[19] Cf. Wade, pp. 205–21.

well known,[20] died early in 1722, but the group maintained its coherence for some time afterwards.

Sainte-Palaye was only twenty-seven years old when he was elected to the Académie des Inscriptions and he had not published a line. It is very likely that he owed his election to his reputation in the Boulainviller group and to the efforts of those of its members who were influential at the Académie. He had become known in academic and scholarly circles soon after his return from Holland. Some time before 1722 he was frequenting the Abbé Massieu,[21] and a little later he began attending the Tuesdays of Father Des Molets. About the same time he joined a group of former students at Juilly —like himself, from robe families—who had banded together to follow out a planned program of literary and historical studies. This group included Denys-François Secousse, Rollin's prize student, and Mauguet de Mézières, later a friend of Madame du Châtelet.[22] The ideas animating these young men were similar to those of Boulainviller's circle.

The Count and his friends were opposed to the classical humanist tradition in historiography, which they associated with absolutism and with the ecclesiastical allies of absolutism, the Jesuits. The leading Jesuit historian of the turn of the century in France, Father

[20] Mathieu Marais, a friend of Boulainviller, wrote to Bouhier of the so-called *Réfutation de Spinoza* (which appeared at Brussels in 1731, nine years after the death of its author), that its apparent orthodoxy "ne trompera personne. Je l'ai vu manuscrit et c'est une étrange idée d'avoir voulu éclairer ce que cet athée avait tenu obscur." (*Journal et Mémoires*, 4:361.) The manuscript version which Marais saw was the *Essai de métaphysique dans les principes de Benoît de Spinoza.*

[21] In 1743 Sainte-Palaye paid tribute to the Abbé Massieu "qui daigna seconder mes premiers efforts dans la carrière des lettres." (*MAI* 18:799.) Massieu died in 1722, so that the association of the two men dates from before then.

[22] Bréquigny 66, fol. 91, Secousse to Sainte-Palaye, 20.8.1722. On Secousse, see Bougainville: 'Éloge de Secousse,' *MAI** 25:289–302, and Villevault: 'Éloge de Secousse,' *Ordonnances des Rois de France*, vol. 9, pp. xxvii–xxx. De Mézières was probably not the Béthisy de Mézières of whom Saint-Simon draws a rather repugnant portrait (*Mémoires*, 14:320–22; 38:181–83) but the grandfather of Madame de Genlis, who in her *Mémoires*—admittedly of doubtful authenticity—writes of him: "M. de Mézières avoit beaucoup d'esprit et étoit un très grand géometre. C'est une anecdote parfaitement connue dans la province que M. de Mézières, voisin de la célèbre Madame du Châtelet, cultiva ses dispositions pour la géometrie et lui donna tous les matériaux pour les ouvrages qu'elle a publiés depuis." (*Mémoires de Madame de Genlis* [Paris, 1825], 1:142.) According to Violet Wyndham (*Madame de Genlis* [London, 1958], p. 22), Monsieur de Mézières, "a lawyer with cultivated tastes" was the *son* of the distinguished mathematician. At all events, he was indeed a good friend of Madame du Châtelet (cf. *Lettres de la Marquise du Châtelet*, ed. Th. Besterman, 2 vols. [Geneva, 1958], 1:50).

Gabriel Daniel, did in fact avow that his *Instructions pour l'histoire* were simply an abridgment of the precepts of the ancients, and despite some concessions to the need for accuracy and critical control of evidence, expressed his own conviction that the value to the historian of manuscripts and of documentary evidence had been exaggerated.[23] Boulainviller never lost an opportunity to ridicule Daniel. Although the outstanding writers and thinkers of the robe had traditionally been *Anciens*, they never liked the classicism of the Jesuits which was heavily weighted in favor of the Latin authors rather than the Greeks, and which stressed the appearance rather than the substance of the classics, their eloquence, rather than those moral virtues which the *Anciens* felt to be implicit in the "simplicity" and "naturalness" of writers less "civilized" than those of contemporary courtly society. They also disliked the Jesuit conception of history as an exercise in rhetoric rather than a science, because it encouraged historical skepticism and gave support to the doctrine that the Church itself at any moment in its history was the living embodiment of Christian truth. This doctrine, which made all historically grounded criticism of the Church or of any aspect of its current teachings or practices irrelevant, was opposed by Jansenists, Gallicans, and free thinkers alike.

Secousse, Sainte-Palaye, and Mézières were thus remaining loyal to an important current in the intellectual life of the magistracy, even as they too rejected the classical tradition in history writing and came down on the same side as the *Modernes*, on the side of *cose* rather than *parole*. Quintus Curtius, Secousse wrote to Sainte-Palaye in 1722, "n'est point un historien . . . c'est un Déclamateur

---

[23] Daniel's "Instructions" are in his *Histoire de France*, 3 vols. (Paris, 1713). Lenglet du Fresnoy (*Usage des Romans* [Amsterdam, 1734], 1:110) makes Daniel's attitude to sources the object of a cutting attack: "Lorsque le père Daniel écrivoit son Histoire, M. Boivin le cadet, l'un des sous-Bibliothécaires du Roy, s'avisa, croyant bien faire, de communiquer à cet habile Jésuite les Recueils de M. de Loménie et ceux de M. le Comte de Béthune. Le premier ce ces Recueils est un dépouillement fait par Mrs Dupuy de tout ce qu'il y a de plus précieux dans le Trésor des Chartes; et le second renferme une infinité de Lettres originales des Rois, Princes, Princesses et autres Seigneurs François depuis le règne de Louis XI. Ces deux Recueils peuvent aller à treize ou quatorze cens volumes in Folio. Le P. Daniel fut deux heures à les parcourir; il ne revint plus à la Bibliothèque du Roy, de peur d'y trouver encore ce Recueil; il dit néanmoins en sortant qu'il étoit fort content de ce qu'il avoit vu. Mais il parla plus sincèrement à un de ses Confrères, en lui disant que toutes ces Pièces étoient des paperasses dont il n'avoit que faire pour écrire l'histoire."

qui a choisi l'histoire d'Alex. comme un sujet illustre . . . Il n'a aucune des qualitez de l'historien. Il n'a mesme pas songé à la chronologie, il ignore les premiers principes de l'astrologie, ce qui lui a fait dire des choses absurdes, et il ne sçavoit pas mesme la Géographie . . . Tous ses discours sentent le Déclamateur, ils sont pleins de lieux communs; il n'a observé ni bienséance, ni caractère et les Perses et les Scythes y parlent comme les Grecs . . . Il manque souvent de jugement." Even Cicero was passed over as a historian, despite his merit as a writer and a philosopher, in favor of Diodorus Siculus. "Les faits secs et decharnez que je trouvois dans celui-ci m'attachoient plus que tous les traits de cette divine éloquence," Secousse declared.[24] Secousse and Sainte-Palaye were so convinced of the predominance of content over form that they recommended reading the Ancients in translation.[25]

It seems likely that this group of young scholars quickly came to the attention of Bignon and his friends, for in 1722 Secousse was elected to the Académie des Inscriptions at the age of thirty-one, with hardly a printed line to his credit, rather as Fréret had been elected some years previously. Secousse was certainly frequenting a circle of scholars whom he does not identify, but who—to judge by his letters—were influential and eager to make proselytes among the young. They also had their eye on Sainte-Palaye, for they had definite plans for him. Secousse wrote to Sainte-Palaye of an evening he spent with these men in late 1722: "Ils disoient que quoique la Nature vous eust donné du talent pour toutte sorte de littérature, cependant il ne paroissoit point que vous eussiez choisi une à laquelle vous estiez le plus propre, que l'estude des choses, des faits et de l'histoire vous conviendroit mieux que celle des mots et de l'éloquence . . . Ils se promettoient bien lorsque vous serez revenu à Paris de . . . diriger vos estudes et de vous former à suivre leurs Veües et leurs Idées particulierres."[26] It is very likely that the circle described by Secousse is that of Boulainviller. That the men in this circle were on the lookout for promising young disciples among the sons of aristocratic families is not surprising, in view of their political inclinations. Boulainviller's own work on French history and institutions was immediately related to the political ambitions

---

[24] Bréquigny 66, fols. 91–94, 20.8.1722.   [25] *Ibid.*
[26] Bréquigny 66, fols. 95–100, 16.11.1722.

of the nobility, and in his *Mémoires au Régent* he proposed a number of reforms that would have been advantageous to the *noblesse d'épée* and the landed *noblesse de robe* alike.

Something of these practical interests can still be detected in a vast program of studies in French history proposed to the Académie des Inscriptions in 1727 by the erudite doctor and professor of medicine Camille Falconet, who may also have been a member of Boulainviller's circle. His program formulates in a remarkable fashion the goals and methods of Boulainviller. Significantly enough, Sainte-Palaye took his cue from it, and all his own research was guided by it. Sainte-Palaye was a close associate and disciple of Falconet until the latter's death in 1762, and the doctor's curious *salon* was one of his regular haunts.

Born into a famous Lyons medical family, Falconet had been brought up by his grandfather, a friend and correspondent of the celebrated Guy Patin, in the traditions of Renaissance humanism, and by the end of Louis XIV's reign he was a familiar figure in libertine circles in Paris. Le Beau in his *Éloge* tells that on his settling in the capital he was admitted by the Duchesse de Bouillon to a "société choisie qu'elle avoit formée chez elle et qui réunissoit le sang le plus illustre de la France avec la plus éclatante littérature." Other guests of the Duchess included Le Sage, Chaulieu, J. B. Rousseau in his early period, Fontenelle, and Paradis de Moncrif, later a favorite of the devout Marie Leszczinska, which did not prevent him from dabbling actively in unorthodoxy.[27] Falconet shared Moncrif's interest in Spinoza—his library contained the complete works together with a rare collection of related texts—and Fontenelle's skepticism and epicureanism.[28] Moving in this aristocratic and libertine milieu, he was naturally on the side of the *Modernes* in the *Querelle*.[29] His skepticism in matters of religion, his sympathy with materialist ideas, the generosity with which he made his large library of physical, medical, and clandestine texts

---

[27] Sainte-Beuve, *Causeries du lundi*, 7ᵉ ed., 2:359; *Mémoires de d'Argenson*, ed. Société de l'Histoire de France, 2:61–62; Grubbs, p. 71; Carré, *Fontenelle*, pp. 555–57. Moncrif was among the Spinozists and free thinkers who met under the aegis of the gallant and philosophical Comte de Plélo, one of the lions of the Regency.

[28] In 1752 he honored his old friend by publishing his *Théorie des tourbillons cartésiens*.

[29] B.N. Français 9457, fols. 64–76, 'Lettre de M. Falconet sur la querelle à l'occasion d'Homère,' dated 10.5.1715.

available to men of letters, and the encouragement he gave to the *philosophes* themselves, made him a great favorite with the *Encyclopédistes*, who thanked him publicly for the assistance he had given them.[30] At the end of his life, Falconet won a spirited tribute from Grimm who observed: "Je n'ai jamais vu de jeune homme plus séduisant que ne l'était notre digne Falconnet à l'âge de quatre-vingt-onze ans."[31] On Sunday mornings a group of literary men and *philosophes* met together at Falconet's home for what was called ironically "la messe des gens de lettres," a title that set the tone of the gatherings. The regulars included—besides Sainte-Palaye and his friend and protégé Bréquigny—Grimm, d'Alembert, and Maupertuis.[32]

Another society which Sainte-Palaye frequented on his return to Paris was that of Rémond le Grec. This Rémond—one of three brothers, the sons of a fermier-général—had belonged to the circle of Ninon de Lenclos, and he counted among his best friends the Abbé Fraguier and Fontenelle. He had lived in England, and he entertained excellent relations with Lord Stair, the British ambassador, as well as with the celebrated Lady Mary Wortley-Montague.[33] Though he sided with the *Anciens* during the *Querelle*, his refined epicureanism, formulated in a *Dialogue de la Volupté*,[34] endeared him to Fontenelle and to other free-thinking spirits of the time. "C'est un homme qui a beaucoup d'esprit et de belles-lettres ... Il joue, il aime les femmes et la cour," Mathieu Marais said of him,[35] though as a good robin Marais did not pass up a chance of deriding him at a later date for his opportunism. During the regency of the Duc d'Orléans he obtained the post of Introducteur des Am-

---

[30] *Encyclopédie*, 'Discours préliminaire,' vol. 1, p. xliv. See also Diderot, *Correspondance*, ed. G. Roth, 1:65, and Jean Mayer, *Diderot homme de science* (Rennes, 1959), p. 55, on the relation of Diderot and Falconet.

[31] *Correspondance littéraire*, ed. Tourneux (Paris, 1882), 5:46.

[32] On Falconet's salon, see Paul Lacroix, *Institutions, usages, et coutumes, 1700–1789* (Paris, 1875), p. 448; C. Le Beau: 'Éloge de Falconet,' MAI* 31:345–57; and *Bulletin de la Société de l'Histoire de France*, 2e série (1861), 3:24–29. It was at Falconet's—Voltaire wrote to König—that Maupertuis read his "long ouvrage contre vous et contre moi, intitulé *la Querelle*." (Besterman, 4860.)

[33] His letters to Lady Mary in Robert Halsband, ed., *The Complete Letters of Lady Mary Wortley-Montague, 1708–1720* (Oxford, 1965), 1:395–96, 446–53. Cf. also Robert Halsband, *The Life of Lady Mary Wortley-Montagu* (Oxford, 1956), esp. pp. 85–86, 102–4, 108–9.

[34] Published in 1736 in *Recueil de divers écrits*, ed. by Saint-Hyacinthe.

[35] *Journal et Mémoires*, 1:283.

bassadeurs,[36] and it must have been about this time that Sainte-Palaye got to know him. On his death in 1741, Sainte-Palaye paid tribute to him in a letter to Bouhier: "C'étoit un homme de beaucoup d'esprit, d'une littérature exquise et d'un commerce infiniment aimable. Comme je jouissois plus que personne du plaisir de vivre dans sa société on ne sauroit plus le regretter que je fais."[37]

Sainte-Palaye frequented other societies of urbane, free-thinking, and pleasure-loving people, similar to that of Rémond le Grec, but even less memorable. At the home of Madame de Mézières, for instance, there was a great deal of gaiety and probably of libertinage.[38] Little known salons such as this played their part, along with the better known ones, and more serious groups like the Entresol and the circle of Boulainviller, in fomenting the *esprit frondeur* that is characteristic of the first half of the century.

Sainte-Palaye remained deeply attached to this witty and skeptical culture. As the century advanced, however, the *Modernes* gave way to the *Encyclopédistes* and to reformers of broader views and more practical intentions. The trend can be observed in some of the societies Sainte-Palaye frequented in the second half of the century.

One of the most celebrated of these was the *paroisse* of Madame Doublet de Persan in the Cour des Filles Saint-Thomas.[39] Sainte-Palaye was a regular and much-loved member of this salon for many years, and he felt particularly at home in it. It was dominated by men of the robe, many of them no longer active in office, but content to be witty and urbane writers, amateurs, or scholars. "On y était janséniste," Grimm wrote, "ou très parlementaire, mais on n'y était pas chrétien; jamais croyant ni dévot n'y fut admis."[40] The tone was set by Madame Doublet herself, talented, intelligent, a

[36] *Journal de Barbier*, 30.3.1721.   [37] B.N. Français 24418, fol. 370, 9.12.1741.
[38] Bréquigny 66, fols. 48, 99. After her husband's death in 1734, Madame de Mézières married the celebrated lover of the Duchesse du Berri, "Beau La Haye."
[39] On this salon, see Edmond and Jules de Goncourt, *Portraits intimes du XVIIIᵉ siècle* (Paris, 1857), 1ère série, pp. 73–76, and the same authors' *La Femme au XVIIIᵉ siècle* (Paris, 1862), pp. 416–17; Feuillet de Conches, *Les Salons de conversation au XVIIIᵉ siècle* (Paris, 1891), pp. 109–17; Grimm: *Corr. litt.*, 9:317–18; unsigned article in *Gazette de France*, 23.11.1898, which protests the piety of Mme Doublet but adds Helvétius to her parishioners; Pierre Manuel, *La Police de Paris dévoilée* (Paris, an II), 1:201 *et seq.*, from which the Goncourts have drawn most of their information. They seem not to have used an invaluable source on Mme Doublet's salon, the correspondence of the Marquis d'Éguilles with Bachaumont and Mme Doublet in Arsenal 4900, fols. 1–103, though this correspondence was published in the *Revue rétrospective* for 1886 (see n. 46 below).
[40] *Correspondance littéraire*, 9:317–18.

worthy member of the wealthy Crozat family, and above all by her lifelong friend the amateur, critic, and memorialist Petit de Bachaumont. Skeptical, ironical, cultivated, Bachaumont was the son of a gay blade, who, to please his father, had accepted a charge of *auditeur des comptes*.[41] Bachaumont *petit-fils* was as little attracted by the dignity of office as his father. "Je suis né avec un bien fort honnête dont j'ai pu disposer dès mes premières années," he declared in a letter to the painter J. B. M. Pierre; "je n'ai voulu prendre ni charges, ni emplois; j'ai voulu rester libre."[42] And in a letter of thanks to an influential lady who had procured him a charge of *premier président* at one of the sovereign courts he vowed to "remuer ciel et terre et employer toutes les manières possibles, tous les souterrains imaginables et tout le crédit que m'a fait obtenir ma charge pour avoir la permission de la vendre."[43]

Around them Madame Doublet and Bachaumont had gathered an extraordinarily tightly knit, devoted group of like-minded people. Sainte-Palaye and his friend Foncemagne were, like Bachaumont, from families of *officiers*, and, like him, they had given up thoughts of office in order to live "noblement" and to pursue in freedom their own interests. Similarly Bimard de La Bastie, a young man from the Dauphiné, had been trained for the magistracy, but unattracted by the exercise of office, had pursued a military career for a while, before settling down to the life of a gentleman scholar. Guided by the Président de Valbonnais, he was introduced to Bouhier's circle at Dijon and became a member of the Académie des Inscriptions. La Bastie held unorthodox opinions in religion and politics. A paper on the Roman *pontifices maximi* which he read to the Académie des Inscriptions caused a mild scandal, because in it he argued that the early Christian emperors by no means broke with

---

[41] The Goncourts' delightful sketch of this "aimable homme accommodant et facile, tout à tous," who was Bachaumont's father is in *Portraits intimes*, 1:54–58.

[42] *Ibid.*, p. 85. Cf. also *Revue universelle des arts* (1857), 5:261. Bachaumont's attitude is characteristic of an important part of the magistracy and expresses one of the ideals of the older bourgeoisie, according to Werner Sombart. (*Der Bourgeois* [Munich and Leipzig, 1913], pp. 200–1 *et passim*.) The ideal of an independent existence devoted to intellectual labors and distractions is certainly common in the seventeenth and eighteenth centuries. Thus, Fontenelle is supposed to have declared "qu'il auroit voulu naître avec cinquante mille livres de rente, et d'être Président de la Chambre des Comptes; car . . . il faut être quelque chose, et que ce quelque chose ne vous oblige à rien." (Trublet, *Mémoires*, in Fontenelle, *Oeuvres* [Amsterdam, 1764], 11:182.)

[43] E. et J. de Goncourt, *Portraits intimes*, 1:77.

the pagan cults. This view was disturbing to many conservative-minded people, including Président Bouhier. La Bastie himself hinted that their suspicion of him was not ill-founded. "Je n'ai pas toujours dit tout ce que je pensais," he wrote to a friend, "mais les gens d'esprit m'entendront, et ce n'est pas pour les sots que j'écris."[44] With his intimate friends he was less restrained. Fréret refers suggestively to the "liberté avec laquelle il disait son senti-ment" and to his "caractère ferme, plein de droiture et de franchise, ennemi de toute dissimulation." Nobility for him meant, above all, courage to face the truth and tell it and disdain for every form of hypocrisy. La Bastie was a particular friend of Falconet and of Sainte-Palaye, whose interest in the Provençal poets he shared.[45]

Also from a distinguished robe family in the South was the attrac-tive young Alexandre Jean-Baptiste Boyer, Marquis d'Eguilles, brother of the more celebrated Marquis d'Argens. The Boyers were an old noble family, which had joined the ranks of the robe. Pre-ferring adventure to a sinecure at the Parlement of Aix, where his father was *procureur général*, he sailed for Edinburgh in October, 1745, as semi-official ambassador of the Court of France to the Young Pretender. He was taken prisoner after Culloden, upon which he was quietly abandoned by his government. His letters to Bachaumont and Madame Doublet, written during Charles Ed-ward's campaigns and from his prison in Carlisle, are full of charm, wit, and affection. They say much for the spirit that bound the members of the *paroisse* together. On the other hand, his official dispatches to d'Argenson reveal him as a lucid and intelligent ob-server of the episode of the '45.[46]

The d'Argentals—Monsieur and Madame—witty, amiable, and intelligent, were pillars of the *paroisse*, and they occasionally brought along their eminent friend, M. de Voltaire. Their back-ground, too, was that of the robe. D'Argental's father had been a *président honoraire* of the Parlement of Metz; he himself held an office of *conseiller* at the *Chambre des Enquêtes* in addition to

[44] Quoted by Gaston Boissière, 'Un Savant au XVIIIe siècle, Jean-François Séguier, d'après sa correspondance inédite,' *Revue des deux mondes*, April, 1871, pp. 446–72.

[45] *Ibid.*, pp. 449–53.

[46] His letters are in *Revue rétrospective* (1886), 3:95–168, 217–57; (1886), 4:121–44, 217–40; (1886), 5:73–96. On his mission, see the article by G. Lefèvre-Pontalis, 'La Mission du Marquis d'Eguilles en Écosse auprès de Charles-Édouard (1745–46),' *Annales de l'École Libre des Sciences Politiques* (1887), 2:239–62, 423–52.

serving, subsequently, as the representative in Paris of the Duchy of Parma. But d'Argental too was inwardly detached from his public office. Since his youth he had had a passion for the theater and before his marriage had constantly courted actresses. Voltaire, considering him a man of letters and of the world rather than a magistrate, repeatedly urged him to get rid of his office: "Vendez vite votre vilaine charge de conseiller au parlement, qui vous prend un temps que vous devez aux charmes de la société; quittez ce triste fardeau qui fait qu'on se lève matin."[47]

More bound to their official posts were two other members of the "parish": Durey de Viencourt, president of the *Grand Conseil*, and his son, Durey de Meinières. The latter, for reasons that are certainly not foreign to the political pretensions of the *cours souveraines*, had made the history of the Parlement his special hobby. He had gone through the registers and compiled over a hundred folio volumes of catalogues and digests of their contents, which he put to use in a fervid statement of the jurisdictional rights of the parlements, published in 1755.[48] More resounding than Meinières' pamphlet was the celebrated denunciation of the Jesuits made in 1761 by the Abbé de Chauvelin, another faithful *paroissien*, before the Parlement of Paris of which he was a *conseiller clerc*. The Jesuits, in Chauvelin's requisitory, were the instruments of pontifical and episcopal despotism, oppressors of the second-order clergy in whose defense the Parlement, as the watchdog of the nation, must act. Chauvelin's attack—which made him something of a popular hero—could not have displeased his fellow *paroissiens*, least of all the Abbé Xaupi, Dean of the Faculty of Theology at the University of Paris. A staunch appellant from the bull *Unigenitus*, Xaupi, like Chauvelin, belonged to an eminent robe family. He did a great deal of research on early Catalán and Spanish texts and put his learning to use in a number of works designed to demonstrate the extensive authority of the *conseil*—the equivalent of the Parlement in his native Roussillon. His dislike of the politics of the

---

[47] Besterman 1319.

[48] 'Indication sommaire des principes et des faits qui prouvent la compétence de la puissance séculière pour punir les évêques coupables de crimes publics, et pour les contenir dans l'obéissance qu'ils doivent aux lois, et dans la soumission qu'ils doivent au roi.' Meinières' wife, one of the few women admitted to the *paroisse*, was also a keen student of history. (Cf. *Correspondance de l'abbé du Bos*, ed. Lombard [Paris, 1913], p. 70.)

bishops made him, again like Chauvelin, a powerful ally of the lower-order clergy. Throughout his life he remained ardently Richerist in his theology, bitterly hostile to the Jesuits, and an attentive reader of the *philosophes*, especially of Rousseau.[49]

Grimm's characterization of the *paroisse* as "très parlementaire" thus turns out to be fairly accurate. What about the supposedly atheist temper of Madame Doublet, Bachaumont and their friends? Both Lanson and Professor Vernière[50] have described Madame Doublet's salon as a hotbed of Spinozist and materialist ideas. Many of the members were at least keenly interested in these ideas. Falconet, as we have observed, owned all Spinoza's works. Bachaumont, in his characteristically casual way, turns out to be unusually well-informed about Spinozistic and materialist literature, and Professor Vernière suggests that he was more than simply well-informed.[51] He was certainly no Christian, this man who, in his youth, had carved on the walls of a garden temple in his grandfather's country estate the motto *Otio, Musis et Amoribus* and who on his deathbed could find nothing to say to the priest but "Monsieur, vous avez bien de la bonté." As for the mistress of the house, we have Grimm's word that "elle a passé quarante ans de suite sans sortir de sa chambre, ne se souciant de faire aucun acte de religion."[52] The Spinozist sympathies of at least one *paroissien*, the scientist Dortous de Mairan, one of the wittiest, most affable, and most sought-after men of the age, are well established.[53] Still another *paroissien*, J. B. de Mirabaud, is usually credited with a number of anti-biblical and anti-Christian tracts. Even the assorted Abbés who attended on Madame Doublet hardly lent an air of orthodoxy to the *paroisse*. The Abbés Voisenon and Legendre were unashamedly and notoriously libertine. The latter, the brother of Madame Doublet,

> Siégoit à table
> Mieux qu'au jubé

in Piron's words.[54] The same might have been said of "notre cher

---

[49] Préclin, pp. 321–24, 331, 331n.
[50] Lanson, 'Sur l'histoire de l'esprit philosophique en France avant 1750,' *RHLF* (1912), 19:1–29, 293–317; Vernière, pp. 394, 617.
[51] Vernière, pp. 617–19.   [52] Grimm, *Corr. litt.*, 9:317–18.
[53] Vernière, pp. 279–86 *et passim*.
[54] Quoted in an article on the Salon of Madame Doublet, *Gazette de France*, 23.11.1898.

abbé de Bernis,"[55] the companion of Diderot's Bohemian youth, who was always more interested in advancing his fortune in this world than in laying up store for the next. None of the remaining *paroissiens* seems to have had more religion than the abbés. Certainly not Pidansat de Mairobert, who had been raised by Madame Doublet and was perhaps her child, or d'Argental's brother, Pont-de-Veyle, the faithful companion of Madame du Deffand. The Comte de Tressan, it is true, belonged to the intimate circle—the society "des Saintes"—of the Queen, but he was a thoroughly worldly and irreverent character, a friend of the *philosophes*, the author of some elegantly libertine adaptations of medieval romances, and a wag whose propensity for satirical verse got him banished from court on occasion.[56] The poet Piron had bouts of religion between visits to the Café Procope, but as in the case of J. B. Rousseau, these seem to have owed more to personal resentments than to divine encouragement, except, perhaps, for the last one which overtook him when he was too old and sick to fight it off. As for Sainte-Palaye himself, there is no indication anywhere in his work or in his letters of anything but indifference to religion.[57] Grimm allowed of only one Christian among the *paroissiens*—Foncemagne. But even he turned to the consolations of religion only after the death of his wife.[58]

What then *was* the creed of the *paroisse* and its priestess? In large measure it seems to have been one of skepticism, criticism, and contempt for official dogmas combined with a love of irreverent and entertaining discussion. "Ce petit monde," the Goncourts write, ". . . vivait sans souci, sans Dieu, sans remords, dans la plus profonde et la plus sereine paresse d'âme. La vie et le présent lui étaient tout. Il n'avait ni peur ni curiosité du lendemain. Il ne demandait point aux choses la raison de l'homme, à l'homme la raison des choses. Le catéchisme d'Epicure lui suffisait. Il vivait en paix avec sa conscience, qu'il n'éveillait pas, en paix avec la religion publique qu'il saluait dans la rue. Les hommes de ce monde n'étaient ni philosophes, ni jansénistes; ils regardaient de la fenêtre jouer la foi à pile ou

---

[55] D'Eguilles to Bachaumont, 24.10.1748, *Revue rétrospective*, 5:79.
[56] Cf. H. Jacoubet, *Le Comte de Tressan et le genre troubadour* (Paris, 1923); also *Lettres du Commissaire Dubuisson*, pp. 431–37, 445.
[57] See ch. 2, n. 53 above.
[58] Cf. *Correspondance de J. J. Rousseau*, ed. P. Plan, 5:43–44, Madame de Verdelin to Rousseau, Feb., 1760.

face, sans parier. Ils étaient des athées nonchalants, des impies sans zèle: ils étaient des indifférents."[59] While not completely inaccurate, the Goncourt brothers' charming portrait is too much colored by the world-weary agnosticism of the late nineteenth century. There was more active questioning, more concern among these men than the Goncourts will allow. Their "patriotism," their interest in reform, their concern with the good of the nation, though not exclusive of sectional prejudices, appear to have been genuine, and their circle can probably be considered a nursery of the so-called Patriot movement of the eighties of the century. Madame Doublet's *paroissiens* were doubtless critical, in the first instance, of what irked them and obstructed their own claims; but in their criticism they accepted for themselves, and encouraged others to accept, ways of thought and standards of judgment that were to lead beyond sectional goals; at the same time they were induced into adventurous speculations, the full consequences of which they did not foresee, and into alliance with men whose interests were not always the same as their own.[60] The *Mémoires secrets* of Bachaumont and Mairobert show strong parliamentary sympathies. At the same time the editors are "enlightened," progressive, and they support the *philosophes*, whom they consider allies in the struggle against "tyranny."

The *paroisse* was distinguished from some other salons and libertine circles by the unusual degree of unity among its members and by its activity as a group. All the *paroissiens* had pet names by which, in mock-conspiratorial fashion, they were known among themselves. All—and occasionally Voltaire—contributed to Madame Doublet's *registres*, a ledger of unofficial news, from which *nouvelles à la main* were made up and dispatched by the d'Argentals' valet to subscribers in Paris and the provinces.[61] These *nouvelles* satisfied a real demand. "Un peuple qui veut s'instruire ne se contente pas de la gazette de France," the author of a work on the *Police de Paris dévoilée*, published early in the Revolution, declared ironically. "Que lui importe que le roi ait lavé les pieds à des pauvres qui ne les ont pas sales . . . que Monsieur ait daigné agréer

[59] *Portraits intimes*, 1:86–87.   [60] Cf. Préclin, pp. 166–67; also Ford, p. 88.
[61] From Frascati Sainte-Palaye remembered to send an account of an audience with Benedict XIV (Arsenal 4900, fol. 308, 24.6.1749). From Brussels Voltaire contributed items "pour . . . orner le grand livre de Mme Doublet" (to Mme de Solar, 5.9.1742, Besterman 2479).

un livre que peut-être il ne lira pas; et que le parlement, en robes, ait harangué un dauphin en maillot? Il veut à la fin savoir tout ce qui se dit et tout ce qui se fait à la Cour, pourquoi et pour qui un cardinal de Rohan s'amusait à enfiler des perles; s'il est vrai que la comtesse Diane nommait les généraux d'armées, et la comtesse Julie des évêques; combien le ministre de la guerre donnait de croix de St. Louis à sa maîtresse pour ses étrennes."[62] What the *nouvelles à la main* provided was something like the "inside story" behind official announcements and official silences. They undermined respect for the Court by revealing or insinuating frivolous motives and causes behind important policy decisions, fostered disrespect and skepticism concerning official dogmas of all kinds, animated the spirit of criticism and inquiry, and contributed to the formation of a public opinion. Madame Doublet's newsletter seriously embarrassed the King on occasion,[63] and in 1753, at the height of his difficulties with the parlements in the affair of the sacraments, the government threatened to intervene, as it had done a few years previously in the case of Father Des Molets' little gatherings, which were disbanded in 1750. Madame Doublet was warned by the lieutenant of police that the King was informed of the scandalous news spread abroad by visitors to her home and of the disrespectful nature of their conversations. She was enjoined "à faire cesser au plus tôt un pareil abus en éloignant de chez elle les personnes qui contribuent à l'entretenir."[64] On another occasion Choiseul, who was related to Madame Doublet through his wife, fulminated against "cette femme, ma très chère tante" and warned her that "s'il sort derechef une nouvelle de sa maison, le Roi la renfermera dans un couvent d'où elle ne distribuera plus des nouvelles aussi impertinentes que contraires au service du Roi."[65] In fact, Madame Doublet was not locked away, and the *nouvelles* continued to

---

[62] Pierre Manuel, *La Police de Paris dévoilée* (Paris, an II), 1:201.

[63] See *Correspondance secrète du Comte de Broglie*, ed. Ozanam and Antoine (Paris, 1956), 1:190–91 on the part played by the *nouvelles* in the complicated affair of the Chevalier d'Éon, Louis XV's personal agent in London.

[64] Quoted in Manuel, 1:204.

[65] Quoted in E. and J. de Goncourt, *Portraits intimes*, 1:75–76. In fact, Choiseul himself was an intimate friend of Madame d'Argental and she—according to the writer and spy Mouhy, who had been appointed to observe Madame Doublet's salon—"tient aussi même bureau de nouvelles" (quoted in Manuel, 1:207). Madame Denis also declared in a letter to Voltaire that "M. de Choiseul est parlementaire. Il les soutient dans toutes les occasions. Cela est inconsevable [sic], mais cela est." (Besterman 14544.)

appear. Only d'Argental's valet Gilet suffered for the vagaries of his masters and after 1759, when d'Argental was appointed Minister of Parma, even Gilet was covered by diplomatic immunity.

Madame Doublet's *paroisse* was different from d'Holbach's later and more radical *synagogue*. As Grimm observed, "on n'affichait pas dans sa maison cette liberté de penser philosophique; on s'en servait sans en jamais parler." The *nouvelles* themselves were intended to have a limited and select circulation, and subscribers were advised to "ménager le secret, autant pour ne pas les avilir et les rendre trop communes que pour ne pas faire de querelles avec les arbitres de la librairie."[66] The *paroissiens*, many of whom had ties with the old libertine circles of the previous century, had no intention of rabble-rousing. Having the public weal in mind, they wished to instruct others no doubt, but they acted cautiously in the tradition of the early Enlighteners. Some of them might even have agreed with Dubuisson who, having given the Marquis de Caumont a detailed account of a manuscript *Lettre sur la mortalité de l'âme*, concluded: "L'on finit en répétant le raisonnement rebattu que les philosophes ne sont jamais dangereux, parce qu'ils n'ont pas le fanatisme d'être chefs de parti; ce qui, selon moi, ne prouve pas que le monde, en général, puisse se passer de religion, mais seulement que les philosophes le peuvent."[67] Mirabaud, on d'Alembert's testimony, was loath to share his ideas and his work even with his friends.[68] La Bastie, as we saw, did not write "pour les sots" but for those who could read between the lines. Such ideas were commonplace in the early eighteenth century. Duclos records that Fréret told him he would be distressed if a certain "dangerous" work of his were to become public. He intended it, he said, only for "des amis *interioris admissionis*."[69] Duclos himself was alarmed by the combativeness of a new generation of *philosophes*, too eager, in his view, to "tirer des cabinets et rendre publics des écrits qui n'en devaient jamais sortir."[70] There was undoubtedly an element of "élitism" in the prudence of the free thinkers—entirely understandable in an age which envisaged reform as coming from above.

---

[66] *Portraits intimes*, 1:75.
[67] *Lettres du Commissaire Dubuisson*, p. 225. Cf. likewise Montesquieu's *Dissertation sur la politique des Romains dans la religion*.
[68] 'Éloge de J. B. Mirabaud,' quoted by Carré, *Fontenelle*, p. 536.
[69] Quoted in Vernière, p. 397n.
[70] Quoted in P. Meister, *Charles Duclos, 1704–1772* (Geneva, 1956), p. 44.

At the same time, this prudence was also in part determined by tactical motives, and it would be wrong to refuse Madame Doublet's parishioners the title of Enlighteners.[71] Grimm was right to salute the old lady of the Cour des Filles St.-Thomas on behalf of the *philosophes*.[72]

Sainte-Palaye also frequented the salon of one of Madame Doublet's *paroissiennes*, Anne-Marie du Boccage, the wife of a *receveur des tailles* at Dieppe. Fontenelle, Clairaut, Voltaire, Dr. Johnson, and Pope Benedict XIV were among her admirers. With some pretension to literary talent—she translated *Paradise Lost* and made her own contribution to the revival of the epic and the *grand goût* with *La Colombiade*—she was not a frivolous woman. The tone of her salon was too earnest for Marmontel, who declared that "le sérieux m'en étouffait et j'en fus chassé par l'ennui."[73] The very moderation which oppressed Marmontel appealed to Gibbon, who preferred her salon to that of her rivals,[74] and to the gentle Barthélémy, who remained faithful to her for fifty years. Sainte-Palaye's protégé and his best friend, the historian Bréquigny, died in her home in 1794. The members included Mairan, Marivaux, Montesquieu, the d'Argentals, the mathematician Clairaut, the philosopher Condillac, the sculptor Bouchardon, and at least one of the Van Loos, a family of successful painters. Sainte-Palaye knew all of these people well. Other regulars with whom he was friendly

[71] On the élitism of Fontenelle and other eighteenth century Enlighteners, cf. some remarks by Robert Shackleton in his preface to Fontenelle's *Entretiens sur la pluralité des mondes* (Oxford, 1955), p. 33, and Krauss, 1:9, 70–75. The former argues that Fontenelle's élitism was fundamentally aristocratic, the latter that it was primarily tactical. The two arguments can probably be reconciled. The early Enlighteners did not believe that the categories of human society could be altered: there would always be a few wise men and a populace of fools, as there would always be masters and servants. On the other hand, the wise men and the masters were not, in their view, a hereditary caste, and it was also the function of the wise in each generation to lead the populace to follow beneficial principles, instead of blindly following harmful ones. On this question see the fundamental study of Bernhard Groethuysen, *Die Entstehung der bürgerlichen Welt- und Lebensanschauung in Frankreich*, 2 vols. (Halle, 1927–30).

[72] It is worth noting that of five societies which Lanson considered breeding grounds of the philosophic spirit in the early eighteenth century—"ceux qui ont pour centres Boulainvilliers, Rémond le Grec, le médecin Falconet, le cercle des Caumartin, le salon de Madame Doublet" ('Sur l'histoire de l'esprit philosophique,' *RHLF* [1912], 19:310)—we have found that the leading medievalist of eighteenth century France belonged to four.

[73] 'Mémoires,' *Oeuvres complètes* (Paris, 1818), 1:468. On her salon, see also Grace Gill-Mark, *Anne-Marie du Boccage* (Paris, 1925).

[74] *The Autobiographies of Edward Gibbon*, ed. Murray (London, 1896), p. 204.

were Buffon, his neighbor in their native Burgundy, the Cardinal de Bernis whom he also met at Madame Doublet's, and the painter Joseph Vernet, whom he had visited in Rome and from whom he had commissioned four paintings. Here, in addition, he rubbed shoulders with La Condamine, Helvétius, Mably, Condorcet, Carlo Goldoni, Lord Chesterfield, and Madame du Boccage's special protégé, the Abbé Yart, an authority on English poetry and one of the founders of the Académie de Rouen.

Several scholars held literary salons of their own. We have already mentioned the Tuesday meetings at Father Des Molets' and the Sunday mornings at Falconet's. Foncemagne, an intimate friend of Sainte-Palaye since the early twenties,[75] had gathered round him a little circle which met regularly at his home in Saint-Cloud. It included Malesherbes, the correct but loyal protector of the *philosophes*,[76] the Prince de Beauvau and the Duc de La Rochefoucauld, two noblemen distinguished by their dedication to the cause of Enlightenment and their patronage of the *philosophes*, Nicolas Desmarets, the geologist—a member of the Académie des Sciences, a contributor to the *Encyclopédie* and a beneficent administrator in the Limousin, where he was inspector of manufactures during the intendancy of Turgot[77]—Mably, Bachaumont, and the antiquarians Quiret de Margency and Grosley.[78] Gibbon, when he was in Paris, enjoyed "the evening conversations of Mr. de Foncemagne," which, he says, "were supported by the erudition and good sense of the principal members of the Academy of Inscriptions."[79]

The discussions at Foncemagne's must have ranged widely over many topics of literature, scholarship, and science. Sainte-Palaye and Gibbon certainly discussed the former's *Mémoires sur l'an-*

---

[75] A letter of 16.6.1725 mentions "mon amy Foncemagne." (Bréquigny 66, fol. 51.)

[76] On the death of Malesherbes' father, the Académie des Inscriptions invited Foncemagne and Paulmy d'Argenson, as those closest to him, to convey to Malesherbes the Academy's condolences. (Registres Ac. Insc. [1772], p. 100.) It was also Foncemagne who composed the epitaph for Malesherbes' father. (B.N. Français, 9457, fol. 13.)

[77] Germain Martin, *La grande Industrie en France sous le règne de Louis XV* (Paris, 1900), p. 96.

[78] On Foncemagne's salon, see Feuillet de Conches, *Les Salons de conversation au XVIIIᵉ siècle* (Paris, 1891), p. 103; J. Brackelmann, 'Die altfranzösische Liederhandschrift no. 389 der Stadtbibliothek zu Bern,' *Archiv für das Studium der neueren Sprachen* (1867), 41:339; also a letter from Desmarets to Grosley of 11.12.1758, B.N. Nouv. Acq. Fr. 803, fol. 95. Only Gibbon testifies to the presence of Mably (*Autobiographies*, p. 314).

[79] *Autobiographies*, p. 262.

cienne chevalerie, for in 1764 Sainte-Palaye wrote to Bréquigny—then in London—inquiring if his work were known and if it had been translated "comme M. Gibbon me l'avoit assuré."[80] But the conversation probably turned quite frequently to politics. Gibbon reports a heated argument he had at Foncemagne's house with Mably over the relative merits of republican government and limited monarchy.[81] The composition of the salon—Grosley was an ardent champion of the Economists and of the Abbé Coyer's thesis in his *Noblesse commerçante,* Desmarets later did well during the Revolution, Beauvau and La Rochefoucauld were subsequently leading figures in the Patriot party and in the so-called *Société des trente* which began meeting at the house of Conseiller Duport in 1788,[82] Malesherbes was the author of a memorandum to the King advising him to convoke not the old Estates General of the fourteenth century, "vieux débris de l'ancienne barbarie," but "les propriétaires d'une grande Nation renouvellée par la civilisation"[83]—indicates that, even more clearly than the *paroisse* of Madame Doublet, it was a forum of liberal ideas and reform projects.

Sainte-Palaye was a member of yet another group of scholars and *philosophes,* centered around Trudaine, the close friend of Helvétius and of Mairan, a member of the Académie des Sciences, a director of commerce under Machault and one of the great liberal administrators of the reign of Louis XV.[84] Here he encountered his old comrade Doctor Falconet, de Jaucourt, the hard-working Protestant who was second-in-command of the *Encyclopédie,* Réaumur the scientist, Madame Dupré de Saint-Maur, the wife of an eminent member of the robe, and Montesquieu.[85] The latter was highly esteemed by Sainte-Palaye, as he was—almost to a man—by the scholars and academicians of the magistracy, of which he was the most illustrious living son. He seems to have visited Sainte-Palaye in Burgundy in 1749, shortly before the latter left on his second Italian journey.[86]

Sainte-Palaye's circle of friends included many men to whom he was drawn by common scholarly interests and activities. At the Académie des Inscriptions he was particularly associated with

[80] Bréquigny 165, fol. 47, 8.6.1764.   [81] *Autobiographies,* p. 314.
[82] Jean Égret, *La Pré-Révolution française* (Paris, 1962), pp. 326–31.
[83] *Ibid.,* p. 322.
[84] On his administration, see Germain Martin, pp. 36–38 *et passim.*
[85] Cf. Cerati, *Elogio,* quoted by Shackleton in *Montesquieu,* p. 185.
[86] *Correspondance de Montesquieu,* ed. Gebelin and Morize (Paris, 1914), 2:234.

Foncemagne and Secousse, the three of them being—as Secousse told Bouhier—"liez tous les trois d'une amitié très intime qui a eu pour premier fondement la conformité de nos gousts et de nos études."[87] Together with Bonamy, Lancelot, and Falconet, they constituted a tightly knit party supporting medieval studies and research into French history at the Academy—"la caballe des partisans de nos antiquités françoises et gauloises," as one commentator put it.[88] As such, they acted in consort to secure the election of like-minded scholars. In this way Le Beuf, Grosley, and Lévesque de la Ravalière were brought into the Academy,[89] as was Sainte-Palaye's special friend and protégé Louis-Georges de Bréquigny. Sainte-Palaye and his group had the support at the Academy of a number of well-wishers. They were particularly friendly with Choiseul's protégé, the Abbé Barthélémy, author of the *Jeune Anacharsis*, and with the Comte de Caylus, the antiquarian and champion of the *goût antique*.[90] Caylus indeed did not disdain to write an occasional paper on medieval literary history.

There were several younger scholars with an interest in medieval literature and history to whom Sainte-Palaye gave friendship and assistance: Court de Gébelin, author of *Le Monde primitif*,[91] Le Grand d'Aussy, whose collection of fabliaux played an important role in spreading knowledge of medieval literature,[92] and the young Paulmy d'Argenson, an intimate of Bréquigny,[93] whose *Mélanges tirés d'une grande bibliothèque* was having a somewhat similar effect, though possibly on a different public.

In the provinces and in Italy Sainte-Palaye had ties with zealous amateurs—all of them noblemen or magistrates—who shared his interest in the troubadour poets. He was in correspondence with Mazaugues at Aix, with Caumont at Avignon, with Séguier at

[87] B.N. Français 24420, fol. 100, n.d. (probably 1741).

[88] B.N. Nouv. Acq. Fr. 803, fol. 174v., Lefebvre to Grosley, n.d.

[89] Archives de l'Académie Française, collection L. H. Moulin, carton 216, Sainte-Palaye to Grosley, 31.5.1761, and B.N. Nouv. Acq. Fr. 803, fol. 174v., Lefebvre to Grosley.

[90] Cf. *Correspondance inédite du Comte de Caylus avec le P. Paciaudi, Théatin (1755–1765), suivie de celles de l'abbé Barthélémy et de P. Mariette avec le même*, ed. Nisard (Paris, 1878), notably 1:374, 2:265, 271, 289, 292, 294, 299, 308–9.

[91] Bréquigny 158, fols. 59, 61, letters from Court de Gébelin to Bréquigny.

[92] Le Grand referred to Sainte-Palaye as his "ami," his "maître," and his "bienfaiteur" (Bréquigny 165, fols. 208–9, Le Grand to Bréquigny; also B. N. Nouv. Acq. Fr. 6231, Le Grand's 'Essai sur la langue, la littérature et les sciences françoises,' fol. 103: "mon respectable ami et maître, Sainte-Palaye").

[93] Bréquigny 165, fols. 175–220, and Bréquigny 65, fols. 37–118, correspondence of Bréquigny and Paulmy.

Nîmes as well as with lesser known but similar figures at Aix, Montpellier, and Toulouse.[94] Bimard de La Bastie, a fellow parishioner of Madame Doublet, was a particularly close friend, and the correspondence of the two men shows that he was a capable textual critic, well fitted to assist Sainte-Palaye in elucidating Old French and Provençal manuscripts.[95] He was to have accompanied Sainte-Palaye and de Brosses on the celebrated Italian trip of 1739.[96] Not surprisingly Sainte-Palaye's relations with these Southern scholars were personal as well as scholarly—they visited each other frequently and entertained each other's families—for they were united by a common background, common interests, and a common way of life.

His friendship with Bréquigny was one of the most enduring things in Sainte-Palaye's life. The two men probably met at Falconet's little academy.[97] Sainte-Palaye immediately took a liking to the talented young historian and set about getting him elected to the Académie des Inscriptions. In March, 1754, he succeeded in having him voted a corresponding member, and from then on he seized every opportunity of building up Bréquigny's reputation at the Academy so that when the hour struck his promotion to the rank of Associate would be a matter of course. The correspondence of the two men provides a glimpse of the warm and loyal affection that bound them together for the whole of their scholarly lives.

Inevitably Sainte-Palaye was associated with the learned Benedictines of Saint-Maur. He had begun to use their rich library early in his career, and by 1733 he was well known to the monks.[98] In the eighteenth century the abbey at Saint-Germain des Prés was still a

---

[94] B.N. Nouv. Acq. Fr. 803, fol. 95, Desmarets to Grosley, 11.12.1758, contains a list of scholars in the South of France, drawn up by Sainte-Palaye and Foncemagne. Grosley was to call on them in the course of a projected journey to the South.

[95] There is an excellent piece of textual criticism by La Bastie in Bréquigny 154, fol. 81, where he corrects Sainte-Palaye's interpretation of a passage in *Floire et Blancheflor*.

[96] Bréquigny 68, fol. 77. Sainte-Palaye to La Bastie, 4.12.1739.

[97] Bréquigny 48, fols. 38–42, and Letter from Bréquigny to Mercier de Saint-Leger in *Bulletin de la Société de l'Histoire de France*, 2ème série (1861), 3:24–29.

[98] In their re-edition of Du Cange's *Glossarium* (1733), the Benedictines were already drawing attention to the work of the young scholar (Henschel ed. [Paris, 1840–50], 1:63). Sainte-Palaye, on his side, paid tribute to the monks in his 'Mémoire concernant les principaux monumens de l'histoire de France,' *MAI* 15:614. On the abbey of Saint-Germain des Prés in the early eighteenth century, cf. E. de Broglie, *Bernard de Montfaucon et les Bernardins, 1715-1750* (Paris, 1891).

rendezvous of erudite men from every country in Europe. Here, Sainte-Palaye met many of his colleagues from the Academy—the Abbé Bignon, Rollin, Nicolas Fréret, the two Fourmonts, Sevin, Gros de Boze the *Secrétaire Perpétuel,* three of his own closest friends—Bimard de La Bastie, the Abbé Rothelin and Foncemagne —as well as those of his provincial friends who happened to be in the Capital, such as Bouhier, Caumont, Valbonnais, Mazaugues, Schoepflin.[99]

The atmosphere at Saint-Germain des Prés was congenial to these scholarly magistrates, especially to the older ones, for the outlook of the Maurist fathers was in many respects very close to their own: questioning, critical, rational, and yet at the same time dominated by a legalistic approach. The criterion of the sound tradition rather than that of reason itself was common to magistrates and many Christian scholars. Dom Mabillon's defense of the value of historical research and criticism against the Trappist Abbé de Rancé had marked an important moment in the history of the Enlightenment as well as in the history of the Church. Confident that the Church had much to gain and little to fear from critical scrutiny of her history, Mabillon had helped to establish the reign of reason, even while combating and deploring what he called its perverse uses by the "esprits forts."[100] The ideal of the Christian scholar, the commitment to a "reasonable piety," the desire for a faith and a form of worship that intelligent men could follow without hypocrisy inspired him as it inspired other churchmen of the period, such as Archbishop Harlay in his reform of the Breviary or the gentle Le Nain de Tillemont in his historiography.[101]

The eighteenth century Benedictines continued to pursue the path mapped out by Mabillon, but in a restless age they were less successful at cultivating the calm sobriety and austere dedication of their master, or at preserving themselves from the subtle infection of new ideas. They did not avoid taking sides in disputes which passionately concerned all parties in the nation. Many of them were signatories to the second appeal from the bull *Unigenitus* in 1718, and in 1727, four hundred of them declared their support for the

---

[99] On visitors to Saint-Germain des Prés, see de Broglie, 1:79 *et seq.*

[100] Cf. E. Raimondi, 'I padri maurini e l'opera del Muratori,' *Giornale storico della letteratura italiana* (1951), 128:429–71; (1952), 129:145–78.

[101] Cf. P. Batiffol, *Histoire du bréviaire romain* (3d ed.; Paris, 1911), p. 355.

Bishop of Senez.[102] An Italian observer—Giovanni Lami—writing in 1730 divided the French "Jansenists" into three groups: "i rigidi" who refused to condemn the five propositions, "i medii" who refused to sign the *formulaire* of Alexander VII, and "i molli" who rejected the *Unigenitus*. Only the last group—the appellants in fact —was really powerful enough to disturb the government, Lami noted, adding that it included the monks, a majority of the secular and regular clergy, and almost all "che si piccano d'un po di spirito." The party in which the monks were thus placed by Lami was not Jansenist in the seventeenth-century sense of the term. Rather it was characterized by its opposition to established ecclesiastical authority, defined by Lami as "i Gesuiti, i Francescani, i Vescovi quasi tutti."[103] The whole "Jansenist" movement of the eighteenth century—and the Benedictine monks were deeply involved in it—was in fact, to a large degree, a movement of opposition to the central authority of Rome and the practices and dogmas that supported it. The defense of the Jansenist position in the *Témoignage de la Vérité* of the Oratorian Vivien de la Borde, for example, was based on a radical interpretation of the role of the lower order clergy and of the laity in Church affairs.[104] Many members of the robe shared the anti-Roman and anti-Establishment feelings of the so-called Jansenists. One of Madame Doublet's parishioners, the Abbé Xaupi, was at one and the same time, it will be remembered, the champion of the parlements and the champion of the lower-order clergy.

Worldly attitudes were also making inroads at Saint-Germain des Prés. The Abbé Prevost was doubtless an unusual case. More revealing was a request made by twenty-eight monks in 1765 that they be relieved of the obligation of wearing their robes, attending night services, and observing fasts. Their request was turned down, but several of them, unwilling to submit, left the abbey and took refuge with Frederick the Great, the most powerful atheist in Europe.[105] "Il semble," Messrs. Préclin and Jarry conclude tersely, "que pour certains d'entre eux (i.e., the Benedictines of Saint Maur) la poursuite de recherches scientifiques ait été mortelle à la piété

---

[102] Préclin and Jarry, p. 469.
[103] M. Vaussard, 'Les Lettres inédites de Giovanni Lami à sa famille sur la France du XVIIIème siècle,' *Revue des études italiennes*, nouvelle série (1954), 1:72-94.
[104] Cf. Préclin, pp. 41-51.   [105] Préclin and Jarry, pp. 231, 469.

chrétienne." In such an atmosphere the intellectual leaders of the robe could feel quite at home.

The milieux Sainte-Palaye frequented in Italy on his two visits to that country—in 1739 and in 1749—were strikingly similar to those he frequented in Paris. His reputation as a scholar and historian had preceded him, and he was far and away the most celebrated of the little band of Burgundians who, in 1739 and in 1740, made their way through the Peninsula.[106] With his usual humor De Brosses admits that if the four companions were welcomed everywhere they went by Princes, Cardinals, and men of letters, they had Sainte-Palaye to thank for their popularity. "Savez-vous," he wrote, "que c'est à crever de rire de voir comment à l'abri du titre d'académicien que porte Sainte-Palaye et de quelques vieux rogatons de manuscrits sur lesquels on nous a vus renifler dans les bibliothèques, nous passons pour de très-scientifiques personnages."[107] Ten years later it was the same story. "Les Éminences nous accablent et Sa Sainteté n'a qu'un cri après nous," Sainte-Palaye wrote to Bachaumont from Rome.[108]

In Milan Sainte-Palaye and his companions were entertained by the leading members of the Società Palatina, which was subsidizing Muratori's *Rerum Italiacarum Scriptores* and other studies of Italian and Milanese antiquities. The members of the Society were drawn from the leading patrician houses of Lombardy, and their enterprise owed much to the same combination of local patriotism and pride of caste that inspired the study of local antiquities in France. The travelers were also welcomed to the celebrated Accademia dei Vigilanti of Clelia Borromeo, where Montesquieu had preceded them and where they met the cream of the Italian intelligentsia, mathematicians, physicists, doctors, and historians.[109] Clelia Bor-

[106] *Novelle letterarie di Firenze*, no. 7, 12.2.1740, col. 97.

[107] Charles de Brosses, *Lettres familières écrites d'Italie*, ed. Colomb (Paris, 1861), 1:274. This passage is slightly different in the edition of the *Lettres* put out by Y. Bézard, 2 vols. (Paris, 1931), 1:317.

[108] Arsenal 4900, fols. 306–7, 16.6.1749.

[109] On Clelia Borromeo and her salon, see Gabriel Maugain, *Étude sur l'évolution intellectuelle de l'Italie de 1657 à 1750 environ* (Paris, 1909), p. 75; Giulio Natale, *Storia letteraria d'Italia: il Settecento* (Milan, 1929), pp. 134–35; Adda Annoni, 'Gli Inizi della dominazione austriaca,' *Storia di Milano*, dir. Conte G. Y. degli Alfieri, 12:147–48 *et passim*; Giovanni Seregni, 'La Cultura milanese nel settecento,' *ibid.*, pp. 572–76; A. Giulini, 'Contributo alla biografia della Contessa Clelia Borromeo del Grillo,' *Archivio storico Lombardia* (1919), pp. 583–92; P. J. Grosley, *Nouveaux Mémoires, ou observations sur l'Italie et sur les Italiens par deux gentilshommes suédois, traduits du suédois* (London, 1764), 1:117–18.

romeo's salon was for the *Modernes* against the *Anciens*, for knowledge based on reason and experience against scholasticism, for *cose* against *parole*. It thus stood, on the whole, for the things the visitors stood for in their own country. The presiding genius of the Accademia dei Vigilanti, the naturalist Vallisnieri, whom Clelia Borromeo had brought to Milan from Padua in 1719, introduced materialist and atheist doctrines which must have struck a familiar chord in the ears of the French visitors.[110] In other respects, too, the travelers might have been reminded of home. Clelia Borromeo's academy was not strange to political intrigue. It was, according to Natale, "il centro della riscossa contra l'Austria per ristabilmento in Milano del regime spagnolo."[111]

Clelia del Grillo was the daughter of a Genoese patrician who had been devoted to the cause of Spain and who held his own fief of Mondragon in the Kingdom of Naples from the King of Spain. Her support of the Spanish Bourbons against the Habsburgs probably owed as much, however, to caste interest as it owed to family tradition. (Her husband Giovanni Benedetto Borromeo was, in fact, a trusted servant of the Habsburgs.) In the early decades of the eighteenth century the Milanese patriciate, which was accustomed to controlling the administration of the city and of the state, found itself threatened both by the growing power of the central authority in Vienna and by an influx of new men into the local magistracy, which Vienna had undertaken to infiltrate with its own creatures.[112] The local and the central authorities entered into conflict with each other and, as in France, the magistracy developed a deep distrust of all the forces that to it seemed connected with the power of Vienna: the new men in the magistracy itself, the increasingly influential and wealthy tax farmers and financiers, and the new administrative cadres being formed from the educated members of the bourgeoisie. For years this conflict took, as it had done in France, the form of interminable disputes about precedence. When several of the Great Powers threatened Maria Theresa, however, and the War of the Austrian Succession broke out, a section of the Milanese patriciate became more adventurous and sought to use the opportunity to establish its position and authority under the protection of the Bourbons. Clelia Borromeo had always been distrusted by the Habsburgs who saw her Academy as a hotbed of

---

[110] Maugain, pp. 176–81, 224–25. [111] Natale, pp. 134–35.
[112] Annoni, pp. 248–52, 263.

political disaffection and intrigue, and these suspicions proved well-founded, for "Donna Clelia" did turn out to be the center of an extensive conspiracy which helped to prepare the victories of the Bourbons in the early stages of the war and which supported the régime of Duke Philip of Milan. The Bourbon interregnum, however, turned out to be of brief duration—from December, 1745, until March, 1746.[113] In the proceedings that were subsequently instituted by Vienna against the plotters and collaborators of 1745–46, Clelia Borromeo was deprived of her possessions.[114]

Intelligent, cultivated, witty, and adventurous, Clelia Borromeo is among the most colorful of those eighteenth-century aristocrats who gave a broader social basis to the discussion of subjects hitherto confined to professionals and specialists and who encouraged the newest and boldest ideas in philosophy while at the same time nourishing extravagant hopes for a revival of aristocratic power and prestige. In her, as in those who in France resembled her—the Duchesse du Maine, for example—the new and the old make strange, nervous, but inseparable bedfellows. Many members of the Milanese patriciate shared her ideas and attitudes, and it is not surprising that the Italian *enciclopedisti* of the second half of the century did not look upon them kindly. In their view, the interest of the patriciate in the new ideas had been frivolous and anarchical.

In 1739, the year Sainte-Palaye passed through Milan, Maria Theresa paid a visit to her Italian capital, which was doubtless the occasion for much political discussion at the salon of Donna Clelia. Sainte-Palaye was probably quite aware of the political sympathies of the salon and of his remarkable hostess, and given his own associations in France at this time, it is not improbable that he shared them, at least in some measure.

One of Donna Clelia's close friends and admirers was the celebrated Veronese nobleman, Scipione Maffei.[115] Maffei was also a good friend of Bouhier, of La Bastie, of Séguier, and of many other men of letters in Sainte-Palaye's circle. When he and de Brosses passed through Verona, they naturally called on him and were disappointed to find he was not at home.[116] Maffei shared many of Clelia Borromeo's political sympathies. His criticisms of the exclu-

---

[113] On this period, see Annoni, pp. 224–27.   [114] *Ibid.*, pp. 235–36.
[115] Cf. Maffei, *Epistolario, 1700–1755*, ed. C. Garibotto (Milan, 1955), 2:916.
[116] De Brosses, *Lettres*, ed. Bézard, 1:141.

sive Venetian oligarchy, for example, were by no means inspired by ideas of democracy. His aims were rather those of the French aristocracy in its relations with the monarchy, or of the Milanese patriciate in its struggle with Vienna. The reforms he asked would have loosened the political structure of the Venetian republic, which, more than any other in Italy, remained a tightly knit city-state, by distributing some of the power concentrated in the hands of a few Venetian families among twenty members of the mainland nobility. "Non suggeriva cioè di eliminare la primazia di una classe ma solo quella di una città," is the summing up of a recent historian of eighteenth-century Venice.[117] Maffei's political activity reflects, in short, as does that of the aristocracy in France, a struggle for power among the privileged orders themselves, as well as a new social and political ideal. Correspondingly, the patriotism which inspired his antiquarian and historical studies, like that which inspired the amateurs of Provençal poetry in the South of France, was inseparable from pride of caste, as Gibbon was quick to discern.[118] Nevertheless, Maffei did favor modernization of the nobility. In his *Della Scienza chiamata cavallaresca* he attacked duels. He was also —unlike his French friends—hostile to Jansenism and to Jansenist ideas on free will, magic, and usury.[119] In these matters he sided with the Jesuits whose views were in fact more "modern" and more "lax" on such questions, and to that degree more tainted with secularism than those of the Jansenists. His association with the Jesuits appears to have been the cause of some coolness in Maffei's relations with certain of his French friends, La Bastie and Montesquieu in particular.[120]

There was less affinity with the Jesuits at Bologna, where the travelers spent their evenings in tête-à-tête with Cardinal Lambertini—later, as Pope Benedict XIV, the darling of the *philosophes*. Lambertini was sympathetic to the ideas of Frenchmen such as Le Beuf and Caylus and of similarly minded men in Italy, many of whom—Muratori, Lami, Maffei, Bottari, Passionei—were his intimate friends. His intellectual affiliations emerge clearly from the

[117] Marino Berengo, *La Società veneta alla fine del settecento* (Florence, 1956), p. 168.

[118] *History*, ch. 39, n. 34.

[119] Arturo Carlo Jemolo, *Il Giansenismo in Italia prima della Rivoluzione* (Bari, 1928), pp. 241–43.

[120] Shackleton, *Montesquieu*, p. 177.

discussions held in the early 1740s between the new Pope and his advisors concerning proposed alterations to the Breviary. While the latter wished to modify the old Breviary, the Pope envisaged a completely new one, based exclusively on Holy Scripture.[121] His attitude was thus in keeping with Jansenist notions of ecclesiastical and liturgical reform. Sainte-Palaye's visit to Lambertini was probably no simple courtesy call. There was a real similarity of interests and of temperament here. A rumor, according to which Benedict XIV owed his election to the Freemasons and was himself a Mason —even if only a wild rumor—suggests that in the public mind the new Pope was readily associated with the Gallican and Jansenist factions in the Church, and through them with the learned and free-thinking circles into which we have already followed Sainte-Palaye.[122]

Not far from Bologna—at Modena—Sainte-Palaye had already chatted and pored over manuscripts with Lambertini's friend, Ludovico Antonio Muratori, one of the most learned men in Italy. "Il est simple, naïf, a de l'esprit, charitable, honnête homme, vrai," Montesquieu had written of him some years earlier.[123] An outstanding disciple of Mabillon and the Maurists, Muratori was carrying forward in Italy the task of clearing away the accretions of legend and superstition that were thought to have disfigured and discredited Christianity. In his *Della Filosofia morale* and his *Della Forza della fantasia umana* he demonstrated the spuriousness of certain widely accredited legends and mocked the "enthusiasm" underlying the visions of many pious persons—"massimamente fra il popolo donnesco." Such visions—Muratori had in mind the so-called revelations of Mary of Agreda and Margaret Alacoque— although they were more common in the past than in the present age, nevertheless continued to occur as a result of various kinds of psychological excitement, Muratori argued: "Il tanto andar meditando di certuni, e di certune, e l'agitar solamente, e con forza

---

[121] Batiffol, pp. 370–412, 415–27.

[122] Cf. F. Weil, 'La Franc-maçonnerie en France jusqu'en 1755,' *Studies on Voltaire and the Eighteenth Century* (1963), 27:1787–1815. This is a prudent article, and the author refrains from premature conclusions as to the composition and significance of the early masonic lodges. He does show, however: (1) that in many places robe and noble members were numerous, if not predominant; (2) that the parlements were not anxious to suppress them; and (3) that there was opposition later to the penetration of 'lower class' citizens into the lodges.

[123] *Oeuvres complètes*, ed. Daniel Oster (Paris, 1964), p. 300.

nell'interno del lor cervello le immagine di Dio, dei Santi, del Paradiso e simili sacri oggetti può produrvi una si profonda impressione, che oltre al far loro dolere il capo, paia anche loro d'essere alzati a visione celesti, reali, e soprannaturali."[124] Muratori was indignant when news was allowed to spread of a supposed miracle that happened in Naples. He wrote to Tamburini, one of the most enlightened of the Cardinals, to ask him to investigate it, as it was probably a fraud: "Meriterebbe che Nostro Signore pubblicamente riprovasse impostori tali, che mettono in ridiculo i santi e la religione." When Tamburini replied that the affair could be treated less seriously, Muratori warned that "lasciando correre si fatta iniquità, diamo da ridere agli eretici ed increduli." A liberal policy of promoting free discussion and rational investigation would do more for the Church—Muratori maintained—than demanding blind submission to Papal decrees. Muratori's correspondence does indeed show a fine eighteenth-century impatience with the inquisition and the censorship. "Meglio è che le diciamo noi le verità," he declared, "piu tosto che sentircele dette con ischierno da nemici. E se noi vogliam far passare per vera una cosa che non sia, nulla guadagniamo, anzi perdiam di concetto. Per grazia di Dio, la Chiesa santa non ha bisogna di menzogne, ne ha paura della verità."[125]

It was not only staunch rationalism and strict critical method that the French lay scholars had in common with eminent Italian ecclesiastics. With all his indebtedness to Mabillon, Muratori was, like Sainte-Palaye, a man of the early eighteenth century. His very style is more mobile, more colorful, less noble than that of Mabillon or Tillemont, and his writings have a practical and polemic turn, on occasion, that is characteristic of the Enlightenment.[126] True, he was more a speculative rationalist than an empirical one,[127] but this is the case with many early Enlighteners. Fontenelle and Falconet, for instance, remained on many points loyal to Cartesianism until the mid-century. It is more important, perhaps, that with Muratori rationalism found ready expression in irony and wit. In the writings

---

[124] *Della filosofia morale*, quoted by Jemolo, p. 233.

[125] Quoted *ibid.*, pp. 234, 235, 236.

[126] Mario Fubini, *Dal Muratori al Baretti*, 2d ed. (Bari, 1954), pp. 1–51, gives a penetrating analysis of the manner in which Muratori's broad human and social interests affected his literary style.

[127] Cf. Alfred Noyer Weidner, *Die Aufklärung in Oberitalien* (Munich, 1957), p. 55.

of Muratori irony infiltrates the prose of the scholar and the churchman,[128] as it infiltrates, with Montesquieu, Bachaumont, Sainte-Palaye, and de Brosses, the grave periods of the magistrate. One of the changes which the growing scope of irony indicates is an increase in social awareness, a desire to take in a wider public than the specialists. Fearful of the "populace" as many early eighteenth century Rationalists may have been, they were nevertheless among the first to broaden the basis of philosophical, religious, and "political" discussion (the last usually in the form of historical and erudite polemic). Although they were later attacked, quite understandably, by the *philosophes* and *encyclopédistes* of the second half of the century, it should not be overlooked that they were partly responsible, as we saw before, for creating the figure of the *philosophe*.

Muratori's *Filosofia morale esposta e proposta ai giovani* (Verona, 1730) stands at the beginning of the popularizing tendency of the Italian Enlightenment. The view of the educative role of the poet and writer expressed in the work also heralds that of the Enlightenment. So, too, Muratori struck the first blow against judicial abuses in Italy with his *Dei difetti della giurisprudenzia* (Venice, 1742). His political testament, *Della pubblica Felicità* (Venice, 1749) which was strongly influenced by the English Tory Bolingbroke, marked no radical new departure for him, but voiced the accumulated wisdom of a man who had always been concerned with the terrestrial welfare of ordinary humanity. As early as 1717 in *Il Governo della pesta* he had shown that he was not too proud to write about simple matters of public hygiene, and though his *Annali* retain the already somewhat obsolete form of the scholarly histories of the preceding century, they contain from time to time admonitions to the reader to thank God for having been born not in the tenth century but in modern times, "non già esenti da i vizj ed abusi; ma tempi aurei in paragone di quelli."[129]

In other ways, too, Muratori shows signs of the inroads of modernity. Like Mabillon, he asked only that Church history be open to free discussion and criticism, and he did not carry his zeal over to Holy Scripture itself. The testimony of the Gospels re-

---

[128] In addition to Fubini, cf. also the remarks of E. Raimondi, p. 159, cited in n. 100 above.

[129] *Annali d'Italia*, 7:242, quoted by Noyer Weidner, p. 155n.

mained inviolate, subject neither to textual criticism nor to rational questioning. Muratori, however, knew troubling questions, and his confidence in the harmony of faith and reason was less serene than Mabillon's had been. "Vi confesso il vero," he wrote to Vallisnieri in 1727, "che meditando sulla dipendenza che ha l'anima dal corpo per le azioni nostre, e per li costumi, mi sono incontrato in grotte, che mi han fatto temere e massimamente pensando all'operar dei pazzi. Ma, per la Dio grazia, ricorro sempre al Credo, e qui starò fino alle ceneri." Five years later the same note recurs in a letter to Girolamo Tartarotti, in which he discusses the point that most struck him in reading Locke—the suggestion that matter may have the power to think: "Probabilmente egli fonda la persuasione sua sopra la osservazione delle bestie credute da noi sola materia. Però il rifugio mio è nel Credo, e col fanale della santa religione nostra, e col *scio cui credidi* di S. Paolo, fò coraggio a me stesso."[130] Though not an impossible one, this is a disturbing position for a "reasonable" man like Muratori. Clearly he was not indifferent to some of the implications of the Cartesian doctrine of the animal-machines, which Frenchmen and some Italians too—Vallisnieri was probably one—had not waited long to discern.[131] It is easy to understand that a real sympathy developed between this thoughtful and scholarly ecclesiastic and the urbane Frenchman who visited him in that fall of 1739. A greater writer than Sainte-Palaye, but one with whom the French robe scholars had much in common, paid Muratori a tribute to which Sainte-Palaye would gladly have subscribed. At the end of Chapter 70 of the *History*, Gibbon recorded in a long note his debt to Muratori "my guide and master in the history of Italy." "In all his works," Gibbon declared, "Muratori approves himself a diligent and laborious writer, who aspires above the prejudices of a Catholic priest." Muratori and Sainte-Palaye remained in contact until the former's death, and the Italian did all he could, morally and practically, to further Sainte-Palaye's study of the troubadours, which he saw as the cornerstone of any future history of the Italian literary tradition.

Florence was close spiritually as well as physically to Modena and Bologna, and the Florentine nobility threw open their doors to the traveling Frenchmen. Montesquieu's friends, the Abbés Nic-

---

[130] Both quoted by Maugain, pp. 224-25.
[131] Cf. A. Vartanian, *Diderot and Descartes* (Princeton, 1953).

colini and Cerati, hastened to establish contacts and offer hospitality. Sainte-Palaye found useful items concerning French history and Provençal literature in the library of the Riccardis and spent pleasant hours in conversation with its learned and witty librarian, the Abbé Giovanni Lami.[132] Lami, professor of ecclesiastical history at Florence, advisor of the Grand Duke of Tuscany on theological and ecclesiastical matters and founder of the influential *Novelle letterarie di Firenze*, which he directed from 1740 till his death in 1770, was even more deeply marked with the spirit of modernity than Muratori. Like the latter, he carried forward the work of purifying ecclesiastical history begun by the Benedictines and the Bollandists, and he drew down on himself the wrath of all the bigots in Florence for questioning the authenticity of various legends concerning local saints and, in particular, for denying that the Virgin in the Church of the Annunziato dei Servi had been painted by an angel.[133] But Lami went further than Muratori. His writing is distinguished by a polemical tone, a mordant irony, and an almost Voltairean skepticism which belong unmistakably to the period of the rococo.[134] Whereas Muratori in his criticism steered clear of Holy Scripture itself, and other eighteenth-century Italian Jansenists maintained a rigorously orthodox position in the matter of scriptural criticism—Concina, for instance, seems ignorant of the seriousness of contemporary biblical exegetics and expresses only indignation at the "two or three heretics" who have dared to doubt Moses' authorship of the Pentateuch—Lami in his *De Eruditione Apostolorum liber singularis* (Florentiae, 1738) not only gives a fairly objective, if prudent, exposition of recent work in biblical exegesis but allows the reader to guess his own position, which was by no means dogmatic. Lami is convinced of John's authorship of the fourth Gospel and of the first Epistle, but he accepts that there is an interpolation in the latter at V, 7–8 and that there is some

---

[132] Cf. *Lettere indedite di Ludovico Antonio Muratori scritte a Toscani dal 1695 al 1749*, ed. F. Bonaini (Florence, 1854), p. 516.

[133] Jemolo, p. 238.

[134] Cf. Maurice Vaussard, 'Autour du jansénisme italien: la correspondance inédite de l'abbé Foggini avec Giovanni Lami à la Bibliothèque Riccardienne,' *Revue d'histoire moderne et contemporaine* (1956), 3:298–303 and 'Les lettres viennoises de Giovanni Lami,' *Revue des études italiennes*, nouvelle série (1955), 2:154–83. On Lami's position between faith and Enlightenment, see the essay by Carlo Pellegrini, 'Giovanni Lami, le Novelle letterarie e la cultura francese,' in his *Tradizione italiana e cultura europea* (Messina, 1947), pp. 103–25.

doubt about the attribution to John of the other two Epistles, and of the Apocalypse.[135]

By insisting that divine inspiration guarantees not the individual words but the substance of Holy Scripture, he was able to reconcile his acceptance of contemporary biblical exegesis with his faith. Where purely philosophical speculation was concerned, however, it was not so easy to keep one's balance, and Lami had to tread carefully. In a letter to his uncle from Vienna in 1728, he writes of the conflicting theories of Descartes, Gassendi, and Newton, and ironically envies the inhabitants of the village where his uncle spends his vacations. They are not troubled by such problems; nor is their peace of mind disturbed by thoughts of the "Chinese" who believe "che Iddio non sia altro che questo mondo sensibile," or by "sommigliante vaneggiamenti di Spinoza che bestemoria essere Dio una sostanza estensa e che pensa; e come estensa essere ciò che di materiale si vede nel mondo, e come cogitante essere le anime." Lami's rejection of Spinoza is tempered with humor and irony. The pious horror of most ecclesiastics is absent. On the contrary, there is a deft suggestion that only simple villagers can be undisturbed by the speculations of Spinoza and the "Chinese," only those who "non temono . . . giammai che degli ignoranti e scimuniti sieno accusati ai tribunali, che dell'inquisizione s'appellano, per avere con tutta ragione detto o che Costantino non è battezzato a Roma; o che Elena non trovò la Croce come si crede, e in quelle circonstanze; o che Cristo non iscrisse mai a Abgaro, ne gli mandò il ritratto; o che S. Luca non fù mai pittore; o che Niccodemo non iscolpiva; o che S. Giorgio, e S. Teodoro e S. Margherita non uccisero mai dragoni; o che Elia non è stato fondatore de' Carmeliti. . . ."[136] Happy the villager who has never been persecuted for saying any of these things—and who has never been bothered by strange philosophies. The device of the innocent villager allows Lami to suggest an association of the rationalist in matters of ecclesiastical history and the rationalist in metaphysics. If Lami was not a Spinozist, he may well have been preserved from becoming one, as others were, by irony and an eighteenth century dislike of metaphysics rather than by fervent faith or theological conviction.

Flexible in questions of biblical exegesis, curious of philosophical

[135] Jemolo, pp. 240–44.
[136] Quoted by Vaussard, *Revue des études italiennes*, 1955, p. 161.

novelty, eager for greater freedom of discussion, Lami was repelled
by dogmatism. He stood some way apart from the more rigid
Jansenists with whom he made common cause on many occasions.
On the question of free will and grace, for instance, he refused to
follow either Jansenists or Jesuits, preferring to leave the question
alone and marveling that "in un secolo così illuminato si continua a
scrivere sopra una questione, che si termina facilmente con poche
parole, cioè con un bel *non lo so.*" His exposition of the question
has a suggestion of irony: "non si dubita che dogma di Fede sia
l'esistenza della Grazia e della Libertà; e non si dubita altresì, che sia
inintelligibile il concorso di queste due virtù motrice dell' operaro
umano."[137] What is an intelligent man like Lami to do about this
piquant problem? The desperate faith of the Christian skeptic does
not appeal to Lami. What he recommends is, in effect, a sort of
spiritual indifference. There are more important things for men to
do than to debate questions that serve only "a tormentare senza
conclusione lo spirito umano." Inevitably one is reminded of the
way Montesquieu, Voltaire, and the early *philosophes* were at this
very time writing of the vain speculations of metaphysicians. Without any thought of a faith based on radical despair, but with complete candor, Lami appears to have shared the desire of those early
philosophes to free reason from its tutelage to theology, and to
employ it in useful research rather than in speculation, in *cose*
rather than *parole*. Perhaps, as a churchman, Lami might have done
better not to have taken this view. He took it, however, and nothing
reveals more clearly his involvement in the ideas of his time.[138]

He shared, too, the combination of wit and common sense that is
characteristic of his lay contemporaries. In one of the letters in
which he described his impressions of France, for instance, he
admires the freedom and popularity of theological discussion in
that country. The *style noble* is as absent from this debonair account
as it is from de Brosses' letters from Italy: "Essendo l'altro giorno
in un osteria di vini, dove soglio andare a bere, mi presi assai piacere.

---

[137] *Novelle letterarie*, 1741, quoted by Jemolo, p. 406.
[138] As the Encyclopaedic movement gathered strength, however, Lami's attitude
changed, and he ultimately became a bitter enemy of the *philosophes* (cf. Ettore
Levi Malvano, 'Les éditions toscanes de l'Encyclopédie,' *Revue de littérature
comparée* [1923], 3:213–56). Probably he stood close to Montesquieu, and it is not
surprising that he advised Foggini to review the *Esprit des lois* favorably in the
Giornale de' Letterati of Rome (Shackleton, p. 371).

Uno de' garzoni discorreva colla Padrona, e dicea che non vi era l'Inferno . . . La Padrona che è buona Christiana e credeva che ci fosse, gli contradisse e gli fece un argomento contro che mi piacque infinitamente; perchè è uno de' meglio argomenti morali che noi abbiamo. San Paolo se ne serve ancor esso, ma a un altro proposito. L'Argomento consisteva in questo: che se non vi è inferno, il vivere più felice, è quello de' più scelerati . . . O ved' ella che uno quà tiene bettola, e si trova in una scuola di Filosofi?"[139] It is not hard to understand that Sainte-Palaye enjoyed the company of Giovanni Lami. They had much in common.

With Domenico Passionei, the champion of the anti-Jesuit forces in Rome in the first half of the eighteenth century, Sainte-Palaye was in constant touch. Passionei entertained him generously on both his Italian journeys, and their correspondence extends from the time of Sainte-Palaye's return from the first journey of 1739 until Passionei's death in 1761.[140] Passionei procured Sainte-Palaye copies of manuscripts in the Vatican library, and he also secured, at Sainte-Palaye's request, the release of his friend Laugier from the Jesuit order. On his side, "Frère Jean," as Passionei called Sainte-Palaye, shared with the mercurial and witty Lenglet Dufresnoy the task of keeping the Cardinal informed of events in Paris and generally acting as his literary agent. He was also partly instrumental in getting Passionei elected to the Académie des Inscriptions.[141]

The son of a noble family from northern Italy, Passionei was

---

[139] Quoted by Vaussard, *Revue des études italiennes*, 1954, p. 91.

[140] A letter from Sainte-Palaye to Passionei is indicated by the Fichier Charavay at the Bibliothèque Nationale (carton 102, no. 206, 1) and dated 5.5.1743. The latest in date of the letters from Passionei to Sainte-Palaye in the Moreau collection (Moreau 1567) bears the date 17.12.1760. Although many of Passionei's letters to Sainte-Palaye have been preserved, Sainte-Palaye's letters to Passionei have been lost. My own attempts to track them—in 1954-56—were unsuccessful. More recently they were hunted by W. Herrmann, the author of a book on Laugier (London, 1962), apparently with no better success. They may have been sold with a collection of 352 letters to the Cardinal from eminent scholars and scientists in 1872. (Cf. Cardinal Mercati, 'Sulla fine della biblioteca e delle carte del Cardinal Passionei,' *Studi e Testi* (1952), 144:89-113.) On Passionei in general, see the *Éloge* by Charles Le Beau, *MAI** 31:331-40; C. P. Goujet, *Éloge historique de Monsieur le Cardinal Passionei* (The Hague, 1763); P. A. Galetthius, *Memorie per servire alla storia della vita del Cardinal Passionei* (Rome, 1762); S. von Lengefeld, *Graf Domenico Passionei, päpstlicher Legat in der Schweiz, 1714-1716* (Zurich, 1900); E. Dammig, *Il Movimento giansenista a Roma nella seconda metà del secolo XVIII* (Rome, 1945), Studi e Testi, vol. 119.

[141] Letter of thanks from Passionei, 14.1.1756, Moreau 1567, fol. 26.

among the bitterest enemies of the Jesuits at Rome. They were—he is reputed to have told Winckelmann—"les pères de la fraude, de l'intrigue et du mensonge."[142] Anyone who had been associated with them was suspect, he wrote to Sainte-Palaye; and on one occasion, when he wanted Laugier to ferret out some information about Jesuit politics for him, he warned Sainte-Palaye that "il faut que vous soyez sûr du susdt Abbé avant de vous ouvrir à lui; . . . il y a de fortes présomptions pour craindre qu'il ne soit toujours animé de ce même esprit."[143] He disliked Clement XII—"trop *coglione*" in his own salty phrase[144]—and was a close friend and partisan of the tolerant and conciliatory Benedict XIV. Passionei affected considerable contempt for most of his fellow Cardinals, whom he considered stuffy and stupidly ambitious. "J'ai ce que je voulois," he told de Brosses. "On m'a tenu trente-deux ans dans les emplois et on m'a fait cardinal à la fin quand il n'a plus été possible de différer. Quelques-uns de mes confrères se moquent de mes manières familières et franches; et moi de leur ignorance, de leurs grimaces et de leur politique." De Brosses, however, saw clearly enough where the Cardinal's own ambitions lay: "Passionei ambitionne beaucoup la réputation d'homme de lettres."[145]

Passionei liked to think of himself as modern and enlightened. He befriended men of letters from every country in Europe and prided himself on the equality that marked those relations. "Er nahm mich mit ausnehmender Höflichkeit auf," the young Winckelmann relates, "und begegnete mich als einen Freunden, d.i. mit der Höflichkeit eines Gelehrten gegen den anderen." He forbade scholars to take off their hats when he entered, Winckelmann added, "damit man weiss, dass aus der Republik der Gelehrten sollten alle Complimente verbannt sein."[146] Passionei, it seems, was more flattered by being considered a member of the Republic of Letters than by any other praise. "La pacifique République des gens qui pensent est répandue par toute la terre," Voltaire wrote him. "Ils sont tous frères, vous êtes à leur tête, et quoiqu'à trois cents lieues de vous, Monseigneur, mon esprit se regarde comme un des sujets du

---

[142] Casanova, *Mémoires*, ed. Flammarion (Paris, n.d.), 4:469–70.
[143] Moreau 1567, fols. 34–35, 12.5.1756.   [144] Casanova, *Mémoires*, 4:469–70.
[145] De Brosses, *Lettres*, ed. Bézard, 2:76.
[146] Quoted by Carl Justi, *Winckelmann und seine Zeitgenossen* (Leipzig, 1923), 2:107.

vôtre."[147] It was doubtless no ecclesiastical brotherhood Passionei had in mind when in a letter to Sainte-Palaye he scolded his "très cher et très vénérable Frère Jean" for neglecting him.[148]

In reality, Passionei was something of a tyrant. Just as Bouhier proposed to rule the roost in Burgundy, so his good friend Cardinal Passionei intended to be the "prottetore d'ogni virtù ed il capo delle accademie romane," as Voltaire cleverly called him.[149] He was jealous of his rich library and of the prestige it gave him, refusing to allow it to be catalogued, and seeing to it that none of his librarians would get to know it well so that scholars might be beholden to him alone.[150] He lost no opportunity of emphasizing the value of his services, as Sainte-Palaye found out when he asked him to use his influence in behalf of Laugier. "Je compte donc que nous viendrons à bout de la translation en question"—Passionei wrote him—"mais je vous proteste que les désagréments qu'elle m'a fait essuyer m'ont bien fait prendre la résolution de ne me jamais mêler à l'avenir d'aucune affaire de cette nature pour qui que ce puisse estre."[151] No doubt Sainte-Palaye was supposed to reply with "une grande lettre de gratitude, dont la substance, noyée dans un océan d'adulations, seroit que vous savez bien que sans lui vous étiez perdu, et qu'avec lui vous êtes certain de ne pas l'être." This was Ambassador Nivernois' advice to Montesquieu concerning the Cardinal. "Éloges, admiration, et remerciements excessifs, c'est là son régime," Nivernois, who knew him well, concluded.[152] Like Bouhier, he was furious if the respect and adulation he demanded were withheld. When a dissertation he sent to Barthélémy for the Académie des Inscriptions was judged unsuitable for publication, he rounded in uncontrolled temper on poor Barthélémy,[153] though the fault was

---

[147] Voltaire to Passionei, 12.10.1745, Besterman 2982.

[148] Moreau 1567, fol. 14, 19.2.1755, and *ibid.*, fol. 9, 17.12.1760.

[149] Voltaire to Passionei, 17.8.1745, Besterman 2952.

[150] In 1755 Passionei succeeded Quirini as director of the Vatican Library. To scholars using the library his goodwill was indispensable, for there were difficulties enough to be smoothed over. Sainte-Palaye, for instance, was obliged to encourage his copyists with gifts (Moreau 1567, fols. 15–16, Testaud to Sainte-Palaye), but even then the going was slow. "Nous sommes dans un pays où il faut de la Flemma," Testaud wrote him. (Moreau 1567, fols. 27–28, 31.3.1756).

[151] Moreau 1567, fols. 23–24, Passionei to Sainte-Palaye, 27.8.1755.

[152] *Correspondance de Montesquieu*, 2:277, Nivernois to Montesquieu, 4.5.1750.

[153] *Correspondance inédite du Comte de Caylus avec le P. Paciaudi*, 2:225, Barthélémy to Paciaudi, 17.7.1758.

certainly not his, since he had been instrumental together with Sainte-Palaye in having Passionei elected in the first place.[154]

Clearly this eminence was not without its cloudier side, and Passionei's high-handed ways provoked the hostility of milder men. "Je sens combien je suis petit en comparaison du Cardinal Scander-berh," Paciaudi wrote bitterly to Caylus. "C'est ainsi que nous appelons à Rome le Cardinal Passionei, qui gronde, qui brave et qui menace toujours."[155] He quarreled with Muratori, and then with Maffei "dopo aver cavato da me tutto qual che voleva," as Maffei remarked angrily.[156] His dismissal of his French secretary Testaud de Bois de Lavaud reveals only too clearly how far Passionei was prepared to associate on equal terms with men of letters. Testaud was an industrious and intelligent worker who had served the Cardinal well for many years and won the esteem of both Barthélémy and Sainte-Palaye. "Je l'ai congédié," Passionei wrote ingratiatingly to Sainte-Palaye, "en lui disant expressément qu'il pouvoit partir et ne plus revenir. J'ai été principalement déterminé à lui parler de la sorte, parce que, soit dit entre nous dans la dernière confidence, je n'étois nullement content de sa conduite, et j'ai pris des mesures à cet egard, madame du Bocage m'ayant promis de m'envoyer dans 5 ou 6 mois une personne capable."[157] While he showed deference to men of reputation, Passionei treated a humble and penniless scholar like Testaud as he would treat his cook.

Sainte-Palaye was well aware of these aspects of the Cardinal's character even before the Laugier and Testaud affairs. In 1739 his friend La Bastie asked him to use his influence with Passionei on his behalf; Sainte-Palaye refused and diplomatically suggested to La Bastie that he approach the Cardinal himself. "M. le Card. P. . . . me traitte avec des bontez infinies; mais je n'ose lui faire l'ouverture dont vous me parlez. Tout est sujet à consequence en ce Pais et je me crois obligé à une réserve qui n'est pas trop dans mon

[154] Cf. *Voyage de Barthélémy en Italie*, ed. Sérieys (Paris, an X), letter vi (11.11.1755). Sainte-Palaye also recognized that Barthélémy was mainly responsible for the Cardinal's election, when he congratulated him on the successful outcome of the negotiations. (Rome, Vatican, Ottoboniani latini 3187, fol. 239, 20.10.1755.) Passionei liked academic titles. He cultivated Formey and Maupertuis with a view to election to the Prussian Academy; cf. Galetthius, pp. 247–48.

[155] Paolo-Maria Paciaudi, *Lettres au Comte de Caylus*, ed. Sérieys (Paris, an XI), p. 94, Paciaudi to Caylus, 5.12.1759.

[156] Scipione Maffei, *Epistolario, 1700–1755*, ed. C. Garibotto (Milan, 1955), 2:880–81, 892.

[157] Moreau 1567, fols. 73–74, Passionei to Sainte-Palaye, 7.11.1759.

caractère. Au reste, je suis seur qu'Amateur de Lettres comme il l'est il recevra toujours avec plaisir touttes les propositions qu'on voudra lui faire."[158]

In Passionei as in Lami it is not fanciful to detect signs of the inward corrosion of the ancien régime. The literary vanity of this ecclesiastical eminence, the camaraderie he affected with men of letters, the contempt which he showed for his own colleagues and which he doubtless thought enhanced his reputation in the world, are so many genuflections before secular idols. In almost every portrait of him, as well as in his own correspondence, Passionei emerges as something of a comedian, acting out the roles prescribed by the writers and wits of the age. The amusing anecdotes that were passed around Rome at the time of the triumphal visit of Madame du Boccage concerning the gallantries of Passionei and Lambertini—then Pope Benedict XIV—were harmless enough from the point of view of the man of the world, but they might have disturbed those who, at the time, were declaiming against the frivolity and worldliness of the Eternal City. "Lorsque le Cardinal sortoit en carosse avec Madame du Boccage," Grosley relates, "il [the Pope] avoit soin de se trouver à sa fenêtre et de les favoriser d'une double bénédiction, en disant: *et homo factus est:* il s'étoit même déclaré rival du Cardinal."[159]

Arrogant, tyrannical, highhanded, and at the same time witty, eccentric, gossipy, and garrulous, Passionei resembled many of the eighteenth-century magistrates and magistrates' sons whom he befriended. Like them, he used dangerous weapons—irony, wit, contempt—to attack positions and privileges that were opposed to those he himself supported, and in so doing he helped, as they did, to ridicule and discredit the social, political, and religious order in its entirety. Like them, although he was deeply affected by the ideas and attitudes of the Enlightenment, he could not pursue them to the end or embrace them fully, for the speculative philosophy of the Enlightenment was, ultimately, bound to clash with the Church as its social philosophy was bound to conflict with the interests of the aristocracy. For those in the Church and in the magistracy who did not have the courage to break with and denounce their old privileges —as Malesherbes did, for instance, when he called on the King to

---

[158] Bréquigny 68, fols. 77–79, Sainte-Palaye to La Bastie, 4.12.1739.
[159] P. J. Grosley, *Nouveaux mémoires*, 2:476–77.

convene a National Assembly, as a higher authority than the sovereign courts—the new ideas might well go no further than a formal mimicry, a rococo bal masqué, at which bishops, princes, and *présidents à mortier* could transcend, in play, their human and social reality. Sainte-Palaye knew such milieux well in Paris. He could not have felt out of place in the even more theatrical Roman circle of Passionei.

Despite divergences of interest among them, the Italian Jansenists, the French Jansenists, the cultured nobility, and the magistracy had much in common. They all wanted to increase some local or particular authority at the expense of some central authority, and they all criticized or mocked the established central authority, appealing for support both to reason and to the past, which became, among many of them, an object of intensive scholarly research. They were at one and the same time conservatives, not to say reactionaries, and rebels. Among the noblemen and the magistrates, in particular, there were many who had used their leisure time to reflect freely upon religion, history, laws, the principles of government and of authority, the nature and organization of societies and other similar subjects. In their minds the ideas of the Enlightenment were bred; by their conversations, by the books they wrote and read, and by the authors they protected, they likewise encouraged the diffusion of new ideas, new values, and new methods of thought and investigation. Sainte-Palaye was intimately associated with this world of critically minded churchmen, magistrates, patricians, and aristocrats. He frequented their literary and intellectual societies, and he reflected in his work their aims, their tastes, and many of their contradictions.

CHAPTER 4

SCHOLARS OF THE *ROBE* AND *PHILOSOPHES*

"Is Montesquieu to be considered one of the *philosophes?*" Robert Shackleton asks in his recent study of Montesquieu.[1] Mr. Shackleton answers the question with a guarded *yes*, in view of the modernity of many of Montesquieu's ideas, his considerable contributions to history and to sociology, and the relations of friendship and goodwill that bound him to many of the *philosophes* and the *Encyclopédistes*. Montesquieu was not in the anti-*philosophe* group of scholars, he concludes. Montesquieu was not alone. Many scholars and many members of the Académie des Inscriptions, including Sainte-Palaye, were in a similar position. Being a scholar by no means implied hostility to *philosophie* or to the *philosophes*. We have already seen, in fact, that Sainte-Palaye and his friends referred to themselves as *philosophes*, and we have noted that even in the early decades of the century the term had several nuances of meaning, according as the person using it inclined more to the *Anciens* or to the *Modernes*, to the Christians or to the secularists, to the Jansenists or to the Jesuits, and as he belonged to the older generation of the robe or to the younger, to the aristocracy of the salons or to the aristocracy of the provinces. As the century progressed the meaning of *philosophe* and of *philosophie* continued to evolve, and the conflict which is generally supposed to have opposed scholars and *philosophes* was actually a conflict *within* the Enlightenment between different conceptions of *philosophie*. Sainte-Palaye's place in the intellectual life of his time and the meaning of his work cannot be grasped without some account, however tentative and subject to revision, of the relations of scholars and *philosophes*.

In his great work on *Die Entstehung der bürgerlichen Welt- und Lebensanschauung in Frankreich* (Halle, 1927–30), Bernhard Groe-

---

[1] Shackleton, *Montesquieu*, p. 386.

thuysen showed how closely the ensemble of values and attitudes which the educated Frenchman of the later seventeenth and eighteenth centuries referred to as *philosophie* is associated with the bourgeoisie—rational inquiry, emancipation from myth and "superstition," confidence in human reason, interest in this world rather than in a world beyond, emphasis on individual merit and achievement and a sense of distinction with respect to the *peuple*, the credulous, superstition-ridden, "enthusiastic" multitude. It is no accident that the earliest "philosophers" are numerous in the ranks of the robe, for in the late sixteenth and seventeenth centuries the robe was the flower of the French bourgeoisie.

Philosophie was never confined to the robe, of course. Even the outlook of the nobility came to be affected by it, for under absolutism the nobility had lost many of its effective social functions. It became in some measure a spectator, and sometimes a critical one, of the state which was run on its behalf. Under absolutism the nobleman became, in a way, a private citizen, more or less reflective, concerned with his own pleasures, and interested in the means of acquiring enough money to pay for them. The "embourgeoisement" of the nobility was deepened as its ranks were more and more filled with recently ennobled members of the bourgeoisie and as its links by marriage with wealthy merchants, bankers, and financiers multiplied. Some of the staunchest supporters of the *philosophes* were found in the well-to-do aristocracy.

In the eighteenth century the force of *philosophie* was somewhat blunted, however, in the hands of the robe. The bourgeois origins of most robins precluded their adopting a warrior ideology, but as they were well established and eager to defend or to restore privileges and prerogatives to which they were "entitled," they were not likely to develop *philosophie* further. They were content with what had already been achieved. It was part of their way of thinking, but it was not, for them, a battle cry, a conscious ideology, a system of values with which they identified themselves wholeheartedly and without reserve. As for the wealthy financiers and *anoblis*, their way of life encouraged them to speculate freely but their close association with the court and the established order led them to seek a compromise between intellectual audacity and practical prudence. While *philosophie* owed much to both groups, therefore, neither could formulate it as a coherent method or way of thought, an ensemble of principles and procedures to be proposed openly to all men in the expectation that any one able to think and judge "impartially" was bound to accept it. It was this that the *philosophes* of the second half of the century undertook to do.

Naturally there were inconsistencies and contradictions at the extreme end of their thinking. Diderot and Rousseau had a hard time reconciling individualism and universality, and Diderot did not easily give up the traditional hierarchical model of social organization. These difficulties are inseparable from *philosophie* in its most self-conscious and highly elaborated form: on the one hand, it invoked reason, universality, and humanity against privilege and exclusiveness, while on the other it was the intellectual arm of a class which continued to define itself in opposition to the mass, the *peuple*. Nevertheless, with all its contradictions, *philosophie* in the hands of Voltaire or Diderot did increasingly present itself as a doctrine, or rather a set of values, which demanded assent and commitment. This was why it could and did constitute a real threat to the doctrines of the Church, for instance, in a way that the *philosophie* of the earlier libertines and skeptics never did. It was not, as we know, the "truth," but it offered itself as such and it had all the force of a coherent ideology.

Neither the robe nor the aristocracy was in a position to create a coherent ideology. Mostly, indeed, they tried to avoid systematic exposition, elaboration, and justification of their ideas, for as they had settled into positions of privilege, purchased offices, titles, and lands, their adherence to the bourgeoisie had become compromised, and with it, their adherence to *philosophie*, their ability to develop it and to accept its implications. They could go so far, but no further. That is why, as we shall see, earnest scholars and witty aristocrats were still more suspicious of "systems" than the empirically minded *philosophes*. Even Montesquieu's great *Esprit des lois*, which was perhaps as near to an ideology as the privileged classes in the eighteenth century came, is a discursive, apparently rather rambling work. Its unity, order, and meaning are not easily discerned—to Voltaire, for instance, it was "de l'esprit sur les lois"— and this, significantly, may be one of the main reasons for its enormous success and influence. It could be all things to all manner of people. Only careful study reveals its strong bias in favor of the established order of society and, in particular, of the parlements. In the works of lesser men than Montesquieu it is even more difficult to detect a coherent ideology. Yet it is possible, I believe, if we bear in mind the complex and ambiguous social position of the robe and the aristocracy, to discern not indeed a conscious ideology but an intelligible ensemble of values and attitudes.

It is because *philosophie,* as we usually think of it, was the most advanced and coherent expression of bourgeois values and aspirations in the eighteenth century that we do not need to be concerned with the social origins of particular *philosophes* in order to account for it. (Most were, as it happens, of bourgeois origin, the upper bourgeoisie of *fermiers-généraux* in the case of Helvétius and Lavoisier, for instance, the artisan class in the case of Diderot, Rousseau, or Beaumarchais.) The doctrine spoke clearly enough for itself, and it was strong enough to attract the entire or partial adherence of many who were not themselves bourgeois. The ideas and attitudes of the robe and the aristocracy, on the other hand, since they never achieved and, indeed, deliberately avoided clear formulation, were hardly capable of attracting any one except perhaps to the degree that they borrowed the accents of the *philosophes.* They could come, more or less consciously as the case might be, therefore, only from the members of the two social groups themselves.

The differences between the new *philosophie* and the older *philosophie* could almost always, however, be glossed over by emphasizing the elements common to both and, for a time at least, especially in the early part of the century, there was a good deal of collaboration as well as friction among all the leading social groups in France. Merchants, financiers, noblemen, and magistrates were all eager to extend their influence and found themselves united in their opposition to the central power. The collaboration of the nobility and the robe in particular was established about this time. By the 1720's, for instance, the peers of the realm were prepared to collaborate with the magistracy, which was demanding, as they were, the restoration of some of the powers and privileges they had had to relinquish under Ludovician absolutism. They began to advocate extending rather than curtailing the influence of the parlements, hoping doubtless to use them to their own ends, so that at the time of the trial of the Duc de la Force in 1721, Saint-Simon and the old guard who still opposed the claims of the parlements found themselves confronting Luxembourg and his allies, who supported them. The understanding between peerage and magistracy is reflected in the membership of the free-thinking and speculative societies that flourished during the period. These included, as we have seen, both great noblemen and many representatives of the magistracy. The magistracy, it is true, remained in some ways the most conservative social group. Tainted with *philosophie* it certainly was, as we have remarked, but it was distinguished by its emphasis on law rather than reason. Since man had fallen from the state of innocence, it was often argued, injustice was his inevitable condition, and the only real choice was between chaos and strict observation of the laws, however unfounded in reason, nature, or God they might be. The backbone of the Jansenist movement and of the *Anciens* in the *Querelle*, the magistrates never tired of decrying every altera-tion to the established order—the mingling of social classes, the attempt to reconcile worldly ambition with religious precept, the confusion of literary genres. But their very complaints only confirm that movement among the social classes was possible for anyone who had the means. In this period *philosophie* tended to justify to the privileged groups which cultivated it the enlargement of the area of their freedom and influence with respect to each other and to the central authority.

In the 1730's, however, there was a notable upturn in economic activity after the long period of relative stagnation that had run from about the beginning of the seventeenth century.[2] The bour-geoisie again began to grow in wealth and in numbers. It became progressively more difficult to satisfy its aspirations by absorbing its wealthiest members into the ranks of the privileged. For one thing, they were too numerous. For another, the new economic condi-tions restored to some extent their confidence in entrepreneurial activity, so that they no longer inevitably wished to sink their capital into the purchase of lands and offices; in this way they came to regard the privileges of others less as something to be acquired by themselves than as something old and pointless to be done away with. Thirdly, many noblemen and magistrates, sensing the threat to their predominance from the swelling tide of prosperous and educated merchants, manufacturers and financiers, tried to fight it

[2] Cf. E. Labrousse, *La Crise de l'économie française à la fin de l'ancien régime et au début de la Révolution* (Paris, 1943), pp. vii–lii.

off by tightening restrictions and progressively closing the doors of privilege.[3] By mid-century criticism of the ancien régime by philosophically inclined writers was ceasing to be a criticism of manners, as that of both the *Anciens* and the *Modernes* had been in the main, and became increasingly a structural criticism. This point is marked by the publication, within a very short time, of a number of crucial works around which the different forces and pressure groups of the ancien régime rallied. Montesquieu's *Esprit des lois* appeared in 1748; in the same year the *Encyclopédie* obtainted its *privilège;* in 1750 Rousseau's first Discourse was published, followed a year later by Voltaire's *Siècle de Louis XIV.*

With the *Esprit des lois* Montesquieu, fusing the two main theories of robe and sword authority, forged a new and up-to-date political doctrine for the aristocracy. The exclusiveness of earlier noble, royalist, or parliamentary arguments was transcended; Montesquieu's theory of the monarchy accommodated all the privileged orders of the ancien régime—the monarch and his court, the nobility, the parlements, and the clergy—and showed that they were all dependent upon each other and part of a single unified system.[4] After this, the parlements could assume the leadership of the aristocratic revival.[5] The crucial role of the sovereign courts was in fact clearer to all—to Louis XV and to ministers such as d'Argenson, to Voltaire and to the nobility of the sword itself—in 1750 than it had been in 1715 when the parlements were just beginning to emerge from a long period of enforced silence and to recover the right to remonstrate, and when the elements of the aristocracy—the peerage, the nobility, and the magistracy—still eyed each other with suspi-

---

[3] Cf. Ford, pp. 124-46; R. Mousnier and E. Labrousse, *Le XVIIIe siècle* [Paris, 1953], pp. 347-49 (Histoire générale des civilisations, vol. 5). Against Ford, Jean Egret argues that there were still many ways for a *roturier* to enter the parlements, for instance, and that the degree of exclusiveness varied considerably from one parlement to another ('L'Aristocratie parlementaire française à la fin de l'ancien régime,' *Revue historique* [1953], 208:1-14). The fact remains, however, that the privileged bodies were becoming more and more exclusive.

[4] We should recall, moreover, that the distinction between robe and sword in the eighteenth century was functional rather than social. Both groups considered themselves and were considered aristocratic; they differed only in their *état* or profession, and they mingled constantly. (Bluche, *Les Magistrats*, pp. 95-96, 303-6, 334-38 *et passim.*)

[5] Ford, pp. 239-45. See also Louis Althusser, *Montesquieu, la politique et l'histoire* (Paris, 1959), and Albert Mathiez's well-known polemical article 'La place de Montesquieu dans l'histoire des doctrines politiques du XVIIIe siècle,' *Annales historiques de la Révolution Française* (1930), 7:97-112.

cion. Yet there was much in the *Esprit des lois* to please the *philosophes*, and this aspect of the work was thrown into relief by the attacks of Jesuits and Jansenists and by the ultimate compliment of being placed on the Index.

Montesquieu's fusion of *philosophie* and feudalism was something of a tour de force. Significantly, it was welcomed with enthusiasm by the French nobility. In the Austrian Netherlands it was immediately hailed by the privileged circles of nobles and patricians who made up the provincial estates and who were fighting for their lives against the encroachments of Vienna. In England it won and retained the favor of noble Whigs and Tories alike.[6] It set the tone for a considerable body of literature, including Sainte-Palaye's most popular works. "Any reasonably objective student," Ford writes, after pointing out the double character of Montesquieu's thought, ". . . must, it seems to me, distinguish between the urbane and likable man of letters and the political theorist whose views were destined to serve the most reactionary groups in France . . . In Montesquieu, the greatest product of the society of courts, academies, and salons, the intellectual heritage of Hotman at last united with that of La Roche Flavin on behalf of the noblesse both of the sword and of the robe. Thereafter, Mirabeau *père* could resume the languishing defense of decentralization, and La Curne de Sainte-Palaye could hold up his portrait of medieval chivalry as an ideal toward which modern society ought to strive."[7]

Three years after the *Esprit des lois* appeared, Voltaire brought out his *Siècle de Louis XIV*, for which, as he was told by Durey de Meinières, the parlements never forgave him.[8] Voltaire's consistent support of the central authority and of enlightened Royal administration is well known.[9] He frequently invoked *la nation* above the King—in the *Siècle* he was, as he said, concerned "moins de la gloire de ce roi que de celle de la nation"[10]—but he never admitted that the parlements had the right to speak for the nation

---

[6] Cf. Shackleton, *Montesquieu*, pp. 356–57; F. T. H. Fletcher, *Montesquieu and English Politics, 1751–1800* (London, 1939); Henri Pirenne, *Histoire de Belgique* (2d ed.; Brussels, 1926), 5:255.

[7] Ford, pp. 244–45. Actually the *Mémoires sur l'ancienne chevalerie*, though published separately in 1751, began to appear in the volumes of the *Mémoires de l'Académie des Inscriptions* before the *Esprit des lois* was published.

[8] Voltaire to Madame de Saint-Julien, 22.1.1772, Besterman 16518.

[9] See Peter Gay, *Voltaire's Politics, the Poet as Realist* (Princeton, 1959).

[10] Voltaire to d'Argental, 1.4.1752, Besterman 4244.

as they claimed to have, and he always took the side of the central authority against aristocratic or parliamentary powers and privileges.

While the privileged classes and, in particular, the landed interests, worked to bend the royal power to their wishes, therefore, Voltaire placed his hopes in an alliance of the King and the well-to-do bourgeoisie. Quite possibly his obstinate refusal to recognize the authenticity of the *Testament* of Richelieu, with its obvious noble preferences,[11] springs from his firm belief that the historic mission of the monarchy was not to harmonize and preserve the nobility but to realize the weal of the entire nation, setting the good of the whole above the interests of any one class, by which he meant furthering the interests of the active and productive bourgeoisie, since these, in his mind, were identical with those of the nation. Inevitably Voltaire ran foul of the parlements, and his relations with the scholars of the robe became increasingly strained. In the 1730's, for instance, he and Meinières were on excellent terms. The President was helping the poet in his *démêlés* with the Abbé Desfontaines. Madame du Châtelet at this time found him "un homme bien aimable"; Voltaire gratefully presented him with a copy of the *Eléments de la philosophe de Newton*.[12] In 1763, however, Meinières took exception to passages concerning the parlements in Voltaire's *Essai sur les moeurs*. At first Voltaire thought the criticisms concerned matters of fact, and he held up production of his book in order to make the necessary corrections to it from a memorandum Meinières had promised to send him. When he received it, he was quickly disabused. "Il respire l'esprit de parti," he wrote to the d'Argentals; and two days later, he added: "Il faut que je vous dise, mes chers anges, que j'ai de la peine à croire que les observations succinctes soient du président de M^{xxx}, qui m'avoit autrefois paru modéré et philosophe."[13]

To the left of Voltaire a still more radical group of thinkers was beginning to make its presence felt, offering sharper criticisms, and raising more fundamental questions than even Voltaire envisaged or, perhaps, desired to raise. This group was also more active and combative than earlier Enlighteners had been. The frontal assault

---

[11] Cf. in particular, 1, iii, 1, ed. Louis André (Paris, 1947), pp. 218–23; also pp. 27–28, 48–56 of the introductory material to this edition.

[12] *Lettres de la Marquise du Châtelet* 1:294, 308, 322.

[13] Besterman 10399, 10403.

of the *Encyclopédie* took the place of the innuendos of the previous generation. By the mid-1740's Diderot had begun to question an earlier aristocratic and élitist idea of Enlightenment. In *La Promenade du sceptique* a group of enlightened friends spend some pleasant hours together discussing questions of morals and metaphysics. The setting, as in Berkeley or Shaftesbury, is a beautiful park, far removed from the turmoil of the everyday world. The participants, again as in Berkeley and Shaftesbury, carry Greek names. One of the friends, however, expresses interest in spreading the ideas of the group beyond its confines. The leader of the group, Cléobule, advises him not to do so: "Ne vous attendez pas que votre ouvrage serve beaucoup aux autres; mais craignez qu'il ne vous nuise infiniment à vous-même. La religion et le gouvernement sont des sujets sacrés auxquels il n'est pas permis de toucher . . . Ariste, si vous m'en croyez, vous préviendrez cet éclat, vous renfermerez votre manuscrit et ne le communiquerez qu'à nos amis." Ariste sees his friend's point, but he is not happy with it. "Imposez-moi silence sur la religion et le gouvernement," he says, "et je n'ai plus rien à dire."[14] A couple of years after the *Promenade du sceptique*, Rousseau published his First Discourse. It was not well understood by many readers, as their comments and criticisms indicate, but instead of leaving well enough alone, Rousseau felt he had to clarify his views in a series of letters to his critics. He had used the language of caution in the Discourse, he explained, not out of diffidence alone, but for tactical reasons. "C'est pour pouvoir tout faire entendre que je n'ai pas voulu tout dire. Ce n'est que successivement et toujours pour peu de Lecteurs que j'ai développé mes idées. Ce n'est point moi que j'ai ménagé, mais la vérité, afin de la faire passer plus sûrement et de la rendre utile." But these tactics had clearly failed. The time had now come, therefore, for plainer speaking: "puisqu'il est tems de parler à découvert, je vais vaincre enfin mon dégoût et écrire une fois pour le Peuple."[15] There is indeed a world of difference between the conniving ironies of Fontenelle, Marivaux, even the early Voltaire, and the democratic, argumentative style of Rousseau's great polemical works or the visible conversion of the reader to a more enlightened and informed point of view than that of fashionable society which occurs in Diderot's *contes*.

[14] Diderot, *Oeuvres*, ed. Assézat and Tourneux 1:181, 183, 184.
[15] 'Préface d'une seconde Lettre à Bordes,' *Oeuvres complètes*, ed. Pléiade, 3:106.

There was thus an increasing diversity of points of view among the various enlightened groups of the eighteenth century. As the word *philosophe* gradually acquired new shades of meaning it could less and less properly be applied to the scholars who remained on the whole rather *philosophes* in the early sense of the term, the sense given in Furetière's dictionary (edition of The Hague, 1727): "esprit ferme et élevé au-dessus des autres . . . guéri de la préoccupation et des erreurs populaires, et désabusé des vanitez du monde; qui aime les honnêtes plaisirs; qui préfère la vie privée au fracas du monde . . ."

Nevertheless, the disagreements among scholars, enlightened aristocrats and magistrates, and *philosophes* proper as they came to be thought of in the second half of the century, should not, as we have already suggested, be simplified. None of these groups was rigorously homogeneous, and there were many shades of opinion and interest, as well as internal tensions, in them. It was, after all, an enlightened aristocracy that in large measure supported the work of the *philosophes*. Moreover, large sections of this aristocracy, including many magistrates, were benefiting handsomely from the economic upturn that had set in in the 1730's. These men were increasingly aware of the possibility of improving the returns from their lands. New techniques were bound to interest them as they interested the *philosophes*, and they could be expected to listen with interest as the Physiocrats proposed the elimination of customs barriers and other restrictions on free trade. As the most immediately effective way they had of profiting from the new economic conditions was, however, the efficient exploitation of their feudal rights and privileges—many of which, long abandoned, were now being eagerly renewed—large numbers of landed aristocrats had one foot in the camp of the *philosophes* and one in that of the conservatives. Yet there were others who were not only convinced of the rightness and usefulness of the *philosophes'* ideas from the point of view of humanity but confident that they themselves could survive significant social change and curtailment of their privileges. A certain number of thoughtful noblemen, who were already making handsome profits from their farmers and sometimes also from mining operations on their lands, seem to have believed that a prosperous and free market would more than compensate them for the loss of their feudal privileges. The royal authority, moreover, continued frequently to unite the critics in opposition to it, blurring the divergencies of view among them. Thus the parlements and the *philosophes* were sometimes allied in the pursuit of apparently common goals. This was notably the case in the 1770's when the parlements in their bitter struggle with the King set themselves up as the champions of the nation and of liberty. Most of the *philosophes* did at this point become their associates, tactically at least, and when the latter came under renewed fire at Court in 1773 we find the *Mémoires secrets* of Bachaumont coming to their defense with the comment that "leur attachement connu au parti patriotique est un grief encore plus grand que leur irréligion prétendue."[16] Many of the scholars, Sainte-Palaye among them, were associated with the liberal wing of the aristocracy as well as with the parlements. Their attitude to *philosophie* was thus by no means negative.

There were a number of issues on which almost all parties were agreed. The scholars disliked government censorship of literature and opinion, and they opposed it insidiously if not always very courageously.

In face of the hostility of Stanislas, the Queen, the Dauphin, and, whenever he turned his mind to it, the King himself,[17] Secousse as *censeur royal* passed the first two volumes of the *Encyclopédie*,[18] to see them immediately attacked by the *Journal de Trévoux*. He had already complained bitterly to his friends of the rigors of the censorship. "Les difficultés se multiplient de jour en jour," he had written, "et le moindre petit in-12 en fait naître une foule. Tout concourt à l'anéantissement des Lettres."[19] Complaining of the proscription of the sixth volume of Condé's *Mémoires*, the respectable scholar and *censeur royal* announced brazenly that he would be "attentif à me saisir du premier qui osera se montrer," and that he had already subscribed to a number of clandestine journals.[20] The docility of the scholars can be exaggerated, and was often more apparent than real. Thus Mercier de Saint-Léger, director of the violently anti-*Encyclopédie Journal de Trevoux*, could advise a German friend: "Votre intention étant de faire une bonne Bibliothèque, vous ne pourriés vous dispenser d'acheter ce livre."[21]

[16] *Mémoires secrets*, 8.1.1773, 6:253.
[17] Joseph Le Gras, *Diderot et l'Encyclopédie* (Paris, 1928), pp. 70–79, 128.
[18] B.N. Français 22139, fol. 104.
[19] B.N. Français 24420, fol. 85, Secousse to Bouhier, 31.3.1744.   [20] *Ibid.*
[21] B.N. Nouv. Acq. Fr. 816, fol. 205, Mercier de Saint-Léger to Polling, 29.4.1763.

Mercier proceeded to offer to obtain a copy of the *Encyclopédie* for his correspondent. The correspondences of Bouhier, Caumont, Mathieu Marais, Passionei, Secousse, de Brosses, Mercier de Saint-Léger, Bréquigny, and Sainte-Palaye, to mention but a few, are full of allusions to and requests for clandestine and prohibited texts. One of the functions of the "literary agent" most provincial scholars had in Paris was to get hold of such texts.

The scholars' interests were wide and worldly. Sainte-Palaye, as we shall see shortly, was active in the artistic controversies of the age, and he was friendly with many painters and men of letters. He was a man of taste. Maffei was the author of a successful tragedy, *Mérope*, which was translated into French by Fréret, who may also have translated the comedies of Lélio.[22] Sinner, the erudite librarian of the Bürgerbibliothek in Berne—one of Sainte-Palaye's Swiss correspondents—published a translation of Congreve and preceded it with a good introductory essay on English literature. We saw signs in Sainte-Palaye's travel notes of his interest in economic and social matters and in manufacturing techniques. We have also mentioned Muratori's writings on hygiene and legal reform. Sinner drew up a plan for modernizing the school curriculum in Berne and prepared a report to the economic society of Berne on coal deposits in the canton.[23] Grosley, whom Sainte-Palaye had elected to the Académie des Inscriptions, was interested in economic and political questions as well as in the history of laws and institutions; he had competed for the prize which Rousseau won from the Académie de Dijon in 1750. De Brosses' essay on the *Terres Australes* earned the applause of the *philosophes*. Bréquigny was keenly interested in the search for a Northwest passage to the Orient. "Nous sommes bien enfans dans la connoissance du globe"—he remarked in a letter to his friend Lord Hardwicke, one of the Trustees of the British Museum—"et nous n'avons même que des idées bien imparfaites des parties orientales depuis long tems connues. Telle est la Chine, que j'espère que nous allons connoître un peu mieux."[24]

Doubtless there was in all this more of an old encyclopaedic tradition, reaching back to the Renaissance and even into the Middle

---

[22] Maffei, *Epistolario*, 2:734, and Frédéric Deloffre, *Une Préciosité nouvelle: Marivaux et le marivaudage* (Paris, 1955), pp. 27–28.

[23] Emil J. Walter, *Soziale Grundlagen der Entwicklung der Naturwissenschaften in der alten Schweiz* (Berne, 1958), pp. 145–47.

[24] Br. Mus. Add. 35617, fol. 129. Bréquigny to Hardwicke, 17.12.1780.

Ages, than of modern science. The scholars clung to an ideal of a universal man and a universal science which, in some ways, expresses the pride of their class, of that parliamentary aristocracy that took its privileges, its superiority, and its right to leadership for granted. But the encyclopaedism of the scholars also carried elements of a more modern desire to take stock of, rationalize, and increase human control over a world newly disenchanted and desacramentalized, in which skills, techniques, and procedures of production and extraction had acquired dignity and interest.

An influential segment of the aristocracy, including the robe, was keenly interested in scientific and technological developments and in their practical applications, recognizing in them, especially in the favorable economic conditions that prevailed after 1730, a means of augmenting its fortune and influence. The shareholders of the *manufactures royales* and of the *manufactures privilégiées*, such as the great glass company of Saint-Gobain, were mainly noblemen.[25] Noblemen also predominated in the mining industry.[26] Many enlightened and well-to-do landowners supported the Physiocrats and, in their own interests as well as in those of the "nation," advocated liberalization of the grain trade and other economic and fiscal reforms.

In several cases we find scholars in the van of the liberal movements of the time. In the Austrian Netherlands, for instance, one of the advisors of the Count of Cobenzl, Maria Theresa's reforming minister, was the Alsatian scholar Schoepflin, whom Sainte-Palaye had known in Strasbourg while on his diplomatic mission and with whom he was subsequently in correspondence on matters of historical scholarship.[27] Schoepflin was behind several of Cobenzl's reforming measures, such, for instance, as the founding of an academy at Brussels to help dissipate "les préjugés invétérés et l'ignorance"

---

[25] Henri Sée, *L'Evolution commerciale et industrielle de la France sous l'ancien régime* (Paris, 1925), pp. 256–60.

[26] *Ibid.*, p. 259; also G. Martin, pp. 210–19; G. Lefebvre, *The Coming of the French Revolution*, trans. R. R. Palmer (New York, 1957), p. 13, and the essay on 'Les Mines de Littry, 1744—an VIII,' in the same author's *Études sur la Revolution Française* (Paris, 1963), pp. 159–96. Labrousse (vol. 1, p. xxvi) holds that the capital accumulated by landowners financed a considerable part of the industrial expansion of France in the eighteenth century. Cf. also Pierre Léon, *La Naissance de la grande industrie en Dauphiné, fin du XVII⁰ siècle—1869* (Paris, 1954), 1:266–68.

[27] Bréquigny 66, fols. 106–7, letters from Schoepflin to Sainte-Palaye.

or the modernization of the University of Louvain.[28] Interestingly enough, the hard working Cobenzl found himself in conflict with the local aristocracies, the patriciates of the towns, and the Estates, all of which were threatened by the efforts of the central government to extend its influence.[29] Schoepflin's collaboration with this enlightened minister was not a unique case. In France itself many of the royal intendants who were so disliked by Boulainviller and who are so often attacked in parliamentary remonstrances, were actually recruited from robe families, although it does appear that increasingly in the course of the eighteenth century they acted in concert with the local aristocracies.[30]

As for the personal relations of *philosophes* and scholars, they were, on the whole, friendly. "Il est fort engoué de vous," a mutual friend wrote Voltaire of Caumont in 1733,[31] and Voltaire returned the compliment.[32] Bréquigny was incensed at the bungling that led to Voltaire's departure from France: "J'ai appris depuis peu le départ de votre célèbre ami M. de Voltaire, et son dessein de se fixer en Prusse," he wrote to Cideville in 1750. "C'est une perte pour la France; les génies y accouroient autrefois: d'où vient en partent-ils aujourd'hui?"[33] Voltaire on his side admired Bréquigny's *Histoire des révolutions de Gênes*, which he read in an Italian translation.[34] Many scholars were consulted by Voltaire when he was writing his own histories. Meinières, Foncemagne, Secousse, and Caumont were invited to criticize and, where possible, to contribute to the documentation of the *Siècle de Louis XIV*. Voltaire's relation with Foncemagne more than any other acquired celebrity as a result of a debate between the two men concerning the authenticity of the famous *Testament politique* of Richelieu.[35] The debate was considered exemplary, in the same way that Hume's debate with Wallace on the populations of the ancient and the modern worlds had been some years earlier. Madame de Verdelin, an intimate friend of Foncemagne's, sent the latter's *Lettre* to Rousseau: "Si elle eût

[28] Pirenne, *Histoire de Belgique*, 5:311, 318, 324.   [29] *Ibid.*, 250–59 *et passim*.
[30] Henri Sée, *La France économique et sociale au XVIIIᵉ siècle* (Paris, 1925), pp. 98–99; also Forster, pp. 27–28.
[31] Besterman 644.
[32] See the correspondence and letters concerning them, Besterman 633, 644, 645, 651, 696, 840, 875, 1076.
[33] Quoted Besterman 18:162n.   [34] Besterman 6255.
[35] Voltaire, *Oeuvres*, ed. Moland, 25:321. Cf. also Tyrtée Tastet, *Histoire des quarante fauteuils de l'Académie Française, 1624–1844* (Paris, 1844), 3:141–44.

renfermé une satire, je ne vous l'aurois pas envoyée; mais le tour et l'érudition m'a paru faites [sic] pour vous plaire et l'amitié que l'auteur a pour moi me fait désirer que vous le goûtiez."[36]

There were also scholars among the friends of Diderot[37] and of Marmontel. It was at the latter's house at Grignan that, during the troubled days of the Revolution, the Abbé Barthélémy "dans ses promenades faisait penser à celles de Platon avec ses disciples." On these walks Barthélémy was accompanied by Raynal, Marmontel, and Bréquigny "qui avait aussi de cette aménité et de cette sagesse antiques."[38]

An interest in botany which was widespread among the men of the robe brought some of them into relation with Rousseau. Malesherbes, for instance, was a passionate botanist, and this was a real bond between him and the *citoyen*.[39] So too, one of Sainte-Palaye's companions on the Italian journey of 1739, Le Gouz de Guerland, likewise an amateur botanist—he had set up a botanical garden at Dijon—was a fervent admirer of the Genevan. Le Gouz was one of those speculative souls in the magistracy who were attracted to nonmechanical, organic, even occult types of science. In addition to his botanical studies he was interested in phenomena of magnetism and electricity, which he studied with the celebrated Abbé Nollet. No doubt he was carrying on the Renaissance encyclopaedic traditions to which we have already alluded. The animistic and wholistic approach of amateurs like Le Gouz did, however, keep alive a tradition on which the more radical *philosophes* drew freely.[40]

Sainte-Palaye himself was on fair terms with several of the *philosophes*. The Duc de Nivernois, the French ambassador in Rome and one of the great liberal aristocrats of the century, was

[36] Rousseau, *Correspondance*, 11:366–67, no. 2248, Mme de Verdelin to Rousseau, 22.10.1764.

[37] See ch. 3, n. 30 above. In a letter to his family, Diderot included among his friends the Abbé Sallier, a prominent member of the Académie des Inscriptions, who also helped him on the *Encyclopédie* (*Correspondance*, ed. Roth, 4:153, 179).

[38] *Mémoires de Marmontel* (Paris, 1818), 2:162–64.

[39] John M. S. Allison, *Lamoignon de Malesherbes, Defender and Reformer of the French Monarchy, 1721–1794* (New Haven, 1938), pp. 16–18, 72–73.

[40] Charles C. Gillispie, 'The *Encyclopédie* and the Jacobin Philosophy of Science,' *Critical Problems in the History of Science*, ed. Marshall Clagett (Madison, 1959), pp. 255–89, and the comments on this paper by Henry Guerlac, *ibid.*, pp. 317–20; also Jean Fabre, 'Diderot et les théosophes' in his *Lumières et romantisme: énergie et nostalgie de Rousseau à Mickiewicz* (Paris, 1963), pp. 67–83.

devoted to him and ranked him with Montesquieu, Helvétius, and Mirabeau among the personalities young Englishmen on the Grand Tour ought to meet in Paris.[41] The Prince de Conti invited him to L'Île Adam and discussed with him and Laugier improvements to his estate.[42] The poet Gresset had an extravagant affection for him.[43] Sainte-Palaye was also well known to and liked by d'Alembert and Voltaire. He invariably sent the latter copies of his works.[44] Rousseau knew him sufficiently well, possibly through de Boze, to seek his advice about some medals which his Genevan friend Jallabert had asked him to sell.[45]

His candidacy for a vacant seat at the Académie Française in 1758 was unopposed by the *philosophes* who, under the leadership of Voltaire and d'Alembert, were already well entrenched there.[46] In a letter to the d'Argentals, who had probably intervened with the great man on behalf of Sainte-Palaye, Voltaire declared himself "aussi honoré qu'enchanté de l'avoir pour confrère."[47] As for d'Alembert, he had been party to the discussion at Falconet's concerning Sainte-Palaye's proposed glossary of Old French, the Prospectus of which, published in 1756, was the immediate justification of his candidacy. Many of the more liberal members of the Academy were his friends—Buffon, Bernis, Gresset, Nivernois, Mirabaud. There was opposition to Sainte-Palaye, but it does not seem to have come from the *philosophes* either inside the Academy or outside of it. It came from the supporters of his rival for the seat, Le Franc de Pompignan, a poet of some reputation and an eminent member of the robe himself. "J'habite Paris," wrote the author of a *Lettre à M. L. . . . F. . . . de Pompignan*, "et cependant je ne connoissois point, ou fort peu, avant cette concurrence le mérite

---

[41] Francis Hardy, *Memoirs of the Life of James Caulfield, Earl of Charlemont* (London, 1810), p. 38, and *Autobiographies of Edward Gibbon*, p. 201. On Nivernois, see the essay by Sainte-Beuve, *Causeries du lundi*, 8:389–411.

[42] Bréquigny 66, fols. 158–59, 'Voyage autour de Paris,' written up by Laugier. Conti was a friend of both Rousseau and Hume and one of the leading liberal spirits of the time.

[43] Bréquigny 159, fols. 103, 105, Gresset to Bréquigny, 11.2.1776 and 21.4.1776, in which Sainte-Palaye is referred to affectionately as "mon Tyran," "mon charmant Ennemi barbare," "mon Barbare adoré."

[44] Besterman 4912, 6287, 6291, 18204.

[45] Rousseau, *Correspondance*, 2:118–19, no. 189.

[46] Cf. Gaston Boissier, *L'Académie Française sous l'ancien régime* (Paris, 1909), p. 100.

[47] To d'Argental, 7.6.1758, Besterman 7054.

littéraire de votre compétiteur . . . Il sembloit donc, Monsieur, à ne
juger que par les yeux et les oreilles, que le choix de l'Académie
devoit tomber sur l'homme que tout le monde connoissoit par son
nom seul, plutôt que sur celui qui faisoit demander en le nommant:
Qui est-il? et qu'a-t-il fait?" Sainte-Palaye was in fact "un sujet
qui n'a ni votre rang dans la société, ni votre mérite dans les
lettres."[48] Collé's arguments were similar: "Devrait-on en effet
balancer entre l'auteur de Didon, et de quantité d'autres ouvrages
de poésie et de littérature, qui tous respirent le goût . . . et le
compilateur de vieux mots françois, le sec et ennuyeux auteur d'un
glossaire . . . C'est vouloir mettre en parallèle Mansard et celui qui a
tiré des carrières les pierres qui ont servi à bâtir Versailles."[49] Collé
was not to be diverted by Sainte-Palaye's affability and gentleness
of manner. "Je connois ce M. de Sainte-Palaye," he announced
charitably; "c'est un très-galant homme, mais ce n'est qu'un pauvre
érudit." The tone of these writings is not that of the *philosophes*
who, when they criticize erudition, oppose it not merely, or even
mainly, to *le goût*, but to *l'esprit philosophique*. It is probably much
more an echo of the old debate of the *Anciens* and *Modernes*.
Inside the Academy, according to the testimony of Bréquigny, the
group opposing Sainte-Palaye and supporting Le Franc was led by
Richelieu, the head of the *dévot* party.[50]

The election of Sainte-Palaye thus appears not to have involved
a really bitter contest between the two parties at the Academy. The
Queen was actively supporting his candidacy, but this fact seems
neither to have won him the support of the *dévots*, as one would

---

[48] This pamphlet in Bréquigny 59, fols. 128–128v.

[49] Charles Collé, *Journal historique ou Mémoires critiques et littéraires* (Paris, 1807), 2:245.

[50] Bréquigny 74, fol. 185. Bréquigny writes: "Lorsque Sainte-Palaye fut reçu à l'Académie Françoise, la Reine avoit dit à M. de M . . . (Mirabaud) qu'elle s'intéressoit à Sainte-Palaye et qu'elle seroit bien aise qu'il fût élu. Lors de la séance le Duc de R . . . (Richelieu) dit tout haut, Messieurs, on nous accuse de vendre, nos voix, il faut ici justifier aux yeux du public la liberté de nos suffrages. En se tournant vers M. . . il ajouta, on sait que la Reine sollicite. Cela est vrai, répondit M. . . , mais la Reine en faisant connoître ses désirs donne l'intention de les remplir. Elle détermine les suffrages sans les forcer. C'est en usant de sa liberté qu'on acquiesce au choix qu'elle indique; et en disant cela il fit voir son bulletin où le nom de Sainte-Palaye étoit écrit de la propre main de la Reine. La M. . . (Marquise?) s'intéressoit pour Lefranc." On Richelieu's role at the Académie Française, see Pierre Mesnard, *Histoire de l'Académie Française* (Paris, 1857), pp. 107–19, and a letter of Mme de Farges, de Brosses' daughter, in which she describes d'Alembert and Richelieu as the leaders of the opposing factions (quoted by M. Tourneux, 'Une Épave du cabinet noir de Louis XV,' *RHLF* [1897], 4:54).

have expected, nor to have alienated the sympathies of the liberals. Possibly the latter were glad of an opportunity to accede without misgivings to the royal wish. Le Franc, indeed, may have owed his election two years later to the Queen's intervention on behalf of Sainte-Palaye. The Academy considered it a duty to elect him—and it did so unanimously—in order to reaffirm its power to choose its members independently.

Le Franc's *discours de réception* or election address was the occasion of one of the great literary scandals of the eighteenth century. It is of interest because it was a clear sign of increasing tensions within the formerly common front of the Enlighteners. Le Franc broke with the compromising, conciliatory stance which the robe intellectuals—great men like Montesquieu as well as lesser ones such as Sainte-Palaye, de Brosses, Foncemagne, Secousse—had adopted until then toward the *philosophes*. He chose to use the opportunity presented by the required *discours de réception* to launch a violent attack on "ce siècle enivré de l'esprit philosophique et de l'amour des arts." The *philosophes* were accused of "l'abus des talents, le mépris de la religion et la haine de l'autorité." Voltaire, Duclos, d'Alembert, and Buffon were virtually designated by name.[51] In the face of this gross attack, the Academy closed its ranks and united in condemning the newcomer. "Le discours de M. Lefranc a fait faire des mines à bien des gens," Nicolas Desmarets wrote to Grosley. "Celui qui en a fait le plus étoit M. de Malesherbes, qui étoit derrière M. de Buffon. Je n'ai démêlé sur le visage de ce dernier et sur celui de Dalembert que du mépris froid . . . Duclos en témoigne publiquement son mécontentement."[52] De Brosses was shocked and disgusted. "La conduite de M. Lefranc a été déplorable," he wrote to Jallabert in Geneva. "Quelle rolle [sic] pour un homme de son rang et de son talent."[53] The King, the *dévots*, and Fréron, on the other hand, were delighted.[54]

Le Franc's outburst was unexpected. His career had hitherto been that of a fairly successful magistrate and man of letters of the robe. He had founded an Academy at Montauban, where he was a

---

[51] Abbé F. A. Duffo, *J. J. Lefranc, marquis de Pompignan, poète et magistrat, 1709–1784* (Paris, 1913), p. 347.

[52] B.N. Nouv. Acq. Fr. 803, fol. 102, Desmarets to Grosley, 28.4.1760.

[53] Yvonne Bézard, *Le Président de Brosses et ses amis de Genève* (Paris, 1939), pp. 234–35.

[54] Duffo, pp. 346–47.

Premier Président of the Cour des Aides, he had spoken out in typical parliamentary style against "abuses," and he was known as the author of some plays, some poems, and a *Prière universelle* adapted from Pope, which endeared him to the Deists. He had received an approving nod from Grimm and some flatteries from Voltaire. The more clairvoyant of the *philosophes* could doubtless see that he used the language of liberty, as magistrates were wont to do, in defense of particular prerogatives.[55] More disquietingly, however, he had disowned the *Prière universelle* and had taken to composing French versions of the Psalms, poems based on biblical prophecies and hymns for religious holidays. It was even said that he was angling for the post of tutor to the Dauphin, the leader of the *dévot* party at court. No wonder Voltaire, who had a good nose for the *infâme*, did not really like him.[56] The fact that in 1758 he was supported by the *parti dévot* at the Academy shows that by that time he had already moved a great way from the center to the right, abandoning the common ground that the robe scholars had hitherto shared with the *philosophes*. In his case the move may well be more significant than in the case of Palissot or the Abbé de Castres. While they turned against the *philosophes* because they found it more remunerative to side with the *dévots*,[57] Le Franc's move to the right and his unheard-of attack on his colleagues in 1760 was a sign that the more conservative parlementarians were becoming alarmed and were drifting away from the *philosophes*, for the latter were also taking up more and more radical positions. Voltaire, anxious to win the authorities over to the cause of reform, could not induce the *philosophes* to give Choiseul and his circle their confidence.[58] The *philosophes'* distrust was not groundless. In 1759 the Parlement had condemned Helvétius' *De l'Esprit* and the *Encyclopédie*. "L'hu-

[55] On his speech, 'Sur l'intérêt public,' and his Remonstrances, see Duffo, pp. 106–11, 307–30. Duffo omits to point out that it was not only or even so much the poor as the landed gentry and the patricians whom Lefranc wanted to protect from the "rapacity" of the tax collectors. Moreover the tax collectors and the landowners were rivals for the meager resources of the peasants. Even a cursory glance at Marion, *Histoire financière*, esp. 1:206–56, shows how common the rhetoric of Lefranc was among the apologists of privilege in the eighteenth century.

[56] Duffo, p. 349.

[57] The King and the *dévots* did their best to buy over writers and scholars; cf. Mesnard, pp. 110–11.

[58] Cf. John N. Pappas, *Voltaire and D'Alembert* (Bloomington, 1962), pp. 22–26, 43–44, 53–54, 57–58.

manité frémit, le citoyen est alarmé," the *Procureur Général* Joly de Fleury had declared in his requisitory, holding up the specter of a veritable conspiracy "pour soutenir le matérialisme, pour détruire la Religion, pour inspirer l'indépendance."[59] Three years later Rousseau's *Émile* was condemned for proposing to justify natural religion, encouraging speculation about religion, and thereby undermining "le principe de l'obéissance."[60] Palissot's satire of the *philosophes* was followed by the imprisonment of Morellet, who had dared to write a reply.

In increasingly difficult conditions Sainte-Palaye and his friends tried to avoid breaking with the *philosophes*. Although a few of them were Christians—like Foncemagne, who was converted after his wife's death,[61]—not many were party to the intrigues of the *dévots* and, in general, they had only contempt for the literary lackeys employed by the court. "L'Abbé Sabbatier . . . se déchaîne contre M. Helvétius qui le nourrissoit et lui faisoit une pension de cent pistoles," one member of the Académie des Inscriptions observed disdainfully of the author of the anti-philosophical *Trois siècles de la littérature*. "Il s'est jetté maintenant du côté de la défense de la religion. *Non defensoribus istis tempus eget.* Plusieurs personnes ont encore des papiers de sa main contre l'existence de Dieu."[62] At the time of the scandal caused by Palissot's *Philosophes*, many scholars sided with the aggrieved party against Palissot. "Je crois qu'à force de jouer les ridicules plus ou moins réels des savants et des gens de mérite, la cour en viendra jusqu'à regarder les sciences comme ne méritant point son attention et qu'elle ne fera

---

[59] Quoted by Pierre Grosclaude, *Un audacieux Message, l'Encyclopédie* (Paris, 1951), p. 90.

[60] Quoted by Henri Wallon in his Introduction to Rousseau's *Émile*, ed. J. L. Lecercle (Paris, 1958), p. 82.

[61] According to Barthélémy, Foncemagne was also an intimate friend of Jean-Pierre de Bougainville, a zealous *dévot*, whom the Académie Française had tried, by a famous maneuver, to exclude from its ranks (*Correspondance inédite du Comte de Caylus*, 2:265, and Mesnard, pp. 75–76). On one occasion Foncemagne came near to joining the ranks of the *dévots*. This was in 1772 when he accepted a pension awarded by the King to him as well as to the Abbé Batteux, an enemy of the *philosophes*, in appreciation of the "sagesse" they had shown at all times. The King declared at the same time that other similar pensions would be forthcoming for all who behaved with "moderation and restraint." The letter announcing the awards also warned academicians to look to the morals and opinions of future academicians before electing them.

[62] B.N. Nouv. Acq. Fr. 815, fol. 163, Ansse de Villoison to Mercier de Saint-Léger, 28.12.1772.

rien pour les savants," Desmarets wrote to Grosley on this occasion.[63]

Sainte-Palaye's behavior was markedly prudent. His *discours de réception*, for instance, in contrast with Le Franc's, struck a moderate note, dealing mostly with the relevance of linguistic history to the normal occupations of the Academy, appealing for consideration of the merits of Clio as well as of gayer muses and giving offense to no one. He did not put up a good fight for his friend de Brosses when the latter tried to enter the Académie Française against Voltaire's wish in 1771. Buffon, de Brosses' principal ally in the Academy, canvassed Sainte-Palaye who at first promised his support[64] and then withdrew it in order not to offend Voltaire. But de Brosses himself had tried hard to maintain neutrality in the conflict of *philosophes* and *dévots*. "Toute cette vilaine dispute"—he wrote to Jallabert of the polemic between Le Franc and the *philosophes*—"fait lever les épaules aux gens sages et honnêtes."[65]

The collaboration of scholars and *philosophes* was most firmly rooted in their common interest in history and in their common adherence to certain fundamental principles of criticism. Both groups rejected a large part of humanist historiography. They no longer believed that history was a belletristic exercise to be entrusted to successful poets rather than experienced historians; they did not accept that fact-gathering was a matter for lawyers and jurists; they felt that the humanist view of history as a storehouse of maxims and lessons for princes and rulers was inadequate; and while they considered factual accuracy more important than fine phrases, they no longer believed they could take facts for granted or establish them easily. The humanists had been concerned with the moral and political message to be learned from history. The scholars and philosophers of the late seventeenth and the eighteenth centuries not only were feeling their way toward a new interpretation of the uses of history, they were convinced that any lessons to be learned from it would be valid only if the factual accounts on which they were based were true.

The scholars ardently championed the spirit of criticism and inquiry. Muratori, for instance, observed with satisfaction how

[63] B.N. Nouv. Acq. Fr. 803, fol. 102, Desmarets to Grosley, 28.4.1760.
[64] Buffon, *Correspondance inédite*, ed. Nadault de Buffon (Paris, 1860), 1:131.
[65] Yvonne Bézard, *Le Président de Brosses et ses amis de Genève*, pp. 234–35.

many errors and prejudices had been exposed in natural philosophy and urged that "i lumi che in questo particolare abbiamo . . . possono bene stendersi agli altri generi di letteratura."[66] In a paper to the Académie des Inscriptions Fréret declared that scholars must acquire "l'esprit méthodique que l'étude des sciences exactes a remis à la mode dans notre siècle." The spirit of inquiry—"l'esprit philosophique" developed by the natural philosophers—must inspire the work of scholars too: "la vraie critique n'est que cet esprit philosophique appliqué à la discussion des faits: elle suit dans leur examen le même procédé que les Philosophes employent dans la recherche des vérités naturelles."[67] In 1761 Caylus wrote to du Tillot, deploring the survival of an outmoded kind of erudition. "Elle charge, elle répète, enfin elle veut briller par des inutilités sans nombre," he declared, "tandis que l'esprit d'ordre et de géometrie ne se permet que le nécessaire."[68] At the Académie des Inscriptions, the parading of useless and irrelevant erudition had been condemned by Fourmont the Elder as early as 1720. The authority of the ancients, he pointed out, is no guarantee of accuracy, and an author's argument is not improved or rendered more valid by extensive quotation.[69] The *philosophes* themselves were not unconscious of this change. In his article on "Erudition" in the *Encyclopédie* d'Alembert remarked that ". . . on vante beaucoup, en faveur des sciences exactes, l'esprit philosophique . . . mais croit-on que cet esprit philosophique ne trouve pas de fréquentes occasions de s'exercer dans les matières d'érudition? Combien n'en faut-il pas dans la critique pour démêler le vrai d'avec le faux?"

The great Benedictine scholars were for *cose* rather than *parole*, preferring collections of well-authenticated documents to the most eloquent arguments in support of a priori theories. Dom Lobineau declared: "Je n'ai d'autre guide que les faits, persuadé qu'un bon historien doit suivre les faits et non pas les amener à ses vues et les tirer par force pour les faire entrer bon gré mal gré dans la structure d'un système que la prévention seule aura formé."[70] Likewise, the directives issued in 1750 to the monks working on the *Recueil des*

---

[66] *Delle riflessioni sopra il buon gusto nelle scienze e nelle arti* (Naples, 1713), quoted by Mario Fubini, *Dal Muratori al Baretti* (Bari, 1954), p. 4.

[67] 'Réflexions sur l'étude des anciennes histoires et sur le degré de certitude de leurs preuves,' *MAI** 6:150–52.

[68] *Correspondance inédite du Comte de Caylus*, 1:277.

[69] 'Des Citations,' *MAI** 5:80.   [70] Quoted by E. de Broglie, 1:46–47.

historiens des Gaules et de la France state that: ". . . l'Éloquence n'est qu'un arrangement de mots qui flatte agréablement l'oreille . . . au lieu qu'un recueil mal digéré mesme, de pièces curieuses et d'une vérité solide nous ouvre l'esprit, nous instruit à fond et nous est infiniment plus utile que les vains ornemens de l'Éloquence qui ne sont propres qu'à nous chatouiller."[71]

Many eighteenth-century scholars went further than the Benedictines. On the whole, they no longer identified, as the Benedictines still tended to do, historical truth with the testimony of the most reliable authorities.[72] Nor did they readily see history as the unfolding of divine providence, and the task of the historian as that of bearing witness. The majority leaned more toward secular forms of determinism, and they sought the causes of historical change in the ambitions of men and in the force of institutions, of geography, of climate, of technical and economic conditions. Boulainviller and Fréret were the leading representatives of a new school of aristocratic historians which profoundly influenced later historiography.

Above all, the new historians emphasized the role of reflection in the writing of history. As the *Modernes* in literature gave increased importance to the subjectivity of the writer while at the same time requiring that he concern himself with the actual world rather than with traditionally accepted literary topics, so the historians, while they recognized the value of scholarly research and factual knowledge, saw little of worth in mere chronological narration. "Un sec et triste faiseur d'annales," wrote Fénelon, "ne connaît point d'autre ordre que celui de la chronologie . . . Au contraire l'historien qui a un vrai génie choisit sur vingt endroits celui où un fait sera mieux placé pour répandre la lumière sur tous les autres." "Le grand point" for Fénelon "est de mettre d'abord le lecteur dans le fond des choses, de lui en découvrir les liaisons . . ."[73] Likewise Boulainviller, though he staunchly defended the need for erudition among historians—and he was at pains to point out that historical erudition cannot be acquired easily or rapidly[74]—insisted equally on the need

---

[71] Bibliothèque de l'Institut, MS 1451, 'Documents ayant servi au Recueil des Historiens des Gaules et de la France.'

[72] Eduard Fueter, *Geschichte der neueren Historiographie*, 2d ed. (Munich and Berlin, 1936), p. 310.

[73] 'Projet d'un traité sur l'histoire,' part of the 'Lettre sur les occupations de l'Académie Française,' *Oeuvres* (Versailles and Paris, 1820–30), 21:230.

[74] 'Première lettre sur les parlements de France,' in *État de la France* (London, 1727–28), 3:5.

for insight into the relations between the facts. "Le véritable fruit de l'Histoire," he held, "se doit prendre dans les tableaux, non pas formez d'une manière romanesque ou tels que les ont faits Varillas et Maimbourg, mais conséquens du récit de leur conduite."[75] In the same way these noblemen insisted on the need to go beyond *parole* to *cose*, to see the endless stream of change behind the stasis of terms. Boulainviller could not condemn the Jesuit Gabriel Daniel strongly enough for failing to take account of the reality of change: "Que juger de sa méthode constante de réduire en toutes occasions les loix et les Usages les plus anciens aux idées et aux pratiques de notre Siècle, sans aucune attention à la différence de quatre ou cinq cens ans et quelquefois davantage."[76] In similar vein Fénelon had insisted on accurate knowledge of each period of history: "Notre nation ne doit point être peinte d'une façon uniforme: elle a eu des changemens continuels . . . Il ne faut jamais confondre les comtés bénéficiaires du tems de Charlemagne, qui n'étoient que des emplois personnels, avec les comtés héréditaires, qui devinrent sous ses successeurs des établissements de famille. Il faut distinguer les Parlemens de la seconde race, d'avec les divers Parlemens établis par les rois de la troisième race dans les provinces pour juger les procès des particuliers. Il faut connoître l'origine des fiefs, le service des feudataires, l'affranchissement des serfs, l'accroissment des communautés, l'élévation du tiers-état. . ."[77]

With a profound sense of history and change, the aristocratic historians were not narrowly legalistic. Well before Montesquieu, Boulainviller had already renounced a defense of the nobility based only on old documents and legal precedents. Standing before their own past as before another civilization, the men of the early Enlightenment were fully aware that the laws which men make are not those that truly govern their destinies. "Le monde," wrote Boulainviller, "est le jouet d'une succession éternelle. Pourquoi la Noblesse, ses avantages, ses possessions seroient-ils hors de la règle commune? Il ne faut point être triste ni jaloux de l'élévation de ces familles obscures qui entrent dans les travaux de nos pères, et qui viennent jouir de la gloire qu'ils ont laissée à leur Patrie . . . La décadence où se trouve à présent l'ancienne Noblesse est une conséquence nécessaire du changement qui s'est fait dans le gou-

---

[75] *Ibid.*, pp. 5–6.   [76] *Ibid.*, p. 9.
[77] 'Projet d'un traité sur l'histoire,' pp. 234–35.

vernement, dans la manière de faire la guerre, et de celui qui est arrivé dans les moeurs et dans les esprits . . ."[78]

The laws which men make are themselves seen as part of history now, and as such, they are understood to be subject to those general laws which govern the evolution of societies. Not the written laws, but the societies and civilizations of which they are part, interested the new historians. This changed outlook gave an enormous impetus to research into customs and institutions, it encouraged the study of societies as complete wholes of interlocking and interdependent parts, and it fitted well with the relativism in social thought which two centuries of travelers' reports had continuously fostered and which proved to be one of the most effective means of undermining the authority of absolutism and justifying reform. Boulainviller charged that the reason for the absence of historical sense among so many historians was fear of offending the government by a favorable or impartial depiction of ages prior to that of absolutism: "Ne semble-t-il pas qu'ils ont eu peur d'offenser le Gouvernement présent, en faisant seulement connoître quel a été celui des Siècles passez: comme si tous les Âges n'avoient pas leurs advantages particuliers qui ne passent point à d'autres Générations."[79]

Nearly every scholar sought to adapt his work to the requirements of the new history. Caylus put forward the right of the antiquary to reflect on his material and to fit it into the larger pattern of the evolution of societies and techniques.[80] Sainte-Palaye pointed out that the romances of chivalry were an important source for the historian of societies and manners. Lévesque de la Ravalière showed how the study of medieval sculpture was relevant to the understanding of the "usages" and of the "génie" of the age that had produced it.[81] Even the products of superstition and ignorance, the fabulous lives of saints, he argued, contain invaluable information about contemporary customs and manners, institutions and modes of thought, which the writers reveal—and all the more preciously— "sans le vouloir."[82] Provincial and local histories, which had hitherto

---

[78] 'Traité sur l'origine et les droits de la noblesse,' in *Continuation des Mémoires de M. Salengre* (1730), 9:84–87.

[79] *État de la France*, 3:43.

[80] *Recueil d'Antiquités* (Paris, 1762), vol. 5, Préface, pp. iii, viii–ix.

[81] *MAI* 18:322, read January, 1745.

[82] 'Notice d'un manuscrit conservé dans la Bibliothèque de Sorbonne,' *MAI* 23:254–55.

been little more than compilations of genealogies, began to take on a more general social and human character. Even the Benedictines tried to swim with the tide. Montfaucon, the successor of Mabillon, recast the original plan of his *Monumens de la monarchie françoise*, with a view to relating items which had originally been "détachez et comme isolez" and showing the historical development of taste and of styles in the Middle Ages.[83] But to many scholars the method of the Benedictines, despite such efforts to bring it up to date, now seemed old-fashioned. Montfaucon—in La Bastie's view—worked "plus du poignet que de la tête."[84] By the middle of the century the new style of historiography was generally established. The semi-official *Mercure* and the *Année littéraire* both praised writers who adopted it.[85]

This historiography is hard to separate from that of the *philosophes*. They too were more interested in the history of man, his societies, and his cultures than in the history of a few princes and royal houses. Voltaire made his views on this score clear in several places. Fontenelle, the leader of the first generation of Enlighteners, had held similar views. Instead of the movement that is visible on the surface of the earth—wars, territorial and political struggles, etc.—"je suis bien aise," Fontenelle declared, "de voir celui qui se fait continuellement dans les esprits des Peuples, ces goûts qui se succèdent insensiblement les uns les autres, cette espèce de guerre qu'ils se font en se chassant et en se détruisant, cette révolution éternelle d'opinions et de coutumes . . . sur-tout si on me montroit comment ces goûts, ces opinions, ces coutumes se produisent ou s'abolissent les uns les autres."[86]

Scholars and *philosophes* were alike united in condemning a cer-

---

[83] *Monumens de la monarchie françoise* (Paris, 1729), vol. 1, Preface, p. i.

[84] Quoted by Boissière, *Revue des deux mondes* (April, 1871), pp. 446–72.

[85] *Mercure*, 2.10.1784, reviewing 3d volume of Papon's *Histoire générale de Provence*, praises the author for having been one of "ces Voyageurs qui parlent peu des Cours, des Princes, mais beaucoups des Peuples, du sol, du climat, des plantes, des loix, du commerce, des moeurs, de la cartographie, des monnoies, et de l'ancienne et de la nouvelle carte. Un bon Historien développera maintenant tous ces objets . . ." The *Année littéraire* (1765), 2:123, reviewing an *Histoire de la ville de Lille*, informs its readers: "Vous ne confondrez point . . . cette Histoire avec la plûpart de celles qui n'ont qu'une ville pour objet. L'auteur a peint les moeurs et l'esprit des hommes; ce qui devient intéressant pour tous les pays."

[86] 'Sur l'histoire,' *Oeuvres* (1761), 9:351–79.

tain fashionable contempt for factual knowledge, and on the whole, both eschewed the popular and often fanciful histories of the loves of kings and queens which were modeled on the productions of the Abbé de Saint-Réal.[87] The *philosophes* had a healthy respect for erudition. They had learned from Bayle that sound scholarship must be the basis of all historical data and fact-judgments, and in practice—despite several jibes at mere scholars—Voltaire recognized the need to get his facts right and to substantiate his arguments; hence his inquiry whether Foncemagne would look over some of his historical work before publication.[88] Lanson has shown that Voltaire did not neglect to follow the discussions at the Académie des Inscriptions,[89] and we have his own word for it that he valued its work highly.[90] The *Siècle de Louis XIV* is full of praise for the great scholars of the seventeenth century, and, as Raymond Naves remarked, these passages illustrate "toute l'attention que Voltaire a portée à ces travaux de bénédictins (ou de jésuites) dans lesquels il voyait la base de toute construction sérieuse."[91] D'Alembert also warned against the abuse of the speculative intelligence. "Il faut avouer," he told the Académie Française, "que dans ces matières obscures l'usage de l'esprit philosophique est tout à côté de l'abus. Aussi combien de raisonnements creux n'a-t-il point produits sur les causes des révolutions des états?"—and d'Alembert goes on to compare abstract theorizing in history with general systems of physics or chemistry which their

[87] The influence of Saint-Réal and Saint-Evremond was by no means wholly bad. In their way, they emphasized that history is a human study and not a mere narrative of events. "Étudier l'histoire, c'est étudier les motifs, les opinions, et les passions des hommes pour en connoître tous les ressorts." (Saint-Réal, 'De l'usage de l'histoire,' p. 4, in Lenglet du Fresnoy, *Méthode pour étudier l'histoire* [Paris, 1713], vol. 2.) But Saint-Réal's own histories bordered on fiction, and it was the anecdotal aspect of his work which enjoyed the greatest success and influence in the eighteenth century.

[88] To d'Argental, 25.12.1751, Besterman 4035.

[89] Gustave Lanson, 'Formation et développement de l'esprit philosophique au XVIIIᵉ siècle,' *Revue des cours et conférences*, April, 1910, p. 248.

[90] 'Siècle de Louis XIV,' ch. 31, *Oeuvres*, ed. Moland, 14:537.

[91] *Le Goût de Voltaire* (Paris, n.d. [1938]), p. 133. Thomas Warton had already emphasized the enormous erudition of Voltaire (*History of English Poetry*, 1778, Hazlitt ed. [London, 1871], 1:107) before Carlyle pointed out that he was "a man of much deeper research than is imagined." (*Essays*, Library ed. 2:221–22.) Voltaire's remark in a letter to Cideville (Besterman 586) that he valued a little poem by his friend more highly than all the productions of the laborious Benedictines should be read with common sense.

authors have constructed in complete ignorance of the facts.[92] D'Alembert was aware that contempt for erudition among his contemporaries was sometimes the expression of a certain aristocratic contempt for science and learning in general. "C'est une espèce de mérite aujourd'hui," he wrote in the "Discours préliminaire" to the *Encyclopédie*, "d'en faire peu de cas; et c'est même un mérite que bien des gens se contentent d'avoir."[93]

Scholarship for the *philosophes* was not irrelevant, or even secondary: it was insufficient. What mattered was how it was used and to what end. The real cause of the tension between *philosophes* and scholars in the eighteenth century was not so much methodological as political. Magistrates and children of magistrates, the scholars were more firmly attached to the existing social order than the *philosophes* proper. However critical they may have been of this or that aspect of it, however eager for reform, however broadminded, they did not put their entire social order seriously or practically in question. The *philosophes*, on the other hand, tried to set themselves outside all existing or historical societies and to examine social relations from the point of view of reason or nature. The details of the evolution of particular societies, with which the scholars were primarily concerned, interested them only insofar as they threw light on the general problem of men's relations with each other in society.

On the very ground, therefore, where they were most in agreement—history and historical scholarship—scholars and *philosophes* were separated by far-reaching points of conflict. Both groups rejected providentialism, both demanded that historical testimony be subjected to rigorous scrutiny and that all historical accounts and explanations be based on study of the actual facts; but they envisaged the scope and the purpose of historical scholarship differently.

---

[92] Réflexions sur l'histoire,' *Oeuvres* (Paris, an XIII), 4:198.

[93] 'Discours preliminaire,' *Encyclopédie*, vol. 1, p. xxx; similarly in n. 1 of his *Éloge de Marivaux*, the jibe at the "jolis écoliers" of his own day. D'Alembert himself actively assisted the scholars. It was he who interceded with Frederick the Great to obtain communication of the famous Breslau MS of Froissart (*Oeuvres posthumes de Frédéric II, roi de Prusse* [Berlin, 1789], 12:28, 30). The celebrated tract known as *Le Philosophe*, which was published in various forms and places from 1743 on and which expresses the main planks of the *philosophes'* program, also stresses the importance of historical and factual knowledge in preference to metaphysical speculation (ed. Dieckmann, pp. 34-35).

The skepticism of the *philosophes* was a controlling discipline, not a pervasive philosophy. Carrying with them a diffuse but growing demand for radical change, they wished to intervene in history and to shape anew, deliberately, and in the light of reason, the forms and institutions of human society which hitherto had always been born in the shadow of ignorance and which had been taken for granted or seemed "natural" on account of their simply being there. They did not, therefore, attack the power of reason itself. On the contrary, reason was an indispensable weapon to them in their struggle for reform, since it provided the principles on which a rational and human social and political order might be built. At the same time, since men had to be persuaded to act according to reason, education was vital. To most of the *philosophes* history would have appeared useless without an educative function. When d'Alembert remarked that "la science de l'histoire, quand elle n'est pas eclairée par la philosophie, est la dernière des connoissances humaines,"[94] he was saying—among other things—that the task of history is both to inspire in men the desire to intervene in the historical process and to teach them the values and principles by which this intervention ought to be guided. Thus, in Voltaire's historiography, evaluative judgments play a large part, dividing the past into dark and bright ages. The entire medieval period, for example, the period of rule by noblemen and ecclesiastics, was summarily dismissed as a virtually undifferentiated chaos in which "la barbarie, la superstition, et l'ignorance couvraient la face du monde."[95] The only reason for studying this lamentable interlude was to learn to despise it and avoid its recurrence.

In their eagerness to change the course of things the *philosophes* were frequently impatient of the details of the structure which they opposed, and the past sometimes became for them a ludicrous masquerade scarcely worth the attention of reasonable men. The lesson—the universal that can be distilled out of the particulars—was all that counted. The rest was dross. Thus d'Alembert wrote, in a passage reminiscent of the skeptical La Mothe le Vayer, that the work of Tacitus "perdroit peu, quand on ne voudroit la regarder que comme le premier et le plus vrai des romans philo-

[94] 'Réflexions sur Christine, reine de Suède,' *Oeuvres*, 4:7.
[95] 'Essai sur les Moeurs,' ch. 94, *Oeuvres*, ed. Moland, 12:123.

sophiques."[96] Similarly, the *abrégé chronologique*, in d'Alembert's view, is all that is required to achieve the ends of history. Further information is simply a concession to idle curiosity. "Il seroit à souhaiter que tous les cent ans on fît un extrait des faits historiques réellement utiles et qu'on brulât le reste."[97] The very rationalism and optimism of the *philosophes* have led here, at this extreme end of one line of their thinking, to a view of history in which the goal of historical research is not to grasp the historical but to transcend it.

Associated as they were with a class which demanded no radical changes but rather a modest rearrangement of the existing forces in society, the scholars tended to emphasize the powerlessness of man before the impersonal forces of history. In their eagerness to substitute a rational human order for what had hitherto resulted obscurely from conflicts of dimly understood wills and forces, the *philosophes* had sometimes emphasized the activity of those men— Alfred the Great, Louis XIV, Peter the Great—who had contrived to make order out of chaos and to impose a human will, even an arbitrary one, on the brute material of history. The scholars, on the contrary, reflecting the view of the magistracy and continuing

[96] 'Réflexions sur l'histoire,' p. 195. La Mothe, while rejecting any sure knowledge of the past, had still accepted the usefulness of history on the grounds that as a source of moral precepts its value was not impaired by inaccuracy any more than the works of Hesiod or Ovid were precluded from being instructive because they were works of imagination. (*Oeuvres* [nouvelle édition; Dresden, 1756–59] vol. 5, pt. ii, p. 476.) Likewise, Rousseau in *Émile*, bk. 2 (*Oeuvres complètes*, Hachette, 2:128, n. 2): "Les anciens historiens sont remplis de vues dont on pourrait faire usage quand même les faits qui les présentent seraient faux. Mais nous ne savons tirer aucun vrai parti de l'histoire; la critique d'érudition absorbe tout: comme s'il importait beaucoup qu'un fait fût vrai, pourvu qu'on en pût tirer une instruction utile. Les hommes sensés doivent regarder l'histoire comme un tissu de fables dont la morale est très-appropriée au coeur humain."

[97] 'Réflexions sur l'histoire,' pp. 192–93; also 'Réflexions sur Christine, reine de Suède,' p. 7. Likewise, Lord Chesterfield considered that a general notion of the medieval period was sufficient for the general, educated reader (*Letters to His Son*, no. 113), and Bolingbroke thought that, while everyone should have some knowledge of the period before the sixteenth century, learned study of it was an affectation. (*Letters on the Study and Use of History* [London, 1752], 1:201.) Fontenelle had envisaged in his essay 'Sur l'histoire' that a full knowledge of human nature would one day make it possible to deduce "toute l'histoire passée et toute l'histoire à venir, sans avoir jamais entendu parler d'un seul événement . . . Cette méthode d'apprendre l'histoire ne serait assurément pas mauvaise," he claimed, ". . . car les principes généraux étant une fois saisis, on envisage d'une vue générale tout ce qui en peut naître et les détails ne sont qu'un divertissement qu'on peut négliger." (In F. Grégoire, *Fontenelle, une philosophie désabusée* [Nancy, 1947], pp. 330–31.) This is surely the most provocative expression of the rationalist point of view.

a long tradition which stretches from Montaigne by way of Boileau to Montesquieu, took pleasure in debunking the heroes and tyrants of the past. Nothing is easily changed, they held, certainly not as men plan, and those "heroes"—princes, kings, or philosophers— who imagine they can impose their will on institutions that were there before them and that will outlive them are time's fools. They are the unwitting instruments of irrational or inhuman forces— passions, ambitions, "fortune" itself—not the creators of new worlds they fancy themselves to be. In the particular sense in which the word liberal is appropriate to the magistracy, this was a liberal tradition, since it emphasized the law and order established by a whole community in the course of its history over the whims of the great, while at the same time it discouraged every attempt to interfere effectively in the traditional and apparently natural workings of things.

The skepticism of the magistracy was thus far more all-embracing than that of the *philosophes*, and it had a long pedigree. In the seventeenth century, Christian and free-thinking magistrates alike had frequently been ready to view the spectacle of history as an object lesson in human folly and in the impotence of the unaided reason of man. This view was the more welcome to them as it stressed the importance of the very instrument which lay in their hands—the law. In a world condemned to imperfection—it could be argued, as Pascal argued—that the law provided the only means of maintaining order and a certain minimal humanity, even if the law itself was neither rational nor natural. Within this context the study of history fulfilled two functions: on one level, the scholarly study of laws and precedents was indispensable for the settling of disputes and the preservation of order; on another level, the infinite spectacle of human passion and prejudice which history revealed served to remind the "philosopher," in one sense of the word, of the dangers to which worldly desire subjects him. The course of wisdom was to refrain from tampering with the world as it is. There was thus a place for historical scholarship in the thinking of the mid- and late-seventeenth-century magistrates, but its practical function was unphilosophical and its philosophical function was un-practical. In so far as historical research was practical, it was undertaken entirely within the existing legal and political tradition; in so far as it was philosophical and established a vantage point outside the tradition, it discouraged any action whatsoever. Not unexpectedly, the *philosophes* rejected this conception of historical scholarship. The idea of history as no more than an endlessly varied record of human absurdity was what led d'Alembert, as we just saw, to question the value of amassing "useless facts."

The scholars of the eighteenth century made a determined effort to go beyond the historical outlook of their predecessors and to bring themselves up to date. They learned to use the new vocabulary of "reason," "nature," and "liberty" in their historical studies, and they succeeded in thoroughly modernizing the traditional conception of law rather than reason as the alternative to chaos. But no matter how sophisticated or "philosophical" their work became, its latent conservatism remained strong. The aim of historical scholarship—as they practiced it—continued to be the seeking out of guidelines in the past to determine the shape of the future. Many of them doubtless believed quite sincerely that they offered a middle way, which could be accepted by both traditionalists and *philosophes*, provided they were of good will. De Brosses' reference to "gens sages et honnêtes"—by which he meant himself and his friends—is characteristic. In fact, however, the middle way was only a variation on existing arrangements, and one which singularly favored the class which advocated it. The magistrates traditionally thought of themselves as the party of the "nation" and the champions of "liberty," and they believed quite genuinely that the political solution they supported—monarchical government tempered by the parlements—could be accepted by all freedom-loving and philosophically minded people. Significantly, however, this particular political arrangement was the only one they envisaged as favorable to freedom, for they worked exclusively with the materials and the categories provided by the past.

The common front of reform obscured but did not diminish the differences between scholars and magistrates on the one hand and *philosophes* on the other. The Burgundian magistrates' brief flirtation with Rousseau in the sixties, for instance, was terminated when it became clear that fundamental disagreement underlay their apparent identity of interests. The author of the *Discourse on the Arts and Sciences* so pleased the magistrates of Dijon, who thought they recognized in Rousseau's work an echo of their own lamentations about the decadence and corruption of the age, that they offered him a job—composing parliamentary remonstrances! De Brosses wrote Rousseau that such a position would be worthy of his "noble liberté" and would give him a marvelous opportunity to serve humanity "dont la magistrature cherche à maintenir les droits par l'exacte observation des loix."[98] Rousseau refused, however, probably because he knew that his idea of liberty and that of de Brosses were very different. The magistrates subsequently became more and more disenchanted with the "citoyen." By 1766 he was no more than a "méchant enfant."[99]

Elsewhere, collaboration was maintained but still the fundamental differences were not eliminated. In Brittany, according to Augustin Cochin, "le Contrat Social s'appelle 'le contrat de la Duchesse Anne,' les Droits de l'Homme sont 'les privilèges bretons.' Nulle part la contradiction ne fut plus criante entre l'esprit et la lettre des doctrines. C'est que tout l'état-major de l'armée parlementaire est attaché à cette lettre et ne conçoit même pas qu'on s'en écarte. Au regard des dogmes, des principes, ils sont aux antipodes des avocats philosophes qui luttent à leurs côtés."[100] The Paris magistracy may have been more truly liberal and enlightened,[101] but not sufficiently so to be free of suspicion. Many members of the liberal and patriotic parties in the eighties believed that robe members should be gotten rid of.[102]

It would be a gross simplification, of course, to say that the circle of Sainte-Palaye and his scholarly friends was a mere intellectual workshop for the parlements. In a good deal of what they wrote, however, the same general tendency can be observed, and the robin is usually discernable beneath the *philosophe*. The case of Bréquigny, Sainte-Palaye's closest friend, is a fairly typical one. In two learned and well-written essays prefixed to volumes XI and XII of the *Ordonnances des Rois de France*—"Recherches sur les Communes" and "Recherches sur les Bourgeoisies"—Bréquigny attacked the old feudal law, judging it counter to natural law, both in its disrespect for property rights and, even more fundamentally,

---

[98] Rousseau, *Correspondance*, 2:33.
[99] Yvonne Bézard, *Le Président de Brosses et ses amis de Genève*, pp. 138–39, de Brosses to Pierre Pictet, 30.8.1757; pp. 244–46, de Brosses to Jallabert, 18.2.1766.
[100] *Les Sociétés de pensée et la Révolution en Bretagne* (Paris, 1925), 1:41.
[101] Cf., however, Bluche, *Les Magistrats*, pp. 356–58.
[102] Jean Egret, *La Pré-Révolution française*, pp. 328–29, 333–34.

in its disrespect for the rights and liberties of the individual. Bréquigny argued that the granting of *coutumes* to townsfolk by the King in the High Middle Ages and the confirmation by him of those granted by the great lords introduced into the "constitution" an element alien to feudalism. The *coutumes* were made by the people and were the expression of its deepest will; they became law through the Prince; but the act by which they became law was one of *souveraineté*—the King legislating as absolute sovereign —and not one of *suzeraineté*—the feudal lord confirming the acts of a vassal. Custom law is thus the result of a kind of collaboration between the people from which the laws come and the King through whose actions they are made effective, against the feudal lords.[103] Bréquigny emphasized that the *coutumes* of the medieval towns represented something akin to a fixed and universal system of legislation, which was to be contrasted with the arbitrariness of feudal law. The bourgeois himself—diligent, hard-working, law-abiding—was contrasted favorably with the tyrannical and rapacious feudal lord—noble and ecclesiastical alike. Bourgeois was not, Bréquigny insisted, a title of inferiority, but a title of privilege[104] to which even noblemen aspired[105] and the bourgeoisie as a whole—"classe intermédiaire entre la classe infortunée de ceux qu'on appeloit *vilains* et la classe tyrannique de leurs oppresseurs les Seigneurs de fief"[106]—was to be considered the source of liberty, prosperity, and culture in France.[107]

It might well seem that Bréquigny was extolling the virtues of the *tiers* against the other two orders, but was he really? The defense of custom law and the attempt to associate it with Royal authority marked no innovation. These were traditional themes of

---

[103] 'Recherches sur les communes,' *Ordonnances des Rois de France de la troisième race*, ed. Bréquigny and Vilevault (Paris, 1769), vol. 11, pp. ii–li, at p. xxxiii. Cf. also p. li: "Le but de cette sorte d'associations étoit de se défendre contre la tyrannie des Seigneurs." The lords and the bishops were almost always opposed to the burghers' demands, Bréquigny insists, and he mocks the attempt of one chronicler to present the bishops as concurring in the founding of burgh charters in order to help the King stamp out brigands. "Il est aisé de juger," he writes, "qu'Oderic ne voyoit que bien confusément du fond de son cloître ce qui se passoit au dehors." (p. xxi.)

[104] 'Recherches sur les bourgeoisies,' *Ordonnances des Rois de France de la troisième race*, ed. Bréquigny and Vilevault (Paris, 1777), vol. 12, p. xviii.

[105] Cf. *ibid.*, pp. xviii–xix. Charles Loyseau, a spokesman for the robe in the early seventeenth century, had likewise sought to narrow the gap between *seigneurs* and holders of offices under the Crown. (See Porchnev, pp. 538–45.)

[106] 'Recherches sur les bourgeoisies,' p. vi.   [107] *Ibid.*, p. xxxii.

the robe since the great jurists of the sixteenth century.[108] Bréquigny also developed another theme dear to the robe—that of a common source in the "general usages" of the nation for the different *coutumes*. In these "general usages" if in anything, the "original constitution" of the realm was to be sought. As Bréquigny appears to have held, along with other champions of the parlements, that all the parlements constituted in essence one single body—*le Parlement*[109]—it is clear that in his system the parlement deserved to be considered the guardian of the "ancient constitution" and of the rights of all Frenchmen. Bréquigny's attacks on the old nobility, his glorification of the authority of the Crown, and his criticism of Boulainviller[110] do not make him an adherent of the old Romanist thesis of the beginning of the century. His arguments rather favored the parlements, which he probably considered, as the sixteenth century jurists had done, *pars corporis principis*. What he objected to in the old feudalism was what he would have objected to in extreme absolutism (or "despotism"): the immediacy of the relation of power and authority and the absence of "intermediary powers." Feudalism had become a system of oppression, he declared, "parce que le pouvoir que rien ne balance, franchit insensiblement les bornes."[111] The echo of Montesquieu is clearly audible here.

What at first seemed to be an apology for the *tiers* thus turns out to be a defense of the parlements. Bréquigny's "bourgeoisie" itself should probably be identified with that earlier bourgeoisie from which the robe was recruited rather than with the contemporary bourgeoisie of merchants and tradespeople. His praise of trade and commerce and his defense of luxury should not mislead. Montesquieu himself attached great importance to trade, commerce, and luxury but distinguished between *commerce de luxe*

---

[108] Cf. Church, pp. 114–18.

[109] Hence, his praise of "la liberté dont nous jouissons sous le meilleur des Rois à la tête d'un Parlement libre" in manuscript fragment entitled "Essai sur la Constitution du Gouvernement d'Angleterre" (Bréquigny 48, fols. 157–58). On the theory of the unity of all the *cours souveraines*, the so-called "théorie des classes," both in the period 1756–71 and in the years immediately preceding the Revolution, see Jean Egret, *La Pre-Révolution française*, pp. 236–45.

[110] 'Recherches sur les communes,' pp. xiii–xiv, where he maintains that no *commune* existed before the twelfth century and that none was granted by the King until Louis VI.

[111] 'Recherches sur les bourgeoisies,' p. iv.

and *commerce d'économie*,[112] discerning shrewdly that only the former could be accommodated easily into the framework of the ancien régime.[113] Bréquigny was as strongly opposed as Montesquieu to any development of commerce that might threaten the interests of that landed aristocracy which his erstwhile bourgeoisie had in fact become. There is reason to fear, he declared after his eulogy of the early bourgeois, lest the drift to the towns "ne fît déserter les campagnes, et que la classe des hommes qui rendent un état florissant n'épuisât celle des hommes qui le nourrissent."[114] This was a common theme of eighteenth-century magistrates.[115]

It is not hard to understand that the patriots of 1788 eyed the scholars with suspicion. "Gardez-nous de l'érudition," Mirabeau wrote to a friend, and Rabaut Saint-Etienne explained why: "On s'appuie de l'histoire; mais notre histoire n'est pas notre code. Nous devons nous défier de la manie de prouver ce qui doit se faire par ce qui s'est fait; car c'est précisément de ce qui s'est fait que nous nous plaignons."[116]

The scholars had nevertheless come a long way from the crude appeals to precedent of an earlier age, and Bréquigny has clearly been touched by *philosophie* in a way that Baluze before him had not. Sainte-Palaye, in his *Mémoires sur l'ancienne chevalerie*—as we shall see in a later chapter—showed a similar emancipation from mere fact-gathering and accumulation of legal or documentary evidence. The scholars had in fact learned to take up a stand outside their own legal and political tradition, both in theory and in practice—to be "philosophical," in short. At the same time they had succeeded in doing so without sacrificing their basic conservatism and attachment to the model of the past. In the work of Montesquieu, rightly looked up to by the scholars as their intellectual leader, this fusion of conservatism and *philosophie*, which provided a new rationale for historical scholarship in the eight-

---

[112] *Esprit des lois*, 20, iv. The distinction is already implied by Sir William Temple in his chapter on the trade of the Dutch in *Observations on the United Provinces* (1673), ch. 4 (Works [London, 1757], esp. 1:183, 191, 195–96), and taken up by Mandeville in the *Fable of the Bees*, remark Q (ed. of F. B. Kaye [Oxford, 1924], 1:187–88). Cf. also A. Morize, *L'Apologie du luxe au XVIII⁰ siècle* (Paris, 1909), pp. 104–6.

[113] *Esprit des lois*, 20, x. Cf. ch. 1, n. 100 above.

[114] 'Recherches sur les bourgeoisies,' p. xxxiii.

[115] Cf. Marion, p. 231 *et passim*.

[116] Quoted by Jean Egret, *La Pré-Révolution française*, p. 332.

eenth century is at once most brilliantly realized and most clearly discernible.

Being outside his own particular tradition and observing it with the cold eye of a philosopher, the historian, as Montesquieu and the new generation of scholars envisaged him, could no longer be said to be subject to its myths or tied to its routines. To the author of the *Esprit des lois* and to the author of the *Mémoires sur l'ancienne chevalerie*, as to Rousseau the *philosophe*, all social systems are human and none can be taken for granted or wear the prestigious title of "natural." But whereas Rousseau invited his reader to consider that man is his own master and that he need not be the slave of his own reified creations, that he is free, if only he will repossess himself, to break the apparently rigorous necessity of the historical world,[117] Montesquieu transformed the various social roles and institutions of the historical world into a kind of second nature.[118] Just as in the comedies of Marivaux there is a limited repertoire of roles and gestures among which the actor may choose, so in the historical world of Montesquieu there is a limited repertoire of political forms among which societies may choose. Montesquieu does not say that just as man cannot speak without language, he cannot exist socially without social forms; he says that the social forms are limited in number and fixed in nature, like an unchanging language offering always the same choice of vocabulary to those who speak it. As the choice for the individual in the comedies of the time is between the roles of the mistress and of the soubrette, of the valet and of the master, so the choice in politics is among monarchy, despotism, and republican democracy—and even this choice is narrowed by Montesquieu when he indicates that the large state cannot operate as a republic. Thus Montesquieu first raises his reader out of the given world, in the manner of the *philosophes*, only to confront him in the end with a limited choice

---

[117] "L'homme s'approprie tout; mais ce qui lui importe le plus de s'approprier, c'est l'homme même." (*Manuscrit de l'Émile*, cited by Henri Guillemin, "L'Homme selon Rousseau," *Annales J. J. Rousseau* [1943-45], 3:7-26.) The idea is, of course, frequently expressed by Rousseau.

[118] Montesquieu's rejection of the current investigation into the origin of society (*Lettres persanes*, 94) is both modern—for it implies a strictly empirical study of man as social in his very nature—and reactionary, for it marks a refusal, motivated in part no doubt by political considerations, to question the existing order of society and the relations among its members, which their very abstract and individualist presuppositions enabled the contractualists to do.

—absolute or tempered monarchy—by which the general framework of the existing social world is stamped as eternal and un-
changeable.

History—the given, the past—thus becomes the rule for the
future, and the possibilities of human organization are defined by
what has already been. The conservative position is regained, but
now in a new and philosophical guise. Here probably is the main
cause of the disagreement in the eighteenth century between
philosophes and scholars, a disagreement which, as we have seen,
rarely came to a clear head and was often masked by common
interests and pursuits: history, as the scholars practiced it, always
seemed to turn out, however philosophical it might be, to justify
and substantiate the existing order, even while defining the possibilities of modifying it.[119]

There is no question that Montesquieu and the eighteenth century scholars provided a more solid basis for historical scholarship
than the *philosophes* could do. In one sense, it is true, Montesquieu's vision is a denial of time and history, for there is no room
for real novelty in it, only a reshuffling of existing elements. But in
another sense, by discovering system and coherency in the actual
events of the past instead of only in the concepts of the mind, it
gave significance to the minutest particulars and, indeed, made the
understanding of the past and of man fully dependent on the study
of particulars. Historical scholarship was thus raised above fact-
grubbing, idle antiquarianism, or legal dispute. Gibbon was one of
those who perceived this most clearly. He rejected d'Alembert's
suggestion that "useless facts" be subject to periodic bonfires: "Ne
suivons point les conseils de cet écrivain qui unit, comme Fontenelle, le savoir et le goût. Je m'oppose, sans crainte du nom
flétrissant d'érudit, à la sentence, par laquelle ce juge éclairé mais

---

[119] An extreme, but characteristic reaction to Montesquieu is that of the pseudo-
Helvétius (probably the Abbé de La Roche): "Je n'ai jamais bien compris les
subtiles distinctions sans cesse répétées sur les différentes formes du gouvernement.
Je n'en connais que deux espèces: les bons et les mauvais; les bons qui sont encore
à faire, les mauvais dont tout l'art est, par différentes moyens de faire passer
l'argent de la partie gouvernée dans la bourse de la partie gouvernante." (On this
celebrated text, cf. R. Koebner, 'The authenticity of the Letters on the Esprit des
Lois attributed to Helvétius,' *Bull. of the Institute of Historical Research* [1951],
24:19–43). Cf. also on the reservations of many *philosophes* with respect to
Montesquieu, Sergio Cotta, 'L'Illuminisme et la science politique: Montesquieu,
Diderot et Catherine II,' *Revue internationale d'histoire politique et constitution-
nelle*, Oct.–Dec., 1954, pp. 273–87, and the same author's *Montesquieu e la scienza
della società* (Turin, 1953), p. 113.

sévère ordonne qu'à la fin de chaque siècle on rassemble tous les faits, qu'on en choisisse quelques-uns et qu'on livre le reste aux flammes. Conservons-les tous précieusement. Un Montesquieu démêlera dans les plus chétifs des rapports inconnus au vulgaire."[120] To Montesquieu and the scholars, however, historical scholarship not only discovered the structures of human culture, it defined— and this rather narrowly—the possibilities of human action and the conditions within which man is free to realize an ordered world of his own choosing. This the most radical of the *philosophes* could not accept without misgivings, and they understandably distrusted those who were so busily engaged in restoring the fences and lines of demarcation which they wished to tear down.

[120] Gibbon, *Essai sur l'étude de la littérature* (London, 1761), p. 105; also p. 98. Gibbon returned to this theme later in his diaries; cf. *Journal de Gibbon à Lausanne,* ed. Georges Bonnard (Lausanne, 1945), p. 261 (entry of 11.4.1764): "J'ai lû Spanheim . . . Il y parle des secours que la Chronologie et la Géographie peuvent tirer des médailles. M. d'Alembert pouvoit bien les ignorer." Bonnard notes that the allusion to d'Alembert escapes him. To us, its meaning should be clear. Gibbon's defense of the "petits traits" is echoed by Robertson's emphasis on the importance of "authenticating the facts which are the foundations of my reasonings" (*History of the Reign of Charles V* [new ed.; London, 1878], Preface, p. ix), and by Pinkerton, who argued—following Gibbon—that the wise philosopher will be able to transform the dross of fact into the gold of history, as Montesquieu did. (*Vitae antiquae Sanctorum qui habitaverunt in ea parte Britanniae nunc vocata Scotia* [London, 1780], pp. iii–iv.)

CHAPTER 5

AMATEUR OF THE ARTS AND ROYAL ACADEMICIAN

Like most educated people in his time Sainte-Palaye was an amateur of the arts. "Nous ne songeons jamais à déjeûner, Sainte-Palaye et moi," de Brosses recounts of their stay in Venice, "sans nous être au préalable mis quatre tableaux du Titien et deux plafonds de Paul Véronèse sur la conscience."[1] The 1766 journey to Holland and Flanders which Sainte-Palaye made in the company of the Abbé Laugier was a kind of artistic pilgrimage. Everywhere the travelers went they hunted down paintings—in churches, in the homes of great statesmen-amateurs such as Cobenzl, and in the private collections of ordinary citizens. In Rome Sainte-Palaye and de Brosses spent many evenings with the director of the French Academy, the painter Jean-François de Troy;[2] and in 1749, on his return to Italy, Sainte-Palaye renewed this friendship. "Nous avons aujourd'hui mon frère et moi disné chez Mr de Troy," he wrote to Bachaumont and Madame Doublet, "avec qui nous avons beu de très bon vin de Bourgogne à votre santé; vous et tous vos amis, sur-tout M. de Valory ont passé en revue dans notre conversation."[3] Bachaumont's friends included many of the leading artists and amateurs in France. Among the former were Coypel, de Troy, and Le Moyne;[4] among the latter Caylus, Mariette, and the chevalier de Valory, a former pupil of de Troy. Sainte-Palaye himself was a particular friend of the Van Loos.[5]

The discussions of artistic questions that took place in private among Sainte-Palaye and his friends—and these must have been

---

[1] De Brosses, *Lettres familières*, ed. Bézard, 1:173. [2] *Ibid.*, 2:217.
[3] Arsenal 4900, fol. 306, 16.6.1749.
[4] 'Correspondance de Pierre avec Bachaumont,' *Revue universelle des arts* (1857), 5:260–64.
[5] Mariette, *Abécédario*, ed. Chennevières and Montaiglon (Paris, 1853–54), 5:362. In a letter to Bréquigny in London, Sainte-Palaye sends regards to "nostre ami Mr. Van Loo." The London Van Loo was the successful portraitist Jean-Baptiste. The same letter contains references to the Van Loo family in Paris.

many in the salon of Bachaumont and Madame Doublet, who was herself an amateur artist of talent[6]—formed the basis of their published contributions to a protracted debate on style and taste which was carried on throughout the century, reaching a climax around the forties and fifties. Sainte-Palaye wrote an essay on taste in the form of a letter to Bachaumont—*Lettre de M. de S. P. à M. de B. sur le bon goût dans les arts et dans les lettres* (1751).[7] Bachaumont's *Essai sur la peinture, la sculpture et l'architecture* of the same year (second edition, 1752) was likewise originally an answer to questions put to him by "un Ami de distinction," whom he identifies in a footnote as "M. de Sainte-Palaye." Sainte-Palaye was also, as we have seen, a close friend of Marc-Antoine Laugier, the author of an important *Essai sur l'architecture* (1753), and the preface to this work contains echoes of an earlier essay by Sainte-Palaye in the form of a letter to the *Mercure—Lettre à M. de la Bruere sur le projet d'une place pour la Statue du Roy.*[8] The work of Sainte-Palaye and his friends thus stands at what the art historian Albert Dresdner considered the beginnings of art criticism in the modern sense. It is predominantly social in origin and in form, continuing in writing debates and discussions that had been begun in the conversations of friends or literary salons.[9]

It is also, implicitly, a rejection of extreme absolutism as significant in its way as that contained in the scholarly works of the magistracy. Sainte-Palaye and his friends were well aware of this, and they took the trouble to spell out their attitude. In his *Lettre à M. de B. sur le bon goût,* Sainte-Palaye denied that any group enjoyed a privileged position with respect to other members of society. Art was not the affair of a clique or a court but of all those who loved and appreciated it, and all had a right to speak and to be heard. All those who frequented, as he did, the circles of Bachaumont and Madame Doublet would have supported this position, and it was the collective view of that urban society, that civilization of salons which had succeeded the courtly civilization

---

[6] E. and J. de Goncourt, *Portraits intimes,* 1:71–72; also Jean-Charles Chassex, 'Madame du Boccage ou la belle inconnue,' *French Review* (1957), 30:297–302. Chassex notes that the original edition of Madame du Boccage's *Colombiade* was decorated with tailpieces by "Madame D."—doubtless Madame Doublet.

[7] B.N. Imprimés ZP 2118.

[8] *Mercure,* July, 1748, pp. 147–53; cf. also Herrmann, p. 19.

[9] Albert Dresdner, *Die Entstehung der Kunstkritik im Zusammenhang der Geschichte des europäischen Kunstlebens* (Munich, 1915), pp. 155 et seq.

of Versailles. Bachaumont himself maintained that since native intelligence and reason had been given to all men alike, anyone could, with application, reflection, and some natural sensibility become "ce qu'on appelle un Connoisseur."[10] Laugier, criticized as an amateur and a "demi-savant," retorted in the same vein that the arts are the concern of others besides artists and that nobody has the right to exact blind acquiescence to his own rules of taste.[11] Echoing La Font de Saint-Yenne,[12] the earliest champion of public art criticism, Sainte-Palaye declared that the amateur even had an advantage over the professional in that his judgment in its search for true beauty is untrammeled by prejudices and particular allegiances. "Je n'ay pris aucun parti," he wrote, "entre les Palladio, les Bramante, les Michel-Ange, les Mansard, les Perrault et autres, pour ne point parler des modernes. C'est peut-être un avantage que j'ay sur les gens de l'art pour mieux juger: la Nature est mon unique guide, et je ne vois que par ses yeux."[13] The views of Sainte-Palaye, Laugier, Bachaumont, and La Font coincided to some degree with those of the *philosophes*. "C'est au poète à faire de la poésie, et au musicien à faire de la musique," Rousseau declared; "mais il n'appartient qu'au philosophe de bien parler de l'une et de l'autre."[14]

Not surprisingly, in view of this conception of the public's role in artistic matters, questions of town planning interested Sainte-Palaye and his friends. New in their ideas was a growing concern for the welfare of private individuals, for social life as distinct from the life of the court, and consequently, for the city as a totality rather than for a few notable monuments. Air, light, and sanitation were important considerations in the thinking of writers like La Font and Voltaire and, increasingly, of municipal authorities themselves.[15] Promenades and gardens were built for public rec-

---

[10] Bachaumont, *Essai*, p. 3; cf. Hautecoeur, 4:56, and G. Wildenstein, 'Goûter une oeuvre d'art en "connoisseur,"' *Gazette des Beaux-Arts*, 1106, April, 1961, Chronique, pp. 1–3.

[11] *Essai* (2d ed.; Paris, 1755), p. 59; cf. also his *Observations sur l'architecture* (The Hague, 1765), p. 4.

[12] Cf. Dresdner, p. 175.

[13] *Lettre de M. de S. P. à M. de B. sur le bon goût dans les arts et dans les lettres* (Paris, 1751).

[14] *Oeuvres*, 13:248. Diderot did try to understand painting from the point of view of the artist, but he intended thereby to enrich his basically lay criticism, not to replace it with a dry professionalism.

[15] Cf. Hautecoeur 3:477–78, 521–22; also P. Lavedan, *Histoire de l'urbanisme: Renaissance et temps modernes* (Paris, 1941), pp. 200–4.

reation, and many writers hoped not only for great new programs of public building, but for the disengagement and proper display of existing public buildings. If the colonnade of the Louvre and the Tuileries could be situated at either end of one principal street, and the Luxembourg and the portal of Saint-Gervais at either end of an intersecting street, an ideal arrangement would be realized, Sainte-Palaye declared.[16] His idea was that public buildings should be seen and enjoyed by all and that their social significance should be expressed by making them visible to the citizens from as many positions as possible. This idea of Sainte-Palaye's was taken up by the Abbé Laugier several years later in a chapter of his *Essai sur l'architecture*.

The *philosophes* readily collaborated with the critics in their campaign for urban improvements. A controversy which broke out around mid-century over two projects, one for the completion of the Louvre and the other for the construction of a new square for the proposed statue of Louis XV, provided a rallying point for all who were concerned with the arts and their relation to society. In July, 1748, in an open letter to the director of the *Mercure*, Sainte-Palaye launched public discussion of these projects by making known a plan by Bachaumont and the architect of the City of Paris, Laurent Destouches, for the completion of the Louvre colonnade and the construction of a square in front of it with one side open to the Seine. Although many different projects for a suitable open space in which to place the King's statue were subsequently presented by members of the Académie d'Architecture and others,[17] Bachaumont, who enjoyed considerable reputation as an art critic,[18] won support for his project from the duc de Gesvres, Governor of Paris, from the *prévot des marchands*, from

[16] 'Lettre à M. de la Bruere sur le projet d'une place pour la Statue du Roy,' *Mercure*, July, 1748, pp. 147–53.

[17] Hautecoeur, 3:504n., declares that these are not known and mentions a collection of 'Divers projets d'une place publique pour ériger la statue de S.M. Louis XV du jeudi 18 janvier, 1753,' which appeared in a catalogue at Saint Petersburg in 1890. The Bibliothèque de l'Arsenal has a collection of plans by academicians —'Recueil de différens Projets et Plans proposés pour la construction d'une place publique destinée à la statue équestre du Roy, MDCCXLIX' (Arsenal 3103). This collection contains marginal comments by Paulmy d'Argenson. Arsenal 4041 contains comments by Bachaumont on some of the plans.

[18] In Arsenal 4041 there is a memorandum presented to Tournehem in 1746, doubtless on request, in which painters and sculptors deserving of support are listed. It was published by Paul Lacroix, who does not indicate where he found it, in *Revue universelle des arts* (1857), 5:418–27. Dresdner (p. 190) describes Bachaumont as "eine Art Orakel" in the artistic circles of the time.

the duc de Richelieu, from de Bernis, and from Madame de Pompadour. Voltaire was enthusiastic. "Je mettrai le feu à Paris," he wrote to d'Argental, "s'il est assez Goth pour ne pas saisir cela avec enthousiasme."[19] The poet Gresset wrote to Bachaumont that he had shared "avec tous les bons citoyens et tous les vrais amateurs des arts le plaisir que leur a causé la lettre de M. de Ste. Palaye sur le projet d'une place pour la statue du Roy."[20] Throughout the protracted debate on the subject, Sainte-Palaye continued to play a prominent part,[21] and though in the end the square was built at the western end of the Tuileries, the basic idea of the open river side was retained, while the completion of Perrault's colonnade, the other main concern of Sainte-Palaye and Bachaumont, received consideration from the government and won popular approval.[22]

Sainte-Palaye's interest in town planning was not limited to the question of a suitable site for the King's statue. What he and Bachaumont had in mind was a program of improvements to the city as a whole, to the advantage of all the citizens.[23] They were entirely in sympathy with the sentiment expressed a year later by Voltaire: "On parle d'une place et d'une statue du Roi. Il s'agit bien d'une place! Paris serait encore très incommode et très

[19] Arsenal 4041, fols. 49–50, 51, 57, 91, correspondence to and from Bachaumont, Madame de Pompadour, Tournehem, Richelieu, and de Gesvres in October, 1748; also *ibid.*, fols. 34–36, two copies of a letter from Voltaire to d'Argental. A further letter from Voltaire to d'Argental on the subject, dated 4.9.1749, is in the *Correspondance* (Besterman 3457). Voltaire's lines 'Sur le Louvre,' *Oeuvres*, 8:520, are also pertinent.

[20] Arsenal 4041, fol. 47, Gresset to Bachaumont, 28.9.1748.

[21] Sainte-Palaye's article in the *Mercure* provoked several replies, some of which were probably by friends. There are copies of them with annotations and occasionally corrections in his hand in Arsenal 4041, fols. 76–78.

[22] Voltaire had already complained about the state of the Louvre in *Ce qu'on ne fait pas* (pre-1745). That the Louvre concerned Bachaumont and Sainte-Palaye as much as the Place Louis XV seems obvious from documents in Arsenal 3036 (extracts from La Font de Saint-Yenne's important *Ombre du grand Colbert* and from articles concerning the Louvre in *Journal des Savants*, *Journal de Trévoux*, and *Mercure*) and Arsenal 4041 (memorandum on the Louvre submitted by Bachaumont to Tournehem in 1746, fol. 124, and letter on the same subject from Bachaumont to Richelieu, urging that the plans for the completion of the colonnade, which Bachaumont says he has discussed with the architect Gabriel, be given speedy consideration, fol. 99, dated 27.9.1749). On the whole discussion, see Lavedan, pp. 198–211, Louis Hautecoeur, *Histoire du Louvre* (Paris, n.d. [1951]), pp. 72–73, Dubech and d'Espezel, *Histoire de Paris* (Paris, 1931), 1:215–16, Sir Reginald Blomfield, *A History of French Architecture, 1661–1774* (London, 1921), 2:183–87.

[23] Cf. Bachaumont's *Essai*, where several other projects are discussed, notably a way of saving the Champs Elysées, as originally planned, from land speculators (2d ed., pp. 53–58).

irrégulier, quand cette place serait bâtie. Il faut des marchés publics, des fontaines, qui donnent en effet de l'eau, des carrefours réguliers, des salles de spectacle. Il faut élargir les rues étroites."[24]

Despite agreement on a wide range of points, however, the attitudes of Bachaumont, Sainte-Palaye, La Font, and their circle were not identical with those of the *philosophes*. Many of the critics were sons of the robe, and they deplored the influence on the arts of the contemporary Maecenases—new-rich *anoblis*, financiers, and *fermiers-généraux*. In 1731 Mariette complained of the decline of artistic standards in an age dominated by acquisitiveness. "Il n'y a pour ainsi dire rien autre chose qui puisse faire travailler les graveurs," he wrote to an Italian friend, "que la perspective du gain: et tout le reste des hommes agit-il autrement? Ils cherchent donc à plaire, et deviennent . . . les esclaves du goût dominant. Celui qui règne aujourd'hui est le joli . . . Cela est tellement vrai, que bien que l'admiration pour Raphael et Michel-Ange soit bien établie, je ne conseillerois néanmoins à aucun graveur, désireux de gagner sa vie, de graver un de leurs tableaux."[25] In 1738 when the painter de Troy was appointed to head the French Academy in Rome, Mariette penned a few comments on this man whose principal successes hitherto, despite a few canvases on traditional Biblical or mythological themes, had been with *tableaux de modes*. "C'est un homme du monde qui en connoist parfaitement les usages et qui sçaura faire honneur à la nation dans le poste qu'il occupe," he noted, adding with barely concealed disapproval: "Un mariage avantageux . . . le met encore en estat de figurer, chose qui est fort de son goust; car il a toujours aimé à frayer avec les gens de finance, et ce qu'on appelle les gros riches."[26]

[24] *Oeuvres*, 23:298.

[25] Quoted by M. J. Dumesnil, *Histoire des plus célèbres amateurs français et de leurs liaisons avec les artistes, Pierre-Jean Mariette, 1694–1774* (Paris, 1858), 1:46–47. There is a similar account in J. B. d'Argens, *Lettres juives* (Amsterdam, 1737): "En effet, les tableaux de Poussin, de Le Brun, et de Le Sueur, sont médiocrement recherchés aujourd'hui; et les peintres, qui travaillent dans le caractère de ces grands hommes, et qui tâchent de donner à leurs ouvrages la noblesse et l'harmonie qui font l'âme du dessein, sont beaucoup moins suivis que ceux qui peignent des tableaux qu'on n'eût osé mettre autrefois dans une antichambre. Watteau a été le Fontenelle et Lancret le La Motte de la peinture." (Quoted from The Hague ed. 1738, 6:59–60, letter 196.)

[26] Mariette, *Abécédario*, 2:101. For a brief but suggestive discussion of de Troy as a painter, see Pierre Francastel, 'L'Esthetique des Lumières,' in *Utopie et Institutions au XVIIIᵉ siècle: le pragmatisme des Lumières* (Paris and The Hague, 1963), Congrès et Colloques, 4.

Caylus blamed the new wealthy class of financiers and *anoblis* for the so-called decadence of taste. De Troy, in his view, was "capable de bien traiter les opérations les plus étendues de l'art et d'étaler tout ce que la fougue du pinceau peut indiquer de plus grand et de plus abondant."[27] But contracts for covering a whole wall or ceiling were few and far between in the years of rococo interior decoration. The use of glass and mirrors left no room for vast paintings on "les grands sujets de l'histoire." "On n'a laissé au plus beau des arts," La Font de Saint-Yenne complained in similar vein, "que quelques misérables places à remplir, des dessus de porte, des couronnements de cheminée et ceux de quelques trumeaux de glace, raccourcis par économie."[28] Artists, Frézier declared, have become the servants of wealthy, but uncultured and unenlightened patrons.[29] As a result their own taste has been corrupted. Baillet de Saint-Julien chose his words carefully when, commenting on some designs by de Troy for the Gobelins factory, he observed that even in that aspect of his work where one could still admire the artist's talent, he was no more than "un riche marchand d'étoffes."[30] As for Bachaumont, he expressed fears for Fragonard. He had heard that "l'appât du gain" had seduced him "et qu'au lieu de travailler pour la gloire et pour la postérité, il se contente de briller aujourd'hui dans les boudoirs et dans les garde-robes."[31]

Nearly all the critics followed La Font de Saint-Yenne, an ardent champion of the hierarchy of the genres, in deploring the decline of historical painting and the vogue of genre painting.[32] Sainte-Palaye and de Brosses had already noticed the popularity of the Flemish and Dutch genre painters, especially with the Englishmen they met in Italy, and de Brosses expressed appropriate sentiments about the decline of taste in his *Lettres*. De Brosses' views on genre painting were common among the critics.[33] Even

[27] Quoted by Gaston Brière, 'De Troy,' in Louis Dimier, *Les Peintres français du XVIIIe siècle* (Paris and Brussels, 1930), 2:16.

[28] 'Reflexions sur l'état de la peinture en France' (1747), quoted by Hautecoeur, *Histoire de l'architecture classique en France*, 4:47.

[29] 'Dissertation sur les ordres de l'architecture' (1738), quoted by Herrmann, p. 222.

[30] Quoted by Brière, p. 28.

[31] 'Sur les peintures, sculptures et gravures . . . exposées au salon du Louvre, le 25 août 1769,' in Bachaumont's *Mémoires Secrets* (London: Adamson, 1780), 13:32–33.

[32] Cf. J. Loquin, *La Peinture d'histoire en France de 1747 à 1785* (Paris, 1912), pp. 138–40 *et passim*.

[33] *Ibid.*, pp. 139–40n.; de Brosses, *Lettres*, ed. Bézard, 1:172.

portraits were regarded as inferior, and La Font was indignant at the growing demand for them. Again, the wealthy private client was blamed for undermining the taste and talent of artists. Portraits, La Font complained, "occupent nos meilleurs pinceaux et nous privent d'excellents peintres qui se distingueraient dans la carrière supérieure et honorable de l'Histoire."[34] Similarly Bachaumont, commenting on what he judged the excessive number of figures in Veronese's *Pilgrims of Emmaus*, on their "expressionless faces" and on the inappropriately grand architectural background that the artist had provided for this humble scene, claimed that it would be wrong "de nous en prendre au Peintre de tous ces petits défauts de convenance. Sans doute nous lui rendrions plus de justice, en pensant que le Noble Vénitien qui lui a demandé ce Tableau ignorant apparemment les convenances, a voulu obstinément qu'il representât une partie de son Palais, de sa Salle à manger, de son beau Buffet. Il l'a obligé de mettre dans ce Tableau, sa Femme, ses Enfans, ses Chiens, ses Domestiques, et même jusqu'à ses Nègres et son Cuisinier. Plaignons les Peintres, quand ils sont forcés de prêter leur main et leur pinceau à de pareils caprices."[35] Even the great portrait painter La Tour was criticized, not indeed for his art, but for the genre he practiced. La Tour, however, shared the sentiments of some of his critics—especially of the more philosophically inclined ones—and as "citoyen et philosophe" he undertook to avoid the genre of portraiture as it was understood by his contemporaries, that is as a means of satisfying the vanity of individuals, and to devote himself to painting "des Hommes illustres" rather than "des gens opulents."[36] In this way the portrait was to become a branch of historical painting. In his study of *La Peinture d'histoire en France* Jean Loquin attributed the preference for *peinture d'histoire* to the fact that the critics were first and foremost literary men, but Loquin may have given too much weight to the opinion of the eighteenth century artists themselves. Historical painting was *public* painting. It concerned not a few wealthy individuals but the whole nation, and this, in part, is what moved the critics. La Font de Saint-Yenne carried his sense of the public nature of art so far as to regard great private collec-

---

[34] 'Sentiments sur quelques ouvrages de peinture' (1754), quoted in Loquin, p. 139n.

[35] *Essai sur la peinture, la sculpture et l'architecture* (2d ed.; Paris, 1752), pp. 18–20.

[36] Loquin, p. 139n.

tions as virtually public property. As early as 1747 he proposed that the King create a public art gallery in Paris where people could always view "les innombrables chefs-d'oeuvre des plus grandes maîtres de l'Europe . . . qui composent le cabinet de tableaux de Sa Majesté, entassés aujourd'hui et ensevelis dans de petites pièces mal eclairées et cachées dans la ville de Versailles."[37] Three years later, Lenormant de Tournehem went some way toward meeting this demand when he opened the *Cabinet du Luxembourg* to the public. But La Font's ideas were more grandiose. In *L'Ombre du grand Colbert* of 1752 he suggested that the *Galerie d'Apollon* in the Louvre be set up as a public gallery. Without directly raising dangerous questions, and possibly without even thinking of them, La Font was taking up a position that was expressed later in more general and more radical forms, which he himself would certainly have rejected. The owners of works of art, La Font's views imply, have a duty to the public; they are not absolute possessors, but rather guardians of a property which in the last resort belongs to the public, and they are as responsible to the public as the King is, for example, for the use of the power invested in him.[38]

In all this there was much to please the *philosophes*, and it is not surprising to find that on a large number of specific points—the influence of new-rich clients, the place of portrait painting, the superiority of history painting, the public nature of art, etc.— Diderot is in close harmony with La Font, with Bachaumont, with Sainte-Palaye. Yet we also find Diderot defending the artist against the critics and refusing to criticize artists publicly.[39] This was also the position of his friend C. N. Cochin, who, as secretary of the Académie Royale de Peinture, found himself engaged at one and the same time in the defense of a privileged body—the Academy —against the claims of society as a whole, and in the defense of the artist against an exacting, powerful, and tyrannical society of wealthy aristocratic patrons on whom the artist was coming more and more to depend for his daily bread. The patronage of the

[37] 'Réflexions,' quoted by Loquin, p. 64.

[38] On La Font, see Roland Desné, 'La Font de Saint-Yenne, précurseur de Diderot,' *La Pensée* (1957), 73:82–96. In his study of *Les Sans Culottes parisiens de l'an II* (Paris, 1958), Albert Soboul remarks that the idea of the farmer and landowner as the trustee rather than the possessor of his crop was widespread in radical circles during the Revolution. It is hard to conceive that La Font would have accepted this extension of his doctrine.

[39] *Salon* of 1763, *Oeuvres*, 10:226.

wealthy—as Cochin saw it—threatened to demote the artist from the high position of honor and respect he had won for himself in the Renaissance as the man of genius whose eyes beheld divine ideas, and to reduce him once again to the mere craftsman he had been during the medieval period. This was also the reason for the attacks of Mariette, Caylus, and the connoisseurs on the wealthy private patron. Mariette's sharpest criticism of de Troy was that, having sold himself to wealthy clients, he had stifled his genius and become a mere artisan: "l'on dira toujours de luy que c'est un practicien."[40] But whereas Cochin saw in the Royal Academies the means by which the artist could be protected from the pressure of the wealthy client, Mariette and Caylus wished to subordinate him to a select group of amateurs or connoisseurs, to whom they themselves belonged and who, they claimed, could speak for the public —a kind of artistic *parlement*. They thus set themselves up, as the parlements had done traditionally, in opposition both to the wealthy financiers and *fermiers-généraux* and to royal "despotism," as the spokesmen of the *nation*. Sainte-Palaye and Bachaumont were willing to broaden the basis of connoisseurship and to remove some of the aura of estericism surrounding it, but in the end their position was only slightly more liberal than that of Mariette and Caylus. It was certainly not Diderot's.

The protests of Sainte-Palaye and his friends against the influence of the wealthy private patron were part of a general assault by the critics on the "chicorée" and the "petite manière" of the day. It was mounted during the second burst of rococo inventiveness in design, which Fiske Kimball placed between 1730 and the death of Pineau in 1754,[41] and it was made in the name of a simpler

---

[40] *Abécédario*, 2:103–4.

[41] Fiske Kimball, *The Creation of the Rococo* (Philadelphia, 1943). The first outspoken criticism was voiced by Voltaire in *Le Temple du goût*. Voltaire was soon joined by a large number of critics, amateurs, architects: J. F. Blondel (*De la Distribution des maisons de plaisance* [1737], and other later works), Frézier (*Dissertation sur les ordres d'architecture* [1738]), de Brosses (*Lettres d'Italie*), Soufflot (in two papers read to the Académie de Lyon: *Mémoire sur l'architecture gothique* [1741], and *Dans l'art de l'architecture le goût est-il préférable à la science des règles ou celle-ci au goût?* [1744]), Abbé Le Blanc (*Lettres d'un Français* [1745], *Lettres sur les ouvrages de peinture* [1747]), La Font de Saint-Yenne (*Réflexions sur quelques causes de l'état de la peinture en France* [1747], and the celebrated *Ombre du grand Colbert* [1749 and 1752]), Caylus (*Réflexions sur la peinture* [1747]) and Bachaumont (*Essai sur la peinture, la sculpture et l'architecture*). In 1754 and 1755, C. N. Cochin delivered what might be considered the death blow with two satires published in the *Mercure*. On the entire debate, cf. Herrmann, pp. 61–67, 221–34, and Hautecoeur, 4:46–50.

style, variously associated with nature, reason, antiquity, and the masters of the reign of Louis XIV. *Philosophes* and critics found themselves on the same side of the fence in this debate, but once again they were united only in their opposition to the rococo. There was no uniformity of view among them, and they were far from sharing a single esthetic position.

All of them were involved to some degree in the culture of which they were critical. Voltaire attacked the rococo in the *Temple du goût* and elsewhere, but he did not escape its charm or influence. Much of his own work, especially his light verse and his *contes,* is in the same spirit of inventiveness, improvisation, and wit as the works of the great artists and decorators of the rococo. Caylus had studied with Watteau for a while, and he had a penchant for amusing erotic tales which were hardly in the grand manner. Similarly Mariette, so severe in his taste, was associated for many years with Watteau and Boucher, and he prepared engravings of their works as well as of those of the masters of the High Renaissance.[42] Boffrand, who declared that the Académie d'Architecture must preserve "ces principes, sur lesquels sont fondées la pureté et la noble simplicité de l'Architecture" from the "folles nouveautés qui s'introduisent,"[43] could still be rococo in Lorraine and in Germany, even if he remained generally more restrained on the soil of France. Blondel was an admirer of Pineau.[44] Even Diderot was occasionally seduced by the charm of the rococo.

But it is not so much in the varying degree of their attachment or opposition to the rococo itself as in the scope of their own ideals and in their awareness of the problems presented by the relation of the artist to society that we can discern where the critics truly stood and how diverse their positions were.

Sainte-Palaye's models—Raphael, Le Sueur, the Carracci—were the divinities of academicism, and it was a doctrine of academic eclecticism which he preached against the rococo. His outlook was not stuffily conservative, however. The influence of Fontenelle, for instance, is perceptible in his belief that, while intelligence and sensibility mark out the connoisseur from birth, only an appropriate stimulus from the outside world, the call of another human

---

[42] Dumesnil, p. 51.
[43] *Livre d'architecture* (1754), quoted by Hautecoeur, 3:139.
[44] Cf. Herrmann, p. 65.

voice in art, in literature, or in philosophy, will galvanize these qualities into action. Sainte-Palaye described his own "discovery" of painting, after years of ignorance, in terms of a sudden illumination, such as struck Malebranche, according to Fontenelle, when he discovered Descartes. For a long time, he recounts, he saw in the sketches his friend Bachaumont had made of the great masterpieces of Raphael, Michelangelo, and the Carracci only "un griffonage . . . de figures à demi tracées, des traits sans liaison . . . quelques coups de plume jettés rapidement et comme au hasard sur le papier."[45] Then one day he was looking at the Le Sueurs in the Cloister of the Chartreux: "Mes yeux se desillèrent enfin, et le voile tomba." The creation no less than the perception of works of art involves a combination of original genius and training, and the greatest writers and artists, for Sainte-Palaye, were those who united an original inspiration—the "sublime"—with technical mastery of their craft, understanding of its rules, and sound composition. The model Sainte-Palaye offered to young artists was Le Sueur, in whom, he held, great expressiveness was combined with the utmost sobriety and firmly structured composition. In the paintings in the Cloister of the Chartreux in particular, Le Sueur had created a truly sublime art with none of the theatrical showiness that Sainte-Palaye associated with the grand manner in his own time. "Je remarquois que deux ou trois personnages dans une cellule, ou dans un paysage aussi simple que la cellule même faisoient tout le sujet. Point de ces attitudes forcées que la Nature désavoue, et que le Peintre met sans nécessité, et seulement pour montrer qu'il se joue du dessein; point de ces expressions outrées et toujours manquées, de ces draperies dont toute la richesse est dans la bizarre surabondance des plis et dans des ornemens superflus; point de ces Palais de Fées qui percent un Ciel brûlant et tout en feu; point de ces contrastes dans l'ordre des groupes, ainsi que dans la distribution des ombres et des lumières, qui ajoutent au fracas, qu'on appelle la Machine."[46] Instead, "un petit nombre de couleurs donne la vie à ces tableaux et n'impose point par un faux brillant: tout y respire la plus grande simplicité." Here, he concluded, were masterpieces which brought before his eyes "l'idée que je me fais de la Peinture des Grecs."

[45] 'Lettre de M. de S.P. à M. de B. sur le bon goût dans les arts et dans les lettres,' p. 3.
[46] *Ibid.*, p. 8.

Similarly Bachaumont, admiring the richness, the color, the facility, the intelligence of Boucher, found his "têtes de femme ... plus jolies que belles, plus coquettes que nobles; ses draperies ... presque toujours trop chargées de plis, de plis trop cassés ... ne flattant pas assez le nu."[47] With Sainte-Palaye, Bachaumont, and their friends—as with Montesquieu, Voltaire, and other writers of the time—the word "joli" characterizes the facile manner of artists who were bent on pleasing nouveaux riches clients and who, accepting their purely social function, treated the traditional themes of Renaissance art ironically and playfully, while "grand" or "noble" is reserved for works in which the great tradition is continued faithfully so that the artist seeks not to please and delight with his wit and with sensuous images but to translate into sensuous form eternal truths. So Le Moyne is "en sculpture ce que Boucher est en peinture: un peu maniéré ... ce qu'on peut appeler un très-joli sculpteur. Il compose finement, élégamment, et spirituellement." Bouchardon, on the other hand, "est ce qu'on peut appeler un très-grand sculpteur, peut-être égal aux meilleurs Grecs et fort supérieur aux Romains." The reason for Bouchardon's greatness? "Il imite le bel antique, et surtout la nature."

Not surprisingly, Sainte-Palaye and his friends followed with keen interest the spate of more or less scholarly works on the architecture and antiquities of Italy, Greece and the Greek colonies, and Egypt which came off the presses around mid-century, and they contributed in their own way to the spread of the new knowledge.[48] Caumont, Le Beuf, and La Bastie did research on the Roman antiquities of Southern France. Sainte-Palaye himself, despite protestations of his ignorance of Greek and Roman antiquities,[49] made careful notes on Roman architecture during his stay in Rome in 1739,[50] and he was quick to grasp the interest of the excavations at Herculaneum, which were not then widely known

---

[47] 'Jugements de Bachaumont,' *Revue universelle des arts* (1857), 5:419–20. These remarks are almost identical to those in the *Corr. litt.* of Raynal and Grimm, 1:462 (*Salon* of 1750).

[48] On the revival of interest in antiquity, see Hautecoeur, 4:1–44; the same author's *Rome et la renaissance de l'antiquité à la fin du XVIIIᵉ siècle* (Paris, 1912); and the older but still useful book by L. Bertrand, *La Fin du classicisme et le retour à l'antique* (Paris, 1877).

[49] Bréquigny 68, fol. 77, Sainte-Palaye to La Bastie, 4.12.1739.

[50] Moreau 1722, fol. 528, 'Remarques sur les fabriques romaines du tems des Empereurs que j'ai veues à Rome et dans les autres villes d'Italie.'

in France.[51] It was at the very time when Sainte-Palaye and de Brosses were in Naples—July and August, 1739—that the frescoes depicting the lives of the gods and scenes from Greek legend were discovered and taken to Portici.[52] Sainte-Palaye immediately informed Bachaumont and asked for instructions from the Académie des Inscriptions,[53] while de Brosses sent Bouhier a *Mémoire sur la ville souterraine d'Herculée*,[54] in which he gave a description of the fresco of Theseus with the slain minotaur at his feet and the women and children around him kissing his hands and knees in gratitude. This fresco was already famous, for a glowing report of it had been spread abroad by Marcello Venuti, who was in charge of Charles III's library and art treasures. "In the excavations near Naples," the Tuscan humanist wrote to a friend in Rome, "the loveliest thing in the world has been discovered: a painted wall with figures in life-size, splendidly and realistically depicted, much more beautiful than the works of Raphael."[55] De Brosses' enthusiasm was considerably more measured. "Les figures," he wrote, "sont d'une grande correction de dessin; l'attitude et l'expression sont belles, quoique la figure principale soit un peu raide et tienne de la statue, mais le coloris n'est pas bon, soit par la faute du peintre, soit qu'il ait été altéré par le temps et le séjour dans la terre."[56] This was also Sainte-Palaye's opinion, for he described

---

[51] It was only thanks to the personal intervention of Marcello Venuti that the travelers had been able to visit the excavations at all (De Brosses, *Lettres*, 1:427). Until the end of the century, scholars and amateurs testify continually to the difficulty of gaining access to the excavations. Caylus and Paciaudi complain frequently and on one occasion had recourse to theft (*Correspondance inédite du Comte de Caylus*, notably 1:59, 114, 116, 128), while Saint-Non had to have one of his illustrations drawn from imagination, because he and his artists were barred from visiting the site. (*Voyage pittoresque de Naples et de Sicile* [Paris, 1781–86], 1:182.)

[52] Marcel Brion, *Pompeii and Herculaneum*, trans. J. Rosenberg (New York, 1960), p. 45; also Egon Caesar Conte Corti, *The Destruction and Resurrection of Pompeii and Herculaneum* (London, 1951), pp. 111–14.

[53] Arsenal 4900, fol. 319, to Bachaumont and Madame Doublet, 18.11.1739; Bréquigny 68, fol. 77, to La Bastie, 4.12.1739.

[54] Dated Rome, 28.11.1739. Together with a 'Mémoire sur les antiquités d'Herculée,' which was submitted to the Académie des Inscriptions in 1749 and which complemented the earlier account sent to Bouhier with a full description of the discoveries—buildings, statues, frescoes, inscriptions, furnishings—condensed from Venuti's *Descrizione delle prime scoperte dell'antica città d'Ercolano* (Rome, 1749). The letter to Bouhier was published as *Lettres sur l'état actuel de la ville souterraine d'Herculée et sur les causes de son ensevelissement sous les ruines de Vésuve* (Dijon, 1750).

[55] Quoted by Corti, p. 114.

[56] De Brosses, *Lettres familières*, ed. Bézard, 1:471.

the newly discovered fresco to Bachaumont and Madame Doublet in identical terms.[57]

The moderate enthusiasm of Sainte-Palaye and de Brosses is characteristic of Bachaumont's circle of friends, none of whom was narrowly "antiquomane," not even Caylus. They did not believe that "correctness" was enough to make a great work of art. An original "genius" or "inspiration" was at least as necessary as technical skill and good training. Rather than strict antiquarians, Sainte-Palaye and his friends had become the representatives in the age of Enlightenment of a somewhat modified version of the academicism of the previous century.[58] Their ideal, reminiscent of that of de Piles, was an art in which color, movement, and expression all had a place. Bachaumont found Vien too cold;[59] similarly, though he admired Noel Hallé for having resisted "la frivolité du siècle," he judged him a mediocre painter, "un pinceau sec qui ne peut rien exprimer de gracieux et de sublime."[60] The artists he liked were Doyen, La Grenée, Casenove, Loutherbourg, Vernet, Hubert Robert, and he shared this taste with most of his friends—Sainte-Palaye had four Vernets in his collection.[61] "Il faut de la vie et du mouvement par-tout," he declared, "et quand un artiste peut joindre l'action théâtrale et l'expression des passions, son ouvrage n'en est que plus parfait."[62]

Bachaumont seems close to Diderot not only in his judgments of particular works and artists, but in his general approach. He judges by the same conventional categories as Diderot—choice of subject, composition, historical accuracy or "costume," expression, color, draughtsmanship, draperies, etc.,[63] and he comes to painting and sculpture, asking the same questions as Diderot: What moment is

[57] Arsenal 4900, fol. 319.

[58] Jean Loquin pointed out many years ago that Caylus was really an eclectic and a traditionalist rather than a strict devotee of classical antiquity (Loquin, pp. 92–94). Similarly Fiske Kimball saw the anti-rococo movement of the mid-century as "a return to academicism." (The Creation of the Rococo [Philadelphia, 1943], p. 204.) Characteristically, de Brosses considered de Piles the very model of a connoisseur (Lettres, ed. Bézard, 1:341).

[59] Salons of 1767, 1769, Mémoires secrets (London: Adamson, 1780), pp. 8–9, 36–37.

[60] Ibid., pp. 10, 29, 35.

[61] According to his will, Sainte-Palaye's small collection of paintings included, besides a Bourguignon and a Jean Jouvenet, four Vernets ordered from the painter in Italy. These four paintings, which have not been traced, are numbered 260, 261, 264, and 265 in the catalogue raisonné of Vernet executed by Florence Ingersoll-Smonse (Paris, 1926).

[62] Salon of 1769, Mémoires secrets, p. 56.   [63] Cf. Dresdner, pp. 206–7.

being represented? What is the emotional relation of the figures to each other? Do the formal relations correspond to and express these emotional relations? Are the setting, the clothing, and the accessories appropriate or only decorative? He also supports, as Diderot did, the hierarchy of the genres.

Bachaumont, however, was considerably more conservative and academic than Diderot. Indeed the interest of his criticism, according to Dresdner, lies in its ordinariness.[64] He admired Bouchardon but, faithful to the *beau idéal*, he objected to what he called Bouchardon's propensity to excessive realism: "Il imite le bel antique, et surtout la nature, mais quelquefois il l'imite peut-être trop exactement, et ne l'embellit pas assez."[65] He had some admiration for Chardin, but was less enthusiastic than Diderot, and his faith in the hierarchy of the genres was never shaken. The two canvases in which Chardin represented *Les Instruments de musique* were, he said, "magnifiques dans leur genre. Mais quel genre!"[66] "Je ne fais pas grand cas du génie concentré dans la nature inanimée," he added later.[67] His attitude to the portrait was also less complex than Diderot's. Diderot was torn in the matter of the portrait, as in the matter of the still life, between different aspects of his own democratic humanism: his longing for a great public painting in tune with a great society, his respect for the humblest elements of reality, his admiration for the genius and vision of the individual artist, and his refusal to bow to traditional hierarchies of value. Bachaumont criticized the portrait in the name of a public art; but he associated public art unquestioningly with the existing society. What was public was what was prestigious in the France of the ancien régime: great scenes from war and religion and figures of noble or notable personalities. He wrote with contempt of the portraits of a "foule obscure de bourgeois" whose names are no more flattering to the ear than their faces are pleasing to the eye[68] while, on the other hand, he objected that Hallé had made the royal children too small in the portrait he painted of them: "On est fâché de voir réduire en petit des princes illustres qu'on ne sauroit montrer à trop de spectateurs à la fois, et dont le peuple avide se dispute sans cesse le coup d'oeil."[69]

[64] *Ibid.*, p. 191.
[65] 'Jugements de Bachaumont,' *Revue universelle des arts* (1857), 5:421.
[66] *Salon* of 1767, *Mémoires secrets*, p. 21.
[67] *Salon* of 1769, *Mémoires secrets*, p. 49.   [68] *Ibid.*, pp. 43–44.
[69] *Ibid.*, p. 47.

The limitations which mark the art criticism of Bachaumont and Sainte-Palaye are also found in the views they and their circle put forward in questions of architecture and urbanism. The ideas of the eighteenth-century planners, amateur and professional alike, bear the characteristic mark of the Enlightenment in their far greater concern with the public weal than with the prestige of a tiny minority of privileged persons or of courts. A dictionary of select words does not make a speech, Rousseau was to remark in his *Dictionnaire de musique*.[70] "Ce n'est point la quantité de beaux bâtimens qui fait une belle ville," Sainte-Palaye declared in 1748, "mais une certaine harmonie et un heureux assortiment des uns avec les autres, comme ce n'est point la quantité de belles figures qui fait un beau tableau, mais une heureuse intelligence à les disposer et à les grouper, tant par elles-mêmes que par leurs lumières et par leurs ombres."[71] A similar idea occurs in Laugier's *Essai*. Laugier's insistence on the relatedness and the equal importance of all the parts of a building, which seems to be a conventional classical viewpoint, was in fact revolutionary in 1753, his biographer declares.[72] In the doctrines of seventeenth-century classicism, as represented by F. Blondel for instance, the "decoration of façades and the study of ornaments" is "the most noble and eminent part of architecture." Blondel never did get around to dealing with "matters relating to solidity and commodity." For Laugier, on the other hand, the "parts of an architectural Order are the parts of the building itself. They must therefore be applied so that they not only adorn but actually constitute the building. The existence of the building must depend so completely on the union of these parts that not a single one could be taken away without the whole building collapsing."

One might be tempted to look for a relation between the notion of a totality of interdependent parts which Sainte-Palaye applied to urbanism and his friend Laugier to architecture, and the social and political ideas of some Enlightenment reformers, of Rousseau, for example, with his vision of the unity of society as a "correspondance interne de toutes les parties" rather than a mere relation "par juxtaposition."[73] The political equivalent of the aesthetic

---

[70] *Oeuvres*, ed. Auguis, 27 vols. (Paris, 1824–25), 13:403.
[71] 'Lettre à M. de la Bruere sur le projet d'une place pour la Statue du Roy,' p. 151.
[72] Herrmann, pp. 20–21.   [73] Article 'Économie politique,' *Oeuvres*, 12:10.

ideas of Sainte-Palaye and Laugier is not, however, the democratic state of Rousseau; it is rather the corporate state in which each order, supposedly, contributes its part to the whole, and in which the relations of the orders are rigorously controlled and balanced, so that the structure is secured and immobilized for all time.

Characteristically Laugier projected this arrangement into nature. The architect, he declared, should take as his model the primitive hut, the simplest, most natural, and most rational form of human shelter against the elements, with its four columns supporting a roof (as Laugier saw it), as well as the masterworks of the architects of the past, who had invariably been guided by this "natural" form. Laugier's rejection of the wall as an essential element of construction was doubtless a rejection of the baroque in which the wall had been used as a plastic, malleable element in the composition of a building;[74] in many ways, however, it pointed backward rather than forward. The young Goethe immediately sensed the conservative nature of Laugier's "reforms." In conscious opposition to the Frenchman, he emphasized the role of the wall as the functional support of the house and derided columns as "belastender Überfluss."[75] The meaning of Goethe's elevation of the wall to the point at which it becomes the primary element of architecture seems clear. The architecture in which the wall is dominant is not, indeed, the architecture of aristocratic humanism, as Goethe saw it; it can only be an architecture resulting from the collaboration of an entire people with the individual creative genius which it brings forth out of itself. Goethe, of course, believed he had found such an architecture in Gothic. His revolutionary ideas, couched in a new, biting, and rousing prose, reveal by contrast the timidity and conservatism of his French predecessor. "Säule," he writes, "ist mitnichten ein Bestandteil unsrer Wohnungen; sie widerspricht vielmehr dem Wesen all unsrer Gebäude. Unsre Häuser entstehen nicht aus vier Säulen in vier Ecken; sie entstehen aus vier Mauern auf vier Seiten, die statt aller Säulen sind, alle Säulen ausschliessen, und wo ihr sie anflickt, sind sie belastender Überfluss. Ebendas gilt von unsern Palästen und Kirchen. Wenige Fälle ausgenommen, auf die ich nicht zu achten brauche. Eure Gebäude stellen euch also Flächen dar, die, je weiter sie sich ausbreiten, je kühner si gen Himmel steigen, mit desto

[74] Cf. Herrmann, pp. 50–52.   [75] 'Von deutscher Baukunst.'

unerträglicherer Einförmigkeit die Seele unterdrücken müssen!
Wohl! wenn uns der Genius nicht zu Hilfe käme, der Erwinen von
Steinbach eingab: vermannigfaltige die ungeheure Mauer, die du
gen Himmel führen sollst, dass sie aufsteige gleich einem hocher-
habenen, weitverbreiteten Baume Gottes, der mit tausend Ästen,
Millionen Zweigen und Blättern wie der Sand am Meer, ringsum,
der Gegend verkündet die Herrlichkeit des Herrn, seines Meisters."

There are not many passages in the literature of the eighteenth
century that are as revolutionary as this magnificent eulogy of the
wall, the mass, against the "useless" ornament of the traditional
orders. Its tone is far removed from that of the essays of Laugier
or Sainte-Palaye.

In general, the circle to which Sainte-Palaye belonged and whose
ideas he expressed was not effective as a source of new ideas for the
future. There is no sign that Sainte-Palaye and his friends hit on
those fruitful contradictions which confronted Diderot and which
pointed toward a new conception of the nature of the work of art
and of the artist's relation to society,[76] no evidence that they went
much beyond the neoclassical esthetic doctrine which the critics
and writers of the magistracy had championed in the previous century. Was the function of art to disclose the eternally true, the
noble ideal, the universally human, and, if so, how was it to do so
without becoming abstract and conventional? Or was it to reflect
the ephemerally but vividly real and existing, the passing particular, and if this was its task, how should it perform it without becoming a fashionable chronicle? Or did art, perhaps, have a social
role to play, revealing to men aspects of reality which they would
not otherwise discern, and inspiring them with a desire to follow
the artist's lead as transformer of reality? What was the relation in
the artist between the craftsman or technician and the man of
genius with his vast general insight? The critics in the circle of
Bachaumont and Sainte-Palaye did not consider these questions on
the same level as Diderot or Rousseau. They opted for a compromise by which the "froid logicien" and the "grand orateur" in
Diderot's pithy phrase[77] would be reconciled. For Diderot and for
Rousseau, on the other hand, despite hesitations, the real problem
was no longer to reconcile these categories but to transcend them.

The failure of Sainte-Palaye and his group to find a new solution

[76] Cf. Dresdner, ch. 6.   [77] 'Essais sur la peinture,' *Oeuvres*, 10:468.

to the problem of the artist's relation to society and of the nature of artistic creation is brought out concretely in their failure to resolve the problem of patronage with any better success than their seventeenth-century predecessors. Taking up a traditional comparison of Le Brun's *Famille de Darius* at Versailles—the highest point of French classical academicism—with its neighbor, Veronese's *Pilgrims of Emmaus*, Bachaumont suggested that Le Brun as a member of the Academy enjoyed greater freedom under his royal master than Veronese who had to yield to the whims of wealthy clients. Yet it did not escape Bachaumont that this "freedom" too had its price. Later in the *Essai*, he discussed the work of Puget and regretted that this talented sculptor had done so little at Versailles. The reason, he declared, was that the sculptors at Versailles had to work from designs given them by Le Brun. Several gifted and respected sculptors accepted this condition, "mais Le Puget ne voulut jamais captiver ainsi ses talens, et il retourna dans son Païs. . . "[78] Puget's gesture highlights a problem that confronted those artists and writers of the seventeenth century who held to the somewhat watered down Renaissance view of the artist characteristic of an important stream in French classicism. Boileau had openly castigated the "gratifiés," those poets who sold their independence and prostituted their talent for a pension, but he himself sought the favor of the King. The fact that he did so by claiming that his very independence, his very refusal to sing to order would enhance his praise of the monarch when it came, reveals only too clearly the ambiguous relation of the "independent" artist to the court—a relation, incidentally, which closely paralleled that of the magistrate to the Royal authority—and it is not surprising that Boileau so frequently expressed shame and guilt at having become a paid poet or that he dreamed of withdrawing from the court and from the world. Puget's withdrawal is thus one pole of a dilemma which the seventeenth-century artist who still believed in the quasi-divine nature of art could not resolve. The eighteenth-century artist no longer viewed his special genius as a vision of transcendent truth; he gloried in his absolute originality. But the problem of patronage was not thereby altered. Bachaumont came no nearer than his predecessors to a solution of it, despite his admiration of Puget's gesture.

[78] *Essai*, p. 40.

Some time later, Bachaumont's successor Mairobert complained that all the efforts of officialdom to encourage *tableaux d'histoire* had produced only mediocre works, and he blamed this failure on the very nature of royal patronage: the direct imposing of his theme on the artist, the setting of time limits and other material conditions, the artist's inevitable desire to flatter the court and win further commissions, the intrigue and corruption that accompany official contracts. Mairobert goes no further toward a solution, however, than Boileau, Puget, or Bachaumont. In place of direct royal patronage he envisages only, as the *Anciens* had done a century before, pensions for those who would devote themselves to the study and imitation of the great models of the past.[79]

Many of the critics were thus driven back by the limitations of their social and political views on the very academicism which they might at first have seemed to be opposing. Academicism—which meant to them the indirect protection by the King of artists pledged to carry forward established traditions—might be expected to achieve in the realm of art a goal similar to that which the intellectual leaders of the robe were pursuing in politics. As the magistrate under the protection of the Crown was the keeper of the ancient laws of the land and the ancient rights, liberties, and privileges of the King's subjects, safeguarding them even from the King himself, so the artist under the protection of the King was the keeper of the eternal laws of art, safeguarding them from all particular and passing pressures, even if they were to come from the court itself.

By the last third of the century, those who sought a middle way between the ideas of the radical *philosophes* and the arch-conservatism of the *dévots* were finding the going more and more rough. "Il semble," Dom Poirier complained to Foncemagne in 1773, "qu'il n'y ait plus de milieu pour la Morale entre les livres impies et les livres de dévotion . . . et nos livres de dévotion au dix-huitième siècle sont d'une platitude insoutenable."[80] The scholars and critics in the circles Sainte-Palaye frequented were not narrow-minded men. Most of them were irreligious, many of them desired some reform of the government. Nevertheless their outlook was more limited and conservative, as we have now discovered in a number of instances, than that of the *philosophes* proper. It is not

[79] *Salon* of 1779, *Mémoires secrets*, pp. 195–97.
[80] B.N. Français 9457, fol. 216, 20.4.1773.

surprising that they found a solution to so many problems in academicism, for the Royal Academies, like the parlements in a way, were at once free and bound, at once critical and traditional, irreligious and respectful, egalitarian and privileged, independent and dependent. Sainte-Palaye, no democrat, could permit himself to express contempt for those who made distinctions *within* the Academy. "Je crains que nous n'ayons des gens qui facent plus de cas des rangs que des vrais titres," he wrote on one occasion to a candidate for a place at the Academy.[81] This kind of equality was not dangerous. It existed within the structure of privileges and ranks, depended on it, and at the same time sustained it. Here, therefore, was one place where the liberal scholars, critics, and intellectuals who were attached to the parlements or to the nobility could continue to reconcile intellectual liberty with conservatism and their desire for reform with traditionalism. In some ways, indeed, the Academies were a version of those isles of reason and equality which the eighteenth century read of in its literature or saw on the stage and tried to capture in its salons, its private theaters, its country retreats. In them the Enlightened man found a provisional escape from his historical condition, and a reconciliation, however precarious, of theory and practice, observation and action.

Sainte-Palaye was a power at the Académie des Inscriptions.[82] Four times its Director,[83] he guided it toward the study of medieval antiquities, and he worked hard to secure the election of young scholars interested in the Middle Ages. His best known and most influential work—the *Mémoires sur l'ancienne chevalerie*—was first presented as a series of papers to the Academy. By the 1770's, however, the generation of old-style *philosophes* to which Sainte-Palaye belonged with his heart and mind was disappearing even from the Academy. The voices of Falconet, Lévesque, Le Beuf, Bonamy, and Lancelot had long been silent.[84] Of the scholars of

---

[81] Archives de l'Académie Française, collection L. H. Moulin, carton 216, to Grosley, 31.5.1761. On the "equality" practiced at the Royal Academies, see the amusing pages of Anatole France in *Les Opinions de M. Jérôme Coignard* (Paris, 1920), pp. 182–95.

[82] "C'est un ami essentiel," Lefebvre de Saint-André wrote to Grosley, who was seeking election to the Academy (B.N. Nouv. Acq. Fr. 803, fol. 169, 5.4.1759).

[83] In 1751, 1754, 1759, and 1767, according to the manuscript registers of the Academy for these years.

[84] Lancelot died in 1740, Secousse in 1754, Le Beuf in 1760, Lévesque and Falconet in 1762, Bonamy in 1770.

Sainte-Palaye's own generation, only Foncemagne remained. The nearest in seniority to the two stalwarts was Barthélemy, who had been elected twenty-four years after Sainte-Palaye, and even he commented sadly on the disappearance of his old colleagues and friends. "Notre Académie s'est presque renouvelée," he wrote in 1775: ". . . nos anciens confrères et amis disparaissent; . . . nous avons encore M. de Foncemagne, M. de Sainte-Palaye, Le Beau, Burigny, Danville; mais leur âge me fait trembler. Il faut mourir ou voir mourir ses amis, ce qui est pis encore."[85]

Sainte-Palaye himself went into a decline after the death of his brother in 1773.[86] Until January, 1777, however, he maintained regular attendance at the meetings in the Louvre, though he had long ceased to contribute anything. In May of that year his intimate friend and collaborator Foncemagne died. Sainte-Palaye was by now practically blind and deaf, and he depended entirely on the good offices of his remaining friends—Bréquigny, Malesherbes, Beauvau, and Madame du Boccage.[87] He died on March 1, 1781.

Dramatically enough, his successor was Chamfort, the man who, a few years later, was to strike a deadly blow at the old Academies and all they stood for. Chamfort's criticisms are not, as is often charged, inappropriate. They are well argued and entirely consistent with his democratic sympathies. With his *Rapport sur les Académies* of 1791, the conflict between the patrician intellectuals and the *philosophes* reached its climax. The Académie des Inscriptions, the special stronghold of the robe, was the object of Chamfort's particular hatred. It was, he declared, "une fille digne de sa mère par le même esprit d'abjection." As long as it dealt with classical and Jewish antiquities, it at least did no harm. "Eh! que ne s'y bornoit-elle. Nous étions si reconnoissans d'avoir appris par elle ce qu'étoient dans la Grèce les dieux cabires, quels étoient les noms de tous les ustensiles composant la batterie de cuisine de Marc Antoine! . . . Certes il valoit mieux faire son éternelle occupation (de ces bagatelles) que d'étudier nos antiquités françoises pour les dénaturer, que d'empoisonner les sources de notre histoire, que de

---

[85] *Lettres du Comte de Caylus*, 2:294, Barthélemy to Paciaudi, 9.6.1775.

[86] According to Barthélemy in 1777, "M. de Sainte-Palaye depuis quelques années ne fait que végéter." (To Paciaudi, 25.7.1777, *ibid.*, 2:308–9.) In 1778 the historian Houard wrote Bréquigny for news of Sainte-Palaye: "M. de . . . me dit que le respectable vieillard dépérissoit de jour en jour. Sort-il encore de chez lui? La tête est-elle toujours saine?" (Bréquigny 160, fol. 132.)

[87] Chamfort, *Éloge*, pp. 382–83.

mettre aux ordres du despotisme une érudition faussaire, que de combattre et condamner d'avance l'assemblée nationale, en déclarant *fausse et dangereuse* l'opinion qui conteste au roi le pouvoir législatif pour le donner à la nation: c'est l'avis de MM. Secousse, Foncemagne, et de plusieurs autres membres de cette compagnie."[88] Chamfort did not appreciate fairly the scholarship of the members of the Académie des Inscriptions. This is hardly to be wondered at in view of the political circumstances in which his report was prepared. It cannot be said, however, that, despite some simplifications, he seriously mistook its political significance. It is entirely fitting that the old Académie des Inscriptions came to an end with the old magistracy.

We have devoted hitherto many pages to the social and intellectual milieu in which Sainte-Palaye lived and worked, and we have emphasized how much he and his fellow scholars were shaped by their social position. We must now emphasize their enormous achievement, not least in bringing to light, making available, and providing the means with which future generations might interpret the sources of medieval history. Their own motives may have been narrow enough, and somewhat contradictory, but as so often happens, their objective achievement transcends their motives.

[88] 'Des Académies,' *Oeuvres complètes* (Paris, 1812), 1:159–60.

PART II

NEW APPROACHES TO MEDIEVAL STUDIES

The scholars of the seventeenth century did a great deal to refine the techniques of historical investigation. As catalogues began to appear describing the great European collections of manuscripts and rare books, Mabillon and Du Cange provided the means by which historians could evaluate the authenticity of the documents on which increasingly they based their accounts;[1] Ezechiel Spanheim, Jacob Spon, and Charles Patin showed how numismatics was relevant to the work of the historian;[2] Jean Chapelain, pursuing an idea already mooted by Fauchet, suggested that works of fiction might be used by the historian interested in certain types of information.[3] While many scholars were preoccupied with the question of authenticity, Spinoza and Bayle insisted on the matter of truth. The fact that an historical account is well authenticated, they argued, does not guarantee that what it says is true. Increasingly in the eighteenth century, scholars learned to be concerned not only with establishing the material soundness of their sources but with critically evaluating their content in accordance with the criteria suggested by Bayle and codified by a number of professional historians, such as the Dutchman Perizonius and the German Bierling, a friend of Leibniz.[4]

[1] The progress of diplomatics is described succinctly in Ludwig Traube, *Vorlesungen und Abhandlungen zur Palaeographie und Handschriftenkunde* (Munich, 1909); cf. also Harry Bresslau, *Handbuch der Urkundenlehre* (2d ed.; Leipzig, 1912), notably 1:25–28 on Mabillon, and David Douglas, *English Scholars* (London, 1939). At the end of the century Le Clerc judged palaeography the most significant single contribution to historical studies. Without it, "historias fictitias pro veris suscipimus, et sic fabulis honorem soli veritati debitum tribuimus." (*Ars critica* [Amsterdam, 1697], 1:18.)

[2] Cf. A. Momigliano, 'Ancient History and the Antiquarian,' *Journal of the Warburg and Courtauld Institutes* (1950), 13:285–315. "Sans les Médailles," wrote Patin, "l'Histoire dénuée de preuves, passeroit dans beaucoup d'esprits, ou pour l'effet de la passion des Historiens, qui auroyent escrit ce qui seroit arrivé de leur temps, ou pour une pure description de mémoires, qui pourroyent estre faux ou passionez." (*Histoire des médailles ou introduction à la connoissance de cette science* [Paris, 1695], p. 8.) Cf. likewise Jacob Spon, *Recherches curieuses d'antiquité* (Lyon, 1683), p. 353.

[3] Fauchet, *Oeuvres* (Paris, 1610), p. 591v. Jean Chapelain, *De la lecture des vieux romans*, written circa 1646, published 1728, in *Continuation des Mémoires de littérature et d'histoire de M. Salengre*, 6:281–342, and again in 1870, by A. Feillet. "Lancelot," wrote Chapelain, "n'est point Tite-Live, par ce que les actions qui y sont racontées sont éloignées de toute vérité. Si toutefois il ne lui est pas comparable par la vérité de l'histoire, n'étant composé que d'événements fabuleux, j'oserois dire qu'il lui pourroit être comparé par la vérité des moeurs et des coutumes dont l'un et l'autre fournissent des images parfaites: l'un des temps dont il a écrit, l'autre de ceux où il a écrit." (Feillet ed., p. 12.)

[4] J. Perizonius, *Oratio de fide historiarum contra Pyrrhonismum historicum* (Lugd. Bat., 1702); F. W. Bierling, *De judicio historico* (Rinthelii, 1703), *De*

The aims of historical scholarship also began to change. Where it had once been almost entirely subordinate to religious and legal debate or to literary and political education in the humanist spirit, history came to be valued less as a record of objective events—the deposit, as it were, of human willing and acting—than for what it told of the historical agent, man himself. To Enlighteners, history was above all a means of freeing men (not necessarily all men, but at least those who had sufficient intelligence) from superstition, from routine and, as far as possible, from the brute force of circumstance by revealing them to themselves as responsible agents, creators of themselves, of their institutions, of their societies, and of all existing or possible explanations of the universe. The very act of self-recognition, it was hoped, would free men to make themselves and their society consciously and deliberately rather than obscurely and in ignorance, to shape a destiny rather than to suffer one. It was not expected that man could arrive at absolute freedom. His own nature, the nature of social living, and the nature of the universe imposed limitations on his freedom, and for this very reason recognition of his own physical and psychical structure and of the laws of nature and society was a condition of freedom. It was important therefore to distinguish the real from the

---

Pyrrhonismo historico (Rinthelii, 1707). In the *De judicio*, which owes much to Leibniz and to Locke, Bierling distinguishes knowledge of rational relations (*scientia*, based on *ratio*), knowledge of God (*fides cordis*, based on *revelatio divina*), and empirical knowledge, including historical knowledge (*fides intellectus*, based on *revelatio humana*). The latter has not the certainty of *scientia*, but it need not be rejected on that account. The key to achieving the greatest possible degree of certainty in this area resides, in Bierling's view, in techniques of investigation. The *De judicio* set forth accordingly four principles that should guide historical research: (1) It should be established which historians are generally reliable and which are not [sec. x]; (2) All historical sources should be exploited once their authenticity has been ascertained, whether they be written or monumental [secs. x, xxv]; (3) Contemporary testimonies should be compared critically [sec. x]; and (4) *Sachkritik* or rational criteria should be applied [secs. xxix, xxx]. The *De Pyrrhonismo* outlined five principles of criticism: (1) No historian should be accepted as in all respects trustworthy; (2) The historian's biography and the probable bent of his prejudices should be established; (3) Improbable fables and legends are not more likely because they are common; (4) Contemporary accounts of causes and motives must be critically examined; and (5) Where different accounts are contradictory, it is prudent to accept only those points which cannot be disavowed by any of the conflicting parties. (*De Pyrrhonismo*, ch. 5.) Bierling was no timid conservative. Leibniz apparently felt he had gone too far. (Cf. Gerhardt's ed. of Leibniz's *Gesammelte Schriften* [Berlin, 1890], 7:486; also L. Davillé, *Leibniz historien* [Paris, 1909], p. 242.) Both Perizonius and Bierling were known in France, partly through Bayle. In 1724, at the height of the Pouilly-Sallier controversy at the Académie des Inscriptions, Bierling's two treatises were reissued.

mythical, so that man might understand where he stood and what he could do. The natural scientists had achieved a great deal, but the historical realm remained to be as thoroughly purged of myths, monsters, and magic as the natural one had been.

Sainte-Palaye came into early contact with all the main currents of contemporary historiography, and he was alive not only to the latest methods of documentary criticism but to the internal criticism of Bayle and to the new orientation of historical studies in general. Bayle, as we saw earlier, had been something of a hero in the Dijon of President Bouhier. He was also a great favorite of Denys-François Secousse, Sainte-Palaye's mentor in matters of criticism and scholarship. The correspondence of the two men shows the older impressing on the younger some of the main lessons of the new history. Diodorus Siculus—he tells Sainte-Palaye—is a better historian than Quintus Curtius. He is "très sensé et très judicieux . . . honnête homme et . . . Philosophe . . . Il est exact dans les faits qu'il rapporte, et il a eu soin de marquer les auteurs qu'il a suivis et qui sont ceux qui méritent le plus de créance. Il rapporte dans les choses importantes les différences qu'il trouve entre les historiens et il s'attache toujours à ce qu'il y a de plus vraysemblable."[5] An enthusiastic appraisal of Dionysius of Halicarnassus throws clear light on Secousse's ideal; "Je ne puis vous exprimer combien j'en suis content," he writes to Sainte-Palaye. "Tel est l'historien que je cherche depuis longtemps. Un homme qui a approfondi la matière qu'il veut traitter, exact, judicieux, qui rapporte les différentes opinions . . . il se détermine pour des raisons solides; à la vérité il est très sec et je n'ai pas aperçu la moindre apparence de pensée. Cette simplicité n'est pas du goust de tout le monde. L'abbé Lenglet a dit de lui: Historien exact mais ennuyeux. Je ne pense pas comme lui. L'histoire est la science des faits, l'exactitude et la discussion sont les devoirs de l'historien. L'ornement n'est qu'un accessoire qui souvent accable le principal, ce qui me paroist un grand deffaut."[6]

On his election to the Académie des Inscriptions in 1724, Sainte-Palaye was thrown into even closer contact with the modern movement in historical scholarship. Indeed, his election came at a time when a crucial battle for the new history was being waged at the Academy.

[5] Bréquigny 66, fol. 91, 20.8.1722.   [6] *Ibid.*, fols. 95–100, 16.11.1722.

In a provocative paper on the *Incertitude de l'histoire des quatre premiers siècles de Rome*, read in December 1722, Lévesque de Pouilly questioned the validity of the very canons of classical history. The legends which fill most histories of distant periods have brought discredit on history as a whole, he declared. "Il seroit donc utile de porter le flambeau d'une sévère critique dans toutes les annales des peuples, pour y démêler ce qu'elles renferment de douteux ou de faux."[7] Lévesque emphasized that his aim was not to attack history at the roots, but only to apply to certain areas hitherto considered sacrosanct the legitimate criteria which must govern any honest inquiry: "Est-ce combattre tous les faits historiques que d'attaquer quelques fables? N'est-ce pas au contraire servir la vérité, que de la dégager de ce qui pourroit nous la rendre suspecte?" Lévesque's concern for accuracy, however, led him to reject the testimony of canonical authorities like Livy, Cicero, Varro, and Dionysius of Halicarnassus.[8]

Conservative scholars at the Academy, alarmed at the implications of their colleague's criticism, rose to the defense of the classical historians. Their spokesman was the Abbé Sallier. Sallier's first reply is disappointing,[9] but in his second paper he exploited Lévesque's methods of criticism to attack Lévesque's own position.[10] By the end of 1724 the two men had come to some agreement on principles, for on December 22 of that year Sallier read a paper on Lévesque's behalf, in which the methods of historical criticism were outlined. "Reconnoissons," Lévesque urged, "que dans l'histoire le faux est mêlé avec le vrai, mais qu'il est des marques ausquelles on peut les distinguer . . ."[11] The methods laid down were those which had already been fully elaborated by Bayle, Le Clerc, and Bierling. In a third *Discours sur la certitude des quatre pre-*

[7] *MAI* 6:14.

[8] The substance of Lévesque's argument was that (1) the authors in question could not know personally and at first hand the events of which they wrote; (2) they contradict each other; (3) they attribute to the Romans the same sort of legendary history that is found among other peoples; and (4) they themselves admit the uncertainty of their accounts.

[9] Sallier expresses only indignation: "Je ne pense pas qu'on ose porter ce jugement d'un Écrivain qui . . ." etc. (*MAI* 6:30).

[10] He criticizes Lévesque's claim that the Romans borrowed their early history from the Greeks by attacking the reliability of Plutarch, on whom Lévesque rested much of his argument. (*MAI* 6:59.)

[11] *MAI* 6:71–72. The *Registres de l'Académie des Inscriptions* for 1724, p. 597, record that the paper was read by Sallier.

miers siècles de Rome (April 10, 1725) Sallier closed the discussion by accepting the validity of Lévesque's method and his right to apply it to all provinces of history, even if he still rejected Lévesque's conclusions.

The high point of the whole controversy was Fréret's *Réflexions sur l'étude des anciennes histoires et sur le degré de certitude de leurs preuves*, which was read to the Academy on April 17, 1724, just three months before Sainte-Palaye's election, and which set forth the principles that were to become the basis of all future historical investigation at the Académie des Inscriptions. The scholars recognized the importance of Fréret's *Réflexions*, and indeed of the whole controversy, by placing all the papers relating to it together under the heading "Fondements de l'Histoire" in a single volume of the Academy's *Mémoires*, even though the contributions were made over a period of three years.

Even before Sainte-Palaye's election, Secousse had written him a full account of the Pouilly-Sallier controversy. His own sympathies lay unequivocally with Pouilly. "Il a sur l'estude de l'histoire des idées justes," he noted, 'qu'il seroit fort à souhaitter que les sçavans qui travaillent dans ce genre voulussent imiter."[12] He himself began subjecting his favorite historian, Plutarch, to the kind of searching investigation he had commended in Pouilly, and in this he was joined by Sainte-Palaye who, immediately after his first paper—a surprisingly uncritical *Vie d'Agathocle, tyran de Syracuse*[13]—appears to have decided to place himself in the position of a disciple and to be guided by his friend and mentor.[14]

The results of this collaboration were a paper on Plutarch's Life of Romulus and a comparison of Livy and Dionysius of Halicarnassus. Alfred Maury, the historian of the Académie des Inscriptions, judged the paper on Plutarch harshly, mainly on the grounds that in his grave discussion of chronological errors and inconsistencies in the Life of Romulus, the young academician completely bypassed the essential question of the veracity of the entire Romu-

---

[12] Bréquigny 66, fols. 95–100.

[13] *Registres de l'Académie des Inscriptions* (1724), p. 545.

[14] At the start of his first paper on Plutarch, read to the Academy on February 8, 1726, Sainte-Palaye explicitly associated himself with Secousse: "Je satisfais avec plaisir aux engagements que m'a fait prendre un confrère, qui a des droits trop légitimes sur mes études . . . J'entrerai dans la même carrière avec lui . . ." (*Registres* [1726], p. 169.)

lus legend.[15] He concluded—quite mistakenly, as we know—that Sainte-Palaye had been little touched by the ideas of Lévesque or by Fréret's critical principles. Sainte-Palaye was not, indeed, as audacious as his older colleagues—we should remember that skepticism about the authenticity of the Romulus story might well be taken to imply skepticism about the authenticity of the Bible stories —but he did observe that "entre plusieurs traditions différentes sur un même fait, il [Plutarch] ne manque presque jamais de se déterminer pour la plus fabuleuse."[16] Nor was Sainte-Palaye afraid to extend his criticism to Livy. "Ce que nous disons icy de Plutarque," he stated, "convient également à Tite-Live, car il lui est entièrement conforme sur tous ces faits; et l'on connoît assez d'ailleurs quelle est sa crédulité et son goût pour tout ce qui s'appelle merveilleux."

The following year, on January 4, 1727, Sainte-Palaye, now settled in Paris, read the Academy another paper on classical historiography, *Observations sur quelques chapitres du deuxième livre de la première Décade de Tite-Live*. This second paper exposed his limitations more glaringly. His comparison of Livy and Dionysius of Halicarnassus, which shows clear marks of Secousse's influence, concluded—as we might expect—in favor of the latter. But the paper reveals a temptation which Sainte-Palaye did not always resist, even in later life. Instead of doing away with the very idea of authority, Sainte-Palaye, like Secousse and Bouhier, seems to have been tempted rather to distinguish between good and bad historians and to grant a kind of authority to those historians whose general reliability had been established.

Another serious limitation in Secousse's teaching was his vision of history, which appears to have stopped at the accumulation and critical evaluation of facts. "J'ai reconnu," Secousse wrote his young friend, "que s'il y a quelque genre de Sciences dans lequel je puisse réussir ce sera dans l'histoire, et que mon goust et mon inclination me portent à la compilation des faits."[17]

In the field of medieval studies, to which the two scholars turned a few years later, a good deal of work of this kind still required to be done. But Sainte-Palaye tried to go beyond the mere accumulation of facts. His association with the literary salons of the day had

---

[15] *L'ancienne Académie des Inscriptions et Belles-Lettres* (Paris, 1864), p. 122.
[16] *MAI* 6:123.   [17] Bréquigny 66, fol. 91, 20.8.1722.

opened his mind to a larger view of history. The Academy itself had tried hard to put its house in order and to adapt to a new style of scholarship. The eighteenth-century editors of the Academy's *Mémoires* are constantly criticizing irrelevant erudition, arguments based on unproven assumptions, and poor arrangement of material.[18] Their purpose was to improve scholarship and to make it more attractive by getting rid of mere erudition and by integrating it into a wider framework of reflection about man and society. Charles Le Beau, one of the Academy's secretaries, defined the object of its endeavors as "l'histoire de l'esprit humain et des divers systèmes qu'il a enfantés."[19]

As Sainte-Palaye turned to the Middle Ages, it was such an aim as this that he had in mind.

A great deal of work on the Middle Ages was done by the scholars and amateurs of the *Grand Siècle*.[20] Much of this work, however, was fragmentary and frequently it was drily legalistic. Many of those who studied the Middle Ages were not aware of a gulf between their own time and the time with which they were concerned in their work. They stood, as it were, in the immediate presence of the past, and they lacked the historical sense, the sense of difference, which characterizes the modern historian. The rise of absolutism did produce, however, a number of writers in whom the sense of the passing of an epoch was acute. Usually these writers were associated with the world that absolutism was leaving behind. The most lively and sympathetic studies of the Middle Ages in the seventeenth century were thus frequently connected with movements of opposition to the court and to absolutism. In contrast to the Jesuit Claude Menestrier, who in his *Traité des tournois* of 1669 had nothing but scorn for medieval carrousels,[21] decked his knights out in classical garb, and had them watched over by the

---

[18] Their comments are to be found in B. N. Nouv. Acq. Fr. 6196. The Academy was thus following the general tendency of the age to break down professional barriers, trade secrets, special languages, and all the trappings of untested and traditional authority. The new attitude had been formulated clearly by Fontenelle when he wrote: "J'ai voulu traiter la philosophie d'une manière qui ne fût point philosophique." (*Entretiens sur la pluralité des mondes*, ed. Shackleton [Oxford, 1955], p. 53.)

[19] *Registres*, for December 3, 1768.

[20] See Nathan Edelman, *Attitudes of Seventeenth Century France toward the Middle Ages* (New York, 1946).

[21] "Ces inventions étoient bonnes en un temps où les gens étoient moitié bestes" (p. 79).

divinities of Greece and Rome, André Favyn in his *Théâtre d'honneur* (1620) expressed with some eloquence the disquiet of important elements of the nobility in the time of Richelieu and Mazarin at the decline of an earlier feudal ethos and at the diminishing political influence of the nobility in general. Favyn stressed the Germanic origins of the Franks, their prowess in battle, their fine stature, beside which the Romans appeared as "nains et pygmées,"[22] and though he did not go into detail on the status of the conquered populations of Gaul, he announced provocatively that "de toute Antiquité les charges principales tant de Paix que de Guerre, de Justice et des Armes, estoient tenues en France par les Nobles seulement, sans que les Roturiers y fussent appellez."[23] Noble sympathies also inspired Favyn's successor, Vulson de la Colombière. The latter's eloquent plea on behalf of the Middle Ages in his *Théâtre d'honneur et de chevalerie* is at the same time an apology for the nobility.[24] Vulson also appealed to the nobility to maintain its old traditions and not to give in to the pleasures of courtly life. The medieval nobles, he admonished, "ne noyoient pas leur ardeur dans les excès de la débauche; ils ne laissoient point croupir leurs courages dans les ordures des voluptez . . . Quelle manie possède aujourd'huy les plus honnestes gens . . . que l'oysiveté semble estre leur plus noble occupation."[25] To the young nobility of France he held up the example of Bayard, the perfect knight and the flower of chivalry.[26]

Throughout the period of absolutism a section of the nobility maintained a serious interest in the Middle Ages. Some time before 1675 Le Laboureur, commissioned by a group of high noblemen,

[22] *Le Théâtre d'honneur et de chevalerie* (Paris, 1620), vol. 1, bk. 2, p. 133. On the long history of the idea of Germanic moral and physical superiority, see Samuel Klinger, 'The Gothic Revival and the German *translatio*,' *Modern Philology* (1947–48), 45:73–103.

[23] Favyn, 1:173.

[24] *Le vray Théâtre d'honneur et de chevalerie ou le miroir héroique de la noblesse* (Paris, 1648), Epître à Monseigneur le Cardinal de Mazarin. If the King will read his book—Vulson declares—"il y remarquera que les moindres divertissemens des anciens Nobles n'estoient jamais sans sueur, non plus que sans laurier et sans victoire; qu'ils ne combatoient jamais que pour le bon droit, et que la protection des veufves, des orphelins et des vertueux opprimez estoient leurs plus glorieux emplois, après le service de leurs Souverains; Il connoistra qu'ils estoient honnestes, modestes et respectueux en leurs amours, généreux et clémens envers leurs ennemis, fidèles et religieux en leurs promesses, protecteurs des foibles, et remplis de piété, de franchise, de libéralité, de civilité, de force et de hardiesse . . ."

[25] *Ibid.*, 'Préface, servant d'Avertissement à la Noblesse.'   [26] *Ibid.*, 1:16.

wrote his *Histoire de la pairie de France,* where he tried to explain how the nobility—which at the time of the conquest of Gaul by the Franks had been on a par with the King—was gradually ousted from its position, and how the original division of powers among equals was replaced by a complex feudal hierarchy.[27] Le Laboureur's plans for reform may have been somewhat chimerical; nonetheless he pointed a way to future constitutional scholars. The private *Académie du Luxembourg,* which was meeting about 1692, did not aim at a return to the status quo of 1,000 years earlier, but it hoped to find guidance for the reorganization of the state by studying the history of government and institutions in France. A program was drawn up to conduct research into the origins of the monarchy, of the parlements, of the offices of the Crown, into the course of the administration of justice, and into the rise of the communes and of the *noblesse de robe.*[28] Fénelon's *Projet d'étude de l'histoire de France* and his *Examen de conscience sur les devoirs de la Royauté* are aspects of the same tendency on the part of the nobility to examine the evolution of the existing form of government.

In robe circles, too, there was considerable interest in the Middle Ages. The robe was understandably less sympathetic toward the chivalric ethos and toward feudalism than the nobility; nevertheless, it was not pleased with absolutism as it had been realized under Louis XIV, and it looked back with regret to an earlier age of hope and promise, usually the sixteenth century. Its decline under absolutism had been, if anything, more marked than that of the nobility; there was, therefore—as indeed we have already seen in an earlier chapter—not only considerable sympathy in robe circles for the literature and art of the sixteenth century, but considerable curiosity about the social and political history of France from the Middle Ages onward. While Le Laboureur and Fénelon investigated the history of the nobility and restated its political claims in the early eighteenth century,[29] the men of the robe also looked into the past to explain the present and to plan for the future. The

---

[27] E. Carcassonne, *Montesquieu et le problème de la constitution française* (Paris, 1926), p. 11.

[28] *Ibid.,* pp. 7–8.

[29] Le Laboureur's *Pairie* was published in 1740; in 1721 Ramsay published a popularization of Fénelon's political ideas in his *Essai philosophique sur le gouvernement civil.*

great constitutional debates of the sixteenth century had produced several writers (Seyssel, Pasquier, Loyseau, La Roche Flavin) who had championed the cause of the robe against the apologists of the King (Bodin) and of the nobility (Hotman), and it is significant that their arguments and historical analyses were revived in 1732, when the struggle between Fleury and the parlements was at its height, in a pamphlet entitled *Mémoire touchant l'origine et l'autorité du Parlement de France, appelé Judicium Francorum.*[30] It is hardly surprising, therefore, that the magistracy was deeply involved in the investigation of medieval history.

As in the nobility and in the magistracy, there were important currents in the Church which were out of sympathy with the world of the court and of absolutism. We have already had occasion to mention several eighteenth-century churchmen, friends of Sainte-Palaye, who looked back for inspiration to the early medieval Church. They were by no means isolated cases. Bossuet himself had marked Augustinian leanings. The respected and celebrated Abbé Fleury, who was called by the Regent in 1715 to be tutor to the young Louis XV, and who was, incidentally, linked to the robe by family connections and by early training, was likewise moved by strong Augustinian sympathies. In his widely read and frequently republished *Discours sur l'histoire ecclésiastique*, he argued that from a Christian point of view the Middle Ages cannot be summarily dismissed: "Les siècles que l'on compte ordinairement pour les plus obscurs et les plus barbares ne l'étoient pas autant qu'on le croit et n'ont été dépourvus ni de science ni de vertu." Developing a characteristic Augustinian theme, Fleury held that the Middle Ages had been thrown into disrepute by men who "ayant plus de littérature que de religion et de bon sens, ne s'arrêtoient qu'à l'écorce, et ne pouvoient rien goûter que les écrivains de l'ancienne Rome et de l'ancienne Grèce." The criterion of good taste and politeness was not the only one, he concluded: "Qu'importe après tout que l'on parle et que l'on écrive mal, pourvu que l'on croie bien et que l'on vive bien? Dieu ne regarde que le coeur: la grossièreté du langage et la rusticité des moeurs ne sont rien à son égard."[31]

---

[30] Cf. Ford, pp. 93–95.
[31] *Discours sur l'histoire ecclésiastique* (nouvelle édition; Nîmes, 1785), 3ème discours, pp. 139–41.

Favyn, Vulson, and Fleury were not concerned with legal precedents or objects of mere antiquarian curiosity. Rather, they looked in the Middle Ages for an attitude, a mentality, a set of values, a whole way of life, which they felt was increasingly alien to the way of life they observed around them. Nevertheless, they wrote from the perspective of the past, and they did not consider that this perspective should be transcended.[32] The eighteenth-century medievalists, on the other hand, were almost all touched by Enlightenment. They had class prejudices and class interests, but they believed their goal was to rise above them and, in studying particular historical societies, to consider the nature and the laws of human society in general. Their vantage point was not to be that of any particular time or society; it was to be that of enlightened humanity, emancipated from all unexamined beliefs and "prejudices."

Significantly, those who, at the Académie des Inscriptions and elsewhere, put forward the case for the study of the Middle Ages, used the language and the arguments of the early Enlighteners; indeed, many of the earliest medievalists were identifiably also *Modernes*, and they wrote of the past not from the point of view of some standard in the past—be it that of the nobility, that of the robe, or that of the Christian community—but from the point of view of an enlightened and sophisticated society, a strange amalgam of aristocracy and bourgeoisie, which felt its modernity and no longer identified itself completely with any age or social group in the past.

The first leader of the medievalists at the Académie des Inscriptions was Camille Falconet. Falconet was not the first to emphasize the amount of spade work that had to be done before any synthetic account of medieval history could be attempted. In a paper read to the Academy at the end of 1724, Foncemagne, announcing that he had decided to turn all his energies to the study of the history of the monarchy, had suggested that such an ambitious project

---

[32] Thus, for instance, it seems fairly clear that Fleury's position is in one important respect opposed to that of the Enlighteners, however much it may have been touched by Enlightenment in other respects. He speaks for the traditional Christian community against those who had set themselves outside it and above it; cf. Bernhard Groethuysen, *Die Entstehung der bürgerlichen Welt–und Lebensanschauung in Frankreich*.

might well be beyond the powers of a single individual.[33] But it was in Falconet's paper *Sur nos premiers traducteurs françois avec un Essay de bibliothèque françois* (read on January 28, 1727) that the call to arms was clearly sounded.[34]

First, Falconet put forward a plea, in terms that reveal his attachment to the movement of the *Modernes*, for the study of the history and antiquities of France as a subject worthy of the attention of the most eminent scholars. "Envisagés le champ que fournit votre seule Patrie," he told the assembled Academicians, "vous le trouverés encore assez vaste pour y exercer tous vos talens et y déployer toutes vos connoissances."[35] There was no reason why the study of classical antiquity should be preferred to that of the national past. "L'autorité des Anciens fraperoit-elle plus que la raison même? Pourquoy nous mépriser et ne pas faire de nous le même cas, que faisoient d'eux-mêmes les Grecs et les Romains. Des Savans de Nations qui se reconnoissent inférieures à la Nation françoise, ont pensé plus noblement de leur pays."

The failure of French scholars to study their own history as something worthy of respect in itself has led to a great deal of ignorance and confusion about the national past. "Les Auteurs qui se sont piqués de Belles-Lettres ont tiré quasi tous nos mots des Langues Savantes: Messieurs de Port-Royal sont tombés dans cette erreur, après Perion, Tripaut et beaucoup d'autres: le Père Thomassin qui a suivi Guichart, est allé bien plus loin en rapportant tout à l'hebreu . . . Mr Ménage, qui avoit un talent particulier pour l'Etimologie a un peu ramené les esprits de l'opinion où l'on estoit que nôtre langue devoit tout aux langues savantes: mais malgré cela je dirai hardiment que Mr Ménage, homme d'une littérature très étendue qui avoit lu beaucoup d'Italien et d'Es-

---

[33] 'Essay de recherches historiques sur le gouvernement des rois de France dans la première race,' read 7.12.1724, *Registres de l'Académie des Inscriptions* (1724), p. 565. Bayle had already pointed to the need for instruments of research, in particular for a bibliography of French literature, in the 'Nouvelles de la République des lettres,' October, 1685, art. iii; *Oeuvres*, 1:388.

[34] B.N. Français 9421, fol. 209, 'Procès-verbaux' of the meetings of the Académie des Inscriptions, gives the precise date. Falconet's program bears a striking resemblance to that devised by another great eighteenth-century medievalist, Humphrey Wanley; cf. Joan Evans, *History of the Society of Antiquaries* (Oxford, 1956), pp. 41–44.

[35] Falconet's paper was reported in abstract in the 'partie historique' of the *Mémoires* (*MAI** 7:292–300). Sainte-Palaye preserved a copy of the complete paper (Bréquigny 61, fols. 10–33), and it is from this that we quote.

pagnol, aussi bien que de Grec et de Latin, n'avoit pas encore assez lu de notre vieux françois." Without solid erudition nothing of substance can be achieved by scholars and historians, and that is why "une bonne partie de ceux qui ont travaillé à nos Antiquités n'ont pas eu le succès que d'ailleurs méritoit leur zèle, par le deffaut de cette érudition qui doit faire la base de toutes les estudes." But the Academy, the repository of French erudition, is capable of doing what isolated individuals living almost two centuries earlier failed to do. "Les vrays, les solides fondements des édifices à bâtir que je vous propose," Falconet declared, "se trouvent dans cette Académie ou ne sont nulle part."

The works of scholarship which Falconet proposed to the Academy were a Glossary of Old French "qu'il faut regarder comme la clé nécessaire pour s'ouvrir le chemin à la composition des deux autres ouvrages," a Geographical Dictionary, and a Bibliography of all the works of literature, learning, or science, written in French. These undertakings were so vast that Falconet believed they could be tackled only if the Academicians were willing to collaborate on them, and he suggested that they should be apportioned out among the members of the Academy.

In addition to these fundamental instruments of research which were intended to prepare the ground for future historians, there were a host of other aspects of medieval history which the scholars of the seventeenth century had barely touched on, and to which the members of the Academy could also contribute. Falconet suggested the following:

1. Histories of the weights and measures in use in the various provinces of medieval France.
2. Accounts of monuments, inscriptions, and buildings of all kinds —civil and ecclesiastical—and of the weapons and tools in use throughout the medieval period.
3. Histories of French literature, of the troubadours who stood at its origins (this was a widely held view), and of the theatre in France from the Middle Ages to the eighteenth century.
4. Histories of the coinage.
5. Histories of the introduction and spread of Christianity in Gaul.
6. Histories of the arts and sciences and of their progress up to the eighteenth century.
7. Histories of customs, usages, manners, and laws.

Both within the Academy and without, Falconet found willing followers. In numerous papers the monuments of the French Middle Ages were discussed and interpreted. Montfaucon, the great Benedictine scholar and an honorary member of the Academy, was encouraged to go ahead with his *Monuments de la monarchie françoise*, the project for which he had published in 1725. Sainte-Palaye worked on the troubadours, Barbazan and later Le Grand d'Aussy on the *fabliaux*. Beauchamps and the Frères Parfaict published between 1735 and 1749 extensive and detailed accounts of the history of the drama in France,[36] the Academy set prize dissertations on the establishment of religion in Gaul and on the state and progress of the arts and sciences in the reigns of the French kings from Charlemagne onward,[37] while to catalogue the works which appeared on laws, customs, and usages would be a major bibliographical undertaking. The *Antiquités françoises* on which Sainte-Palaye and Secousse collaborated can certainly be considered a contribution to this part of Falconet's program.

Of the major works, the *Bibliothèque françoise* appeared in 1772–73 in the form Falconet had suggested—that is, a new and up-to-date edition of La Croix du Maine and du Verdier. The editor of the new *Bibliothèque*, Rigoley de Juvigny, while recalling the pioneer work done by Bernard de La Monnoye in the field of bibliography, admitted that he had got the idea of taking the project up again himself from Falconet's paper. Others who had also been moved by the paper came to the help of the new editor. Foncemagne secured La Monnoye's manuscript for the Académie Française and made it available to him. Sainte-Palaye and Bréquigny also assisted.[38] The *Dictionnaire géographique* was undertaken by

---

[36] P. F. G. Beauchamps, *Recherches sur les théâtres de France depuis 1161 jusqu'à présent*, 3 vols. (Paris, 1735), François and Claude Parfaict, *Histoire du théâtre françois depuis son origine jusqu'à présent*, 2 vols. (Amsterdam, 1735–36), continued through 15 vols. in the edition of Paris, 1745–49; the same authors' *Dictionnaire des théâtres de Paris*, 6 vols. (Paris, 1756).

[37] In 1797 Anquetil thought it worthwhile to go through the essays submitted for these prizes, in order to obtain a general picture of the state of the arts and sciences in the Middle Ages, which he communicated to the new 'Classe des sciences morales et politiques' of the *Institut*. (*Mémoires de l'Institut, Classe des sciences morales et politiques*, 4:35.)

[38] *Les Bibliothèques françoises de La Croix du Maine et de du Verdier*, nouvelle édition, revue et augmentée d'un Discours sur le progrès des lettres en France, et des remarques historiques, critiques et littéraires de M. de la Monnoye et de M. le Président Bouhier, de l'Académie Françoise, de M. Falconet, de l'Académie des Belles-Lettres. Par M. Rigoley de Juvigny (Paris, 1772–73), 1:7–9, Préface.

Falconet himself in collaboration with Sainte-Palaye,[39] while the Glossary, the cornerstone of the whole edifice, as Falconet recognized, was entrusted to Sainte-Palaye.

Had Sainte-Palaye's work been confined to the Glossary, the Geographical Dictionary, the History of the Troubadours, and the Dictionary of French Antiquities, his contribution would have been notable enough. He was engaged in many other historical projects, however, and at the Academy he endeavored to integrate these into the pattern sketched by Falconet. After 1727 his papers were exclusively concerned with medieval subjects—institutions, manners, literature, historical sources, and materials.

The influence of Falconet's paper has not been exaggerated. As late as December, 1789, it was still remembered by Mercier de Saint-Léger who, in a letter published in the *Journal des Savants* for October, 1791, recalled it and deplored that its provisions had even then hardly been carried out.[40]

Sainte-Palaye can be considered Falconet's chief executive, and then his successor. At the Académie des Inscriptions he tried to build up a body of younger scholars who would carry on the work he and his friends had begun under Falconet. Falconet's vision of the Académie des Inscriptions inspired his own remarkable *Plan de travail pour l'Académie des Belles-Lettres.* In this plan he complains that too many academicians are still gleaning after the giants of sixteenth- and seventeenth-century scholarship. As a result their contributions to learning are often unconnected and slight. Sainte-

---

[39] The *Dictionnaire géographique* (the manuscript is in Bréquigny 144, 145) was conceived like the earlier dictionaries of classical geography of Ortelio and Cluverius as a guide to the interpretation of texts; cf. Roberto Amalgià, 'Le origini della geografia storica,' *Rivista geografica italiana*, 1915, 22:141–47. By 1737 Falconet was already putting it together, according to a letter from La Bastie to Mazaugues of 10.4.1737. ('Les Provençalistes du XVIIIᵉ siècle,' p. 192.) Sainte-Palaye, on his side, brought back material for the dictionary from Italy. (Sainte-Palaye to Falconet, 6.7.1749, B.N. Fichier Charavay, carton 102, no. 205.) Moreover, many entries in the manuscript are in his hand, most of the sources used for it are obviously drawn from his reading, while he himself marked all the passages relevant to the dictionary in his own copies of manuscripts with a marginal G. Bréquigny also assisted, and most of the manuscript is, in fact, in his hand. D'Expilly's *Dictionnaire géographique, historique et politique des Gaules* (Paris, 1762–70), may owe something to the work initiated by Falconet. But neither Falconet's dictionary, nor d'Expilly's made use of more than generally available printed sources. As yet there is no sign of archival or archaeological research on the spot.

[40] Reprinted in *Bulletin de la Société de l'Histoire de France*, 1861, 2ᵉ série, 3:22–23.

Palaye proposed that the Academy should devote more of its energies to the study of the national past, where an immense amount of essential work still remained to be done. Some members were already engaged in this task, but if it were not for their own enthusiasm, the contempt with which modern and medieval studies were regarded by part of the company would have long since driven them to abandon their work: "Nos vieilles Chroniques, nos anciens Poëtes n'ont pas encore acquis auprès d'un certain ordre d'Érudits la considération que donne l'avantage d'être au monde depuis trois mille ans. Cependant si l'on vouloit estimer les choses par leur difficulté ou par leur utilité, l'Étude des monumens qui concernent notre nation devroit avoir le pas sur toutes les autres, et il me semble qu'il n'en est point de plus digne d'une Académie établie en France."[41]

The voice of the Enlightenment is clearly audible here. Humanist scholarship must yield to historical scholarship, Sainte-Palaye is arguing, and the isolated labors of individuals must find their significance in a larger historical vision.

Sainte-Palaye's aim—like his master's—was to transform the Académie des Inscriptions into a national institution which would undertake important collective works of scholarship, and which would be at the same time a forum for the exchange of ideas and information among scholars. "Je voudrois que l'Académie s'occupast bien plus à faire de vrais ouvrages qu'à composer de petites dissertations," he remarked in his *Plan d'Études*, "et que chaque membre attaché à un plan d'études suivi se proposast un but et rendist compte à la Compagnie du progrès de son travail, de ses découvertes et de ses difficultés. La matière alors ne manqueroit pas, et l'on remédieroit à un autre défaut de cet établissment . . . Il consiste en ce que, dans les travaux de l'Académie, il n'y a point d'ensemble . . . chaque pièce, chaque mémoire est une partie isolée qui ne concourt point à la formation d'un tout . . . De là il arrive que chaque Académicien suivant une route à part, sans se proposer aucun but, ils ne se rencontrent jamais pour s'aider les uns les autres, pour se guider mutuellement."[42] To expedite the work of scholarship, Sainte-Palaye suggested the division of the Academy into classes on the model of the *Académie des Sciences*, a proposal which was put into effect after the Revolution.

[41] Bréquigny 62, fol. 203.   [42] *Ibid.*

Sainte-Palaye's own notion of history reveals that he was familiar with the ideas of the *philosophes*, and that he had thought a good deal about the relation of scholarship to history-writing proper. In a note among his papers he declares that one of the objects of the historian is to study institutions, which can be thought of as the expression of man's endeavor at all times and in all climates and conditions to overcome his weakness as an individual through social action. This is the origin of language, of societies, of the arts and sciences, "qui . . . se perfectionnent et se diversifient à l'infini, parce que la somme des besoins augmentant avec les moyens de les satisfaire, chaque moyen devient à la fois la source de nouveaux besoins et de nouveaux moyens."[43] The dialectic of progress outlined here was common coin among the Enlighteners of the first half of the eighteenth century. Similarly, it is an Enlightened view of scholarship that Sainte-Palaye professed in his *Discours de réception* before the Académie Française in 1758. The aim of scholarship, he declared, is not to amass isolated, or merely chronologically related, facts. Man, himself, in his many historical manifestations, is the subject of the historian's investigation: "L'histoire d'un peuple consiste moins dans le récit de ce qu'il a fait que dans la peinture de ce qu'il a été."[44]

Nevertheless, in practice, Sainte-Palaye was more interested in particular peoples than in man in general, and he devoted much more of his attention to establishing particular facts about French history than to drawing general lessons. Compared with the scholars of the seventeenth century, he had been "emancipated" by Enlightenment from narrow loyalties, as had most of his colleagues. But this emancipation was limited. Sainte-Palaye never questioned fundamentally the social order of which he was part and whose evolution and variations he described with loving care. This underlying conservatism may well have affected the whole of his work. On the one hand, it encouraged him to examine the history of his own society concretely, with a real curiosity for its particular manifestations, but, on the other hand, it may have prevented him from realizing that history of the French *nation* which was his ultimate goal. Like most of his contemporaries Sainte-Palaye saw

[43] Moreau 1722, fol. 297.
[44] *Discours prononcés à l'Académie Françoise le lundi 26 juin MDCCLVIII à la réception de M. de La Curne de Sainte-Palaye* (Paris: Brunet, 1758), in B.N. MS Clérambault 1076, fols. 203–11, at fol. 205.

his society as an association of traditionally separate elements; there is no evidence that he had any conception of the nation as a single unified whole or of the dynamic relations among the elements in it. Doubtless his failure to arrive at such a conception was largely determined by the historical conditions of his age. There were not many in Sainte-Palaye's time who would have been willing to class themselves with the despised *peuple,* and it is hard to imagine what was meant concretely by those who, in the heat of enthusiasm, invoked *la nation* and appealed to "tous les Français." Only the most advanced *philosophes,* perhaps, were able to transcend imaginatively the social order of the ancien régime and to formulate the goal of a truly unified nation. Sainte-Palaye may well have been too attached to the existing order to think of the nation in any other categories than those provided by that order. Whatever the explanation of it, Sainte-Palaye's limited view of the nation may well have been one of the factors which caused him to confine himself to fairly narrowly defined historical problems and prevented him from achieving a major work of synthesis.

If the underlying conservatism of the aristocracy kept its historians from realizing that truly national history which their advanced theories set before them as a goal, its thorough penetration by contemporary thought and its complete transformation by contemporary modes of life made it incapable of understanding or sympathizing deeply with the civilization of the Middle Ages. Its attitude to the Middle Ages was very often tinged with irony. The final memoir of Sainte-Palaye's *Mémoires sur l'ancienne chevalerie,* in which he offered some criticism of chivalry, was not, as Cheruel believed, an external concession to Enlightenment. On the contrary, the eighteenth-century aristocracy, which, as we have frequently suggested, can in no sense be identified with the ancient blood nobility, was itself in large measure "bourgeois" and enlightened. It tended, therefore, to view the Middle Ages with a certain degree of detachment and disdain. Despite his immense material contribution to the study of Old French and Provençal literature, Sainte-Palaye himself remained largely insensitive to this literature. He ferreted out the manuscripts, read them, classified them, and did not love them. The limited success of aristocratic medievalism in the eighteenth century throws an interesting light on the fact that a deeper understanding of the Middle Ages was achieved only some considerable time after the Revolution and the end of the ancien régime.

With these limitations in mind, we can now turn to the individual works through which Sainte-Palaye made his contribution to medieval studies.

PART III

WORKS OF MEDIEVAL SCHOLARSHIP

CHAPTER I

LANGUAGE

The problem of language was doubly important to Sainte-Palaye. As a medievalist he knew that a sound knowledge of medieval Latin and Old French was a prerequisite of any serious study of the sources of medieval history. Like most of his contemporaries, moreover, he felt that the civilization of a period was reflected in its language, and he thought of the history of the French language as in some way the history of the French people. He appears to have been only moderately interested, on the other hand, in the more general question of the relation of language and thought— the question that was closest to the hearts of the *philosophes*. As we shall see, it took the prodding of several of his friends to get him to view the history of the language in the way the *philosophes* wished it to be viewed. In the century of philosophy, his interest in language remained predominantly an aspect of his interest in history.

He believed with most contemporaries that the French language, like French society, had reached near-perfection, but like many people in the late seventeenth and early eighteenth centuries he regretted a kind of impoverishment that seemed to have affected it. There was a richness in the language of the preclassical period that had gone out of French—he thought—and he was one of those who wished to bring some of it back. His linguistic work was not unrelated to this aim. In his view of language as a constant process of change, the classical phase of French could enjoy only a relative, not an absolute privilege. It became one moment in an ever-changing pattern, rather as in the long view of the nation's history which the scholars were taking, the classical period of absolutism was considered a high point of civilization, but was at the same time firmly inserted into a context of analyzable historical development. It is understandable that as a consistent *Moderne* Falconet conceived the historicization of the language and the demystification of its classical phase as an important part of his over-all plan.

In Sainte-Palaye's work on language the contradictory strands we discovered earlier in the historiography and in the art criticism of his milieu again come together. The weakening of the classical rhetorical tradition, which was one of the aims and consequences of his work, freed the language to some degree to adjust and adapt itself to the changing needs of an age concerned with many new and practical questions, and eager to extend communication and discussion of these questions to a wider public than ever before. At the same time it left the door open for a great deal of aristo-cratic "preciosity" and modishness, which the *philosophes*, inci-dentally, were among the first to condemn.[1] It is not certain that the *Modernes* of the first half of the century achieved or, indeed, desired anything like the changes that were made to the language by the generation of Diderot, Rousseau, and Beaumarchais.[2] Similarly, the work of Sainte-Palaye and his colleagues revealed, alongside the literary tradition of absolutism, the literary tradition of the early nobility and, to a lesser degree, of the medieval and Renaissance bourgeoisie. Sainte-Palaye and his friends thereby contributed to the ideology of the so-called feudal reaction, and in some senses this was their aim. But they also opened up a wider notion of culture than the classical humanist one, and at least eased the way for what they themselves did not achieve—a view of a national culture which was ultimately to include not only the poetry of the troubadours but folk poetry and folk myths.[3] Hum-

---

[1] Similarly in Italy, the *philosophes* who fought for the introduction of French and English words, for neologisms and syntactic reform, were the first to criticize the fashion for French words in modish circles. (Maurizio Vitale, *La Questione della lingua* [Palermo, 1960], p. 102.)

[2] Cf. F. Gohin, *Les Transformations de la langue française pendant la deuxième moitié du XVIII* siècle—1740–1789 (Paris, n.d.).

[3] The modern conception of culture was only beginning to form in the eight-eenth century. Archaeologists, for instance, point with dismay to the narrow spirit in which the early excavations at Pompeii were carried out. The *objet d'art* was the goal of eighteenth century researchers, and they ignored whatever was not "beautiful." (Marcel Brion, *Pompeii and Herculaneum*, trans. J. Rosenberg [New York, 1960], p. 59; see also Stanley Casson, *The Discovery of Man* [London, 1940], p. 141.) The interest of the Northern European gentry and bourgeoisie in its own past, notably in medieval architecture and poetry, may have promoted an expan-sion of this narrow notion of culture. By the end of the century some antiquarians, such as Pownall in Ireland, were already beginning to envisage prehistorical cul-tures. (See Glyn Daniel, *The Idea of Prehistory* [Pelican Books, 1964], pp. 24–27.)

drum and technical as it may seem, Sainte-Palaye's language work is thus of considerable moment.

1. The Glossary of Old French

Du Cange's *Glossarium* had laid a solid foundation for the consideration of a large number of medieval literary and documentary sources. Not all of these were in Latin, however, and knowledge of medieval French was insufficient to deal with those which were not. Even experienced palaeographers, Sainte-Palaye claimed, were not capable of turning out satisfactory editions of texts when these were in Old French. Mabillon's 1719 edition of the *Sermons françois de Saint Bernard*, for instance, which Sainte-Palaye had carefully collated with the manuscript in the Bibliothèque du Roi,[4] was far from perfect: "Les méprises qui lui sont échapées . . . prouvent que cet habile Antiquaire ne connoissoit pas aussi parfaitement le vieux François que la Latinité du moyen âge."[5] Sainte-Palaye frequently complained that texts of vital historical importance had been published in corrupt and unintelligible versions.[6] It was not good enough, he claimed, to go to texts in the vernacular with only a knowledge of medieval Latin palaeography. Numerous research projects which had been set on foot or taken up again— the *Gallia Christiana*, the *Ordonnances des Rois*, the *Recueil des historiens*, the *Histoire littéraire*, histories of towns and provinces, of jurisprudence, of the coinage, of manners and customs—all required a Glossary of Old French. Above all, the ambitious collection of the Benedictines, the *Recueil des historiens*, had reached the

---

[4] Sainte-Palaye's annotated copy in B.N. Moreau 1678.

[5] *Projet d'un Glossaire François* (Paris, 1756), in-4°, ii+30 pp. Copies are rare (one at B.N. Réserve La 3). References here are to Favre's reprint in his edition of the Glossary, vol. 1, pp. iv–xii. This passage on p. v. The *Projet* was read to the Académie des Inscriptions on 30.3.1756, and again at the *assemblée publique* of 27.4.1756. (*Registres de l'Académie des Inscriptions* [1756], pp. 54, 62.)

[6] E.g., Bréquigny 165, fol. 47, Sainte-Palaye to Bréquigny, 8.6.1764: "J'ai leu à dix fois les loix de Guillaume, et il y a un bon tiers où je crois qu'il est impossible de rien entendre, parce que l'éditeur lui mesme n'a pas scu les lire et n'avoit pas d'idée du langage." Similarly in his 'Projet d'étude sur l'histoire de France' (Bréquigny 62, fols. 211–12, and two further copies in Foncemagne's papers, B.N. Français 9457, fols. 136–39 and 146–48), drawn up in collaboration with Foncemagne some time before 1740, he had already asserted that ignorance of Old French was the main obstacle to the proper study of the sources of medieval history.

point where many of the relevant materials were in the vernacular. A Glossary was indispensable "si l'on veut qu'elle paroisse avec toute la correction et la fidélité qui font le mérite des premiers volumes."[7]

Sainte-Palaye himself never lost sight of this initial function of the Glossary as an instrument in the hands of editors of texts and scholars engaged on research among the source materials of history. In the Preface he prepared for the Glossary some time after 1760[8] he reiterated the arguments sketched out in the *Projet* of 1756. Regretting that he had not had time to examine still more manuscripts in order that his list of variants might be extended, he expressed the hope that others might later add to and improve upon his work. At the same time he endeavored to clear himself of the "reproche qu'on pourroit me faire sur l'exactitude minutieuse et scrupuleuse, si l'on veut mesme superstitieuse, avec laquelle j'ai rapporté à la teste de chaque article les différentes orthographes sous lesquelles je l'ai trouvé écrit." There were good reasons for this, he declared: "Outre que cette exactitude étoit nécessaire pour retrouver ces mots, il ne sera peut-estre pas inutile de savoir en quel temps ces changements se sont introduits. On pourra le découvrir en parcourant les mots où ils se rencontrent et ce sera un moyen, ou un secours de plus pour démesler la fausseté ou l'autenticité de nos anciens actes et de nos anciens Écrivains."[9] If these were good reasons for compiling the Glossary, they were not, however, the only ones.

Sainte-Palaye's interest in language was primarily historical. While he studied the changing characteristics of French, he accepted its existence—the fact of language—without question and without surprise. But Descartes and the Cartesians had seen in language, above all, the instrument by which men were enabled to think conceptually and to communicate and develop their ideas.

[7] *Projet d'un Glossaire*, p. vii. Sainte-Palaye was not alone in proclaiming the need of a new dictionary of Old French. One would-be editor of a new edition of the *Roman de la Rose* wrote to the *Mercure* in April, 1724 (p. 652) of the difficulty of improving upon earlier editions. Sinner, the learned librarian of Berne, likewise complained in the *Avertissement* to his *Extraits de quelques poésies du XII, XIII, et XIV siècles* (Lausanne, 1759), p. 3, of the absence of a good dictionary of Old French.

[8] Fragmentary notes for this preface in Moreau 1722, 1723, 1724. A coherent plan in Moreau 1724, fols. 175–80. The first part of the Preface was read to the Académie des Inscriptions in 1760. (*Registres, 1763*, p. 39.)

[9] Note for the Preface, Moreau 1724, fol. 138.

It was thus language, in large measure, which for the Cartesians distinguished the human from the animal realm. Many people in the eighteenth century may have known little of the Cartesian meditation on language, but in an age which laid greater emphasis than any other on social life—to the point that the individual considered in isolation seemed almost to vanish into nonexistence—men experienced concretely through the language arts, conversation and writing, their most intense awareness of their humanity. Nearly everybody would have agreed that a person's humanity could be measured by the skill and elegance with which he handled language; the state of a society's language was likewise taken as the measure of its civilization (whence so much discussion of the "merits" of French as opposed to other languages, ancient and modern, and so much concern that it might be in decline). Court de Gébelin expressed the feelings of many contemporaries when he opened his *Dictionnaire étymologique de la langue françoise*— part of his vast study of *Le Monde primitif* (1773–96)—with a salute to language: "Les mots sont les liens des Sociétés, le véhicule des lumières, la base des Sciences, les dépositaires des découvertes d'une Nation, de son savoir, de sa politesse, de ses idées: la connoissance des mots est donc un moyen indispensable pour acquérir celle des choses." Voltaire had already paid his tribute to the instrument he handled so adroitly. In *Les Oreilles du Comte de Chesterfield*, one of the less well-known *contes*, Sidrac invites the luckless Goudman to forget his misfortunes in pleasant and interesting conversation: "Venez dîner avec moi . . . votre faculté pensante aura le plaisir de se communiquer à la mienne par le moyen de la parole: ce qui est une chose merveilleuse que les hommes n'admirent pas assez." It was thus the general and anthropological question of the nature of language itself as a system of signs, rather than the history of any particular language, which interested the men of the Enlightenment, Christians like Beauzée, who contributed the article "Grammaire" to the *Encyclopédie*, and a host of secular thinkers—Du Marsais, Condillac, Rousseau, Turgot, de Brosses, and Court de Gébelin, to mention only a few.[10]

[10] Maurizio Vitale, 'Sommario di una storia degli studi linguistici romanzi,' pp. 66–67, in A. Viscardi *et al.*, *Preistoria e storia degli studi romanzi* (Milan–Varese, 1955). On this question see also Theodor Benfey, *Geschichte der Sprachwissenschaft und der orientalischen Philologie in Deutschland* (Munich, 1869), pp. 299–302; René Hubert, *Les Sciences sociales dans l'Encyclopédie* (Paris, 1923), p. 33;

These men tried to understand the nature and functioning of language as such. De Brosses studied the relation of language to the physiological mechanisms of speech. In an effort to forge a linguistic theory compatible with the new individualism and with the genetic approach of the empiricists, Condillac saw language developing from a primitive system of communications by which the human animal indicated its most simple needs into the complex system of signs required by modern men in a modern environment. Rousseau, while accepting Condillac's thesis, questioned the adequacy of the psychological and individualist presuppositions which he himself shared with Condillac. In the Second Discourse he declared that he could see no way of bridging the gap between so-called natural language (cries, calls, etc.), which men might be held to share with animals, and structured language, of which only human beings living in society appear to be capable. Whatever their approach, it was the phenomenon of language itself that fascinated these men. The goal of all linguistic inquiry, Turgot declared, must be "la théorie générale de la parole et la marche de l'esprit humain dans la formation et le progrès du langage." This general theory, Turgot went on, "est la source, d'où découlent les règles de cette grammaire générale qui gouverne toutes les langues, à laquelle toutes les nations s'assujettissent en croyant ne suivre que les caprices de l'usage, et dont enfin les grammaires de toutes les langues ne sont que des applications partielles ou incomplètes."[11] This conception of language, which is an extension of Descartes', did not rule out detailed study (for Turgot the general theory of language "comme tout autre, a besoin, pour n'être pas un roman, d'être continuellement rapprochée des faits");[12] it did mean that the ultimate justification of linguistic studies lay in their contribution to the philosophy of language, which the men of the Enlightenment, like some scholars in our own time, saw as the cornerstone

---

Guy Harnois, *Les Théories du langage en France* (Paris, n.d. [1928?]), p. 49; Louis Kukenheim, *Esquisse historique de la linguistique française et de ses rapports avec la linguistique générale* (Leiden, 1962), pp. 31–33. On the distinction between the rationalist (Beauzée) and the sensationalist-materialist schools (Condillac), see Maurizio Vitale, *La Questione della lingua* (Palermo, 1960), pp. 106–7 *et passim*. Vitale argues that the latter was more interested in and more able to deal with modes of expression and forms of communication other than the purely logical. It was, in this sense, doubtless more bourgeois, more attuned to the inner life of the individual, than the rationalist school.

[11] Turgot, art. 'Étymologie,' *Encyclopédie*, 6:107–8.
[12] *Ibid*. Cf. Benfey, pp. 281–94, and Harnois, pp. 53–54 on de Brosses.

of the general anthropology they were seeking. Thus Buffon hinted gently that in his view de Brosses' *Traité de la formation mécanique des langues* was a more important contribution to linguistic studies than Sainte-Palaye's Glossary: "Entre nous, il est sûr qu'en fait de grammaire, il y a autant d'esprit dans votre livre qu'il y a de matière dans celui de Sainte-Palaye."[13]

To some extent Sainte-Palaye himself followed the trend of most eighteenth-century thinking about language. He once described language as a system of communication by signs rather than a mere inventory: "Les langues ne sont que les interprètes de l'esprit et les moyens dont ils se sont servis (i.e., les esprits) pour communiquer leurs pensées. Ces pensées regardent autant les choses conceues par l'esprit que celles qui tombent sous les sens." In this way, he argued, "les langues rentrent dans le ressort de la métaphysique."[14] Although he remained primarily interested in philology—the study of the French language and literary tradition as an entity in itself, independent of any general considerations concerning the nature of the mind or of language or literature—and in the application of the fruits of linguistic study to the interpretation of texts, he was therefore willing to make an effort to associate his work with the current philosophical inquiry into language as such. The story of the Glossary is in large measure the story of this effort to reconcile the two approaches and goals of language studies, the philological and the philosophical.

At first Sainte-Palaye was so taken up with amassing material that he can hardly have envisaged the final product of his labors except along the broadest lines. He had set to work zealously on the manuscripts at the Royal and Saint-Germain libraries, compiling lists of words, elucidating meanings, and selecting examples for illustration, so that by 1737 his notes and copies of manuscripts already formed "des recueils immenses."[15] Two years later the Glossary itself filled six volumes folio.[16] These folio registers were no more than the depositories in which Sainte-Palaye filed and classified his material,[17] but they give a clue to the points which

---

[13] Buffon, *Correspondance inédite*, 1:104, to de Brosses, 27.6.1766.
[14] Moreau 1722, fol. 296.
[15] 'Les Provençalistes du XVIIIe siècle,' p. 190, Bimard de La Bastie to Mazaugues, 17.3.1737.
[16] *Novelle Letterarie di Firenze*, no. 7, 12.2.1740, col. 97 *et seq.*
[17] The complete set is in B.N. Moreau 1524–54.

interested him from the very beginning of his work on the Glossary. They show that he was carefully noting all the orthographic variants and shades of meaning he could find. It is likely that at this early stage he proposed to follow the "méthode ordinaire des glossaires et . . . rien de plus," in Bréquigny's words, that is to "rassembler tous les mots de notre ancienne langue, qui se trouvent dans les livres imprimés ou manuscrits, de les ranger par ordre alphabétique et d'assigner à chaque mot l'acception qu'il jugeoit convenable, et de l'appuyer par une citation."[18] The manuscript shows that the numbering of the entries to suggest the semantic development of each word was a later addition. There is not even any sign in these manuscript registers of the short historical essays that accompanied a considerable number of entries in the finished Glossary, although these may have been in Sainte-Palaye's mind at the outset. He could hardly have ignored the example of Du Cange, and he may also have been influenced by Carpentier's plan for an Old French Glossary on the model of Du Cange.[19]

By 1756 when he published a Prospectus of the Glossary with one eye on a *fauteuil* at the Académie Française, he had definitely made up his mind to include historical essays in it. Rejecting de Valois' criticisms of the historical excursus in Du Cange, he declared that they constitute "la partie la plus riche et la plus précieuse" of the *Glossarium*.[20] At the same time he also decided to indicate the historical development of the meanings of the words in his Glossary. "Je m'étois proposé dès le commencement de mon entreprise," he wrote, not quite accurately, "de classer si j'ose parler ainsi, les significations de chaque mot, en les rangeant autant qu'il seroit possible dans l'ordre selon lequel on peut supposer qu'elles soient nées. Par là je mettois le lecteur à portée de saisir d'un coup

[18] *Bull. Soc. Hist. de France* (2ᵉ série, 1861), 3:24–29, letter from Bréquigny to Mercier de Saint-Léger of 26.12.1793, in answer to latter's criticism of Sainte-Palaye in *Journal des Savants*, October, 1791.

[19] According to Carpentier the aim of a good glossary "ne se borne pas à la simple interprétation des termes, mais y applique les usages qui doivent servir de fond à l'histoire." (B.N. Français 12763, fol. 18, Carpentier to Saint-Vincent, *président à mortier* of the Parlement of Aix, 10.12.1749.) An undated autographed note by Sainte-Palaye indicates that he shared this view. "L'usage que bien des gens de Lettres ont fait du Glossaire Latin de Du Cange nous fait espérer qu'on pourra aussi tirer le même avantage de celui que nous présentons." (Moreau 1723, fol. 319.) For this reason, he noted, he intended to provide his Glossary with an historical index. Carpentier's Glossary was reduced in the end to a guide to the Old French terms in Du Cange.

[20] *Projet d'un Glossaire*, p. xii.

d'oeil les rapports réciproques . . . la marche de l'esprit qui les a engendrées et conséquemment les progrès successifs de la langue."[21]

Sainte-Palaye's revised plan of 1756 indicates his desire to keep abreast of the current interests of his day. Inevitably it involved delays. Apart from the labor of organization and composition, the historical articles on certain institutions could not fail to be controversial. The article devoted to the word *Aide*, for instance, had to be altered so as to avoid giving offense to Malesherbes.[22] The article *Apostole* also caused trouble. It had to be severely cut, and its militant Gallicanism suppressed between the first printer's proof and the final version.[23] Most probably other entries would have encountered similar difficulties.

Even so, the Glossary might have been published by the 1760's. The *Projet* had won Sainte-Palaye his seat at the Académie Française, the public had received it well on the whole,[24] and Voltaire, to whom Sainte-Palaye had sent a courtesy copy as he did of all his works, had signified approval and even proffered advice.[25] Reassured by the recognition of the world of letters, Sainte-Palaye had forged ahead with determination, and in 1760 he was writing confidently to Bréquigny that "il n'est pas impossible que nous ne voyions enfin le but auquel je tens depuis quarante ans de travail."[26] Before handing his manuscript to the printer, however, he wanted the final approval of his friends and colleagues. As a result of the discussions which took place at Falconet's in 1762 in the presence of Falconet himself, together with Foncemagne, Bréquigny, and d'Alembert, it was decided to make still further alterations to the Glossary and to hold up publication until these had been successfully carried through.[27] Bréquigny later described the gist of the proposals of which he was the author. "D'abord on devoit placer la principale orthographe, puis toutes celles qui s'en sont peu à peu éloignées, et chacune devoit être appuyée de la citation du livre imprimé ou manuscrit, où cette orthographe a été employée.

[21] Bréquigny 62, fol. 215.
[22] Letters, notes, and correspondence regarding this article in Moreau 1797, fols. 1–84.
[23] B.N. Réserve X 232 contains various proof sheets.
[24] Bréquigny 165, fol. 26, letter of 27.8.1756.
[25] Voltaire to d'Argental, 18.8.1756 (Besterman 6287), and to Thiériot, 20.8.1756 (Besterman 6291).
[26] Bréquigny 165, fol. 36, letter of 27.9.1760.
[27] *Bull. Soc. Hist. de France* (2e série, 1861), 3:24–29.

"Les acceptions devoient être rangées ensuite selon l'ordre le plus probable de la génération des idées, par extension, par allusion, par métaphore et autres métonymies. Chacune de ces acceptions devoit être aussi justifiée par un passage qui servît de preuve et d'exemple."

In this way it was hoped to "présenter en quelque sorte l'histoire physique de chaque mot, par la génération de ses orthographes, et l'histoire métaphysique, par la génération de ses acceptions."[28] Bréquigny was writing some three decades later, and his memory may not have been too good; at any rate Sainte-Palaye describes the new proposal more precisely: "Les conseils d'amis éclairés m'ont déterminé à m'engager dans une carrière plus laborieuse et plus longue. Ils ont désiré que sans me borner aux détails des changemens que chaque terme a éprouvés soit dans ses Ortho-graphes, soit dans ses significations, j'essayasse de faire connoître les motifs et les causes qui ont amené ou produit ces variations . . . Le Lecteur, ajoutoient-ils, vous saura gré de lui faire trouver par intervalles de quoi exercer les facultés de son Esprit, sa raison et son jugement."[29]

This last remark gives a clue to the probable motive for the new proposals. It was hoped to expand the Glossary so that it would contribute to some of those wider aspects of language study which Turgot, for instance, had outlined in his article on Etymology in the *Encyclopédie*.[30] As Bréquigny himself argued, his plan seemed "non seulement remplir l'objet de celui qu'on avoit suivi, mais l'aggrandir, l'ennoblir même, en envisageant la langue sous un point de vue philosophique."[31] The Glossary would thus fall into line with the general aims of such compilations as Diderot had set them forth in the article "Encyclopédie."

Sainte-Palaye's attitude to the new proposals was somewhat

---

[28] The aims of Court de Gébelin in his *Dictionnaire étymologique*, composed somewhat later in the century, were the same as those which animated Bréquigny and d'Alembert. In existing dictionaries, writes Court de Gébelin, "nulle liaison, nul rapport entre les mots; rangés par ordre alphabétique, ils sont tous isolés, et la connoissance de l'un est nulle pour la connoissance des autres: chacun d'eux semble tombé du Ciel, et on ne voit pas pourquoi on attacha telle idée à tel son, quel rapport secret, quel charme les enchaîna l'un à l'autre . . ." (*Le Monde primitif* [nouvelle édition; Paris, 1787], 'Discours preliminaire,' vol. 5, p. i).

[29] Bréquigny 62, fol. 215.

[30] According to Turgot the best way of defining a word is not to give all the possible meanings, which is to tell nothing illuminating, but to give the original idea or concept it was designed to express and to trace how this developed.

[31] *Bull. Soc. Hist. de France* (2ᵉ série, 1861), 3:24–29.

reserved. On the one hand, there was his understandable fear that he might not survive to complete the work to which he had devoted the best years of his life.[32] On the other, there were technical and scholarly considerations of some importance.

Where Bréquigny appears to have believed that there was a correct and uniform usage in Old French, and that variants were corruptions of standard forms, Sainte-Palaye had argued that it was often more prudent to talk of less common and more common forms, since many had existed and been used simultaneously, sometimes in different provinces, sometimes in the same province, sometimes even by the same author or indeed in the same text. More clearly than Bréquigny he seems to have been aware of the linguistic variety of the Middle Ages, and of the difficulties in the way of tracing the phonetic development of Old French words to their modern equivalents through a maze of orthographic variants.[33]

Again, he objected, if all the derivatives and variants of each word were grouped together under one article, how could the Glossary be used as a Glossary? Bréquigny's solution, a complete alphabetical index of variant and derivative forms, would have provided an answer, but it was never compiled.

In the end a compromise was reached. The final version has the variants listed not in some conjectural order of development, but in simple alphabetical order, though the principle of grouping them in one article was adopted. Occasionally, however, Sainte-Palaye contrived to place important variant or derivative forms in the general alphabetical arrangement of the Glossary.

The proposed additions to Sainte-Palaye's plan proved not only ill-conceived but unfortunate. Bréquigny himself admitted that the writing up of the causes and principles of the semantic changes, which Sainte-Palaye would have been content simply to list without explanation, was bound to delay publication considerably, and his forecast turned out to be only too accurate. Sainte-Palaye's attempts to modify the new arrangement of the Glossary in the interest of speedier publication were unsuccessful.[34] The work was

---

[32] Bréquigny 165, fol. 68, Sainte-Palaye to Bréquigny, 17.6.1765.

[33] *Projet d'un Glossaire*, p. ix.

[34] In a letter to Bréquigny of 17.6.1765 (Bréquigny 165, fol. 68) Sainte-Palaye suggested that the new plan be implemented in full for the first two or three letters only, the semantic development being indicated in each subsequent section "au moyen de l'ordre régulier que nous mettrions dans la suite graduelle de nos significations." This suggestion, apparently, was rejected.

not published until over a century after the *Projet* was read to the Académie des Inscriptions, and over eighty years after Sainte-Palaye's death.

There was no lack of diligence on the author's part. Falconet had originally suggested that the Glossary should be a co-operative venture,[35] and Sainte-Palaye did receive help from other scholars. Bréquigny's part in its composition cannot be measured exactly but it is certain that entire sections were largely his work,[36] while many suggestions written into the manuscript of the Glossary in his hand indicate that he and Sainte-Palaye collaborated closely. Another collaborator was the Academician Dupuy, who relates in his "Éloge" of Sainte-Palaye that he worked on several entries, in particular under the letters *G* and *Q*.[37] The celebrated Dupré de Saint-Maur communicated odd words and phrases. As the Glossary was well known throughout the learned world of France and of Europe and was followed with interest by both scholars and *philosophes*, it is likely that there were many such contributions to it from individual persons.

Sainte-Palaye's idea of co-operative work was nevertheless somewhat aristocratic. On two occasions he attempted to coerce humble provincial scholars into handing over the fruits of their research to him. Having heard in 1757 that a certain Le Clerc de Douy of Orléans had compiled a glossary from medieval deeds and charters in his care, Sainte-Palaye immediately set about procuring it for himself. He had useful connections at Court. Silhouette, then chancellor of the Duke of Orléans, and Belle-Isle, then *contrôleur des domaines,* brought pressure to bear on the hapless Le Clerc who, after some vain resistance, was forced to yield up his property to the Royal Academician.[38] Sainte-Palaye also persuaded the Crown to try to acquire the manuscript of a Glossary which was being compiled by his countryman Étienne Barbazan, a modest citizen of limited means. He did not, this time, succeed in obtain-

---

[35] 'Essai de Bibliothèque Françoise,' MS version, Bréquigny 61, fol. 29.

[36] Sainte-Palaye's correspondence with Bréquigny shows that the latter was co-operating actively on the Glossary by 1760. Numerous notes in the MS, and almost the whole of the article 'Chaoir' (Moreau 1597, fol. 227 *et seq.*) are in his hand.

[37] Dupuy, 'Éloge de Sainte-Palaye,' *MAI** 45:117, note *a*.

[38] On Sainte-Palaye and Le Clerc de Douy, see G. Vignat in *Bull. Soc. Arch. de l'Orléanais* (1875), 6:190–204, reprinted in Favre's edition of Glossary, vol. 10, pp. xix–xxii.

ing the manuscript, but he destroyed his rival's chances of competing with him, for Barbazan's publisher was thereafter unwilling to go ahead with the publication of his client's manuscript.[39] Sainte-Palaye's attitude was not, unfortunately, uncommon among aristocratic scholars and at the Royal Academies in general. He conceived of himself as the director of an enterprise. He was good to those who worked for him and accepted their help with gratitude, but he tolerated no competition, especially from inferiors.

To expedite the task of going through the manuscripts and printed works, annotating them, and compiling word-lists from them, Sainte-Palaye employed a number of scribes and assistants, on whose co-operation and intelligence he depended heavily. These men had to be competent palaeographers, familiar with the script and language of texts and documents in Old French. Such qualifications were not easy to come by, and even the best of his assistants made mistakes in transcribing manuscripts, as countless marginal queries in Sainte-Palaye's own hand indicate. Two of them won a certain degree of eminence in the world of letters. One was Georges-Jean Mouchet, of whom Sainte-Palaye always wrote with affection and respect, the other was Pierre-Jean-Baptiste Le Grand d'Aussy,[40] who later published a well-known collection of *fabliaux* and who always freely acknowledged his debt to his "premier maître."[41]

Sainte-Palaye himself continued to play an active part in all aspects of the work, despite his resolve after the adoption of the new plan in 1762 to restrict his role to that of collecting new material and supervising the work of his collaborators.[42] By 1769 the first printed proofs were being corrected, and by 1780 two-

---

[39] Moreau 1436, fol. 6, letter in which Sainte-Palaye argues that the Crown should acquire Barbazan's manuscript for the Royal Library. Cf. also letter from Mercier de Saint-Léger to Tobiéson-Duby, December, 1789, reprinted in *Bull. Soc. Hist. de France* (2ᵉ série, 1861), 3:22–23.

[40] P. C. Lévesque, 'Notice historique sur Le Grand d'Aussy,' p. iv, in *Vie d'Apollon de Tyane*, par Pierre-Jean-Baptiste Le Grand d'Aussy (Paris, 1807).

[41] Bréquigny 165, fols. 208–9, letter from Le Grand to Bréquigny, 26.3.1781.

[42] *Bull. Soc. Hist. de France* (2ᵉ série, 1861), 3:24–29. Sainte-Palaye's continued activity is attested to both by his correspondence with Bréquigny in 1764–65, which is full of reports on the progress of the Glossary and shows his mood varying as he feels the work is advancing or being held up, and by notes, queries, additions, and suggestions in his hand in the manuscript. Moreover, most of the articles were written up in the first person, which suggests that they were prepared from notes by Sainte-Palaye; two complete articles are in his hand entirely ('Hait,' Moreau 1616, fols. 110–15, and 'Langue,' Moreau 1619, fols. 667–707).

thirds of the first volume had come off the presses. In the spring of 1781, however, Sainte-Palaye died, entrusting the completion of his life's work to his favorite pupil Georges-Jean Mouchet, who had worked with him for twenty years.

After Sainte-Palaye's death the fortunes of the Glossary went from bad to worse. He had sold his copies of manuscripts to the King, retaining the use of them during his lifetime only. Soon after he died they were transported to the *Dépôt des Chartes* in the Place Vendôme, and Mouchet was left with only the alphabetical lists compiled by Sainte-Palaye before the new plan was adopted in 1762.[43] As Mouchet had constantly to refer to Sainte-Palaye's manuscripts and transcripts of manuscripts, all of which had been annotated with a view to the Dictionary, this was a grievous blow. Bréquigny asked Moreau to intervene,[44] but the latter had no interest in the Glossary and would do nothing.[45]

Mouchet had recourse to the original manuscripts at the Royal and Saint-Germain libraries, but with the best will in the world he could not have finished the Glossary without Sainte-Palaye's own copies. Publication was finally made virtually impossible by the outbreak of the Revolution.

In the early years of the nineteenth century, however, the re-constituted Institut National des Sciences et Arts began to consider compiling an historical *Dictionnaire de la langue française* as a companion volume to the *Dictionnaire de l'Académie Française*. In the course of the discussions Camus recalled Sainte-Palaye's unfinished work and suggested that the material, which was pre-served at the Bibliothèque Nationale, could be used as a basis for the new Dictionary, and the main lines of Sainte-Palaye's plan adopted. Copies of the part of the Glossary which had been printed were circulated among the assembly, whereupon "elle a exprimé son voeu pour que le dictionnaire fût continué."[46] The task was entrusted to Mouchet, as was only right, but within a short time poor Mouchet also died. The project was allowed to lapse,[47] and

[43] *Bull. Soc. Hist. de France* (2ᵉ série, 1861), 3:24–29.

[44] Bréquigny 66, fols. 171–75 contains several drafts of a letter in which he begs financial assistance to allow Mouchet to finish the work.

[45] Moreau's reply, dated 14.2.1781, is in Bréquigny 163, fol. 183.

[46] *Mémoires de l'Institut National des Sciences et Arts, Section Littérature et Beaux-Arts* (an XII), 5:26–27.

[47] Four volumes of a *Dictionnaire historique de la langue française* were in fact published by the Académie Française from 1865 to 1894. The editors avowed their

lay forgotten for nearly three-quarters of a century until Favre took it up again in 1875. By that time the practical value of Sainte-Palaye's work had been considerably reduced.

Nevertheless, the results obtained by Sainte-Palaye both in scope and in precise definition stand up well to comparison with other contemporary dictionaries of the medieval languages. They far surpass anything available until then in French. There were various glossaries accompanying historical compilations (Lobineau's *Histoire de Bretagne*) and re-editions of early texts (the *Roman de la Rose*, the *Chansons* of Thibaut de Navarre, Beaumanoir's *Coutumes du Beauvaisis*, Joinville's *Histoire de Saint-Louis*, the *fabliaux*, Villon, Rabelais, Marot, etc.), but these were sparse and had a strictly limited application. Lacombe's *Dictionnaire de l'ancien langage françois* (1766) was a small work aimed at the general reader and designed to facilitate understanding of common medieval literary texts.[48] It listed only meanings and was in no sense an instrument of research. Lacombe did not aim at completeness. In the Old French dictionary he compiled from Du Cange's *Glossarium*, Carpentier offered only the skeleton of a finished work. Where Du Cange had provided generous coverage of the medieval Latin vocabulary and had handled its variants and Romance forms fairly attentively, Carpentier failed to do justice to either vocabulary or variants. Even Barbazan's projected dictionary, which alone might have offered serious competition to Sainte-Palaye's Glossary, was apparently in no sense a completed work. Like Sainte-Palaye, Barbazan had cast his dictionary on historical lines "ayant eu soin," as his publisher remarked, "de marquer les différens siècles où les Auteurs qu'il cite ont écrit,"[49] and it was intended to include some 25,000 words with their etymologies.[50]

debt to Sainte-Palaye's manuscript (vol. 1, 'Avertissement,' p. viii), and drew on his material to illustrate pre-seventeenth-century usage and for early idiomatic expressions. In general, however, this dictionary did not look further back than the sixteenth century. Publication ceased at the letter *Az* and was never resumed.

[48] Lacombe claimed a great deal for his dictionary. It was to be "utile aux Légistes, Notaires, Archivistes, Généalogistes, etc. Propre à donner une idée du Génie, des Mœurs de chaque siècle et de la tournure d'esprit des Auteurs; et nécessaire pour l'intelligence des Loix d'Angleterre, publiées en France, depuis Guillaume le Conquérant jusqu'à Edouard III" (title-page of the 1766 edition). It could hardly have fulfilled any of these functions well.

[49] 'Avis du libraire' in 1756 edition of *Fabliaux et contes*, reprinted in 1808 in Méon edition, vol. 3, pp. i–ii.

[50] E. Barbazan, *Fabliaux et contes*, ed. Méon (Paris, 1808), Préface, vol. 3, p. xxvi.

But Mercier de Saint-Leger, who knew Barbazan's work and admired it, declared that it "ne peut pas être considéré comme un livre fini à beaucoup près. Un très grand nombre de mots y manque; plusieurs articles y sont absolument croqués."[51]

To Sainte-Palaye completeness seemed vital, both with regard to vocabulary and with regard to variants.[52] He reproached earlier editors of glossaries not so much with ignorance, as Barbazan had done, as with having shirked or omitted difficult words and with having neglected to seek out variants.[53] The plan he adopted allowed for a far greater amount of information about each word than any dictionary had hitherto supplied. First, the word was defined grammatically, and any peculiarities, like change of gender, duly noted. A brief summary of meanings followed, in the most likely order of evolution. The variant forms were then listed, and an attempt made to trace the etymology of the word. Each meaning was then taken in turn, enlarged upon, illustrated by quotations from texts, and guaranteed by precise references. Occasion-

---

[51] *Bull. Soc. Hist. de France*, (2ᵉ série, 1861), 3:24–29. A suggestion by Déy in *Bull. Soc. des Sciences Historiques de l'Yonne*, 1858, reprinted by Favre, vol. 10, pp. xxvii–xxviii, that Bréquigny's 1762 plan owed something to Barbazan, and that the latter's work was an improvement on the original plan seems to have been denied in advance by Bréquigny, who wrote of Barbazan's work: "Il est composé selon le plan des lexiques ordinaires, qui ne ressemble en rien à celui qu'on avoit suivi dans la rédaction du Glossaire de M. de Sainte-Palaye. D'ailleurs je sais que toutes les fois que M. Mouchet, qui a entre les mains l'ouvrage de M. Barbazan, a voulu y avoir recours, il n'y a rien apperçu qui ne soit parmi les matériaux que M. de Sainte-Palaye avoit rassemblés." (*Bull. Soc. Hist. de France*, 2ᵉ série, 1861, 3:29.) The MS of Barbazan's glossary is in B.N. Français 9189.

[52] Even while the MS was being remodeled to make it conform with the 1762 plan, he continued to search for new variants. (Bréquigny, 165, fol. 57, to Bréquigny 23.6.1764: "J'ai fini . . . les 3 glossaires particuliers des XI et XII siècles et des commencements du XIII." Also *ibid.*, fol. 74, to Bréquigny, 10.3.1766: "Je viens d'achever les insertions que m'ont fourni [sic] les auteurs et les titres des 11ᵉ, 12ᵉ et 13ᵉ siècles.") Some articles (e.g. 'Occasion,' Moreau 1625, fols. 63–70, 'Raembre,' Moreau 1635, fols. 232–34) contain a large number of additional variants written into the margins or on paper slips glued to the quarto sheets of the MS. Even between the MS and the printed version new variants were added. The printed version, for instance, contains references to Berne MSS 354 and 389, though these are not found in the MS. Similarly, new variants were written into the margins of the printer's proofs to be incorporated in the final text.

There was also constant revision of the meanings, e.g., the article *Soudée* (Moreau 1641, fols. 493–98) which carries the indication—"Examiner soigneusement et faire plusieurs changements dans l'ordre des significations." Several articles were altered or added to between the first or second proofs and the final text.

[53] Bréquigny 62, fol. 215. A sample of entries under the letters AA–AB in the dictionaries of Ménage, Carpentier, Lacombe, and Sainte-Palaye gave the following figures: Ménage 15, Carpentier 108, Lacombe 61 plus 91 in the *Supplément*-152, Sainte-Palaye 219. The results of this sample will be found to be valid generally.

ally, an effort was made to explain how the word developed semantically. The fifth part of each entry was taken up with idiomatic or particular uses, common expressions, and proverbs. Finally, when the entry was a verb, there was a sixth section, in which every attested form of the verb was listed in alphabetical order and its place in the conjugation determined. All words or variants, from parts of verbs to idiomatic expressions, were accompanied by at least one textual reference, noted with minute precision.

The sources of the Glossary were immensely rich and varied. Manuscript romances, *fabliaux* and *coutumiers*, legal documents, historical works, and chronicles in private and public collections in France, Switzerland, and Italy were drawn upon, as were also early printed editions and the dictionaries and compilations of Borel, Bourgoing, Corneille, Du Cange, Laurière, La Martinière, Ménage, Monet, Nicot, Pasquier, Oudin, and Trippault. No stone was left unturned. Dialect survivals or parallel modern usages were invoked to help explain Old French expressions,[54] and even monumental evidence was exploited on occasion.[55] Such lacunae as there are in Sainte-Palaye's sources were on the whole unavoidable.

The weakest part of the work was the etymological part. Sainte-Palaye was not guilty of some of the grosser misconceptions of his contemporaries about the morphology of Old French,[56] but no eighteenth-century scholar could claim to have mastered it. It was not generally realized, for instance, that French words usually derive from the *casus communis* of the Latin—though Barbazan did occasionally refer to an ablative form. This led to etymological

---

[54] E.g., articles *Aire* (Moreau 1589, fols. 97–98), *Brandon* (Moreau 1594, fols. 260–62), *Chaitiver* (Moreau 1597, fol. 62).

[55] E.g., article *Jacque* (Moreau 1618, fols. 22–29) where he refers to an "estampe tirée d'après un ancien monument du 12ᵉ ou 13ᵉ siècle." He does not appear to have used coins, seals, or tombstones, however.

[56] Cf. *Mercure*, June, 1741, pp. 1358–68, 'Dissertation par le R. P. Texte sur le jour du décès et le lieu de la sépulture du coeur de la Princesse Jeanne de Chatillon.' Following the passage "li Evesques d'Orliens, M. de Chatillon, li Connestables, li Chantres de Bayeux" the author comments: "Le pluriel pour le singulier étoit alors une élégance." (!) Some Academicians were no wiser, e.g., Duclos in a 'Mémoire sur l'Origine et les Révolutions des Langues Celtique et Françoise' (*MAI* 15:565 et seq., 17:171 et seq., 1740 and 1741): "On peut faire une remarque sur nos anciens écrivains, soit en vers, soit en prose; c'est qu'ils écrivent presque toujours les pluriels sans *s*, et qu'ils en mettent au singulier. C'est peut-être à cet ancien usage qu'il faut rapporter celui d'écrire avec une *s* finale la seconde personne du singulier de l'indicatif des verbes dont l'infinitif se termine en *-er: tu aimes, tu enseignes*, etc." (17:186).

confusions. Thus Sainte-Palaye gave *antecessor* (instead of *antecessore–m*) as the etymology of *ancesseur*, while for *ancestre* (*antecessor*) he had to suppose a combination of *ains* and *être*. This was pure conjecture, based neither on any attested form nor on understanding of the general principles of development from Latin to French.

The phonology of Old French was just as imperfectly known to eighteenth-century scholars as its morphology, despite efforts by Sainte-Palaye and others to determine pronunciation by an examination of the rhyme and meter of medieval vernacular poetry.[57] On the whole, scholars concentrated on external features and relied almost entirely on orthography as a guide to the etymology of words. In the absence of a firm grasp of morphology and phonology, however, spelling was a treacherous guide. Sainte-Palaye's derivation of *adaiser* from *doigt*, for instance, reveals a whole chain of superficial analogies. The form *adoiser* led him to *doigt*, he relates, and this derivation seemed substantiated by a parallel development of the noun and of the verb, *doigt* and *dés*, which he considered doublets, having given rise to the twin forms *adoiser* and *adeser* (or *adaiser*). Rough and ready semantic connections, unsubstantiated by any historical evidence, made the hypothesis appear reasonable. Many other examples bear witness to the same haphazard method of conjecturing.[58]

History, orthography, semantics, and the comparison of medieval Latin and French versions of the same text were not enough to determine the origin of words with precision, and eighteenth century etymology, despite rejection of the excessive Hellenism,

---

[57] Sainte-Palaye tried to determine pronunciation by analyzing the rhyme and meter of medieval verse (Moreau 1724, fol. 105); Mouchet (Moreau 1722, fols. 124–40), Barbazan ('Dissertation sur l'origine de la langue françoise,' in his *L'Ordène de Chevalerie* [Lausanne, 1759]) and Sainte-Palaye (article 'Z' in Glossary, Moreau 1644, fol. 371) investigated orthographic changes and tried to find regular patterns.

[58] The frequent coupling of *tout* with *adies*, a variant of *ades*, led him to suppose that *adies* was Lat. *tota dies*, which had undergone the same semantic change as *incessamment*. (Cf. *Projet d'un Glossaire*, p. x.) He seems to have had second thoughts in this instance, however, and later reverted to Ménage's *ad ipsum tempus*. It was spelling and semantic associations, likewise, which made him derive *fief*, from "fié, fier, et fiance, termes qui répondent à fidel ou féal, fidélité ou féauté. Ce sentiment peut estre appuyé sur ce qu'on trouve dans les plus anciennes éditions fié sans f à la fin." (Moreau 1611, fol. 529.) For other examples, see my article 'Old French Scholarship in the Eighteenth Century,' *French Studies* (1959), 12:346–61.

Hebraism, or *celtomanie* of some earlier scholars, still had the character of a hit-or-miss conjectural art, rather than that of a scientific method. Political prejudices rather than scientific hypotheses were still at the root of many etymologies. Barbazan, for instance, introduced the Romanist-Germanist debate about the origins of the monarchy into language studies by rejecting Pasquier, Fauchet, and Du Cange, expressing contempt for Ménage, of whose etymologies he claimed only 25 per cent were accurate,[59] and maintaining obstinately that all the words in French derive from Latin.[60] Thus he traced *mark* to Latin *margo* (*margine–m*), *franc* to *fractum* (p.p. of *frangere*), *troupe* to *turba*, and *bourg* to *urbs*, rejecting the customary Frankish derivations *mark*, *frank*, *thorp*, and *burg*.[61] An example of his reasoning in matters of etymology is the word *bec*, the origin of which he discovered, not in Celtic, where it was usually sought, but in Latin *vectum* (*vehere*). "Qu'est en effet un bec," he asks, "sinon un conduit, un canal pour introduire la nourriture des oiseaux dans leur estomac?"[62] Sainte-Palaye was capable of committing errors every bit as gross as Barbazan's, as for instance, when he derived Old French *oil* from *ou il, je l'oi*, meaning *je l'entends, cela est entendu!*[63]

At best, Sainte-Palaye can claim to have been less sanguine or affirmative than some of his contemporaries and to have introduced his etymologies as no more than tentative suggestions, sometimes refraining from publishing them altogether if he felt they were too conjectural,[64] and frequently presenting a case for several possible theories.

Despite limitations, the Glossary was the most ambitious lexicographical undertaking of the century, and its appearance was anticipated eagerly by scholars and *philosophes* throughout France. Barthélémy considered it "un travail si prodigieux qu'il est difficile de concevoir qu'un seul homme ait pu former et exécuter ce

---

[59] Barbazan, 'Dissertation sur l'origine de la langue françoise,' p. 3, in *L'Ordène de Chevalerie* (Lausanne, 1759); and 'Dissertation sur la langue des Celtes' in *Le Castoiement ou l'Instruction d'un père à son fils* (Lausanne, 1760), pp. 62, 97.

[60] *Fabliaux et contes*, vol. 3, Preface, p. xxvii.

[61] 'Dissertation sur la Langue des Celtes,' p. 21.   [62] *Ibid.*

[63] 'Remarques sur la langue françoise,' *MAI* 24:682, and in the Glossary. (Moreau 1625, fol. 696.)

[64] Thus, under *Hait* (Moreau 1616, fol. 113v.): "A l'égard de l'etymologie de *hait* je n'en parlerois pas. Je soupçonne pourtant qu'il vient de l'Italien *aitare, aider* (du Latin *adjutare* et *aita, aide*) et qu'on a dit *cela me haite* comme on a dit en latin *hoc me juvat, cela me plaît*."

projet."[65] Bréquigny wrote that it "paroît par son importance mériter de faire époque dans l'histoire de la littérature françoise."[66] Court de Gébelin considered it greater than anything achieved by antiquity, a triumph of modern research and scholarship. Regretting that Varro did not make a complete Latin dictionary, he observed that "il étoit réservé à notre siècle de produire un Ouvrage de ce genre et plus étendu encore; un Ouvrage qui offre tous les mots de la Langue Françoise depuis dix siècles: et ce qui est plus surprenant encore, une seule personne a eu le courage de l'exécuter: cinquante ans de travaux n'ont pu la rebuter: que l'Antiquité eût été fière d'un pareil travail!"[67]

The lexicographers of the nineteenth century knew of the Glossary and exploited the manuscript freely. Roquefort criticized his predecessor's disproportionate preoccupation with fifteenth- and sixteenth-century sources as compared with those of the twelfth and thirteenth centuries. Nonetheless, he pleaded that Sainte-Palaye's work should be completed. "Le vaste recueil de Sainte-Palaye est un prodigieux amas de matériaux qui n'attendent plus qu'une Société laborieuse pour les mettre en oeuvre," he declared.[68] He himself consulted Mouchet and used the manuscripts at the Bibliothèque Nationale for his own work.[69] A decade later Raynouard was making efforts to obtain one of the rare copies of the eighteenth-century volume.[70] He may very well also have consulted the manuscripts. Littré paid generous tribute to his predecessor and acknowledged his indebtedness to Sainte-Palaye's manuscripts.[71] Only Godefroy, curiously enough, does not mention Sainte-Palaye's manuscripts in the Preface to his Dictionnaire de l'ancienne

---

[65] Correspondance inédite du Comte de Caylus, 2:272.

[66] Bréquigny 66, fol. 171.

[67] Monde primitif, 'Grammaire universelle' (2d ed.; Paris, 1774), 2:415.

[68] J. B. Roquefort, Mémoire sur la nécessité d'un glossaire général de la langue française (Paris, 1811).

[69] J. B. Roquefort, Glossaire de la langue romane (Paris, 1808), vol. 1, Preface, pp. iv–v.

[70] In Francis Douce's copy of Roquefort's Glossaire at the Bodleian Library in Oxford, there is inserted a letter dated "Paris ce 5 7bre, 1817" and addressed to "Monsieur Raynouard, Secrétaire Perpétuel de l'Académie Françoise, au Palais de l'Institut." The text runs: "Monsieur, La personne qui nous avoit vendu le volume du glossaire in folio n'en avoit plus il y a déjà longtemps, ce ne seroit donc que par hazard que nous pourrions en retrouver un. Nous allons le faire chercher, et si nous pouvons l'avoir, nous vous le remettrons aussitôt." The letter is signed de Burie frères, Libraires du Roi et de la Bibliothèque du Roi. It is likely that the Glossary in question was Sainte-Palaye's.

[71] Littré, Dictionnaire (ed. 1863), vol. 1, Preface, p. xxxix.

langue française, but a considerable number of articles in this work do contain acknowledgements to Sainte-Palaye for quotations and references.

2. Contributions to the History of the French Language

By the eighteenth century, Fauchet's advice that the search for the universal *Ursprache* should be abandoned had largely been followed.[72] To Enlightenment scholars, reared on Bayle and Fontenelle, the universal *Ursprache* belonged to the domain of unverifiable speculation and of fable. Falconet spoke for most of them when he declared that it was enough to investigate the immediate sources of the French language "sans rechercher trop curieusement le premier lieu d'où elle coule, et par là s'exposer au risque de se perdre dans l'antiquité la plus reculée."[73]

There was no contradiction between the interest of the eighteenth century scholar in general questions such as the relation of language and thought and his refusal to entertain far-reaching and unverifiable hypotheses about the historical origins of existing languages. The investigation of remote origins almost always involved supernatural or mythical elements; the scholars were determined to avoid these and to reason empirically, if not always from observed facts, then at least from hypotheses which were in principle verifiable and which the existing body of knowledge seemed to render plausible. The study of the historical sources of French meant the study of the relations between the modern Romance tongues and the languages of ancient Greece and Rome, the Germanic and Nordic languages, and the tongues of the indigenous peoples who had inhabited the territory of the Romania before the Roman conquests.

As linguistic questions were politically significant, research into the origins of the Romance tongues had begun at an early date. Although there were some who argued that French was descended mainly from Celtic, Frankish, or even Greek, two principal theories dominated scholarship from the Middle Ages onward. According to one of them, the Romance tongues derived from classical Latin corrupted by the Barbarian invaders; according to the other, they

[72] *Recueil de l'origine de la langue et poésie françoise: rymes et romans* (ed. Espiner-Scott, Paris, 1938), p. 27.
[73] 'Principes de l'étymologie par rapport à la langue françoise,' *MAI* 20:8.

owed very little to the Barbarians but had grown naturally and uninterruptedly out of a different Latin from classical Latin. The first theory, it might be said tentatively, was better suited in France to the political theory of the nobility or even of the corporate state, the second to that of a strong monarchy, allied to the bourgeoisie. Dante in the thirteenth century, Aretino in the fifteenth, Henri Estienne in the sixteenth, Celso Cittadini in the early seventeenth held one form or another of the second theory, namely that classical Latin was an artificial literary and grammatical creation which had been forged out of the vulgar spoken Latin of Rome at a certain point in history but which had in no way superseded the spoken tongue.[74] The latter continued to develop along its own lines throughout the "classical" period of Roman letters—it was argued—and, according to Cittadini, traces of it were visible in Plautus, even in Virgil and Cicero, as well as in the late Latin of the last centuries of the Empire and of the Dark Ages. The origin of the Romance vernaculars was to be found in this spoken Latin and not in classical literary Latin corrupted by the Barbarians. Cittadini's theory was revived in the early eighteenth century by Scipione Maffei. According to Maffei, the phonological and grammatical evolution which differentiated the Romance languages from Latin (dropping of final *m*, break-up of declensions through confusion and use of prepositions, formation of the periphrastic past tense, etc.) had been completed before the Barbarian invasions and before the political disintegration of the Empire. On the basis of this elaboration of Cittadini, Maffei believed he could affirm vigorously that "tutta da capo a piedi è Latina la lingua nostra."[75]

Cittadini and his predecessors gave little weight to either superstratum or substratum. Other scholars, however, emphasized the role of the Barbarian invasions. One of the earliest Italian antiquaries, Flavius Blondus, had argued against Aretino that, while there was a popular speech in ancient Rome, it differed only in

[74] Dante, *De Vulg. Eloq.*, 1, 9, ed. Marigo (Florence, 1938), pp. 72–73; M. Vitale, 'Sommario di una storia degli studi linguistici romanzi,' pp. 13, 44–47, in A. Viscardi etc., *Preistoria e storia degli studi romanzi* (Milan-Varese, 1955), and F. Brunot, *Histoire de la langue françoise des origines à 1900* (Paris, 1905), 1:4.

[75] *Verona illustrata* (Verona, 1732). 'Dell' Istoria di Verona,' bk. 11, col. 320. On the whole question of Vulgar Latin, see Urban T. Holmes, 'The Vulgar Latin Question and the Origin of the Romance Tongues,' *Studies in Philology* (1928), 25:51–61.

tone and not in substance from classical Latin.[76] The vulgar Latin of Imperial Rome, he claimed, was far removed from the contemporary languages of Italy, France, and Spain. In Blondus' view, the modern tongues derived from classical Latin transformed by the Barbarians. The process of change had begun in the provinces and among Romans with Barbarian slaves, and had then set in in Rome herself on the fall of the city.[77] Blondus' theory was widely held in the Italian *Quattrocento*, and by the sixteenth century had become a commonplace in France and Spain too.[78] But the question of the prehistory of the Romance languages, more obvious in the case of France and of Spain than in that of Italy, was also considered by Fauchet and by Spanish writers like Juan de Valdés. Fauchet recognized the existence of a Celtic substratum in French, though he did not determine its precise role.

In the work of Ménage and Du Cange, the ideas of sixteenth-century scholars such as Fauchet and Pasquier were given a substantial foundation in careful research among the written sources of the Imperial, and above all, of the Early Medieval periods. Ménage looked for most of his etymologies in Latin, but particularly in "la basse Latinité," while he also took account of "un nombre infini de mots Gaulois et Allemans qui sont demeurez en nostre langue."[79] Du Cange, with his stupendous knowledge of early medieval Latin and of Old French, was able to give the most carefully documented account of the development from Latin to modern French which had yet appeared. He accepted that even in classical times Latin was subject to mutations and alterations, but he seems not to have questioned that these mutations and alterations were made to classical Latin. For him, the main causes of the corruption of Latin (the phrase itself is significant) were the different local speech characteristics in the Roman Provinces and the invasions of the Barbarians. The decline of the political power of Rome, he argued, accelerated a process of corruption which had already started with the weakening of the classical tradition in

[76] Flavius Blondus, 'De Verbis Romanae Locutionis,' in the form of a letter to Leonardo Bruni in 1435, in *Scritti inediti e rari di Biondo Flavio*, ed. B. Nogara (Rome, 1927), sec. 9, p. 121 (*Studi e Testi*, 48).

[77] *Ibid.*, sec. 25, p. 129.

[78] Cf. Vitale, pp. 34–42; and Harri Meier, *Die Entstehung der romanischen Sprachen und Nationen* (Frankfurt a.M., 1941), p. 10.

[79] *Origines de la langue françoise* (Paris, 1650), 'Épistre à Monsieur du Puy, Conseiller du Roy en ses Conseils.'

Imperial times. While Du Cange thus saw the origin of the modern vernaculars in a corruption of literary Latin itself, he had a vivid picture of the uninterrupted historical development of which the existing vulgar tongues were the end product. For him they were, in fact, a living form of Latin. Latin was in this sense not extinct, since it had simply devolved into the languages of the erstwhile provinces of the Empire.[80]

Du Cange's views dominated French linguistic scholarship in the seventeenth century. The question of the differentiation of French from its Latin parent remained largely a question of the influence of Celtic substratum and Frankish superstratum on classical Latin. French was widely held to be a synthesis of Latin, Celtic, and Germanic, a view which paralleled in a remarkable way the theory of the corporate state held by many men of the parlements. Few, however, of those who expounded this theory at the end of the seventeenth or the beginning of the eighteenth century—Huet, Fénelon, Massieu[81]—explained the precise nature of the synthesis. Even in the mid-eighteenth century amateurs like Duclos and Lacombe[82] remained vague about it.

At the turn of the century, however, a re-examination of the process by which French became differentiated from Latin had been begun in scholarly circles, prompted partly by a controversy among ecclesiastics, between advocates and opponents of reform, as to whether Latin had become unintelligible to the people at an early stage or whether—as the reformers argued—it had still been widely used as late as the eleventh century,[83] and partly by a growing interest among critics and defenders of absolutism alike in the social and political history of France in the Merovingian period. Most of the research was carried out by the Benedic-

[80] 'De Causis Corrupt. Lat.' in *Gloss. Med. et Inf. Lat.*, ed. Favre (1883), vol. I, pp. xx–xxix.

[81] P. D. Huet, *Origine des romans* (Paris, 1711), p. 160; Fénelon, 'Lettre sur les occupations de l'Académie Françoise' (1714), *Oeuvres* (Paris, 1821), 21:161; Abbé Massieu, *Histoire de la poésie françoise* (Paris, 1739 [posthumously published]), pp. 98–112.

[82] Duclos, 'Mémoire sur l'origine et les révolutions des langues celtique et françoise,' *MAI* 15:565 (read in 1740); Lacombe, 'Coup d'oeil sur l'origine, sur les progrès de la langue et de la poésie françoises,' etc. in *Supplément au Diction-naire de l'ancien langage françois* (Paris, 1768), p. i.

[83] Cf. Dom Liron, *Singularités historiques et littéraires*, 2:103–33 (Paris, 1738), 'De l'origine de la langue françoise, dissertation où on recherche en quel temps elle a commencé à devenir vulgaire.' The essay was directed against points in Arnauld's *Défense de l'Écriture sainte* (1688). For a general account see Brunot, 1:1–17.

tines and by the members of the Académie des Inscriptions, and several important papers were read at the Academy's meetings. Sainte-Palaye followed these carefully before stepping into the arena himself.

Developing an idea already propounded by Trippault in his *Celt-Hellénisme*, and more recently by Pezron in his *Antiquités de la nation et de la langue des Celtes* (Paris, 1703), Lévesque de la Ravalière urged that the problem of the differentiation of French from Latin was a spurious one: Latin had never been widely spoken in Gaul and had always had to be acquired even by the upper classes as a foreign tongue. Though there had been an immense accretion of Latin words to the Celtic infrastructure of French, the basis of the language—the morphology and the syntax —had not been altered. For Lévesque, French was a continued development from Celtic, a development of which the Roman occupation of Gaul was only one phase, albeit—he admitted—an important one.[84]

Although Lévesque's ideas were not taken very seriously by scholars,[85] the fact that he had read his paper at the Académie des Inscriptions made a public reply from his opponents necessary. It came from the pen of Dom Rivet, the Benedictine editor of the *Histoire littéraire de la France*.[86]

Lévesque had distinguished between Latin, which had always been a learned language in Gaul, and the spoken language ("la naturelle et la populaire") which, according to him, "fut d'abord la Celtique, ou Gaulois pur, sur lequel les Romains et les Francs ont enté, pour ainsi dire, la leur alternativement." Rivet, on the other hand, set out to prove that the difference between the written and the spoken language of Gaul was not nearly so great as Lévesque supposed and that a real distinction between Latin and the vernac-

---

[84] Lévesque de la Ravalière: 'Sur la langue vulgaire de la Gaule,' *MAI** 23:244. Lévesque's ideas are summarized by Dom Rivet in the 'Avertissement' to vol. 7 of the *Histoire littéraire de la France*, where a letter from Lévesque to the Benedictines expounding his views is also printed (p. ii).

[85] Lévesque readily agreed that "toute son Académie est contre lui." (Nouv. Acq. Fr. 803, fol. 160, Lefebvre to Grosley, 16.1.1748.) He had a reputation as a lover of paradox (*ibid.*, fol. 205, Dom Tallandier to Grosley, 13.6.1743), and his friends at the Academy seem to have thought at first that he was playing an amusing game in reviving this old controversy. When it became apparent that he was serious, they were embarrassed and deserted him *en masse*. (*Ibid.*, fol. 174, Lefebvre to Grosley, undated.)

[86] *Histoire littéraire de la France* (1746), vol. 7, pp. vi–lxxxiv.

ular arose only in the ninth and tenth centuries. He adduced two main arguments to support his contention. In the first place, the use of Latin by the Church at a time when it was trying to convert the pagan populations of the Empire to Christianity was inexplicable—Rivet claimed—if it is assumed that the people did not understand Latin; and since there was little opportunity for education among ordinary people, they could only have understood Latin by constant use of it in their daily lives. Rivet admits that in all probability this spoken Latin was "ni pur ni poli." Nonetheless, it remained recognizably Latin. "Il en est de même de notre langue Françoise, de nos jours," he explained. "On la parle dans toutes nos Provinces, où elle a différents dialectes. Il y a cependant quelques gents de la campagne qui ne l'entendent pas encore, et un plus grand nombre qui l'entend et ne la parle point. Elle n'en est pas moins la langue vulgaire du Roiaume."[87] Secondly, Rivet claimed, if Latin had been a language which was not spoken in daily life but learned according to grammatical rules and only by the educated, it would be hard to account for its constant evolution throughout the period from the fifth to the tenth centuries. The fact is that through all its changes it was still felt to be Latin, and consciousness of a vernacular tongue distinct from Latin emerged only about the ninth century, when the vulgar began to be cultivated for its own sake. Thereafter, Latin did become a learned language, Rivet concluded, and there is no further evidence of change after that date.

A similar account of the evolution of French from Latin had already been read to the Académie des Inscriptions by Sainte-Palaye's friend and fellow citizen Jean Le Beuf in 1741. In his *Refléxions sur les plus anciennes traductions en langue françoise*, Le Beuf had argued that a clear awareness of French as a language different from Latin is attested only in the ninth century. Although earlier documents hint at a growing separation of the written and the spoken language before this time, nevertheless, many of the changes one can suppose took place in the spoken language were reflected—Le Beuf claimed—in the written documents. As early as the sixth century endings were disappearing, syllables were being dropped or contracted, and demonstrative adjectives were taking on a new function as articles in charters, decrees, and an-

[87] *Ibid.*, p. xx.

nals. By the ninth century Latin had become so "rustique" that it no longer bore any resemblance to the Latin of the classical writers.[88] The very equation of "latin rustique" with "roman," however, indicates that Le Beuf saw French not as a new language but as a living phase of Latin, the slow maturing of which could be traced through the written sources of the whole Merovingian period.

Neither Rivet nor Le Beuf had questioned that classical Latin was at the origin of the entire movement toward modern French. It was this assumption which Bonamy set out to challenge in two papers he read to the Académie des Inscriptions in 1751: *Réflexions sur la langue latine vulgaire* and *Mémoire sur l'introduction de la langue latine dans les Gaules sous la domination des Romains.* Bonamy may or may not have been aware of the theories of Aretino and Cittadini; he was certainly familiar with the work of Muratori, which had been published in 1739, and about which Sainte-Palaye himself may well have informed his colleagues.

Muratori had not questioned that the Romance vernaculars grew out of the corruption of Latin, but he had been curious about the timing and the manner of the evolution of one language into so many.[89] He had accepted for France and Spain the current theory that the substratum had considerably altered the character of the language introduced into these territories by their Roman conquerors and that the Gothic and Frankish invaders accelerated and left their mark on a process of corruption that was already in full swing. But the causes by which Du Cange had been able to account for the beginnings of the French dialects—the isolation of the province and the collapse of Roman power—could not, in his view, account for the growth of the Italian dialects, especially those of central Italy and of Rome herself. Muratori had, therefore, looked for the origin of these dialects further back in a vulgar speech contemporary with classical Latin and in many cases strongly influenced by pre-Roman Italic substrata.[90] He had thus bypassed classical Latin and set the earliest origins of dialectalization in the common speech of the people of Rome and of the Italian provinces during the classical period itself.

[88] *MAI* 17:710–12.
[89] *Antiquitates Italicae Medii Aevi* (Milan, 1739), vol. 2, col. 989.
[90] *Ibid.*, col. 992; also col. 989, 1011, 1013–14.

Taking his cue from Muratori, Bonamy contended that Rivet and Le Beuf had not solved the problem of the origins of French fully: "Ce n'est pas assez de dire que la langue latine a été la langue dominante dans les Gaules depuis la conquête des Romains: on laisse toujours subsister les difficultés, si l'on ne commence par attacher une idée nette à ce que l'on entend par ces mots, la langue latine."[91] According to Bonamy, the Latin which was spoken in Gaul was at no time classical Latin, but a popular Latin learned from the soldiers and merchants who had daily contact with the inhabitants of the provinces of the Empire. These merchants and soldiers did not speak the Latin of Livy and Cicero. Theirs was a vulgar form of Latin which had developed steadily, somewhere below the level of the consciously elaborated literary language, from the language of the preclassical period. The documents in which one can find traces of this vulgar tongue are not those where only a few letters have been altered (as *minoere* for *minuere*, *basileca* for *basilica*, *scilecit* for *scilicet*, etc.) but those in which "la construction est absolument contraire à toutes les régles de la grammaire latine, où les verbes et les noms ont des inflexions différentes de celles que les Auteurs latins ont employées, et où l'on n'a aucun égard aux cas, aux genres et aux nombres des noms."[92] Gregory of Tours tells of such a Latin, but, though his language is full of barbarisms, his own writings still fit into a living literary tradition. The vulgar tongue is best sought not in semi-literary productions, which, far removed as they are from the refinements of classical Latin, are nonetheless still written in an elevated style, but in non-literary documents into which elements of the vulgar speech were able to percolate more freely. "Cette latinité . . . où l'on n'avoit égard ni aux genres, ni aux cas, ni aux régimes des verbes et des prépositions, òu les génitifs, les datifs et les ablatifs ne sont point désignés par les terminaisons qui leur sont propres, mais par les prépositions *de, ad, a* et *ab,* qui répondent aux articles François qui différencient nos cas; cette latinité, dis-je, est celle d'un grand nombre de titres, de donations, de jugemens et même de lettres de nos Rois de la première race, lorsqu'elles étoient écrites par des secrétaires qui n'avoient point étudié les règles de la grammaire, et

[91] 'Mémoire sur l'introduction de la langue latine,' *MAI* 24:583.
[92] *Ibid.*, p. 586.

qui ne savoient que *le latin d'usage*."[93] This was Bonamy's first point. Against Rivet, he argues that the origin of the vulgar language of Gaul was not classical Latin; against Lévesque, he argues, on the other hand, that it was not Celtic but a vulgar form of Latin which had grown out of the popular speech of the Romans themselves.[94]

Bonamy's second point is equally interesting. The vulgar Latin of Gaul was common to the entire Romania, he declared: "Ce n'étoit que la langue vulgaire que l'on parloit dans les Gaules, en Espagne et même en Italie. Ce qui différencioit ce jargon étoit la prononciation particulière aux peuples qui l'avoient adopté. J'ai dit même en Italie, car les Italiens dès le sixième siècle n'avoient pas une langue commune plus épurée que les Gaulois: pour s'en convaincre, il n'y a qu'à lire plusieurs titres de ce temps, concernant quelques villes d'Italie . . . On y verra le même Latin dont j'ai donné des exemples (for Gaul). Aussi la langue Italienne n'a-t-elle point une autre origine que la nôtre."[95]

Against the commonly held view that the different Romance languages began to develop independently on the fall of the Empire and the Barbarian invasions, Bonamy puts forward the thesis of a limited linguistic unity in the Romania until a fairly advanced stage, with some variations in pronunciation. Numerous constructions not found in classical writers are common to all the Romance languages, Bonamy observed. The periphrastic past is one, the form *il y avoit* is another, as also is the passive form *j'avais été aimé, j'ai été aimé.* Where modern French exhibits a different form of these constructions from Italian or Spanish (as in French *j'ai été,* Italian *son stato*), the forms adopted by the latter are frequently observed to have been used in Old French as an alternative to the form which ultimately dominated and may sometimes still be found in dialects of modern French. Bonamy felt the novelty of these constructions with respect to classical Latin or even to preclassical

---

[93] 'Réflexions sur le langue latine vulgaire,' *ibid.*, p. 618. Bonamy seems to have come close to the notion of a *lingua dell'uso*, intermediary between the spoken tongue and the literary language; See G. Devoto, *Storia della lingua di Roma* (Bologna, 1940), pp. 345–46, and the same author's *Profilo di storia linguistica italiana* (Florence, 1953), pp. 5–6.

[94] 'Réflexions,' *MAI* 24:640: "Je ne puis trop le répéter, c'est de la langue parlée des Romains que les Gaulois ont appris à parler latin."

[95] *Ibid.*, p. 619.

Latin, in which, following Estienne and many of the Italians, he tended to look for the origin of vulgar Latin vocabulary and syntax.[96] While he rejected the idea that the Germanic invasions provoked a radical change from a classical-type to a vulgar-type Latin, he was thus forced to suggest tentatively, for lack of any other explanation, that the new constructions might be attributed to the influence of the Celtic substratum and/or the Germanic superstratum.

Bonamy's two papers mark a notable contribution to the history of the Romance languages. But they left the question how the vernacular tongues did become differentiated largely unanswered, as he himself acknowledged. "S'il est vrai que dans le cinquième et sixième siècle le peuple parlât la langue Latine, et entendît ceux qui la parloient purement, comment est-il arrivé que quatre ou cinq cens ans après, les descendans de ce même peuple, sans qu'une nouvelle Nation se soit introduite dans les Gaules, en soient venus au point de ne plus entendre la langue de leurs ancêtres?"[97] This was the question which faced Bonamy. "J'avoue que la difficulté est embarrassante," he wrote, invoking somewhat weakly Dante's old idea of the changeableness of all human institutions.

Bonamy had argued himself into a position which posed new problems. Modern scholars who have propounded similar views—notably H. Pirenne[98]—have sought to answer his question in political terms. But Pirenne's ingenious and brilliant account of the shattering of the unity of the Romania has not gone unchallenged, and many scholars hold that it cannot in any case be considered the only factor making for dialectalization.[99]

Writing in the eighteenth century, Bonamy did not fully grasp the variety of the factors which could be brought forward to account for the gradual evolution of the Romance tongues out of vulgar Latin—the substrata, the date of colonization by the Romans, the bilingualism or isolation of certain areas, the decentralization of power within the Empire itself, especially after the reforms

[96] *Ibid.*, pp. 632–35.   [97] *Ibid.*, p. 638.

[98] H. Pirenne, *Mahomet et Charlemagne* (3d ed., Paris and Brussels, 1937), pp. 111–12, 251–52 *et passim*. See also H. F. Muller, *A Chronology of Vulgar Latin* (Halle, 1929), *Zeitschrift für romanische Philologie*, Beiheft 78, and the same writer's more recent *L'Epoque mérovingienne, essai de synthèse de philologie et d'histoire* (New York, 1945).

[99] G. Devoto, *Storia della lingua di Roma* (Bologna, 1940), lays great stress on the substrata and on the effects of Diocletian's administrative reforms.

of Diocletian, the influence of the superstrata, etc. Nor did he per-
ceive the complexity of the relations between the literary language,
the *langue d'usage*, and the language spoken in small intimate
groups.[100] The difficulty of reconstructing the elements of the various different layers of vulgar Latin from the Merovingian texts
consequently also escaped him. Nevertheless, given these limitations, he did see that many late Latin texts like Gregory of Tours
are still closely bound to a literary tradition and do not themselves
represent the spoken language of the period, and he seems to have
appreciated the need to approach the problem of vulgar Latin from
two angles: from the study of texts (literary texts and documents)
on the one hand, and from the comparative study of the medieval
Romance tongues on the other.

Three days after Bonamy read his *Réflexions sur la langue latine
vulgaire* to the Académie des Inscriptions, Sainte-Palaye showed,
in a paper on *La Langue françoise des XIIe et XIIIe siècles comparée avec les langues provençale, italienne et espagnole dans les
mêmes siècles*, what results could be expected from the comparative
method.[101]

Sainte-Palaye was fully apprised of the disagreement between
Lévesque de la Ravalière and the Benedictines. Lévesque, in fact,
tried to persuade him to arbitrate in the dispute,[102] and on Sainte-
Palaye's request supplied a reasoned statement of his arguments.[103]
Although Sainte-Palaye declared that he refused to descend into
the lists in this quarrel,[104] the paper he read in March, 1751, was,
as it turned out, a polite rejoinder to Lévesque. Sainte-Palaye's own
reading rarely took him to texts earlier than the twelfth century,
and he was in no sense a classical philologist. His treatment of the
question of the origins of French was based not on a study of Late
Latin texts, but on a comparative study of the medieval vernacular

---

[100] Cf. Christine Mohrmann, 'Les Formes du latin dit "vulgaire," essai de
chronologie et de systématisation de l'époque augustéenne aux langues romanes,' in
Latin vulgaire, latin des chrétiens, latin médiéval (Paris, 1955), pp. 1–10.

[101] *MAI* 24:671–86.

[102] Lévesque sent Sainte-Palaye an essay in which he expounded his ideas and
the difference between "les RR PP B(énédictins) et moi." A copy of these
'Observations sur la langue parlée dans les Gaules' in Lévesque's hand is in Bréquigny 154, fols. 44–54. Another copy is in Moreau 1723, fols. 239–48.

[103] Bréquigny 154, fol. 46: "Mr DSP demande que je fixe ce que j'entends par
Langue Vulgaire," and fol. 51: "Mr. DSP souhaite encor que je dise de quels mots
étoit composée cette langue vulgaire."

[104] 'Remarques sur la langue françoise des XIIe et XIIIe siècles,' *MAI* 24:672.

tongues themselves. By comparing five of these (Provençal, Italian, Spanish, French, and Gascon) he was able to show that both their vocabulary and their syntax are so strikingly similar that the supposition of a common origin of them all is extremely reasonable. Lévesque's attempt to give French a basis of its own, distinct from that of the other languages of the Romania, was thus dealt a severe blow.

By a more thorough application of the comparative method, Sainte-Palaye also achieved more accurate results than Bonamy. The latter had claimed that in spoken Latin indicative and subjunctive were used indiscriminately, and that this gave a clue to the construction of the Romance future tenses, which were made up, not of the future perfect of deponents, nor from the future of nondeponents—as some had suggested—but from the perfect subjunctive of nondeponents.[105] Examination of medieval texts in the vernacular convinced Sainte-Palaye, on the other hand, that the hypothesis already put forward by Castelvetro and Régnier Desmarets was correct.[106] The Romance futures, he argued, were formed from the infinitive of the verb and the present indicative of *habere*.[107] He adduced examples from Provençal which clearly demonstrated that the future had in fact been constructed from these two component parts: *comptar vos ai* (je vous compterai), *dar vos n'ai* (je vous en donnerai), *cresser vos a d'armes* (il vous accroîtra d'équipages), etc. This construction, like several others, is the same in all five languages, Sainte-Palaye claimed, and facts of this kind must be taken into consideration when considering their origin. Recent scholars have tended to attribute to Raynouard the first serious study of the periphrastic future with *habeo*,[108] just as Raynouard has also been credited with the first edition of Rambauld de Vaqueiras' *Discors plurilingue*.[109] In fact, here as else-

---

[105] Bonamy, 'Réflexions,' *MAI* 24:614.

[106] L. Castelvetro, *Giunta fatta al ragionamento degli articoli e de' verbi di Messer Pietro Bembo* (Modena, 1563), pp. 55–56; Régnier Desmarets, *Grammaire françoise* (Paris, 1706), p. 368 et seq.

[107] 'Remarques,' *MAI* 24: 684–85.

[108] Vitale, p. 89; Carlo Tagliavini, *Le Origini delle lingue neolatine* (2d ed.; Bologna, 1951), 1:9. But Schlegel had already pointed out that Sainte-Palaye discussed the formation of the periphrastic future at length before Raynouard. (A. W. de Schlegel, *Observations sur la langue et sur la littérature provençales* [Paris, 1818], p. 33, n. 18.) Schlegel also observed that the famous *rule of s*, usually attributed to Raynouard, was in fact known to eighteenth century scholars who had studied the Provençal grammar of Ugues Faidit.

[109] Angelo Monteverdi, *Manuale di avviamento agli studi romanzi* (Milan, 1952), pp. 172–76.

where, Raynouard was preceded by Sainte-Palaye. The *Discors plurilingue* was the starting point of almost everything Sainte-Palaye wrote in the 1751 paper and was originally published there.

Sainte-Palaye had taken the first step toward an effective comparative method in philology. It is easy to underestimate this achievement. Interest has shifted in our day from the history of individual linguistic and literary traditions, from philology back to general linguistics, and we can now look with new eyes at the vast comparative schemes proposed by Leibniz and other rationalists and attempted in works such as Chamberlayne's *Oratio dominica in diversas omnium fere gentium linguas versa* (Amsterdam, 1715).[110] But while we have gained by ridding ourselves of the incomprehension displayed by many nineteenth century scholars toward this kind of enterprise, we should lose if we failed to appreciate the originality and the importance of Sainte-Palaye's application of a genetic and comparative method to reconstruct empirically a phase in the historical development of the Romance tongues. Sainte-Palaye could not claim to have settled all the disputes about the origins of French. Indeed, the common future, passive, and preterite constructions of the Romance languages raise problems of which he was only dimly aware.[111] But he had indicated a method which was to prove productive of results in the following century.

In this same paper Sainte-Palaye questioned the idea that Provençal had once been spoken all over France, an idea first mooted by Fauchet, and still held by some of Sainte-Palaye's contempo-

---

[110] Leibniz, a fellow-member with Chamberlayne of the Royal Societies of London and Berlin, may well have prompted Chamberlayne to undertake his work. (See the 'Dissertation' by Leibniz appended to Chamberlayne's *Oratio dominica*, p. 22.) Similar schemes for linguistic comparisons in the *Nouveaux Essais sur l'entendement humain*, bk. 3, and in a letter to Peter the Great of 1716 (*Selections*, ed. P. Wiener [New York, 1957], p. 599), where it is suggested that a compilation be made of the Lord's Prayer, the Ten Commandments, and other common texts in all the languages spoken by the Czar's peoples. For a general account of Leibniz's method, see Guy Harnois, *Les Théories du langage en France de 1660 à 1821* (Paris, n.d.), pp. 76–79.

[111] See H. F. Muller, *A Chronology of Vulgar Latin*, pp. viii, 103, and *L'Époque mérovingienne*, pp. 188–89. The elaboration in common of these constructions is the pivot of Muller's argument in favor of the continued linguistic unity of the *Romania* until about the eighth century. Those who argue in favor of earlier dialectalization (e.g., Devoto, *Storia della lingua di Roma*, pp. 350–52) find some difficulty with this question. Bonamy does seem to have sensed the problems raised by these common constructions, though he offered no considered solution.

raries.[112] Even Le Beuf propounded a version of this theory in his *Recherches sur les plus anciennes traductions*. "Dans la pluspart des provinces des Gaules," he wrote, "on parloit vulgairement une langue peu différente de celle des Provençaux, des Périgourdins, des Limousins. Je pense que cela dura jusqu'à ce que le commerce de ces provinces avec les peuples du Nord et de l'Allemagne, et surtout celui des habitans de l'Armorique avec les Anglois, vers le XI siècle, eussent apporté dans la langue romaine rustique une dureté qui n'y étoit pas auparavant."[113] It is not clear whether Le Beuf thought that the language he claims was spoken throughout Gaul in the ninth and tenth centuries was a common parent of the Northern and Southern dialects, or whether he believed it actually had the characteristics of Provençal. Fauchet had said that this language actually was Provençal, which was later pushed back beyond the Loire and the Rhone. Sainte-Palaye freely admitted the close similarity of the two languages in the early stages of their growth. Even in the twelfth century, he claimed, they were not radically different: "On voit dans quelques . . . poésies . . . des vers purement François entre-mêlés avec des vers Provençaux, tant il étoit aisé de confondre ensemble la langue Françoise de ces temps-là avec la langue Provençale."[114] This was not to say, however—as Le Beuf seemed to imply—that Provençal had once been universally spoken all over Gaul and the Provincia.[115] On the contrary, in Sainte-Palaye's view the Northern and the Southern dialects began to assume their distinctive characteristics at about the same time. His rejection of Provençal as the mother of Old French was patent to his contemporaries. Papon, who held the opposite view, declared that "il laisse entrevoir une opinion dont je m'écarte avec d'autant plus de regret, que penser comme lui sur ce qui regarde les moeurs et la littérature de nos pères, c'est presque une preuve qu'on a découvert la vérité."[116]

---

[112] Claude Fauchet, *Recueil de l'origine de la langue et poésie françoise; rymes et romans*, ed. Espiner-Scott. (Paris, 1938), pp. 56–60. Voltaire appears to have adopted Fauchet's view. ('Essai sur les moeurs,' *Oeuvres*, ed. Moland, 12:57–58).

[113] *MAI* 17:718.   [114] 'Remarques,' *MAI* 24:680–81.

[115] Le Grand d'Aussy, a pupil of Sainte-Palaye, claimed that this was what distinguished Sainte-Palaye's ideas from those of Le Beuf (Le Grand, 'Essay sur la langue, les sciences et la littérature françoises,' B.N. Nouv. Acq. Fr. 6231, fols. 102–5).

[116] Abbé Papon, 'Dissertation sur l'origine et les progrès de la langue provençale,' in his *Histoire générale de Provence* (Paris, 1777–86), 2:472. According to Jean Stefanini, the theory that Provençal was the mother of French, Spanish, and

According to Sainte-Palaye, the difference between the two groups of dialects began to be felt clearly about the end of the twelfth and the beginning of the thirteenth centuries. In support of this thesis, he quoted a *tenson* of Albert de Sisteron which already distinguishes between the *langue d'oc* of Catalonia, Gascony, Provence, Auvergne, Arragon, Limousin, and Dauphiné (Viennois), and a *langue d'oil* spoken in the provinces subject to the two kings (i.e., Northern France and Poitou, between them subject to the Kings of France and England). "Il y a grande apparence," he concluded, "que ces deux dénominations (of *langue d'oc* and *langue d'oil*) avoient été en usage avant une ordonnance de Philippe le Bel de 1304 ou 1305."[117]

One outcome of these discussions, and not the least important, was a growing awareness of the geographical and historical variety and complexity of linguistic phenomena. Brought up in the climate of a humanist culture to think of language as fixed and exemplary, disregarding nonliterary language, the scholars were discovering that the fixed and exemplary language was a kind of epiphenomenon of linguistic reality, an ideal construction resting on a vastly varied, constantly shifting and changing base. The Italian scholars pointed this out in their discussion of classical Latin. The French scholars did so in their investigation of their own language, by showing that it was by no means a single structure with a uniform history. Le Beuf argued that Old French is simply a loose term covering a number of provincial dialects. "Il ne faut pas croire," he had written, "que dans les Gaules, ou même dans ce qui composoit en particulier le royaume de France, le langage vulgaire fût uniforme: la différence des dialectes de la langue romance, ou vulgaire françoise, étoit si grande au XII siècle que le françois qu'on parloit dans le Poitou, par exemple, étoit tout différent de celui qu'on parloit au fond de la province de Reims dans le pays boulonois."[118] Sainte-Palaye was as aware as Le Beuf of the dialectal variety of Old French, and he showed that it was visible even at the level of

---

Italian was almost *de rigueur* among members of Southern academies, although what was usually meant was a cultural and literary, rather than a linguistic priority. ('Le Provençal, langue mère ou langue soeur,' *Actes et Mémoires du 1ᵉʳ Congrès International de langue et littérature du Midi de la France* [1957], pp. 208–11.)

[117] 'Remarques,' *MAI* 24:683, note (i).
[118] 'Recherches sur les plus anciennes traductions,' *MAI* 17:728.

literary expression.[119] This discovery by the scholars of the Enlightenment of the rich linguistic subsoil supporting literary cultures and of the many problems it posed for the historian was bound, sooner or later, to modify the very notion of culture.

If we leave the Glossary out of account, the *Remarques sur la langue françoise des XIIe et XIIIe siècles* were Sainte-Palaye's most valuable contribution to the study of the Romance languages. The Preface to the Glossary was to have included a history of the French language,[120] but it has come down to us only in an extract which appeared in the *Journal historique* (July, 1763)[121] and in some notes among his papers. Nevertheless it is fairly certain that it would have been marked by considerable caution and would have contained little that was new. He himself confessed that it was to be largely an amalgam of the views of colleagues whose erudition he respected highly—Dom Liron, Dom Rivet, Le Beuf, Bonamy, and Muratori.[122]

Prudent Sainte-Palaye certainly was. Indeed, it was for his prudence as well as for his vast erudition that he was regarded by his colleagues as a judge and arbiter in their disputes. Yet in his methods of research he was something of a pioneer. He had some idea that phonology is indispensable in language studies,[123] and he appears to have realized that orthographic changes do not always accurately reflect changes in pronunciation. Aware of the variety of dialects in Gaul, he suspected that the phonetic changes from Latin were manifold and complex. By examining the rhyme and meter of poetry, he made a groping attempt to establish patterns of pronunciation at different periods and in different regions.[124] He also appreciated the importance of the historical syntax and historical grammar of Old French, investigating the formation of tenses, the evolution of prepositions, the use of conjunctions and pronouns.[125] In semantics, he drew up a list of points to watch for: "mots ayant deux significations contraires parce que la chose com-

---

[119] Bréquigny 154, fol. 10. Sainte-Palaye points out that Old French poets adopt the dialect of their province or even of their locality.

[120] Moreau 1724, fol. 175, plan of the Preface.

[121] Reprinted in Favre's edition of the Glossary, vol. 9, pp. xii–xv.

[122] Moreau 1724, fol. 162.

[123] 'Observations générales sur le caractère de notre ancienne langue et sur le stile de nos anciens auteurs.' (Bréquigny 154, fols. 14–15.)

[124] Moreau 1724, fols. 105–11.

[125] Moreau 1723, fols. 92–97.

prise dans les deux cas étoit accompagnée des mesmes circonstances (*congier* pour *dire adieu* et pour *accueillir*); mots corrompus par l'altération des anciens que l'on entendoit mal (*chat maigre* pour *char nègre*); mots qui ayant signifié une espèce très particulière d'un mot générique ont esté employez pour exprimer le genre mesme dans toute son estendue; articles confondus avec le mot (*l'ombril, le lombril, le nombril*); mots qui ont signifié le simple et qui depuis ont marqué l'abondance ou l'excès (*trop* pour *beaucoup*, puis *à l'excès*); mots composez de deux verbes ou de deux mots synonymes (*virevolter*) . . ." Or there could be contamination of one word by another. In this way *magis* (*mais*) acquired a restrictive meaning as a result of its constant association with *sed*.[126] Like Fauchet, Ménage, and several of his own associates he recognized the importance of studying the dialects still spoken in the France of his own day. His papers contain many notes from poems in dialect and from dialect dictionaries.[127]

There were weaknesses in the methods of Sainte-Palaye and his contemporaries. Nevertheless, they had made progress, and in the course of their work they had come to a clearer understanding than earlier scholars had had of the nature of the linguistic problem that interested them and of the need for new tools with which to tackle this problem. Sainte-Palaye had made a real contribution to linguistic studies by going beyond isolated words and demonstrating the structural relationship of all the Romance tongues, by suggesting that the comparative method might be used to reconstruct earlier phases of a language, and by demonstrating that while all the Romance languages developed along parallel lines, no one derived from another. His work is the immediate prelude, in some respects, to that of Raynouard and of Diez, although the former chose to disregard what he had said about the equal position of French and Provençal in relation to their common source.

[126] *Ibid.*, fols. 134, 140–45.

[127] Moreau 1723, fols. 47–51, 'Table des mots de patois bressan tiré du livre intitulé *Lo Guemen dou pouro labors de Breissy'*; Moreau 1725, fols. 112–19, 'Noels en langage savoyard'; *ibid.*, fols. 124–29, 'Poésies auvergnates de feu messire Gabriel Pastourel'; *ibid.*, fol. 131. 'Noei . . . en patois dijonnois.' In a letter to Bouhier about a manuscript of Gérard de Roussillon at Sens he noted: "L'on y voit un rapport très sensible avec le patois bourguinon sur tout avec celui des environs de Vézelai." (B.N. Français 24418, fol. 374.)

CHAPTER 2

THE PUBLICATION OF DOCUMENTS RELATIVE TO FRENCH HISTORY

The eighteenth-century medieval scholar not only had to provide the bare means of reading sources in the vernacular, he had to discover and catalogue those sources themselves. The importance of catalogues had been recognized in the late seventeenth century by those scholars and historians who felt the need to establish history on a more solid basis than it had hitherto enjoyed. Mabillon, Jacques Lelong, Montfaucon, and Humphrey Wanley set out to discover and list the manuscript sources of history. Sainte-Palaye continued this work.

The principal manuscript sources to be catalogued were of two kinds: documents (charters, diplomas, treaties, etc.) and texts (annals, chronicles, literary works in prose and verse). Sainte-Palaye and his colleagues worked with both.

In 1746 Secousse, Sainte-Palaye, and Foncemagne set a proposal before the *Contrôleur Général* Machault for a *Table chronologique des diplômes, chartres, titres et actes imprimés concernant l'histoire de France*.[1] Bréquigny, who took over the direction of the project in 1763, later explained the motives which prompted the three scholars to make their suggestion. "Ceux qui veulent étudier à fond notre Histoire," he wrote in his Preface to the first volume of the *Table*, "doivent puiser leurs connoissances dans deux sources différentes: les Ecrits historiques qui contiennent les récits des faits; et les Diplômes, les Chartes et autres Pièces authentiques, qui servent de preuve ou de supplément à ces récits."[2] Hitherto—he added—historians who have written of the general history of

---

[1] Moreau 1436, fol. 9. Also *Table chronologique* (Paris, 1769), Preface, vol. 1, pp. iv–v.
[2] *Table chronologique*, Preface, vol. 1, p. iii.

France, while they have not absolutely neglected these sources, have drawn back aghast at the magnitude of the task facing them if they were to make full use of the original documents. The *Table chronologique* was conceived as an attempt to facilitate this task, and was to be considered as a supplement to Lelong's *Bibliothèque historique*.[3]

Compared to Leibniz's *Codex juris gentium diplomaticus* (1693) or to the even greater undertaking it inspired, Rymer's *Foedera*, the scheme was a modest one. It was to be simply an inventory of all the material which had been published in existing histories or collections of documents, such as those of Labbe, d'Achery, Baluze, or Mabillon. Bréquigny emphasized that, though much of the material in these collections concerned the ecclesiastical antiquities of France, it was also relevant to the general history of the *nation:* "Si on examine avec soin les Chartes dont nous ne pouvons indiquer que le sujet principal, on n'en trouvera presque aucune qui ne renferme incidemment des traits propres à répandre du jour, soit sur les parties essentielles de l'Histoire générale, la Chronologie, la Géographie, les Généalogies; soit sur les parties les plus intéressantes de l'Histoire particulière, les Loix, les Usages et les Moeurs de nos ancêtres."[4]

The task of the editors of the *Table chronologique* was thus not a purely mechanical one. It required a systematic classification of the material, indicating where and in what sources information about or reference to specific points of history was to be found. The editors appreciated that this was largely a problem of indices. Secousse had always set great store by indices, and had spent much time on those for the *Ordonnances des Rois de France*,[5] while Bréquigny stressed in his Preface to the second volume of the *Table* that the indices were intended to transform the work from a simple inventory into a genuine tool of historical research.[6] The *Table chronologique* was a remarkable and imaginative scheme precisely because it was an attempt to relate a great deal of isolated material, published for a diversity of reasons, mostly political or religious, in

---

[3] *Ibid.*, p. vii.   [4] *Ibid.* (Paris, 1775), Preface, vol. 2, p. iii.

[5] Secousse describes the tedium of compiling indices and at the same time the importance he attached to them in a letter to Bouhier of 3.3.1744. (B.N. Français 24420, fol. 82.)

[6] *Table chronologique*, Preface, vol. 2, p. iii.

accordance with the historical viewpoint of the Enlightenment.[7]

Shortly after Sainte-Palaye took over the direction of the project
from Secousse, on the latter's death in 1754, Bertin, the comptrol-
ler-general of finance, and Moreau, the historiographer royal,
spurred on by the success of Rymer's *Foedera*,[8] conceived the idea
of a *Cabinet des Chartes*, in which copies of all the deeds and
charters relative to French history in provincial, private, and foreign collections would be deposited.[9] At a later date, it was planned
to publish a selection of the more important of these in a work of
far greater scope than either the *Foedera* or Leibniz's *Codex*.[10] To
the Benedictines was assigned the task of combing the provincial
and private archives of France, Bréquigny was sent to London,
Dom Berthod to the Low Countries, and finally La Porte du Theil
to Rome. By 1762, the work had been set on foot in France, and
by 1764, the Benedictines were proceeding apace. If time was not
to be lost copying documents already available in print, the publication of the *Table chronologique*, which had now become an
adjunct to the far more ambitious scheme of Bertin and Moreau,
became an urgent necessity. As early as 1762, Moreau began clam-
oring for it. Sainte-Palaye, who was busy with other projects and
unable to give the *Table* his undivided attention, resigned the edi-
torship in favor of Bréquigny,[11] but the following year, when
Bréquigny left for London, Sainte-Palaye again found himself in
charge of the *Table*. Throughout this period Moreau constantly
badgered him to publish.[12] Sainte-Palaye protested that, though the
work was well under way—we have Bréquigny's word that when
he took over again from Sainte-Palaye in 1763 this was indeed so—

---

[7] Cf. F. M. Powicke, *Modern Historians and the Study of History, Essays and
Papers* (London, 1955), p. 186: "A characteristic of the best modern work upon
texts is its regard for the relation between the texts and general history. Texts
are no longer flung out as the useful Hearne flung them out. The days of the
indiscriminate thesaurus or anecdota or miscellanea are gone. We demand an
intelligent purpose, even though it can only be revealed in an index."

[8] Bréquigny in *Table chronologique*, Preface, vol. 1, pp. iv–v; and Pardessus,
ibid., Preface, vol. 4, p. iv.

[9] Langlois and Stein, *Archives de l'histoire de France* (Paris, 1891), pp. vi–x.

[10] Nouv. Acq. Fr. 20255, fols. 1–2, 'Projet de travail pour la Table des Chartes
MSS de l'histoire de France,' sec. 5. From the charters collected by the Benedictines a selection will be made comprising those "qu'on croira devoir entrer dans
le corps des titres de l'histoire de France lorsqu'il s'agira de le publier."

[11] Moreau 1436, fol. 11, letter to Moreau, dated only 1762.

[12] Bréquigny 157, fol. 228, Sainte-Palaye to Moreau, 21.7.1764.

it would be a mistake to publish it as it stood. A mere list of documents available in print would be useless to the historian, he explained, and he begged for time to complete the subject index and
the indices of place-names and of persons, which would open up
the documents to the general historian.[13] Bréquigny had been in
charge of an important part of Bertin's scheme since 1762—he was
overseeing the research of the Benedictines[14]—but he appears to
have shared the views of his older colleague. In 1766 he wrote
Sainte-Palaye from London asking him to supervise the printing
of the first part of the *Table*.

The outbreak of the Revolution interrupted publication at the
beginning of the fourth volume, but the reconstituted Académie
des Inscriptions thought it worthwhile to resume and complete the
work on the basis of notes left by Bréquigny. It was finished in
1876, thanks to Pardessus and Laboulaye, filling by then eight folio
volumes. To this day it is a useful source book for historians of the
first seven or eight centuries of the French monarchy.[15]

[13] Moreau 1436, fol. 10.
[14] Nouv. Acq. Fr. 20255, fol. 3, 'Instructions sur les recherches des chartes MSS.'
These indicate that all communications are to be addressed to Moreau, who will
pass them on to Bréquigny. In Bréquigny 157, fol. 239-41 there is a copy of a
circular in which Bréquigny advises the monks how he wants the work done.
[15] René Dussaud, *La nouvelle Académie des Inscriptions et Belles-Lettres, 1795–
1914* (Paris, 1946), 1:172.

CATALOGUES OF MANUSCRIPTS RELATIVE TO MEDIEVAL HISTORY: THE *NOTICES DE MANUSCRITS*

The problem of literary sources was somewhat different from that of documentary sources. The latter, it is true, were open to forgery and had to be authenticated. Literary texts, however, were subject to a more insidious process of corruption. Being in a sense public property, they could be altered and touched up at will to suit the changing tastes of successive generations of readers. Sainte-Palaye was impressed by the discrepancies he discovered between fifteenth or sixteenth-century printed editions of medieval texts and the early manuscripts of which he had cognizance. At the beginning of a paper on the *Jouvencel*, he drew these to the attention of his fellow-Academicians.[1] The 1529 edition of this work, he declared, was "un amas informe de fictions romanesques, dont le texte, tronqué presque par-tout, ne présente aucun plan raisonnable, aucun discours intelligible." The manuscripts, on the other hand, offered "une source abondante de lumières pour l'histoire de notre milice." "Les manuscrits que j'ai vus" he explained, "m'ont appris que cette espèce de roman étoit, pour ainsi dire, le testament militaire d'un des plus grands hommes qu'ait eus notre Monarchie."[2]

It was important to point out that in many cases the printed texts were not identical with the earliest manuscript sources—

[1] 'Notice de deux MSS du Livre intitulé Le Jouvencel conférés avec l'exemplaire imprimé,' *MAI* 26:700–1: "On n'est point assez en garde contre la negligence, pour ne rien dire de plus, avec laquelle ils ont publié les premiers ouvrages sortis de leurs presses . . . J'ai vû des Imprimeurs confondre ensemble les productions de plusieurs auteurs sous le nom d'un seul, et par-là donner lieu à des erreurs grossières: j'ai vû des pages entières d'ou dépendoit l'ordre du discours, totalement supprimées ou transposées dans d'autres endroits où elles ne pouvoient former aucun sens; j'ai vû, encore plus souvent, des mots mal lus et mal entendus par l'éditeur, remplacés par d'autres mots qui avoient une signification toute contraire à celle que demandoit la phrase où ils étoient employés."

[2] *Ibid.*, pp. 702–3.

though the distinction was a crude one and barely touched on the difficult problems of textual tradition[3]—and historians needed to be told that they could not take the language, style, and ideas of the former as fairly representing the latter. Chapelain, for instance, who, in the seventeenth century, had put forward a plea for greater consideration of medieval romances such as *Lancelot* and *Perceforest*, did not consider the question of the textual tradition at all. To Sainte-Palaye, on the other hand, failure to take account of the difference between the printed versions and the earliest manuscripts was bound to lead to error. It is in the early manuscripts, he held, that "nous puiserons la véritable connoissance des moeurs de nos Ancêtres, toujours défigurées et travesties à notre mode par des Ecrivains modernes."[4]

If the historian was to profit from these warnings, it was the scholar's duty to discover and catalogue the manuscript sources, many of which were unknown or inaccessible. Sainte-Palaye knew that it was not enough to glance at the first title in a codex or to make a cursory examination of the contents. As early as 1728, in a paper on a thirteenth-century Life of Charlemagne, he was pointing out to the Academy "combien de morceaux différens se trouvent rassemblez dans un seul volume. On en compte près de vingt dans celuy-cy, qui pour la pluspart n'ont aucune liaison entre eux et qui pourtant n'ont souvent rien qui les fasse distinguer les uns des autres; de sorte qu'il faut une extrême attention pour tirer de ces sortes de monuments tout l'avantage qu'on en peut attendre: combien donc se trompent ceux qui croyent qu'il suffit de les parcourir légèrement!"[5] Modern scholars who have studied the production of manuscripts have explained how phenomena like the running together of different texts in one manuscript arose (perhaps, for instance, through an initial failure to rubricate the manu-

---

[3] The *mises en prose*, described in detail by Georges Doutrepont ('Les Mises en prose des épopées et des romans chevalresques du XIVᵉ au XIVᵉ siècle,' *Académie Royale de Belgique, Classe des Lettres, Mémoires*, 40 [1930]) did not form the object of any special study by Sainte-Palaye.

[4] 'Observations générales sur le stile de nos anciens Auteurs,' unpublished, Bréquigny 154, fol. 39. Sainte-Palaye returned again and again to this point; cf. the 'Projet d'études sur l'histoire de France,' drawn up in collaboration with Foncemagne (Bréquigny 62, fol. 211): "À la lecture des ouvrages imprimés, nous avons jugé qu'il falloit joindre celle des MSS françois du XIIᵉ, du XIIIᵉ et du XIVᵉ siècles, source peu connue et où il est indispensable de puiser, pour approfondir les antiquités de la 3ᵉ race de nos Rois."

[5] *MAI** 7:286.

script, with the almost inevitable consequence that generations of scribes have copied the various texts it contained in one piece).[6] Sainte-Palaye himself made no attempt to account for the phenomenon he described, and probably could not have done so. But at least he was aware of it and had some idea of the points the cataloguer of manuscripts must look for.

He also knew from his own experience that the historian required a better idea of the contents of a manuscript work than could be provided by a bare statement of the title. He undertook, therefore, to prepare analyses or notices of manuscripts which would indicate the sort of information they contain and the period to which they are relevant.

In the early thirties of the eighteenth century he began working on the manuscripts at the Royal Library in Paris, and gradually extended the range of his research to the great libraries of Italy and to the principal private collections in France. Thus, while notices 1–1547 in his collection concern manuscripts in the Royal Library, notices 1701–1900 are of manuscripts in the library of Saint-Germain des Prés, a large number are of manuscripts in Bouhier's library (1901–83), others describe manuscripts in other private collections.[7] Numbers 1998–2000 relate to acquisitions of the Royal Library since 1738, indicating that Sainte-Palaye was keeping a close watch on the movements of manuscripts. Letters he wrote to Bouhier from Rome show that during the 1739–40 visit to Italy he did not neglect the opportunities afforded by the Italian libraries. He complains bitterly to Bouhier that despite Passionei's assistance, "Je n'ai presque rien fait pour nos anciens historiens qui m'intéressoient plus que tout le reste . . . Je n'avance guère par la lenteur de M^{rs} les Italiens et par le mauvais ordre qui règne dans tous les MSS, sans compter la grande difficulté qu'ils ont à en donner la communication."[8] We have also de Brosses' word for it that Sainte-Palaye spent much of his time in the Vatican and other Roman libraries and that he made a point of examining the collections in every town they passed through.[9] The 1749–50 journey to Italy was the occasion for another harvest of notices of manuscripts. In addition, as the correspondence with Passionei and Testaud de Bois de Lavaud shows, Sainte-Palaye had made arrangements to aug-

---

[6] A. Dain, *Les Manuscrits* (Paris, 1949), pp. 34–35.
[7] The collection is in Moreau 1654–61 (in-folio) and 1662–76 (in-quarto).
[8] B.N. Français 24418, fol. 360, to Bouhier, Rome, 31.12.1739.
[9] *Lettres d'Italie,* ed. Bézard, 2:258, *et passim.*

ment his collection through the work of copyists and amanuenses in Italy. The total result of his work in Italy is impressive. All the great Italian libraries are represented: the Royal Library at Turin, the Ambrosian at Milan, the Ducal library at Modena, the Saibante library at Verona, the San Marco at Venice, the Laurentian and Riccardi collections in Florence, in Rome the Vatican together with the Ottoboni, Chigi, and Strozzi collections, and the Royal Library of Naples (Notices 2001–3273).[10]

Sainte-Palaye's attempt to provide a solid basis for his own research by summary investigation of potential material fell in with a plan for providing the Bibliothèque du Roi with a good catalogue.

Clément's Catalogue of the Royal Library, which had been brought up to date in 1729[11] and published by Montfaucon in 1739 in his *Bibliotheca Bibliothecarum*,[12] had given only the briefest indication of the contents of the manuscripts listed. Clément himself regarded it as only provisional, for in 1688 he had proposed a new catalogue which would divide the King's manuscripts into four classes and provide for full description of the material in each by a team of competent specialists.[13] With the acquisition by the Royal Library of important new collections between 1682 and 1732 the new catalogue became an urgent necessity, and in February, 1733, Maurepas instructed Jean-Paul Bignon, the King's librarian, to bring it to completion.[14] Clément's memoir reveals that the Oriental, Greek, and Latin manuscripts had been fairly well covered even by 1698, and in 1739 it was possible to publish a four-volume folio catalogue of this part of the Royal collection. The catalogue

---

[10] Jules Camus, 'Notices et extraits des manuscrits français de Modène,' *Revue des langues romanes* (1892), 35:169–260, holds that Sainte-Palaye was the first scholar to put the Modena collection to use and shows how his copies and extracts were used by later editors, such as Raynaud (*Bibliographie des chansonniers français*) and the editors of the *Histoire littéraire des croisades* (B.N. Français 9070, fols. 353, 361).

[11] *Catalogus librorum manuscriptorum Hebraicorum, Syriacorum, Arabicorum, Turcicorum, Persicorum, Graecorum, Latinorum, Italiacorum, Gallicorum etc. Bibliothecae Regiae* (Nouv. Acq. Fr. 5410). This is simply a list. The title of only one MS work is given for each codex. Other material bound up in the same codex is not described and was probably not even explored. The left-hand pages contain new entries since 1729.

[12] *Bibliotheca Bibliothecarum*, 2:709–66, 782–921.

[13] Henri Omont, *Anciens inventaires et catalogues de la Bibliothèque Nationale* (Paris, 1921), Introduction, pp. 42–44, quoting from Clément's 'Mémoire sur le catalogue de la Bibliothèque du Roy,' in Nouv. Acq. Fr. 1328, fols. 272–73.

[14] This correspondence, in B.N. Français 22235, fols. 280–81, is quoted in *Revue des bibliothèques* (1895), 5:103–4.

of French manuscripts, however, was nowhere near completion. Clément had been able to do next to no work on it, and Bignon, who knew of Sainte-Palaye's interest in medieval French manuscripts, invited him, together with Secousse and Lancelot, to undertake this part of the catalogue. Although Bignon wrote to Maurepas that "ces . . . Messieurs ont témoigné tant de zèle qu'ils n'ont demandé aucune récompense particulière pour ce travail," and looked forward to the early completion of the work, two years later—in December, 1735—he had to admit to Maurepas that it was still far from ready. "A l'égard des (MSS) françois," he confessed, ". . . nous n'avons pas encore les notices superficielles de la moitié."[15]

In the event by far the lion's share of the task fell to Sainte-Palaye. Lancelot died in 1740 without apparently having contributed very much. In 1737 La Bastie wrote to Mazaugues that Sainte-Palaye was going through the manuscripts of the Bibliothèque du Roi but made no mention of Secousse.[16] In fact Secousse appears to have been responsible for only some 25 per cent of the notices of manuscripts in France (Nos. 1001–1547) and almost all of these were of short pieces—charters, diplomas, title deeds. But the most striking difference between the contributions of Secousse and Sainte-Palaye lies in the manner in which they approached their task. Secousse is content with sketchy notes. Sainte-Palaye's notices are full, detailed, well-ordered, and models of their kind. It is typical of his methodical approach that before embarking on this work, he carefully studied the techniques and materials used in manuscript production throughout the medieval period.[17] First, he gives a complete physical description of the codex, then, with the aid of palaeography, language, information available in the text and references to it in other texts, the manuscript is dated, miniatures and vignettes are described with care, and an attempt is made to identify the original owner and subsequent history of the manuscript. The contents are described with the help of generous quotations which marginal notes suggest Sainte-Palaye hoped to extend still further. Finally the manuscript is compared with others of the same work where these exist.

Sainte-Palaye came nowhere near covering all the French manu-

[15] *Revue des bibliothèques* (1895), 5:109, 112.
[16] La Bastie to Mazaugues, 10.4.1737, in 'Les Provençalistes du XVIIIe siècle,' *Revue des langues romanes* (1880), p. 191.
[17] Moreau 1722, fols. 83–87, contains his notes on the production of manuscripts.

scripts at the Royal Library, however. Even Le Grand d'Aussy, to whom the *Notices* were certainly available, complained that he had no means of tracking down all the *fabliaux* in the Library.[18] The difficulty probably lay in Sainte-Palaye's attempt to combine analyses of manuscripts with an inventory. He must have become increasingly aware of this difficulty, for around 1751 in a *Plan de travail pour l'Académie des Belles-Lettres*[19] he brought the new catalogue of the Royal Library to the attention of his colleagues and invited them to assist in making the descriptions of manuscripts more exhaustive, so that the catalogue would be a useful source book for historians in its own right.

Foncemagne took up this proposal and incorporated it in a memorandum, which he presented to the government.[20] The memorandum stressed the value such a collection would have in bringing to light lost or forgotten manuscripts, making known the contents and the importance of manuscripts, encouraging the study of Old French and of Oriental languages, and stimulating Academicians to more earnest labors. But Foncemagne had already separated the two goals of Sainte-Palaye—the detailed analysis and the cataloguing of manuscripts. What he suggested was not a catalogue but a series of notices of manuscripts which might be published annually, he said, in a volume of some 600 or 700 quarto pages as a supplement to the proceedings of the Académie des Inscriptions.[21] In 1785 Beauvau announced that work would start on a collection of *Notices et extraits* and that a committee had been appointed to supervise it.[22] In 1787 the first volume appeared. In their introduction the editors went over most of the points in Foncemagne's memorandum, taking care, however, to emphasize that "ce travail n'a rien de commun avec celui qui a lieu à la bibliothèque du Roi, pour la confection du Catalogue." It was intended, they declared, to procure the enjoyment of that for which the Catalogue whetted the appetite. This series ceased publication only recently.

As for the Catalogue, it was completed only at the end of the

[18] Le Grand d'Aussy, *Fabliaux ou contes du XII*e *et du XIII*e *siècles* (nouvelle édition; Paris, 1781), vol. i, Preface, p. xcvi.

[19] Bréquigny 62, fols. 203–4.

[20] Nouv. Acq. Fr. 3294, fols. 218–21.

[21] Mouchet, however, continued Sainte-Palaye's attempt to combine the two; cf. a description of his notices of part of the Baluze collection, *Bibl. École des Chartes* (1920), 81:119–20, 127–28.

[22] *Notices et extraits des manuscrits de la Bibliothèque du Roy* (Paris, 1787), vol. i, Preface, p. i.

nineteenth century (1868–1902) by Taschereau. Taschereau could not have been unaware of the volumes of *Notices* compiled by Sainte-Palaye, and many of his entries bear a striking resemblance to those of the earlier scholar, although in general they are less exhaustive. It is a tribute to Sainte-Palaye that Taschereau's work represents no advance on his, except on occasional points of detail that a further hundred years of scholarship had illuminated.

Sainte-Palaye continued to interest himself in catalogues of medieval manuscripts. He probably met the learned librarian of the Bürgerbibliothek in Berne, the patrician Sinner, during the latter's visits to Paris in 1765 and 1770. In any event, he assisted him in the preparation of material for his *Catalogus Codicum MSS Bibliothecae Bernensis* (Berne, 1770)[23]—one of the best catalogues of its kind produced in the eighteenth century and still useful today—and he had him elected a corresponding member of the Académie des Inscriptions.[24]

This work on catalogues might appear a matter of dull routine. At this early stage especially, however, it was not a matter of manipulating slips of paper and glue or of computer machines, but a real test of erudition and critical judgment. Works such as Humphrey Wanley's *Critical and Historical Catalogue of Anglo-Saxon Manuscripts* (1705) or the same author's Harley Catalogue, which appeared after his death in 1759, were major achievements in European scholarship. Sainte-Palaye did not lag behind his English counterpart. He showed better than any of his contemporaries how to go about analyzing and describing a manuscript and the series of *Notices et extraits*, which grew out of his work, has served scholars well for over a century.[25]

---

[23] There are acknowledgements to Sainte-Palaye in Sinner's *Catalogue*, 2:391, and 3:344, 351. Sinner would send Sainte-Palaye the manuscripts, and the latter returned them with notes and comments.

[24] Berne, Bürgerbibliothek, MSS Hist. Helv. X–106 (14), Sainte-Palaye to Sinner, Paris, 27.4.1774. On Sinner, see Adolf Burri, *Johann Rudolf Sinner von Ballaigues* (Berne, 1911).

[25] A. Dain, p. 77, writes: "Composée dans une bibliothèque ou dans un institut de recherche (la notice de manuscrit) présente, si elle est courte, la forme à peu près exacte de la description de catalogue. Mais on peut concevoir des notices plus développées. . . . Il est regrettable que la précieuse publication académique des Notices et extraits de manuscrits soit tombée dans un sommeil qu'on craint définitif. Il y avait là une formule heureuse qui, au prix de quelques rajeunissements, pouvait rendre encore de grands services."

CHAPTER 4

PROBLEMS AND METHODS OF EDITING MEDIEVAL TEXTS

Many of the earliest printed editions of texts—classical or medieval —had simply been reproductions of contemporary manuscripts, and in this sense had constituted no more than an additional phase in the manuscript tradition. By the seventeenth century variant readings of classical texts were being collected with unflagging enthusiasm, but in published editions they were usually relegated to the notes. The texts themselves were taken over lock, stock, and barrel from a manuscript of accepted authority. At the turn of the century, however, Richard Bentley questioned this undiscriminating faith in the value of the written tradition and proposed a method of "conjectural criticism" which rested on careful examination of the texts themselves and above all on the editor's knowledge of the linguistic and historical background of the text in question.

Bentley's method was characteristic of the Enlightenment. It subordinated the search for an authoritative text, objectively present in some one manuscript, to the search for a correct text which the critic should be able to reconstitute by analyzing the inner structure, style, meter, and language of a work or author.[1] Bentley's suggested emendations to Étienne's *textus receptus* of the New Testament, in the *Remarks* upon Anthony Collins' *Discourse of Free-Thinking*, are revealing. He first adduces linguistic and historical arguments to support his conjectures, and then, deferentially since he is dealing with a sacred text, hints that a diligent search among the manuscripts might show that his conjectures could in fact be substantiated by written evidence. Bentley is cautious, but

[1] R. C. Jebb, *Bentley* (pocket ed.; London, 1904), pp. 212–13; also Jacob Maehly, *Richard Bentley* (Leipzig, 1868), pp. 9–10; M. L. Clarke, *Greek Studies in England, 1700–1830* (Cambridge, 1945), pp. 48–50.

the trend of his criticism is clear. " 'Tis plain indeed," he wrote, "that if emendations are true, they must once have been in some manuscripts, at least in the author's original; but it does not follow, that because no manuscript now exhibits them, none more ancient ever did."[2]

Of the three criteria outlined by Hermann Kantorowicz for the *recensio* and *emendatio* of manuscripts—the literary criterion (*der literaturgeschichtliche Massstab*), the criterion of the manuscript tradition (*der überlieferungsgeschichtliche Massstab*), and the psychological criterion (*der psychologische Massstab*)—it was thus the first which dominated the best textual criticism in the eighteenth century.[3] The evidence of manuscripts was used to support the conjectures of the more confident editors or to provide the timid with material from which they could make a selection. The psychological criterion can be discounted entirely.[4]

The pre-eminence of the literary criterion is not surprising. Just as to Locke and the empiricists ideas in the mind were no longer identical with the objects they were thought to represent, so to scholars and historians the past was no longer unproblematic, a series of events without any mystery. On the contrary, the past had to be reconstructed painfully and critically from the debris that was left behind and, at the same time, the elements of the debris—the facts—acquired significance only as they were set in relation to other facts. As the past lost its immediacy, its different aspects were increasingly difficult to deal with in isolation from each other. It was not enough to check the authenticity of the document reporting an event; to be credible and intelligible the

---

[2] Richard Bentley, 'Remarks upon a late Discourse of Free-Thinking, in a letter to F. H., D. D. by Phileleutherus Lipsiensis' (London, 1713), reprinted in *The Works of Richard Bentley*, ed. A. Dyce (London, 1838), 3:287-474, sec. 32, p. 356.

[3] Hermann Kantorowicz, *Einführung in die Textkritik* (Leipzig, 1921), pp. 9-36. Kantorowicz remarks (p. 14): "Der literaturgeschichtliche Massstab führt zur Bevorzügung derjenigen—überlieferten oder nicht überlieferten—Lesart, die der Sprache und der Sache nach die grösste geschichtliche Wahrscheinlichkeit der Richtgkeit für sich hat. Er misst also nach der 'Richtigkeit' der Lesarten, sie mögen 'echt' sein oder nicht."

[4] Although in the opinion of modern scholars the psychological criterion is not the least important (cf. Giorgio Pasquali, *Storia della tradizione e critica del testo* [2d ed.; Florence, 1952], pp. 471-72; also A. Dain, *Les Manuscrits*, pp. 37-51), nobody in the eighteenth century, it seems, had realized that a method of criticism could be evolved from systematic research into copyists' errors, with the possible exception of a group of German Protestant scholars, who had hit on the notion of the *lectio difficilior*. (Pasquali, pp. 10-11.)

event had to be consistent with the wider patterns of nature and, in a more limited way, it had to fit into an historical pattern of causes and effects. In the same way, Bentley felt that the *word* could not be treated as an isolated problem. Its environment had to be taken into account—the general patterns of the language of which it was a part, and the particular patterns of the individual style characterizing one user of that language, the author. Textual emendation thus became part of general linguistic and cultural history; the whole structure of a work or even of a language and a culture was invoked to explain the smallest parts, even as the parts were sought out in order to reconstruct the whole.

Sainte-Palaye did not go as far as Bentley did. His task was not to improve a tradition of scholarship, but to found one. Nevertheless, his methods were similar to Bentley's in that they derive from that historical consciousness which was common to all the men of the Enlightenment.

The early editors of medieval texts, on the whole, either printed directly from a contemporary manuscript or touched up and modernized their model when they had to work from a manuscript of some antiquity. As Sainte-Palaye pointed out, the literary heritage of the Middle Ages was not regarded with anything like the respect and awe granted to the works of classical antiquity, but continued to live and evolve until about the seventeenth century.[5] Sainte-Palaye was not the first to draw attention to the interest of medieval French texts, but he was the first to approach them in a truly historical spirit and to point out that they posed the same problems and required the same kind of treatment from scholars as classical or medieval Latin texts. Having argued that the historian cannot take the Renaissance editions of medieval French texts at their face value but must look behind them to the manuscript sources, he went on to warn that late manuscripts are just as subject to error and inaccuracy through the ignorance of copyists and

---

[5] 'Notice de deux MSS du Livre intitulé Le Jouvencel,' *MAI* 26:700: "Je ne parle pas des livres Grecs et Latins, auxquels des Savans du premier ordre ne dédaignoient point d'employer leurs soins et leurs talens, afin qu'ils parussent avec toute la correction et la fidélité qu'ils méritoient; je parle de nos anciens auteurs François, pour lesquels nos premiers Imprimeurs ne se crurent point obligés d'emprunter des secours étrangers: persuadés qu'un manuscrit qu'ils avoient découvert, et dont l'écriture et la langue leur étoient en quelque façon familières, n'avoit pas besoin de plus grandes lumières pour en risquer l'impression, ils l'imprimèrent souvent sans avoir su ni le lire ni l'entendre."

scribes as the early printed editions are—as he claimed—through the ignorance or indifference of printers. The scholar, he concluded, cannot be satisfied with the examination of one manuscript: "Je crois devoir recommander également aux Savans qui voudront connoître les écrits de nos anciens auteurs, et à ceux qui voudront les publier, non seulement de ne point se fier aux anciens imprimés, mais de ne point se contenter de la lecture d'un seul manuscrit et d'en conférer le plus qu'ils pourront les uns avec les autres."[6]

From the collation of manuscripts two results could be expected: first, that all the elements of a text could be reconstituted in their entirety, and second, that the text could be restored to its original form. In the case of collections like the troubadour poems, the *Chansons* of Thibaut de Navarre, or the *Fabliaux,* each manuscript contained a different selection of works, and Sainte-Palaye's primary aim was to recover as many items as possible from all the available manuscripts.[7] While he duly entered variants in the margins of his copies, he did not attempt to reconstitute correct readings on the basis of the manuscript tradition itself. It is unlikely that this restraint was due to any feeling that the manuscripts he possessed or had examined were equally valid and authoritative editions of the text, that is to say, that there was more than one exemplar. Such an idea is too sophisticated to have been held by an eighteenth-century medievalist. Quite simply Sainte-Palaye had no material basis for preferring one reading to another. When he did query the texts, his proposed emendations were in reality independent of the manuscript tradition—marginal queries and suggestions are found even when he was working from a single manuscript—and they were grounded, like Bentley's emendations, in the editor's knowledge of the author and his medium. Sainte-Palaye's studies of the style and language of the Old French authors, his attempt to distinguish the various phases through which Old French passed, and the changing forms and meanings of its vocabulary are completely in line with this approach to the texts. But it is unlikely that he would have incorporated his emendations

---

[6] *MAI* 17:787.

[7] In a short appreciation of Dacier's edition of Froissart, Molinier states that this was the aim of much textual work in the eighteenth century. (*Sources de l'histoire de France,* 4:16.)

in a text which he intended to have published. For the most part, indeed, he was querying the work of the scribe who had copied the manuscript for him, and though this *implied* the right to emend, it is not certain that Sainte-Palaye would have used it. On the whole, he employed the methods of internal criticism as Mabillon had done, in order to detect interpolations and major structural alterations to the text by later hands and to date his manuscripts. The notices of manuscripts which he continued to compile until the end of his life bear witness to the sureness with which he combined the evidence of language and style with more strictly palaeographic evidence to date a manuscript and spot changes made to it by later copyists.[8]

Nineteenth century scholars commented on the soundness of Sainte-Palaye's criticism. In 1867–68 J. Brackelmann published Sainte-Palaye's transcription of the Berne manuscript (no. 389) of the *Chansons* of Thibaut de Navarre and drew attention to his attempt to restore the proper order of the verses of one of the songs ("C'est dou conte debair e docenin son ganre"), which had obviously been copied incorrectly in the manuscript. Although Sainte-Palaye did not solve the problem, Brackelmann declared,[9] he pointed it out, and Brackelmann contrasted his approach with that of Paulin Paris, who had published the poem in the form in which it stood in the manuscript without so much as commenting on the question of the verse order,[10] even though he had in fact consulted Sainte-Palaye's transcription of the manuscript.

Bentley had argued against Collins that far from leading to uncertainty and justifying Pyrrhonism, a large number of manuscripts, containing a large number of variant readings, provided a surer means of reconstructing an original text than a single manuscript. "If there had been but one manuscript of the Greek Testament at the restoration of learning about two centuries ago," he asked, ". . . would the text be in a better condition then, than now

---

[8] Additional notices of MSS in Moreau 1474, fols. 345–402; Moreau 1723, fols. 92–93; Moreau 1725, entire volume.

[9] *Archiv f.d. Studium d. neueren Sprachen* (1868), 42:317.

[10] Paris's edition of this song in *Histoire littéraire de la France* (1856), 28:773. It was also published in the same order of stanzas by C. Hofmann in a paper read to the Bavarian Academy. (*Sitzungsberichte der bayerischen Akademie zu München* [1867], 2:486–527.)

we have 30,000 (variant readings)?"[11] But Bentley did not have in mind that the manuscript tradition itself could be studied historically. Sainte-Palaye was in a similar position. In a number of cases —Froissart's Chronicles, the troubadour poems, the *Fabliaux*,[12] the *Chansons* of Thibaut de Navarre[13] and several thirteenth century romances[14]—he gathered together with considerable success all the versions, written and printed, on which he could lay hands.

But, having done so, he found himself confronted with the problem of recension. Since Lachmann, scholars are accustomed to construct a genealogical table or tree (*stemma*) of the entire written tradition and to establish the relationship between the different manuscripts of a tradition on the basis of their origin. This method of work was unknown to the scholars of the eighteenth century.[15] To many of them the age of a manuscript still constituted the best guarantee of its reliability. This was not an unreasonable supposition in the case of medieval manuscripts. Since they had long been regarded as part of a living tradition, they had constantly been modernized with respect to language, to style, and even to content

---

[11] 'Remarks upon a Late Discourse of Free-Thinking,' sec. 32, p. 349.

[12] See below, Appendices nos. 2, 3, and 4.

[13] His copy of songs by Thibaut in a collation made by the printer Coustelier of three MSS (Clairambault, Baudelot, and Noailles; Pb⁵, Pb¹¹ and Pb¹⁷ in Raynaud's *Bibliographie des chansonniers français*) is now in Moreau 1679, fols. 1–123. In addition, he collated this with MSS in the Vatican (Reg. Suec. 1490 and Reg. Suec. 1522; R¹ and R² in Raynaud), in the Estense library at Modena (R. 4, 4; M in Raynaud) and at Berne (389; B² in Raynaud). As late as 1770 he was still interested in MSS containing O.F. *chansons*, for when he learned of one in the possession of Noblet at La Clayette, he immediately sought permission to consult it (draft of his letter to Noblet in Bréquigny 65, fol. 168). The permission was granted (*ibid.*, fols. 170–73). Sainte-Palaye's copy (Arsenal 6361) is of great value now, the original MS having disappeared. A complete account of Sainte-Palaye's work on this MS by Paul Meyer, *Notices et extraits des manuscrits*, 1ère partie (1890), 33:1–9.

[14] Arsenal 5871, fol. 25, contains a list of MSS and printed editions of the "Romans de la Table Ronde." (*Saint-Graal, Merlin l'Enchanteur, Artus de Bretagne, Chevalier au Lyon, Tristan, Perceval* and *Lancelot*.) Over twenty MSS are listed, including most of those at present in the B.N. Français (94–123, 1422–24, 1426–28), but then more widely dispersed in private collections. Each MS was carefully described, its age established, and a comparison made with other MSS of the same text. Omissions, substitutions, and additions were noted, and allusions which might help to identify the author or the owner of the MS were listed. An attempt was made to trace the history of the MS. A similar examination was made of fourteen MSS of the *Roman d'Alexandre*. (Bréquigny 154, fols. 123–25.)

[15] But cf. Pasquali, pp. 9–10 on Bengel, Griesbach, and Wettstein, the German scriptural scholars.

for the benefit of later generations of readers. The tendency to modernize medieval manuscripts has been pointed out by many modern critics, but eighteenth century scholars like Sainte-Palaye or Capperonnier were quite aware of it.[16] Again, unlike the classical scholar, the medievalist might hope to discover a manuscript contemporary with the *Urschrift*, even a direct apograph of it. Respect for the age of a manuscript was not therefore altogether unjustifiable, particularly if the author and his date were known.

Closely associated in the mind of the eighteenth-century medievalist with the notion of age was the notion of quality. A good manuscript was one which had been copied faithfully and which had suffered few alterations, interpolations, and stylistic or linguistic corrections. A bad manuscript was almost invariably a late one, which had been altered to suit the requirements of a later generation of readers. The idea of the good manuscript was the counterpart in textual studies of the idea of the reliable historical authority. Faced with the need to assess each historical testimony on its merits and to discard the idea that all classical historians were canonical authorities, many scholars at the end of the seventeenth and the beginning of the eighteenth century had tended to look for a convenient measuring-rod, and after carefully investigating the reliability of a number of sources, usually lighted on one which they considered superior to all others and could apply with confidence on all occasions. We have already observed how Bouhier selected Herodotus, and Sainte-Palaye Dionysius of Halicarnassus, in this way.

How was a text established on the basis of these two closely related criteria of age and quality? Careless editors, like Lenglet du Fresnoy, for instance, might work from a printed edition, making arbitrary corrections here and there on the basis of manuscripts in their possession, which they referred to vaguely as "ancien" or "très ancien" but of which they rarely gave an adequate description.[17] Others, more scrupulous, like Capperonnier, would reject

---

[16] 'Notice de deux MSS du . . . Jouvencel,' *MAI* 26:700; *Histoire de Saint-Louis, par Jehan sire de Joinville*, ed. Melot, Sallier, Capperonnier (Paris, 1761), Preface, pp. vii–viii.

[17] *Le Roman de la Rose, par Guillaume de Lorris et Jean de Meun dit Clopinel, revu sur plusieurs Editions et sur quelques anciens manuscrits. . . .* ed. Lenglet du Fresnoy (Paris, 1735).

late manuscripts out of hand and take as their basic text the oldest manuscript available.[18] The weakness of this method of basing a text on an authoritative manuscript became apparent, however, when editors were confronted with a number of more or less equally "good" (that is, linguistically convincing) manuscripts of approximately equal age.

At this point editors usually resorted to the methods of the classical scholars: i.e., the selection of one manuscript for the text, and the piling up of variants in the notes. This was by and large the method followed by Lévesque de la Ravalière for his edition of Thibaut de Navarre, and there is little reason to doubt that if Sainte-Palaye had published the poems of the troubadours in a complete edition he would have used the same method. The idea that it was possible to base a text on a study of the relations between the manuscripts had occurred to no one. The *recensio*, as it became known to nineteenth-century scholars, was never practiced by the medievalists of the eighteenth century. The best editions were preceded, not by a classification, but by an "Examen" of the manuscripts.

Sainte-Palaye's series of studies of Froissart includes such an examination of the manuscripts of the Chronicles. This examination reveals an acute sense of language and of style, and the ability to use this sense in order to advance beyond the concept of antiquity; it also shows up the limitations of Sainte-Palaye's method.

In general Sainte-Palaye accepted the common criterion of antiquity. Thus, he wrote of two manuscripts of the first book of the Chronicles (Bib. Reg. 8318, 8331, now B.N. 2641, 2662, Luce A8, A18) that "quoyqu'il manque plusieurs choses dans l'un et dans l'autre, l'ancienneté doit leur faire donner la préférence."[19] On the other hand, his feeling for the linguistic and stylistic character of a manuscript led him to reject this criterion on occasion in favor of what is implicitly a criterion of origin. Discussing a manuscript of the third book of the Chronicles (Bib. Reg. 8325, now B.N. 2650) he remarked: "Ce manuscrit qui n'est que du milieu du XV siècle est celuy où le langage du vieux temps est le mieux conservé: *apparemment il a esté copié sur quelque autre plus ancien, et meilleur que ceux qui nous restent* . . . C'est encore l'ancien langage

---

[18] *Histoire de Saint Louis*, Preface, pp. viii–xiii.
[19] 'Jugement de l'histoire de Froissart,' *MAI* 13:574–75.

qui me porte à regarder le manuscrit 8329 (now 2654), quoyqu'il ne soit guère que de la fin du XV siècle, comme le meilleur que nous ayons pour le quatrième volume."[20] [Italics added.] Sainte-Palaye did not push this reasoning any further. As it stands, however, it is sufficient to demonstrate that he was dimly conscious of the question of the filiation of manuscripts.

The idea that a late manuscript might stand closer to the *Urschrift* than a number of older ones, arrived at on the basis of a Bentleian type of criticism, implied that a more refined kind of external criticism might be applied to the manuscript tradition than that used by the seventeenth-century scholars,[21] but there was no theory behind this insight and no attempt to develop it systematically. This is clear from the way Sainte-Palaye dealt with the Froissart manuscripts, treating them on the whole singly, in isolation from each other, or simply listing them without comment. It is hard to see how he could have established a text of the Chronicles, if that had been his intention, on any other principles than those currently followed by his contemporaries. His discussion of the famous Breslau manuscript of the Chronicles, which had recently been rediscovered, and for which extravagant claims were being made,[22] reveals how far he was from abandoning the conven-

---

[20] *Ibid.*, p. 575.

[21] In a letter to the Dutch scholar D'Orville of August 1, 1732—immediately before Sainte-Palaye read his paper on Froissart—Jeremiah Markland made a similar observation to that of Sainte-Palaye: "You were mentioning a MS Propertius which you have . . . You seemed to think that it is of no great value; it is possible that it may be very modern, and yet taken from a good copy." Markland expresses his opinion "that modern MSS often help us out where more ancient ones leave us in the dark," respectfully and deferentially, as if he were putting forward a new idea. Markland's letter is printed in Euripides' *Supplices Mulieres, cum notis Jer. Marklandi integris* (Oxon, 1811), pp. 295-96. I am indebted to Professor G. Giarrizzo for drawing my attention to it.

[22] On the Breslau MS, see A. Schultz, *Beschreibung der Breslauer Bilderhandschrift des Froissart* (Breslau, 1896); A. Linder, *Der Breslauer Froissart* (Berlin, 1912). These works deal mainly with the miniatures, but have useful historical introductions. According to Sainte-Palaye, it was claimed that the Breslau MS "déceloit par tout la mauvaise foy de Sauvage qui dans son Édition de Froissart avoit corrompu tous les anciens mots, les noms propres et les noms de lieux, altéré et perverti tous les faits et tellement tronqué cette précieuse histoire qu'on y reconnoissoit à peine la dixième partie de celle qu'on trouvoit dans le MS de Breslaw." (Bréquigny 48, fols. 292-93.) Sauvage's edition had been judged unsatisfactory even by some contemporaries, and a new edition was planned in 1563-65 by the Antwerp printer Christophe Plantin. This would have used the Breslau MS, then at Schoonhoven, South Holland, to correct the text of Sauvage. (Cf. G. Raynaud, 'Une édition de Froissart projetée par Christophe Plantin,' *Mélanges Julien Havet* [Paris, 1895], pp. 515-19.) Sainte-Palaye did well, how-

tional treatment of the manuscript tradition. He questioned the
authority of this manuscript on two main grounds—antiquity and
conformity. The Breslau manuscript, he declared, "ne remonte
guère au delà de la fin du XV siècle et . . . il est par conséquent
d'une médiocre autorité." The combined weight of "plus de 40
MSS de Froissart que j'avois maniez et dont plusieurs devoient
estre d'autant plus fidèles qu'il n'y avoit pas lieu de douter qu'ils
n'eussent esté faits les uns pour le Roy et les autres pour la Reyne
d'Angleterre à qui il paroissoit que l'autheur mesme les avoit pré-
sentez" was, understandably, even more damning. The Breslau
manuscript would have to be regarded, therefore, with great caution: "On ne se persuadera pas aisément que le seul Manuscrit de
Breslaw contienne seul des différences si considérables."[23] These
comments were made in 1735, before he had received any but the
scantest information about the Breslau manuscript. Shortly after-
ward he took steps to obtain a collation of this manuscript with
Sauvage's edition of the text.[24] Unfortunately the most valuable
part of a paper he prepared on the results of this collation has been
lost, but from what remains of it, it would appear that he had not
altered his opinion.[25] For the first book of the Chronicles, the only
manuscripts he knew were of the first, unrevised version of the
work ("A" manuscripts in Luce's edition), but for the second
book, of six manuscripts he consulted, four represented the revised
version ("B" manuscripts in Luce), and the Breslau manuscript
also fell into this category.[26] The idea that there might be two

---

ever, to insist that early editors should not be criticized glibly (Cf. Lenglet du
Fresnoy on Sauvage in *Méthode pour étudier l'histoire* [Paris, 1713], 2:104), and
that the value of their work must be assessed only after careful examination of
their methods and sources.

[23] *MAI* 13:578. Also Bréquigny 48, fols. 292–93.

[24] A directive indicating which passages he wanted to have collated is in
Bréquigny 48, fols. 288–91.

[25] Bréquigny 48, fols. 292–93: "Je dis alors (i.e., in 1735) dans mon Mémoire que
je persistois dans mon sentiment jusqu'à ce qu'on nous eust fait voir quelqu'un de
ces passages importans du MS de Breslaw qui manquoient dans l'Edit. de Sauvage.
Enfin nous avons eu touttes les prétendues additions ou augmentations de ce
fameux MS. Je les ai soigneusement examinées. Et si je ne me trompe, voici le
jugement qu'on en peut porter, aujourd'hui avec une pleine connoissance de
cause . . ." The MS breaks off at this point, but it is clear that Sainte-Palaye had
not altered his previous opinion. Sainte-Palaye's assessment of the Breslau MS
was accepted by Dacier and by Buchon in the early nineteenth century; cf.
Chroniques de Froissart, vol. 1, Preface, pp. xiv–xvi. (Collection des chroniques
nationales françaises [Paris, 1824–28].)

[26] See Appendix 2.

stages of Froissart's text and two manuscript traditions never entered Sainte-Palaye's head, however, and he could not, therefore, appreciate the importance of the Breslau manuscript. Those who claimed that the Breslau manuscript invalidated all the others showed, of course, no greater understanding.

Although mistakes were made, the tremendous breakthrough in understanding and methodology accomplished by the scholars of the eighteenth century commands respect. Their textual criticism, based on their knowledge of the general structures—historical, linguistic, stylistic—of which any given text, passage, or word was a part, was often of a high order, and if their understanding of the material aspects of textual tradition was limited, they at least did not suffer from the obsession with them which afflicted many scholars in the nineteenth century. They remained thoroughly conscious of their responsibility as critics. It is interesting that in recent years a number of scholars have shown themselves increasingly critical of the *recensio* as it was practiced in the nineteenth century and have re-emphasized the importance of confronting every element in a manuscript with the totality of our knowledge of the language and the literary and cultural traditions to which the text belongs.[27]

Within its historical limits, Sainte-Palaye's work on medieval texts was particularly valuable. He was probably the first scholar in France to study texts in the vernacular with the care that had hitherto been reserved for classical texts, combining exhaustive examination of all the elements of the tradition—which in the case of

[27] In a famous article published in 1928, Joseph Bédier declared himself totally skeptical of the possibility of any truly scientific study of manuscript tradition, and advocated a return to the methods of the humanists—i.e., publishing the text of a 'good' manuscript with a minimum of alteration. ('La Tradition manuscrite du *Lai de l'Ombre,*' *Romania* [1928], 54:161–96, 321–56.) A more moderate view has been put forward recently by the English classical scholar George Thomson. In words reminiscent of Bentley, Thomson declared, in his 1938 edition of the *Oresteia,* that "whether a particular reading is true or false is a question to be decided in the light of the whole body of the linguistic and literary evidence, which is independent of the authority of particular MSS. Our opinion of the relative value of the MSS must be determined by that evidence and cannot be used to override it" (2:361–62). As a modern scholar, however, Thomson naturally rejects the critic's "feeling for style" as a valid criterion and looks rather for help to scientific study and classification of errors and to improved application of linguistic controls as well as of our knowledge of the traditional themes and ideas of the culture of which the text in question is part. (Cf. 'Marxism and Textual Criticism,' *Wissenschaftliche Zeitschrift der Humboldt-Universität zu Berlin,* Gesellschafts-und Sprachwissenschaftliche Reihe [1963], 12:43–52.)

medieval works especially, he realized, must include early printed versions as well as manuscripts[28]—with the careful internal criticism which Bentley and the English school had developed to a high degree of refinement.

[28] Sainte-Palaye had the foresight to see that early printed editions are worth consulting for readings which they may have preserved from MSS subsequently lost. He praises Sauvage because "il a eu la précaution de rapporter en marge l'ancienne leçon toute défectueuse qu'elle étoit." (*MAI* 13:569.) This respect for *all* the elements of the written tradition is characteristic of his approach. At the same time he set great store by translations and carefully listed all the translations of Froissart which he knew of, believing that they could help to identify place and proper names.

CHAPTER 5

STUDY OF THE CHRONICLE SOURCES OF MEDIEVAL HISTORY

The idea of compiling a collection of chronicle sources of French history had occurred to seventeenth-century scholars like the Pithous and the Duchesnes, but neither the two Pithou brothers nor André Duchesne and his son had been able to realize it. Toward the end of the seventeenth century, Colbert asked Du Cange to draw up a plan for the continuation of the work begun by Duchesne.[1] Colbert's scheme foundered when Du Cange, offended by some criticisms of his plan, withdrew from it. Louvois' efforts to set the work on foot again were attended with even less success.[2] In 1717 the new chancellor d'Aguesseau instructed the Abbé Joachim Legrand to draw up another plan, and the task of collecting and editing the material was assigned to the Benedictine monks. In 1723 Dom Bouquet, a pupil of Montfaucon, took over the direction of the collection. D'Aguesseau this time appointed a group of scholars to supervise the work of the monks. According to Foncemagne this committee consisted of Du Bos, Secousse, Sainte-Palaye, and Foncemagne himself. Notes on the *Recueil des historiens* among Foncemagne's papers suggest that the committee took its supervisory duties seriously,[3] and in the Preface to the first volume (1738), Dom Bouquet himself acknowledged that he had received valuable assistance from it. In fact, the plan ultimately

---

[1] Bibliothèque de l'Institut, MS 1451, 'Documents ayant servi au Recueil des Historiens des Gaules et de la France: observations de l'abbé Legrand.' This account of the early history of the *Recueil* contains information not available elsewhere.

[2] Nouv. Acq. Fr. 3294, fols. 212–17, paper by Foncemagne on the publication of the medieval chronicles. According to Foncemagne, Louvois wanted to put Mabillon in charge of the project but the Benedictine scholar "s'en excusa."

[3] B.N. Français 9457, fols. 125–32; and 9355, fols. 237–40.

adopted for the *Recueil* was attributed by Dom Brial, a later editor, to Foncemagne.[4]

Sainte-Palaye was thus immediately involved in an immense project designed to recover and make available a large body of historical material pertaining to the Middle Ages. The texts themselves had to be studied with care so that an accurate version might be obtained, but the content of the testimony had also to be subjected to scrutiny. Sainte-Palaye turned the methods of historical criticism which he had acquired, under the guidance of Secousse, from Le Clerc and Bayle to the study of the chronicle sources of medieval history. To this end he prepared and published in the *Mémoires* of the Académie des Inscriptions an important series of analyses of these materials. Some were used by the successive editors of the *Recueil des historiens* and of the *Histoire littéraire de la France*, with or without acknowledgement, and may well have been intended for them.[5] Others dealt with works that had already been published by André Duchesne and his son in the five-volume *Historiae Francorum Scriptores*.[6] In the first of these papers, Sainte-Palaye made a clear statement of the principles which were to guide him in all the subsequent ones: "L'histoire n'est fondée que sur le témoignage des auteurs qui nous l'ont transmise. Il importe donc extrêmement pour la sçavoir, de bien connoître quels estoient ces auteurs. Rien n'est à négliger en ce point; le temps où ils ont vécu, leur naissance, leur estat, leur patrie, la part qu'ils ont eue aux affaires, les moyens par lesquels ils en ont esté instruits, et l'intérêt qu'ils y pouvoient prendre, sont des circonstances essentielles qu'il n'est pas permis d'ignorer; de-là dépend le plus ou

---

[4] Foncemagne's 'Plan pour la nouvelle collection des Historiens de France' (B.N. Français 9355, 237–40) is not listed under Foncemagne's name in the B.N. catalogue of French Manuscripts, but is in a volume of letters collected by Dom Brial.

[5] The introduction by the Benedictines to the *Chroniques de Saint-Denis* is avowedly an abridgement of Sainte-Palaye's paper in the *MAI*. (Cf. *Recueil des historiens* [1741], vol. 3, Preface, p. xii and p. 145.) The 'Mémoire concernant les principaux monumens de l'histoire de France,' which is essentially a short, critical description of the principal literary sources of French history from Gregory of Tours on, may have been submitted to the Benedictines as a guide to assist them in their research. The *Novelle letterarie* of Lami (12.2.1740, col. 97 *et seq.*) suggest that Sainte-Palaye's work on the historians was undertaken with a view to the *Recueil*.

[6] (Paris, 1636–49.) These were: Helgaud (4:59), *Gesta Ludovici VII* (4:390), *Historia gloriosi regis Ludovici* (4:412), Continuation of Guillaume de Nangis (2:626), Guillaume le Breton (5:326, 516), Glaber (4:1), *Chronique de Morigny* (4:359).

moins d'autorité qu'ils doivent avoir, et sans cette connoissance on courra risque très-souvent de prendre pour guide un historien de mauvaise foy, ou du moins mal-informé. C'est sur ce principe que m'estant proposé de faire une lecture suivie des historiens de la troisième race de nos Rois, j'ay cherché à m'instruire autant que j'ay pu, de tout ce qui concerne leurs personnes et leurs ouvrages."[7] He proceeded to do this for Rigord, for Guillaume le Breton, for Glaber, for Helgaud, for Guillaume de Nangis and his continuators, for the *Gesta* and the *Historia Ludovici VII*, for the *Chronique de Morigny* (*Chronicon Mauriniacense*), for the *Chroniques de Saint-Denis*, and for the *Jouvencel*. In all his works Sainte-Palaye employed the same technique: his essays on the poems and chronicles of Froissart rely to a large extent on his biographical investigation of the man, he supplemented his edition of the *Voeu du Héron* and the accompanying essay with a monograph on the life of Gautier de Mauny (or Walter Manny), while the *Histoire littéraire des troubadours*, as he envisaged it, included the Lives of the Troubadours alongside examples of their work. For Sainte-Palaye these biographical monographs served a dual purpose: on the one hand, they established a guide to the interpretation of historical texts; on the other, they revealed the real context in which the men of the past lived and acted. Thus, he remarked of his portrait of Glaber: "Ce portrait n'est pas le seul qu'on puisse envisager icy, on y retrouve en même temps celuy de tout un siècle et de toute une nation."[8]

To establish the authorship of a text, Sainte-Palaye employed a variety of techniques which, taken together, remain to this day the basis of all such investigations. The simplest of all is the use of chronology, and it was chronological inconsistencies which led him to throw doubt on the attribution to Suger, by Belleforest, Vossius, and Le Long, of the *Historia Gloriosi Regis Ludovici VII.*[9] Com-

---

[7] 'Mémoire concernant la vie et les ouvrages de Rigord et de Guillaume le Breton,' *MAI* 8:528. The idea occurs frequently in Sainte-Palaye's writings. It is stated expressly in the 'Projet d'étude' (Bréquigny 62, fol. 211) where he declares that biographical information about authors is one of the things he is constantly looking out for in his reading. Moreau 1722, fols. 1–21, contains a list of medieval and Renaissance writers, with their dates and some summary biographical data.

[8] *MAI* 8:553–54.

[9] *MAI* 10:568–69. Sainte-Palaye had been content to deny Suger's authorship of a part of the *Historia gloriosi regis Ludovici*. The editors of the *Histoire littéraire* (1763), 12:403, and Dom Brial in the *Recueil des Historiens* (1818), vol. 12, Preface, p. xii, cast doubt on Suger's authorship of any part of the *Historia* or the

mon sense reasoning on the basis of as much information as it is possible to find about the author and the work is indispensable, and finally stylistic analysis can help to detect breaks in the continuity of a work, changes of author, and even to some extent the education and training of the author. The way Sainte-Palaye argues that Helgaud's *Épitome du Roy Robert* is not an abridgement of an earlier work provides a brief illustration of these two points. First, he suggests that the title of the manuscript copy—"Helgaldi . . . Epitoma Vitae Roberti Regis, ex alterius Monachi scriptis"—is due to the ignorance of the copyist who misunderstood the sense of "epitoma," and himself added "ex alterius Monachi scriptis." Then he points out that Helgaud speaks in the first person as a witness of what he relates and never mentions any other historian; that a contemporary author frequently refers to Helgaud's *Épitome*, which he would probably not have done had there been a primary source; and finally that the style, intricate and detailed, is not that of an abridgement. Sainte-Palaye concludes that the work came at the end of a history of the abbeys of St. Aignan and Fleury as a token of gratitude to Robert, who had been a generous benefactor to them.[10]

Although some of Sainte-Palaye's conclusions have been rejected since he wrote, the very arguments adduced against him have been arrived at by the application of methods of which he himself was one of the pioneer users. His work was solid enough to form the basis of nearly all nineteenth-century criticism of sources, and even today it still has to be taken into account.[11]

Gesta. For a re-examination of this question on which Sainte-Palaye did pioneer work, see A. Coville, 'Observations sur deux sources du règne de Louis VII,' *Revue historique* (1885), 27:351–57.

[10] *MAI* 10:558.

[11] The nineteenth-century editors of the *Histoire littéraire de la France* rejected earlier analyses of Rigord's History by Vossius, Cave, Oudin, Fabricius, Legendre, and Dom Félibien as "incomplètes et inexactes," while appreciating Sainte-Palaye's work and generally accepting his findings concerning the author's life (1832), 17:6, 19–20. His paper on Guillaume le Breton was appraised in similar fashion (*ibid.*, p. 355). The editors of the *Recueil des historiens* also drew frequently on Sainte-Palaye, usually without explicit acknowledgment. (See the prefaces to Rigord and Guillaume de Nangis, *Recueil* [1818], vol. 12, ii–iii; [1840], vol. 20, pp. xlvii–lii.) Sainte-Palaye's attribution of the last of the so-called continuations of Guillaume de Nangis to Jean de Venette was generally accepted in the nineteenth century and has only recently been contested. (See Alfred Coville in *Histoire littéraire de la France* [1949], 38:333–35.) On Jean de Venette's poem, *Les trois Maries*, to which he was the first to draw attention, he remained the sole authority through-

Above all, he had indicated clearly to contemporaries that the medieval chronicles could be put to use by serious modern historians provided they considered them critically. Fables and legends, for instance, were obviously to be rejected out of hand and those historians who reported them to be read with caution. Thus, he observed ironically of Jean de Venette, whom he considered one of the continuators of Guillaume de Nangis: "Il est en général assez crédule sur les miracles, les prodiges, les prophéties et les présages. Je laisse aux Naturalistes l'examen de ce qu'il rapporte, que depuis la peste de 1349 tous les hommes qui naquirent n'eurent plus que 22 dents, au lieu de 32 que les hommes nez avant cette époque avoient toujours eues; j'observeray seulement que le même fait ou la même fable, se trouve rapportée par Rigord sous l'an 1187 comme une suite de l'enlèvement que les Sarrasins firent cette année de la vraie Croix sur les Chrétiens."[12]

The author's standpoint has to be taken into account. Guillaume le Breton and Helgaud, for instance, were writing eulogies—Helgaud of King Robert, and Guillaume le Breton of Philip.[13] This need not always affect the veracity of the narrative, but it may create a false emphasis. Although Guillaume le Breton's *Philippide* is not extravagantly fabulous, "cependant il faut toujours observer que c'est un Poëte qui parle, et un Poëte qui ne s'est proposé d'autre but en composant que la gloire du Prince dont il rapportoit la vie. Si l'on ne peut donc luy reprocher d'avoir altéré essentiellement la vérité de l'histoire, ni d'avoir avancé des faits démentis par d'autres auteurs, il n'a pas toujours négligé de prester les belles couleurs à ceux qu'il a trouvé véritables."[14] It will not do, Sainte-Palaye insisted, to dismiss these sources out of hand as beneath contempt. They provide us with an essential part of our information about the early history of the modern European nations, and it is the task of the modern historian to sift off the pure gold of history from the dunghill of medieval legend. "Je préviens une réflexion qui s'offre naturellement à l'esprit en lisant ce mémoire,"

---

out the nineteenth century and in Coville's analysis of the work—published recently—he was still being quoted (*ibid.*, pp. 362–66). The papers on Froissart, which contributed to the vogue of Froissart in the Romantic period, have been largely superseded, but even in 1870 Kervyn de Lettenhove said he had been much helped by them. (*Chroniques de Froissart* [Brussels, 1867–77], 1:534.) The currently used bibliographies of Molinier (Paris, 1902–06) and Potthast (Berlin, 1896) invariably refer to Sainte-Palaye's discussions of medieval chronicle sources.

[12] *MAI* 8:575.   [13] *Ibid.*, p. 544; also *MAI* 10:558.   [14] *MAI* 8:544.

he began, introducing his memoir on Jean de Venette. "On gémira sur le sort de notre histoire, qui a esté si longtemps livrée à des Écrivains si grossiers et si crédules. Mais il faut distinguer ce qu'une dévotion mal entendue et de mode leur faisoit dire, d'avec ce qu'ils rapportoient nuement et simplement des faits qui se passoient sous leurs yeux. Jean de Venette luy-même en est une preuve sensible: son histoire paroît sincère, et ne s'écarte de la vraysemblance que dans les endroits où il est question de miracles et de prodiges."[15]

Nor is there any need, he declared, to despair of detecting and correcting the tendentiousness of medieval writers. Usually their statements can be checked against those of their contemporaries. In this way, if one feels that Gregory of Tours may have been swayed occasionally by prejudice, "Frédégaire qui l'abrégea, et qui écrivit peu de tems après lui dans des sentimens opposez, l'ayant quelquefois éclairci et quelquefois contredit, fournit aux Critiques éclairez les moyens de percer les Nuages de l'Histoire, et de démêler la vérité à travers des témoignages contradictoires qui semblent l'obscurcir."[16] So too the great reputation enjoyed by the *Chroniques de Saint-Denis*, the fact that historians like Philippe Mouskes and Guillaume Guiart based their writings on them while poets like Adenet le Roi appealed to them to give an air of veracity to their own writings, can act as a pointer to the reliability of the *Chroniques* as sources.[17]

Sainte-Palaye's achievement in laying the foundation of a critical approach to medieval sources is considerable. Nevertheless, there is a flaw in his attitude to the sources. We have already had occasion to remark that he shared with Bouhier and Secousse a tendency to regard a text as authoritative, once its general reliability had been demonstrated. There was in this a danger that specific problems, which required the application of all the resources of historical criticism, might be solved superficially by appeal to the newly established authorities, and that these authorities might be taken as the last word on virtually every aspect of the history of the age they described. All the qualities and defects of Sainte-Palaye's attitude to sources are present in the three memoirs on Froissart's Chronicles, which he read to the Académie des Inscriptions between 1733 and 1735.

He began characteristically with a *Mémoire sur la vie de Frois-*

---

[15] *Ibid.*, p. 526.   [16] *MAI* 15:583–84.   [17] *Ibid.*, p. 590.

sart, based on information which he extracted by dint of pains-taking study from the poems and Chronicles.[18] In 1734 followed a *Mémoire concernant les ouvrages de Froissart,*[19] in which he ex-amined the various stages in the composition of the Chronicles and the influences which might be expected to have affected Froissart's presentation of the facts. The division into four books he attributed to Froissart himself, but all the subdivisions were, he claimed, the work of copyists and especially of printers. "Je tâcheray d'assigner à chacune de ces parties le temps qui luy convient," he wrote, "et de déterminer quand elle fut commencée et achevée, combien d'Années l'auteur y employa et les intervalles pendant lesquels il discontinua d'écrire. Je crois tous ces détails essentiels. Froissart parcourut beaucoup de pays, dans plusieurs desquels il séjourna un temps considérable; il fut attaché en différents temps à des Cours, dont les intérêts estoient fort opposez; il fréquenta un grand nombre de Princes et de Seigneurs de divers partis. Il seroit bien difficile qu'il ne se fût pas laissé prévenir, ou d'affection pour les uns ou de haine pour les autres. Si l'on veut se rappeler les circon-stances de la vie de notre Historien, rapportées dans mon premier Mémoire, et qu'on les rapproche des temps ausquels il travailla à la composition des différentes parties de son histoire; non seulement on verra les instructions qu'il avoit esté en état de prendre, tant par rapport aux lieux que par rapport aux personnes qu'il avoit vues: mais on jugera encore des partis ausquels on peut le soupçonner d'avoir incliné. Ces connoissances une fois bien établies, seront d'un grand secours pour faire apprécier plus au juste les différents degrez d'autorité qu'il mérite, suivant les différentes matières qu'il a traitées, et les temps ausquels il les a traitées . . . Tout lecteur pourra faire l'application de cette règle, à mesure qu'il avancera dans la lecture de Froissart; elle luy servira de guide à chaque pas; elle le garantira de l'erreur ou de la séduction."[20]

Equally important for assessing the reliability of the *Chroniques* is the question of Froissart's own sources. Sainte-Palaye recalls that he had the confidence of many princes and servants of princes, and that consequently he had direct access to the sources of policy. In addition, he made use of state papers and charters.[21] Froissart's only basic mistake—according to Sainte-Palaye—was to have writ-ten at all about things of which he could not possibly have been

[18] *MAI* 13:520.   [19] *Ibid.,* p. 539.   [20] *Ibid.,* p. 540.
[21] *Ibid.,* pp. 546–47.

well-informed, and his most blatant errors occur in his accounts of distant lands—Tartary, Hungary, Africa, the Orient—of which he had no direct knowledge.[22] The confusions in his chronology, consequent upon his use of different modes of calculating years (from January 1, from Easter, from Palm Sunday) and the time of day (which he sometimes divided into the canonical hours, sometimes into broad periods like "haute" and "basse") should be watched but can be remedied once the reader is aware of them.[23]

Sainte-Palaye had already alluded in the second memoir to the vexed question of Froissart's partiality, observing circumspectly: "Il s'agira de voir s'il a observé aussi fidellement qu'il le promet cette loy qu'il s'estoit imposée qui est le premier devoir de tout historien"—the law of impartiality. In the third memoir, the *Jugement de l'Histoire de Froissart*—read to the Academy in 1735 —he attempted to answer this question. He began by noting the notoriety into which Froissart had fallen, and the common opinion that he was in the pay of the English. "Bodin, Pasquier, Brantôme, Sorel, la Popelinière, le Laboureur déposent contre luy dans les termes les plus formels."[24] What justification is there for their criticism, he asks. Sainte-Palaye reduced to the years 1329–69, years spent in familiarity with the King and Queen of England, the period of Froissart's possible anti-French bias, and brought forward key passages, taken from this period of the Chronicles, for examination. The account of the accession of Philippe de Valois to the throne of France, for example, is quite objective—he argued—although this event raised a storm of protest in England. "Tout ce passage," Sainte-Palaye comments, "ne présente rien qui ne dût faire admirer le courage et la bonne foi de l'Historien."[25] Having discussed several passages of this kind, he concluded that the imputation to Froissart of an anti-French bias is unfounded. He does not overlook the possibility that in later years, when he was no longer in the service of the English, Froissart might have written with an anti-English bias. After scrutinizing a number of passages where such a bias, if it had existed, might have been expected to show itself, he again concludes that the evidence does not justify any accusation of serious partiality in one direction or

---

[22] 'Jugement de l'Histoire de Froissart,' *MAI* 13:564.
[23] 'Mémoire concernant les ouvrages de Froissart,' *ibid.*, pp. 550–51.
[24] 'Jugement de l'Histoire de Froissart,' *ibid.*, p. 555.   [25] *Ibid.*, p. 559.

another. In this way Froissart is cleared of the suspicion that he sold his pen to his patrons.

As we saw earlier in our discussion of Sainte-Palaye's treatment of the Froissart manuscripts, it did not occur to him that there might be more than one *authentic* version of the Chronicles, that Froissart might have revised his work in later life and completely redrafted it in his old age, altering on both occasions his attitude to the French and the English. For Sainte-Palaye, in short, the history of the Chronicles themselves was not problematic. Inevitably his arguments have been weakened by the discoveries of later scholars concerning the composition of the Chronicles.

The last part of the third memoir concerns the manuscripts and editions of the Chronicles. Sainte-Palaye here inquired into the validity of the text in current use (Sauvage's edition of Lyon, 1559, 1560, 1561) and concluded that, though it could be improved upon, it was not seriously misleading. The shortcomings of this analysis have already been discussed. The fact that it was considered an indispensable part of a serious study of Froissart's value for modern historians is evidence of Sainte-Palaye's keen awareness of all the problems which needed to be reviewed before the reliability of an historical text could be established. Chapelain, for instance, in the preceding century had completely overlooked the question of the purity of the text itself.

Sainte-Palaye was too intelligent a critic to conclude from the favorable results of his analysis of Froissart that historians could be given carte blanche to draw on him as they pleased. On the contrary, he warned against jumping to this conclusion. Four points had to be borne in mind by the historian using Froissart, he declared. First, the reader must remember that Froissart was only human, and that occasionally his presentation of his material might have been affected by unconscious bias: "L'on ne doit, autant qu'il se pourra, jamais perdre de vue, je le répète . . . les détails de sa vie, ses divers attachements à certains Princes et à quelques Seigneurs . . . les circonstances dans lesquelles il écrivit son Histoire, quels volumes furent entrepris à la sollicitation du Comte de Namur, partisan des Anglois, et quels sont ceux qu'il composa par l'ordre du Comte de Blois ami de la France . . . Je ne dois pas négliger d'avertir que sa prévention se fait quelquefois sentir dans des détails plus particuliers; comme on peut s'en convaincre par les éloges qu'il fait de la piété et des autres vertus du Comte de Foix, bien opposez aux actions de cruauté qu'il avoit rapportées auparavant."[26]

Second, it should not be forgotten that even if his impartiality has been established, Froissart, like all the historians of his age, lacked the critical sense demanded of modern historians: "Mais quand un Historien, dégagé de toute passion, tiendroit toujours la balance égale entre les différens partis; quand à cette qualité il joindroit celle qu'on ne peut refuser à Froissart, j'entends une attention continuelle à vouloir estre informé de tous les événemens et de toutes les particularitez qui peuvent intéresser les lecteurs: il sera toujours bien loin de la perfection, si ses connoissances ne sont éclairées d'une saine critique, qui dans cette multitude de récits différents, sache écarter tout ce qui s'éloigne de l'exacte vérité: son ouvrage sera moins une histoire, qu'un tissu de fables et de bruits populaires."[27] The reader must consequently be on his guard against the chronicler's own credulity and lack of critical sense.

Third, the reader should consider that Froissart wrote his Chronicles in an age avid for color, pageantry, and high romance. The text reflects in this respect the tastes and activities of its author and his time: whence the long descriptions of pageants, tournaments, jousts and chivalrous exploits; many of his expressions are "phrases qui se lisent, presque à chaque page, dans les Romans de Chevalerie de la Table Ronde."[28]

Fourth, in a remarkable passage of the second memoir, Sainte-Palaye warns against accepting the testimony of any historian, however reliable, as in itself sufficient evidence of the truth of what he relates. "Jamais Historien eut-il des garants plus certains des faits qu'il a rapportez? Jamais en fut-il un, en qui l'on doit prendre plus de confiance qu'en Froissart, dans cette partie de son Histoire? Cependant vous vous souvenez, Messieurs, des fautes que M. Lancelot a relevées dans plusieurs articles qui concernent l'Histoire d'Angleterre de ces mêmes temps. Sa critique est fondée sur les actes originaux qu'il a eus entre les mains, et dont l'autorité est incontestable. J'appuye sur cet exemple, parce qu'il me paroît plus propre qu'aucun autre à faire sortir une vérité importante pour notre Histoire et qui a esté tant recommandée par les Auteurs les plus versez dans cette étude: je veux dire l'extrême nécessité d'accompagner la lecture des Historiens, de la comparaison des actes

---

[26] *Ibid.*, p. 563.   [27] *Ibid.*   [28] *Ibid.*, p. 564.

originaux des mêmes temps . . . c'est de ce concours que résulte toute la certitude dont les veritez de cette nature sont susceptibles par rapport à nous."[29]

These memoirs on Froissart reveal the very considerable merits of Sainte-Palaye as a critic. The four points on which he advised caution show that he was alive to the need for the continual exercise of criticism and that he realized the scholar could not be absolved by any general critical evaluation of an historian's testimony from meeting each historical problem with all the resources of judgment at his command. Indeed Sainte-Palaye's constant concern to remind the reader of this is one of the most impressive aspects of the memoirs.

Yet he himself was the first to fall into the very vice he warned against. He so far ignored his own account of the quality of romance in Froissart that his *Mémoires sur l'ancienne chevalerie* are to some degree marred by his excessive and unquestioning reliance on the testimony of Froissart. Similarly the biography of Walter Manny, which he appended to his edition of the *Voeu du héron*,[30] is rendered completely inadequate as a result of his total dependence on Froissart's chronicles for information about his hero. If he had cared to look into the documents which he himself declared were an indispensable corrective to the testimony of historians, he would have been able to turn out a more complete and more accurate piece of work. Nor were these sources inaccessible. Dugdale's *Baronage* and Rymer's *Foedera* both contain material concerning Manny. But perhaps the most revealing instance of his uncritical admiration for Froissart is provided by his reaction to Hume's skepticism concerning the episode of the six burghers of Calais. When he discovered Hume's judgment of this passage in the Chronicles and his poor opinion of Froissart in general (*History*, chapter 15, note [*H*]), he immediately wrote to Bréquigny, who respected Hume greatly, rejecting the philosopher's criticism on the grounds that "si jamais historien a esté instruit de ces tems-là c'est lui (Froissart) contemporain, compatriote et serviteur de la Reine d'Angleterre."[31] Nineteenth century scholars have, in general, vindicated Froissart on this point,[32] but what remains

---

[29] *Ibid.*, p. 554.
[30] *Mémoires sur l'ancienne chevalerie* (Paris, 1781), 3:21–72.
[31] Bréquigny 165, fol. 66, to Bréquigny, 25.3.1765.
[32] *Chroniques de Froissart*, ed. S. Luce, vol. 4, p. xxv, n. 1.

striking about Sainte-Palaye's attitude is his conviction that Frois-sart must be right, and his slowness to consult other evidence. Bréquigny himself was to question the truth of the story, invoking in evidence a number of documents in Rymer's *Foedera*,[33] and Dacier, while supporting Froissart, did not leave the documentary evidence out of account.[34] Rymer's *Foedera* were widely available to scholars in the eighteenth century—a synopsis had even been published in French (The Hague, 1737–1745)—and Saint-Palaye had no excuse for not consulting them.

Sainte-Palaye's love of Froissart can be explained by the pleasure he took in the lively and picturesque style of the Chronicles, a pleasure he shared with many others on both sides of the Channel. His defense of their historical reliability, and his excessive depend-ence on them in his own historical studies were to have a con-siderable effect on medieval historiography in the early years of the nineteenth century.[35]

[33] Bréquigny, 'Deuxième mémoire pour servir à l'histoire de Calais,' *MAI* 50:618–22, read on 29.2.1780.

[34] *Chroniques de Froissart*, ed. Bon-Joseph Dacier, p. 351, n. 2. Dacier's edition was interrupted at p. 632 of vol. 1 and never taken up again. The few remaining copies have no title page and no date. One, which belonged to the early nineteenth century English editor of Froissart, Thomas Johnes, is in B.M. 1850.c.24.

[35] The gist of the papers on Froissart was reproduced in Niceron (*Mémoires*, [1741], 42.210–29), and by the editors of the *Almanach des muses* [1778], 1:53–54). In 1829 they were reprinted by Buchon in his *Collection des chroniques*, vol. 2. In England the poet Thomas Gray was one of those who shared Sainte-Palaye's love of the picturesque in Froissart (*Correspondence of Thomas Gray*, ed. Toyn-bee and Whibley [Oxford, 1935], letter 308, 23.1.1760). Gray was familiar with Sainte-Palaye's studies, since he recommended them to a young friend and de-clared that his own knowledge of the chronicler came from them (*ibid.*, letter 543, to Nicholls, February, 1771). In the second year of the nineteenth century, the papers on Froissart were collected into one volume and published in English translation—*Memoirs of the Life of Froissart with an Essay on His Works and a Criticism of His History, translated from the French of Mr. de la Curne de St. Palaye, by Thomas Johnes* (London, 1801). There was a second edition in 1810. This translation of the Froissart papers was also published by Johnes in his edition of the Chronicles (London, 1802–5), and in a second edition (London, 1805–6).

CHAPTER 6

STUDY OF THE LITERARY SOURCES OF MEDIEVAL HISTORY

The Enlightenment view of history as the history not so much of politics and wars as of culture—"l'histoire de l'esprit humain et des divers systêmes qu'il a enfantés," to quote, once again, the Academician Le Beau—was accompanied, as one would expect, by an extension not only of the type of information which the historian could look for in traditional sources but also of the range of his sources.

Sainte-Palaye grasped that points of real interest may lie unnoticed amid a mass of apparently uninteresting and valueless material. In the *Chronique de Morigny*, for instance, there is a passage describing the activities of one of the monks of Morigny who was responsible for managing the abbey's lands. The passage recounts how the monk Baudouin cleared, settled, and husbanded an estate which the abbey had acquired from the nuns of Saint-Eloy.[1] Sainte-Palaye believed that information such as is found in this account of agrarian economy in the thirteenth century would help to define the context of contemporary politics, laws, institutions, and manners, and it was this kind of information which he sought in many minor chroniclers, like Jean de Venette.[2] Indeed he claimed that some documents which are almost valueless from the point of view of political history remain useful if they are considered in this light.

To go on from here to the study of nonhistorical fictional texts for information about the past was an easy and almost inevitable step, which Sainte-Palaye did not hesitate to take. In 1743 he was writing to Bouhier of two manuscripts of Gérard de Roussillon, one of which he estimated to be two hundred years older than the other: "Je voudrois donner un Mémoire où je comparerois l'un

[1] *MAI* 10: 544–45.   [2] *MAI* 13:520 *et seq.*

avec l'autre et comme ils contiennent bien des détails géographiques de la Bourgogne, et parmi un grand nombre d'usages anciens, des choses importantes sur les droits et les devoirs des Fiefs, mon intention est de faire voir que la lecture des anciens Romans de Chevalerie n'est pas aussi inutile que bien des gens le pensent communément."[3]

In the *Mémoire concernant la lecture des anciens romans de chevalerie* which was the direct outcome of these remarks, and which was read to the Académie des Inscriptions at the end of the year, Sainte-Palaye pointed to the eminent sixteenth- and seventeenth-century scholars—Fauchet, Le Laboureur, Du Cange—who had already defended the old romances as historical sources.[4] Moreover, Galland's treatment of the theme in an early paper read to the Academy was certainly known to him,[5] but he himself admits that he had not read Chapelain's *Dialogue*,[6] and he makes no mention of two papers by Fourmont the Elder on *L'Étude de nos anciens romans*, presented to the Academy in May, 1727.[7] There was at any rate nothing original in the basic principle underlying the *Mémoire concernant la lecture des anciens romans de chevalerie*, and it did not need a man of rare talent to think of it. The merit of the old romances, Sainte-Palaye declared, is to provide "la connoissance générale . . . du génie et du goût des siècles dans lesquels ils furent écrits." Since the *Querelle des Anciens et des Modernes* this idea had become a commonplace, as Sainte-Palaye recognized. "Tout le monde," he wrote, "sent assez que chaque siècle se peint dans les ouvrages d'esprit et d'imagination qu'il a produits ou qu'il a fait revivre."[8]

[3] B. N. Français 24418, fol. 382, to Bouhier, 21.9.1743.

[4] *MAI* 17:787. Others quoted include Pasquier, Duchesne, Favin, Vulson de la Colombière, Chantereau Le Febvre, Catel, Caseneuve, and among contemporaries, Dom Vaissette and Dom Calmet.

[5] Galland's paper is in *MAI* 2:673. Sainte-Palaye refers to it *MAI* 17:789.

[6] Chapelain's *Dialogue* appeared in *Continuation des Mémoires de littérature et d'histoire de M. Sallengre* (1728), 6:281–342. Sainte-Palaye says he learned of it only after he completed his own paper (*MAI* 17:790).

[7] *Registres de l'Académie des Inscriptions* (1727), pp. 249, 251. Neither of these papers was copied into the *Registres* or published in the *MAI*. They were read on May 13 and 16.

[8] *MAI* 17:796. Cf. likewise Helvétius: "Ce n'est pas que les anciens romans ne soient encore agréables à quelques philosophes, qui les regardent comme la vraie histoire des moeurs d'un peuple considéré dans un certain siècle et une certaine forme de gouvernement." (*De l'Esprit*, vol. 2, p. xix, n. 1, *cit.* Werner Krauss, 'Zur französischen Romantheorie des 18. Jahrhunderts,' *Nachahmung und Illusion*, ed. H. R. Jauss [Munich, 1964], pp. 60–71.)

The originality of Sainte-Palaye's paper lies in the fact that he advocated not haphazard reference to fictional sources, but systematic study of them: "Qu'il me soit permis de souhaiter que quelques gens de Lettres se partagent entre eux le pénible travail de lire ces sortes d'ouvrages, dont le temps détruit tous les jours quelques morceaux, d'en faire des extraits, qu'ils rapporteront à un système général et uniforme; afin que, cessant de prendre des routes différentes, on ne soit point obligé de recommencer souvent les mêmes lectures. On pourroit ainsi parvenir à avoir une bibliothèque générale et complète de tous nos anciens Romans de Chevalerie."[9] Where Chapelain and Galland had simply suggested that it might occasionally be useful to consult the literary monuments of the Middle Ages, Sainte-Palaye was proposing that they be treated with the same method and in the same spirit of criticism as traditional historical sources. Accordingly, he stressed the need to establish the date of composition of the text and its authorship, to describe the author's birth, education, ideas, and prejudices, and to identify the prince or nobleman for whom the work had been written and whose interests the author could be expected to have served. Last, but not least, the manuscripts were to be consulted as well as, and often in preference to, the printed editions. As Sainte-Palaye experienced in his examination of the *Jouvencel*, consultation of the manuscripts might have the effect of altering the character of a work and revealing a text of far greater interest to the historian than the better known printed text.[10]

What sort of information did Sainte-Palaye expect to find in literary texts? First, precise information about specific points of history, about political events, wars, royal marriages, births, deaths, etc. Second, information about manners, customs, and institutions: "C'est dans nos Romans . . . que l'on trouvera les connoissances les plus détaillées sur l'ancienne manière de faire la guerre, sur les droits et la dépendance des différents degrés des Feudataires, sur les gages de bataille, sur l'administration de la justice, sur la noblesse et sur la chevalerie, les armures, les armoiries, les tournois etc."[11] Third, information about the arts and sciences ("le progrès des Arts et des Sciences"). There are thus three phases in the examination of literary sources: (1) the collection of factual data; (2) the study of manners and laws; and (3) the evaluation of the style and language in which the texts were written. Sainte-Palaye emphasized that information was not always provided explicitly in the old romances, and that the scholar must read them attentively. With remarkable historical insight he pointed out the value of their very anachronisms: "Ceux qui les ont composés n'étoient point, heureusement, assez habiles pour connoître et observer le costume; ils appliquoient presque toujours au temps dont ils faisoient l'histoire vraie ou fabuleuse, les usages du temps où ils vivoient; semblables à nos anciens Peintres venus après l'invention de la Poudre, qui n'ont presque jamais représenté dans les miniatures le siège de Troie, sans y joindre quelque pièce de notre artillerie."[12]

Sainte-Palaye made out a better case than anyone had yet succeeded in doing, for bringing the literary texts of the Middle Ages into the orbit of serious historical studies. He had also shown greater acuteness than his predecessors in suggesting how they could be exploited by the historian.[13] He had recognized that the resources of traditional historical material had not been exhausted by earlier scholars, and that, approached in a different spirit, this material could be brought to bear profitably on problems which had hitherto received scant attention. He had also suggested on another occasion that the relevance of some material might be appreciated only by subsequent scholars. This was to say, in direct opposition to d'Alembert for instance, that the meaning or usefulness of a document, or fact, for the historian cannot be summarily determined for all time. Yet, his own proposal that the old literary texts be published in a library of extracts ran directly counter to this principle, since the extracts he envisaged were to be selected according to a "système général et uniforme." Sainte-Palaye did not, apparently, reflect that this system in itself was bound to be historically determined and that his extracts would consequently be more revealing of the interests and ideas of his own age than of

[12] *Ibid.*

[13] There are echoes of this paper in Paul Henri Mallet's *Introduction à l'histoire du Danemarck* (Copenhagen, 1755–56), one of the more important works of the Montesquieu school of historians. I quote from the Percy translation (*Northern Antiquities* [London, 1770], 1:56): "It is needless to observe, that great light may be thrown on the character and sentiments of a nation, by those very books, whence we can learn nothing exact or connected of their history. The most credulous writer . . . while he falsify the histories of his contemporaries, paints their manner of life and modes of thinking, without perceiving it. His simplicity, his ignorance, are at once pledges of the artless truth of his drawing, and a warning to distrust that of his relations."

the age they were supposed to illumine. Nor did he see that a selection of this kind would be of limited use to succeeding generations.

The nature of his own interest in literary texts can be judged by his *Dictionnaire des antiquitez*, in which poems, *chansons*, and *fabliaux* are among the sources combed for references to political events, to religious observances and disputes, to manners, customs, arts, sciences, dress and indeed almost every aspect, material and moral, of medieval life, or by his paper on Froissart's poetry in which he tells us that the *Pastourelles* contain "beaucoup de détails . . . concernant les habillements de ce siècle-là, les instruments de Musique champêtre, et divers usages de cette espèce" as well as allusions "à des événements historiques, tels qu'une fabrication de monnoye, l'arrivée du Roy Jean en Angleterre . . . etc."[14] Another poem by Froissart, *L'horloge amoureuse*, was the starting point of a lengthy disquisition on medieval horology.

The same *Notice des poésies de Froissart*, read to the Académie des Inscriptions in 1738, shows how Sainte-Palaye approached the literature of the Middle Ages when he was not looking for information of a political or social nature. The idea that medieval poetry might be studied for its own sake was hardly entertained. Sainte-Palaye's views are typical of the *Modernes* of the early Enlightenment: "Il conviendroit que . . . ceux qui se livrent aux études historiques, tournassent aussi quelquefois leurs vues de ce côté-là, et que pour l'utilité de ces mêmes arts, ils s'étudiassent à montrer par quels moyens et par quels degrés ils se sont élevez au point où nous les voyons aujourd'hui; et que pour la gloire de ceux qui les cultivent ils nous fissent sçavoir combien les modernes ont laissé loin derrière eux ceux qui les avoient précédez."[15]

He showed a certain appreciation of the poems, which he read, as most of his contemporaries read medieval poetry, in the spirit of Fontenelle's well-known essay on Pastoral. He noted "beaucoup de délicatesse et d'agrément" in the *Dit de la Marguerite* and praised the Pastourelles warmly: "Froissart n'a réussi dans aucun genre de Poésie aussi bien que dans les Pastourelles. Cette gaieté naïve et légère, qui presque toujours fait le caractère de son esprit, a passé tout entière dans le coeur de ses bergers et de ses bergères." In the *Rondeaux* "l'expression vive ou tendre est toujours simple,

---

[14] *MAI* 16:223.   [15] *Ibid.*, p. 222.

et rend parfaitement la passion dont son âme est agitée." The final judgment is not altogether unfavorable: "L'invention pour les sujets lui manquoit autant que l'imagination pour les ornemens; du reste le style qu'il employe, moins abondant que diffus, offre seulement la répétition ennuyeuse des mêmes tours et des mêmes phrases pour rendre des idées assez communes: cependant la simplicité et la liberté de sa versification ne sont pas toujours dépourvues de grâces, on y rencontre de tems en tems quelques images et plusieurs vers de suite dont l'expression est assez heureuse."[16]

It is appropriate that this essay on Froissart's poetry closed with a general account of the state of the arts and of letters in the thirteenth and fourteenth centuries—noteworthy mostly for the evidence it contains that Sainte-Palaye paid close attention to manuscript miniatures—of the kind which is a feature of almost all general histories in the eighteenth century and which, as yet, provided the most common framework for the study of medieval literature as literature.[17] Within this framework the critic could appreciate two things: he could appreciate the seeds of future refinement in early poetry much as the observer of the child might watch in him for the earliest signs of the speculative intelligence, and he could appreciate, in the spirit of the pastoral, those "naïvetés" which afforded him an opportunity to escape in play from the complex demands of a highly sophisticated social life into an imaginary world of simplicity and spontaneity.

[16] *Ibid.*, pp. 223–25.

[17] Sainte-Palaye reveals here once more his adherence to the esthetics of his time. It is the lack of inventiveness and originality, the routine quality of medieval art, that condemns it in his eyes: "Les Peintres au sortir de la plus grossière barbarie, saisissant d'abord en détail tous les petits objets que la nature leur présentoit, s'attachèrent aux insectes, aux fleurs, aux oiseaux, les parèrent des couleurs les plus vives, les dissinèrent avec une exactitude que nous admirons encore dans les vignettes et les miniatures des Manuscrits; lorsqu'ils vinrent à représenter des figures humaines, ils s'étudièrent bien plus à terminer les contours et à exprimer jusqu'aux cheveux les plus fins, qu'à donner de l'âme aux visages et du mouvement aux corps; et ces figures, dont la nature la plus commune fournissoit toujours les modelles, étoient jettées ensemble au hazard, sans choix, sans ordonnance, sans aucun goût de composition. Les Poëtes aussi stériles que les Peintres, bornoient toute leur industrie à sçavoir amener des descriptions proportionneés à leurs talens, et ils ne les quittoient qu'après les avoir épuisées; ils ne savent guères parler que d'un beau printems, de la verdure des campagnes, de la clarté et de la vivacité d'une belle fontaine, ou d'un ruisseau qui murmure: quelquefois cependant ils rendent avec naïveté les amusemens enfantins des amans, leurs ris, leurs jeux, les palpitations ou la joie d'un coeur amoureux; ils n'imaginent rien au delà, incapables d'ailleurs de donner de la suite et de la liaison à leurs idées" (*ibid.*, p. 226.)

With all their limitations, however, the scholars and historians of the Enlightenment were the first even to consider that the arts and sciences formed part of history. Sainte-Palaye's studies of Froissart's poetry and of the *Jouvencel*, Le Beuf's paper on Guillaume de Machaut and Sallier's on Charles d'Orléans, Zurlauben's account of the Swabian *Minnesänger*[18]—among a number of papers on literary subjects read to the Académie des Inscriptions—were the first attempts made by scholars to study medieval literature with the seriousness which had hitherto been reserved for political history.

[18] *MAI* 20:377–98; *MAI* 13:593–606; *MAI** 40:154–69.

CHAPTER 7

THE PUBLICATION OF MEDIEVAL TEXTS

The *Recueil des historiens*, the *Table chronologique*, the *Recueil des ordonnances des rois de France*, Bertin's grandiose plan to outdo Rymer and a proposal to launch a collection of the *Historiens des Croisades* bear witness to the fact that eighteenth century scholars did not underestimate the importance of publishing the main sources of medieval history. Sainte-Palaye himself contributed texts to the editors of the *Historiens des Gaules et de la France*,[1] and of the projected *Historiens des Croisades*.[2] Since literature had been acknowledged as an additional source of material for the historian, one would expect that a significant part of Sainte-Palaye's activity as a medieval scholar would have been devoted to publishing good editions of the literary texts of which he had a wider knowledge than almost anyone else in the France of his day. He had had copies made of the manuscripts of many works which had never been printed, as well as of others of which only corrupt printed editions were available; he had himself collated and annotated these copies. Yet the list of texts published by him is meager.

The discrepancy between Sainte-Palaye's private research on the one hand and his actual achievement in print on the other can be explained, in part at least, by his own attitude to the literary texts of the Middle Ages. Sainte-Palaye was not completely insensitive to them, but his taste, like that of his fellow medievalists at the

---

[1] Moreau 1725, fols. 37–41, for instance, contains material intended for the Benedictines.

[2] Moreau 1723, fols. 92–93, copy of an O. F. version of *Quoties et a quibus capta fuit Jerusalem*. Sainte-Palaye has noted in his own hand: "On a copié cet article du MS de Berne pour être employé dans la partie du Recueil des Historiens de France qui concerne les Croisades, à laquelle on travaille à l'abbaye de Saint-Germain des Prés." The Benedictines' copy of this text (B. N. Nouv. Acq. Fr. 3537), dated 1770, bears references to Sainte-Palaye. On the early stages of the *Historiens des Croisades*, see M. Michaud, *Bibliothèque des Croisades* (Paris, 1829), pp. vi–ix.

Académie des Inscriptions and elsewhere, was the taste of his age and of his social class.[3] References abound in his notes, papers, and printed works to the grossness and barbarity of the texts he had to deal with. "Que peut-on attendre des Siècles ténébreux dont j'entreprends de retracer l'image," he exclaimed.[4] A man of the salons and a latter-day aristocrat, he accepted the world of his own time wholeheartedly. There was no question for him of making a profound criticism of it, social or cultural, and he had no intention of contrasting any early writer favorably with modern ones. "Que les Partisans des Siècles qu'ils n'ont ni vus ni connus nous vantent l'heureuse simplicité de nos Aieux," he wrote. "Que leur mauvaise humeur s'exhale en vaines déclamations contre la subtilité de nos Écrivains modernes. Pardonnons à ceux-ci leurs écarts peut-être trop ingénieux et trop raffinés; mais ne regrettons pas ceux qui les ont précédés. Comparons les Écrits de ces temps barbares avec ceux que l'Imprimerie depuis 200 ans environ a mis entre nos mains. Soyons pénétrés de reconnoissance sur-tout pour ces hommes respectables qui, vers le milieu du siècle dernier ont achevé d'épurer notre langue."[5] As for Sainte-Palaye himself, "on voit bien que mon dessein n'est pas de disculper nos anciens Auteurs françois de la Barbarie qui leur a été si justement reprochée."[6] The medieval writers never achieve the "diction noble, pure et élégante" of the classics. Nonetheless, they have something else to offer: "En lisant nos anciens Auteurs, un esprit curieux et Philosophique rencontrera à chaque pas des instructions utiles, y pourra faire des découvertes intéressantes. Ces Auteurs dans leur style barbare donneront avec ingénuité les éclaircissemens nécessaires pour percer les ténèbres de notre ancienne histoire."[7]

On the whole, therefore, Sainte-Palaye was not interested in medieval literature as literature; he was interested in it as a source of information for the historian. The way he envisaged editing and publishing medieval literary texts reflects the historical orientation

---

[3] Gröber's attribution to Sainte-Palaye of a real feeling for the literary value of the Old French texts (*Grundriss der romanischen Philologie* [2d ed.; Strassburg, 1904–6], 1:41) was generous but probably mistaken, at least in the sense in which Gröber intended it. Samuel Rocheblave was closer to the truth when he declared (*Essai sur le comte de Caylus* [Paris, 1889], p. 79) that Sainte-Palaye and his colleagues at the Académie des Inscriptions were "surtout des linguistes et des historiens. Le point de vue littéraire leur est absolument indifférent."

[4] Bréquigny 154, fol. 6.   [5] *Ibid.*, fol. 26.   [6] *Ibid.*, fol. 5.
[7] *Ibid.*, fol. 39.

of his research. Great works of art, he argued, cannot be published in extract without suffering grievous damage. Works of mediocre or uneven quality, however, would lose nothing by being published in this way, and in their case "il est aisé de faire un choix des choses utiles et curieuses qui s'y trouvent, comme par hasard."[8] Sainte-Palaye's plan, referred to in the previous chapter, was to study the literary texts systematically and publish extracts from them containing "tout ce qui paroîtroit de quelque usage pour l'Histoire, pour les Généalogies, pour les Antiquités françoises et pour la Géographie." These were precisely the points which he noted with meticulous care in the margins of his own copies.

Within the framework of his predominantly historical outlook, Sainte-Palaye had some tolerance for the literary qualities of medieval literature. His favorable assessment of Froissart's *Pastourelles* and *Rondeaux* has already been alluded to. Even to Guillaume le Breton's *Philippide* he gave considerable praise. "Les récits, les portraits, les descriptions, tout y est parlant et animé," he declared; "la versification aisée semble couler de source, elle a du nombre et de l'harmonie."[9] The reserves he placed on Guillaume's poetic achievement were those currently being placed on the work of Chaucer or Spenser in England, and on that of Charles d'Orléans in France.[10] According to Sainte-Palaye Guillaume was "un poëte de premier ordre, mais tout se ressent . . . du mauvais goût qui régnoit du temps de l'auteur."[11] In short, though the age was barbarous there were some writers who succeeded in transcending it at times. Sainte-Palaye was therefore prepared to admit a few texts or parts of texts into the proposed Extracts on account of their literary merit: "On pourroit y conserver aussi tout ce qu'il y auroit de remarquable du côté de l'esprit et de l'invention; quelques tours délicats et naifs, quelques traits de morale et quelques pensées ingénieuses."[12]

From the point of view of the medieval scholar, in other words, the literary texts of the Middle Ages did not warrant publication.

---

[8] 'Mémoire sur la lecture des anciens romans,' *MAI* 17:797.

[9] 'Mémoire concernant la vie et les ouvrages de Rigord et de Guillaume le Breton,' *MAI* 8:544-45.

[10] Cf. Sallier on Charles d'Orléans (*MAI* 13:592): ". . . la plûpart de ses défauts ne viennent que de l'imperfection du goût de ces permiers temps; l'idée des beaux vers n'estoit pas encore venue à l'esprit, et elle estoit réservée à un siècle plus poli."

[11] *MAI* 8:544-45.   [12] *MAI* 17:798.

All that was required was an abstract of their historical content and, occasionally, a few lines of particular note or charm.

Even if there had been a desire in learned circles for carefully edited medieval literary texts, there would have been little chance of satisfying it. There was no public for serious works of medieval scholarship.[13] "Il faut s'accoustumer au goût de son siècle," Secousse wrote to Bouhier, "et présenter des aliments proportionnés aux estomachs qui doivent les digérer. Il n'en faut point de trop forts, de trop solides et de trop succulents pour les nostres, qui ne peuvent supporter que des viandes légères et agréables."[14] In England Walpole's advice to Pinkerton was in the same vein.[15] Since medieval literary texts were less likely than purely historical materials to be subsidized from the royal exchequer,[16] they were almost invariably published in modern versions adapted to the taste of the times, and in this form they enjoyed considerable popularity. Despite the jibes of eighteenth century novelists, the romances of Mlle de Scudéry, La Calprenède, and Honoré d'Urfé were still favorites with the reading public of the eighteenth century. Fontenelle and Rousseau, for instance, were both ardent readers of *L'Astrée*. There was thus a ready market for piquant versions of the old romances and

[13] The *Mercure*, for instance, declined to publish a fourteenth-century manuscript which the editors had received from Italy and which they recognized to be of interest. To be useful, they declared, it would have to be published in full "pour mettre les lecteurs à portée d'en tirer toutes les inductions possibles." But this was out of the question. "Si notre soin à cet egard pouvoit faire plaisir à quelques-uns, il déplairoit au plus grand nombre, qui, n'aimant que les lectures agréables ou l'érudition facile, n'aiment point à s'enfoncer dans ces recherches toujours ténébreuses, souvent inutiles et que l'on peut appeler les broussailles de l'antiquité." (*Mercure*, Dec., 1746, p. 48.) Dom Clément complained to a fellow-scholar that no work of learning could count on a good sale in Paris: "La littérature frivole étouffe aujourd'hui l'érudition" (cit. Lecomte, p. 50). Bréquigny foresaw difficulty in publishing his findings from research undertaken in the libraries and archives of England. "Nos libraires accoutumés au débit rapide et lucratif de la littérature frivole sont peu friands des livres d'érudition." (To Lord Hardwicke, a trustee of the British Museum, B.M. MSS. Add. 35, 613, fol. 193, 20.11.1776.)

[14] B. N. Français 24420, fol. 96, to Bouhier, 29.12.1745. The same complaint again, *ibid.*, fol. 82.

[15] *Literary Correspondence of John Pinkerton* (London, 1830), 1:227, Walpole to Pinkerton, 14.8.1789: "If you would adapt antiquities to the taste of those who would read only to be diverted, not to be instructed . . . you must treat them with digressions little or nothing to the purpose."

[16] The scholars themselves accepted that medieval literary texts did not warrant royal subsidies; cf. a letter from La Bastie to Mazaugues, 27.5.1737: "Le Roy ne contribue en façon quelconque à la transcription des MSS des Troubadours. Vous sentés bien que ce n'est pas un objet assez intéressant et qui est plus de simple curiosité que d'utilité réelle." (Quoted by J. Bauquier, *Revue des langues romanes*, 3e série [1880], 4:194.)

chansons in the medieval or chivalric tradition—authentic or invented—and several writers were kept busy supplying it. Mlle L'Héritier, Mlle de Lubert, Tressan, and Moncrif popularized and adapted early poems and romances of chivalry, the latter usually from fifteenth-century prose versions. There were re-editions of *Le Petit Jehan de Saintré* (1724), of *Gérard de Nevers* (1728), of *Cléomadès* (1733), of *Flores et Blancheflor* (1735), of *Tiran le Blanc* (1737). The periodical press followed the fashion. The *Mercure* (from about 1743) and the *Année littéraire* (from about 1750) led the way in printing "medieval" or frankly pseudo-medieval novels and verse. In the second half of the century, ambitious collections were published, often on a subscription basis. Monnet's *Anthologie françoise* (1763) was followed by a revived *Bibliothèque bleue* in 1770. In 1775 Paulmy and Tressan launched the *Bibliothèque des romans*. Three years later the *Almanach des muses* began publication and devoted the first volume to the poetry of the Middle Ages. In 1779 Paulmy started publishing his *Mélanges tirés d'une grande bibliothèque.*

All these works enjoyed considerable success. Monnet's *Anthologie* pleased the critics[17] and the *Bibliothèque des romans* won almost universal applause, the doubts of some reviewers having been removed by Tressan's facile but delightful adaptations.[18] In 1782 the *Mercure* and the *Journal étranger* attested the popularity of the series.[19] Marie Antoinette herself was a reader of the "vieux romans,"[20] while Madame du Deffand confessed to Voltaire that she was guilty of a passionate enthusiasm for the *Amadis.*[21]

Few readers, however, cared much whether the text which gave them pleasure was the original text or a much altered and corrupted version. Even works that were relatively well known, by reputation at least, such as the poems of Villon or the *Roman de la Rose*, were republished in editions which marked scant improvement on those of the Renaissance. Lenglet's edition of the *Roman de la Rose* (1735), for instance, despite vague allusions to manu-

---

[17] *Avant-Coureur* (1765), p. 453.

[18] *Année littéraire*, 1775, Pt. 6, p. 241; *Mercure*, June, 1776, pp. 108–36; *Journal étranger*, July, 1776, pp. 91–100; Grimm, *Corr. litt.* 13:118 (April, 1782).

[19] *Mercure*, Dec., 1782, pp. 126 *et seq.*, April, 1777, Pt. 1, pp. 146–48; *Journal étranger*, Jan., 1782, pp. 352 *et seq.*

[20] There is a copy of *Artus de Bretagne*, bound with her arms, at the Bibliothèque de l'Arsenal.

[21] *Correspondance*, 2:688, to Voltaire, 3.5.1779.

script sources, reproduced substantially the text of the Vérard edition of 1500, which in its turn was based on a fifteenth-century manuscript.[22] Lévesque de la Ravalière's edition of the *Poésies du Roy de Navarre* was exceptional in aiming at a reasonable standard of textual accuracy and at the same time gaining a place on the bookshelves. Lévesque was helped by the curiosity which the romantic legend of Thibaut's love for Queen Blanche aroused in a public voracious for anecdotes of the loves of princes. Barbazan's edition of *Fabliaux et contes*, which did not have this advantage, was coldly received. Barbazan showed some courage in refusing to publish his texts even in a literal translation. It was, he maintained, ". . . plus utile d'interpréter les vers les plus obscurs, qui paroissent inintelligibles, et de donner une juste explication des mots hors d'usage . . . Nos anciens avoient des mots et des expressions très énergiques que nous n'avons plus . . . et que nous ne pouvons rendre que par de longues et fades périphrases, de sorte qu'il est très difficile d'exprimer les beautés qui se rencontrent dans ces originaux par des traductions littérales."[23] The public, however, was neither anxious to be instructed in Old French, nor willing to purchase its pleasure at the cost of a little application. As Le Grand d'Aussy put it: "De bonne foi, peut-on se flatter qu'il se trouvera des gens assez courageux pour entreprendre une lecture dans laquelle dix fois à chaque phrase, il leur faudra consulter un Vocabulaire. Ce n'est pas connoître les lecteurs français que de leur présenter un pareil travail."[24]

Le Grand might be suspected of trying to justify his own edition of the *Fabliaux* in translation, but his observation is not an isolated one. In 1764, Samuel Formey, giving advice on the building up of a good private library at moderate cost, observed that "il y a peu de personnes qui puissent s'amuser à la lecture des anciens Romans en vieux style."[25] Likewise, the editors of the *Almanach des muses*,

---

[22] Yet Lenglet's edition was highly esteemed. A MS note in the copy at the Bibliothèque de l'Arsenal (8° 8676) probably by Paulmy or one of his librarians runs: "Certainement voici la plus complette édition et la plus chargée de recherches qui ait paru sur le Roman de la Rose."

[23] Étienne Barbazan, ed., *L'Ordène de chevalerie* (Lausanne, 1759), Preface, pp. ix–x.

[24] Le Grand d'Aussy, *Fabliaux ou contes*, vol. 1, Preface, p. xcii. Cf. *Partenopeus de Blois*, ed. Crapelet (Paris, 1834), Preface, p. 10.

[25] *Introduction générale aux sciences avec les conseils pour former une bibliothèque peu nombreuse mais choisie* (Amsterdam, 1764), p. 121.

introducing the first volume in 1778, apologized for the difficulties it presented to the ordinary reader, and explained that "pour adoucir la fatigue de cette Lecture . . . nous nous sommes permis d'élaguer et même de corriger quelquefois le style des Pièces que nous avons recueillies."[26]

Moving as he did in the leading literary and social circles of the Capital, Sainte-Palaye knew and shared the tastes of his contemporaries in a way that a provincial scholar of humble station such as Barbazan could not. It was easy for him to come to terms with public demand. In 1752 he published a translation of *Aucassin et Nicolette* in the *Mercure*.[27] He was the first French scholar to recognize the value of this text, but he did not present it in the original Old French. The reception accorded to his translation fully justified his decision to translate it, for it was republished separately in the form he gave it in 1756 and again in 1760, eliciting favorable reviews from the periodical press.[28] The choice of the text in itself and the subtitle—*Les Amours du bon vieux temps*—indicate the author's sense of what the public wanted, but in order that there should be no misunderstanding, a well known rondeau by Clément Marot was appended to the 1756 and 1760 editions setting the tone of the entire work.

> "Au bon vieux temps un train d'amour régnoit,
> Qui sans grand art et dons se démenoit,
> Si qu'un Bouquet donné d'amour profonde,
> C'estoit donner toute la terre ronde:
> Car seulement au coeur on se prenoit.
> Et si par cas à jouir on venoit,
> Sçavez-vous bien comm' on s'entretenoit,
> Vingt ans, trente ans: cela duroit un monde
> Au bon vieux temps.
> Or est perdu ce qu'Amour ordonnoit.
> Rien que pleurs faints, rien que changes on n'oyt.

---

[26] *Almanach des Muses*, vol. 1, Avertissement, p. vi.

[27] *Mercure*, Feb., 1752, pp. 10–64. The translation appeared anonymously in the *Mercure* and in the 1756 and 1760 editions. There is no doubt that it was by Sainte-Palaye, however. A copy of some notes for the printer is preserved among his papers (Arsenal 4834, fol. 10v), and it was intended to be included in the third volume of the *Mémoires sur l'ancienne chevalerie* (cf. Moreau 1797, fol. 219).

[28] Notably from Fréron's *Année littéraire*, 1756, Pt. 2, pp. 338 *et seq.* The fact that Sainte-Palaye planned to publish it once more with the *Mémoires sur l'ancienne chevalerie* bears witness to its popularity.

Qui voudra donc qu'à aymer je me fonde,
Il faut premier que l'Amour on refonde
Et qu'on la meine ainsi qu'on la menoit
Au bon vieux temps.

These familiar verses leave no doubt that Sainte-Palaye's *Aucassin* was directed at a sophisticated, aristocratic public eager for the extreme pleasure of artful simplicity. No demands were made upon it, and no effort was required to read the text.

Although it was an honest translation and had little of the playful eroticism with which Tressan spiced his versions of the old romances,[29] Sainte-Palaye's *Aucassin* was intended to amuse. The translator's disavowal of any literary ambition and his reference to the historical value of the work—"il ne s'agit pas de donner un ouvrage sans défaut . . . il s'agit de faire connoître nos anciennes moeurs"[30]—justified his presenting the public with the kind of thing it enjoyed reading but could not and did not attempt to fit into the categories of serious literature. There is no reason to suppose that Sainte-Palaye did not share the taste of his public. Indeed, the *Aucassin* probably owed its success to the close association of translator and public.

Three further texts were later published in full, and three, in extract, in Sainte-Palaye's *Mémoires sur l'ancienne chevalerie*. The thirteenth century *Voeu du héron* was printed for the first time, in an honest translation from which, however, all the poetic passages of the original had been sedulously eliminated, leaving only the bare essentials of the plot.[31] Similarly, the *Dit des trois chevaliers et del canise* from a manuscript in the Royal Library in Turin appeared in a literal translation.[32] A fifteenth century text—*Les Honneurs de la Cour*—which was of greater historical than literary interest and which held few language difficulties, was presented as it stood in the manuscript, with explanation of occasional difficult

---

[29] Cf. Mario Roques, *C'est d'Aucasin et de Nicolete. Chantefable du XIIIe siècle transcrit d'après le manuscrit de la Bibliothèque Nationale, par Mario Roques, avec une traduction du XVIIIe siècle par La Curne de Sainte-Palaye. Images et ornements par Joseph Hemard* (Librairie Lutétia: Paris, 1936), p. 154. Henri Jacoubet also noted the honesty of the translation in his *Le Comte de Tressan et le Genre Troubadour* (Paris, 1923), pp. 170–72.

[30] Ed. 1760, Avertissement, p. 7.

[31] *Mémoires sur l'ancienne chevalerie*, 3:1–20.

[32] *Ibid.*, 3:138–64. Two MSS copies of the translation are in B.N., the first draft Moreau 1653, fols. 59–73, and a more polished version fols. 39–51v.

words in the margins or footnotes.[33] Two Provençal texts from
manuscripts, in the d'Urfé library,[34] and the *Conte du bachelier
d'armes* from a manuscript in the Royal Library in Paris[35] were
published in abstract only, with a few meager quotations from the
text. The original text of the *Voeu du héron* with translations of
difficult words in the margins was indeed included "en faveur des
amateurs du vieux langage," but it was thrown to the end of
the notes and was clearly admitted only as a curiosity.[36] It is characteristic that the first publication of this important text should
have taken such a form.

If he showed little respect for these texts as literature, Sainte-
Palaye did treat them, as an historian, with care. (The *Mémoires*
had originally been presented at the Académie des Inscriptions and
had to satisfy a scholarly as well as an urbane public.) The Preface
to *Les Honneurs de la Cour* identified the authoress, assessed her
reliability as an observer, and underlined the interest, for a predominantly aristocratic public, of the questions of precedence
which are the subject of the work. Marginal notes accompanying
the text briefly identified the personages who were alluded to in it,
and a fairly detailed biographical index was provided at the end of
the work. The "Observations" on the *Voeu du héron* aimed to determine the historical significance of the poem by comparing the
action with the testimony of historians, while once again explana-
tory notes of considerable length established the identity and traced
the biography of the most important characters, or elucidated
allusions, the meaning of which was no longer clear.[37] The "Observations" on the *Dit del canise* contained a reasoned conjecture
as to the identity of the author and showed how the story illuminated several aspects of medieval chivalry as Sainte-Palaye himself
had described it in his *Mémoires sur l'ancienne chevalerie*. The
Provençal poems were not annotated, but they carried headings
indicating briefly their relevance to the arguments developed in the
Mémoires. These few texts and fragments constitute the sum total
of Sainte-Palaye's own publications of medieval texts.

Serious work on medieval literature in the eighteenth century
took, on the whole, the form of historical studies of authors or of

[33] *Ibid.*, 2:171–267.   [34] *Ibid.*, 2:141–62.   [35] *Ibid.*, 2:163–67.
[36] *Ibid.*, 3:119–37.
[37] The *Vie de Mauny*, (*ibid.*, 3:21–72) a biographical study of Walter Manny,
can also be considered part of the notes to the *Voeu du héron*.

groups of authors. As the *Histoire littéraire de la France* reached
the High Middle Ages only in the nineteenth century, the Académie des Inscriptions provided the principal forum for discussion of
medieval literary questions, and its *Mémoires* long formed the only
medium in which research on medieval literature could be published. It was here that Le Beuf and Caylus first drew attention to
Guillaume de Machaut;[38] that Zurlauben revealed something of
what German and Swiss scholars had been discovering in a paper on
the *Minnesänger*;[39] that Caylus wrote about the *fabliaux*,[40] albeit
without much profundity; that La Bastie and Menard discussed
Petrarch;[41] and that Sallier presented the work of Jean Lemaire des
Belges and of Charles d'Orléans.[42] These papers were illustrated
with generous quotations and extracts, but no texts were published.
Sainte-Palaye made a copiously annotated copy of the Guillaume
de Machaut manuscript,[43] but at no stage does he seem to have
envisaged its publication. Similarly, although he was the first to
recognize the importance of Eustache Deschamps and executed a
careful copy of the Royal Library manuscript of his poems,[44] he
appears never to have thought of publishing them. He was content
to prepare a paper in which he planned to outline the biography of
Deschamps, establish a bibliography of his works—"de ceux qu'il
dit avoir composez et de ceux qui nous restent encore aujourd'hui"
—indicate the points of interest they hold for the historian, and

---

[38] Le Beuf, 'Notice sommaire de deux volumes de poésies françoises et latines
conservés dans la Bibliothèque des Carmes-Déchaux de Paris, avec une indication
du genre de musique qui s'y trouve.' *MAI* 20:377–98; Caylus, 'Deux Mémoires sur
Guillaume de Machaut, poète et musicien dans le XIVe siècle, avec une notice de
ses principaux ouvrages,' *MAI* 20:399–439.

[39] 'Observations sur une manuscrit de la Bibliothèque du Roi, qui contient les
chansons des Trouvères ou Troubadours de la Souabe ou de l'Allemagne, depuis
la fin du XIIe siècle jusque vers l'an 1330,' *MAI* 40:154–69. The starting point for
Zurlauben's paper was the *Sammlung von Minnesingern aus dem Schwaebischen
Zeitpuncte*, published by Bodmer and Breitinger in 1738 from the MS in the
Bibl. du Roi. Zurlauben was friendly with Sinner and with Tscharner, an en-
thusiastic disciple of the Zürich professors; see Enid Stoye, *Vincent Bernard de
Tscharner 1728–78* (Fribourg [Suisse], 1954), pp. 74–109 *et passim*.

[40] *MAI* 20: 352–76.

[41] Bimard de la Bastie, 'Vie de Pétrarque,' *MAI* 15:746–94, 17:390–490; Menard,
'Mémoire sur l'origine de Laure célébrée par Pétrarque,' *MAI* 30:756–76.

[42] 'Observations sur un recueil manuscrit des poésies de Charles d'Orléans,' *MAI*
12:580–92; 'Recherches sur la vie et les ouvrages de Jean le Maire,' *ibid.*, pp. 593–
624.

[43] Arsenal 3297. (Annotations in Sainte-Palaye's hand.) Space was left in this
copy for the musical notation.

[44] Arsenal 3291–93. (Annotations in Sainte-Palaye's hand.)

bring out the degree to which traces of Renaissance ideas and tastes are already apparent in Deschamps' work.[45] The paper would undoubtedly have been based on close study of the manuscript of the poems, but the suggestion thrown out by a modern editor of Deschamps that Sainte-Palaye did not have time to publish the poems is not supported by evidence.[46] The manner in which the copy of Deschamps at the Arsenal was annotated is no different from that of many other copies of manuscripts in Sainte-Palaye's collection. Comparison of the Glossary and the *Dictionnaire des antiquités* with these copies of manuscripts leaves almost no doubt that all Sainte-Palaye's transcripts, with their meticulous linguistic control of the text and their historical and geographical observations, were intended simply to provide material for his historical studies, for the Dictionary of Antiquities, and for the Glossary. There is no reason to believe that he at any time planned to publish the texts which he studied with such care and zeal.[47]

Although little was published in the eighteenth century and that little often in "adaptations" that had no pretension to historical accuracy, the work done by the scholars of the Enlightenment was far more vast in scope and careful in execution than is commonly known. In the conditions of the eighteenth century its effect was necessarily limited, but in the altered conditions of the following century it began to bear richer fruit. Sainte-Palaye's enormous collection of annotated manuscripts, in particular, was exploited with success by generations of medievalists after him and played a sig-

---

[45] Moreau 1653, fols. 7–35, notes for a paper on Deschamps.

[46] *Poésies d'Eustache Deschamps*, ed. Queux de Sainte-Hilaire, and subsequently Gaston Raynaud (Paris, 1873–1903), 11:2–3.

[47] Brackets marking off passages in many of Sainte-Palaye's copies indicate suitable quotations for the Glossary of Old French or points to be referred to in the *Dictionnaire des antiquités*, not extracts for publication. This can be checked by comparing the references in the Glossary and the *Antiquités* with the copies. The question whether Sainte-Palaye intended to publish his collations of O. F. texts has puzzled many scholars. P. Meyer believed it must have been his ultimate aim, but admits that "il ne paraît pas qu'il ait jamais formé à cet égard de projet bien défini." (*Notices et extraits de manuscrits* [1890], 1ère partie, 33:2.) Meyer concludes that the indifference of the reading public was responsible for the insignificant output of medieval texts in the eighteenth century. But a purely external factor like this may not be sufficient to explain the paradoxical situation in which scholars spent their lives making extensive copies and collations of MSS while eschewing all plans for publishing them. The attitudes of the scholars themselves must also be considered.

nificant part in that recovery and popularization of the literature of the Middle Ages which was one of the greatest achievements of nineteenth century scholarship. In the early years of the nineteenth century the pioneer Provençalist Raynouard relied entirely on his predecessor's transcripts for the manuscripts of the troubadours in Italian libraries, and Paul Meyer claimed that the same scholar's *Lexique Roman* "n'est guère complet que pour les poésies des troubadours dont Sainte-Palaye avait fait un dépouillement exact."[48] Bréquigny quoted exclusively from Sainte-Palaye's copy of Wace, which was based on a collation of manuscripts, in his *Notice du Roman de Rou et des Ducs de Normandie*,[49] and the first scholar who acted on Bréquigny's suggestion that Wace's work be published, the Danish professor Peter Brøndsted, admitted that all his notes and explanations of difficult passages in the text were taken from Sainte-Palaye's copy at the Arsenal.[50] In 1832 Crapelet drew attention to Sainte-Palaye's copy of the poems of Eustache Deschamps, and, while he considered the annotations often wide of the mark and the copy itself "souvent défectueuse," he probably made use of both in preparing his own edition.[51] Paul Meyer was more favorably disposed to Sainte-Palaye's copy of the Provençal *Girartz de Rossilho*, esteeming it "en général fort exacte." Indeed, it was his opinion that Sainte-Palaye's copy could be used with profit to restore a number of words which had become illegible owing to the deterioration of the original manuscript.[52] Sainte-Palaye was incidentally the first to draw attention to the Provençal epic.[53] Meyer also used Sainte-Palaye's copy of a manuscript of the

[48] Raynouard, *Choix de poésies des troubadours* (Paris, 1816), vol. 1, Appendice, pp. 344–48. P. Meyer, 'Études sur la Chanson de Gérard de Rossillon,' *Bibliothèque de l'École des Chartes*, 5ᵉ série (1861), 2:33.

[49] *Notices et extraits des manuscrits*, (an VII), 5:21–78.

[50] P. O. Brøndsted, *Bidrag til den Danske Historie og til Kundsgab om Danmarks aeldre politiske Forhold, af udenlandske Manuscriptsamlinger* (Copenhagen: 1817), Heft 1, p. 23.

[51] *Poésies morales et historiques d'Eustache Deschamps* (Paris, 1832), pp. lxvi–lxvii.

[52] 'Études sur la Chanson de Gérard de Rossillon,' *Bibliothèque de l'École des Chartes*, 5ᵉ série (1861), 2:41. Raynouard published some extracts from the Provençal *Gérard* in his *Lexique Roman* (Paris, 1838), 1:174–224. He does not indicate his MS, nor does he mention Sainte-Palaye's copy, but he probably knew of the latter.

[53] Chorier, *Recherches des antiquitez de Vienne* (Lyon, 1659; 1st ed., 1658), pp. 434–35, discusses a MS of *Gérard de Roussillon* which he considered was "composé il y a plus de cinq cents ans," but this was the O. F. *Gérard*.

Hystoria albigensis by Pierre de Vaux-de-Cernai for a partial publication of the text in the *Notices et extraits de manuscrits*.[54] Of
the two manuscript copies of the oldest translation of this work,
the one which was in Noblet's library at La Clayette, and from
which Sainte-Palaye made his copy, is now lost. The editors of a
recent complete edition have consequently established their text on
a collation of Sainte-Palaye's copy with the only surviving early
manuscript in the Royal Library at Brussels.[55] Sainte-Palaye was
also the first to recognize the importance of the manuscript of
Guillem de Tudela's *Chanson de la Croisade* in verse. Only the
fifteenth century prose version had been known to Dom Vaisette,[56]
but Fauriel was wrong in supposing that the earlier version was
discovered in the nineteenth century.[57] Raynouard, who published
some fragments of Tudela's poem in 1838, must have known of
Sainte-Palaye's copy, and it is likely that in this case, as in others,
the starting point for Raynouard's research was that of his eighteenth century predecessor.[58]

The currently used text of the *Voeu du héron* is still substantially that established by Sainte-Palaye from the Berne manuscript
(no. 323) and published by him in the third volume of the
Mémoires sur l'ancienne chevalerie. Thomas Wright considered
this a fairly accurate transcription and reproduced it with few
changes in his *Political Poems and Songs*.[59] Although Jubinal

---

[54] Première partie (1890), 3:77–79. Sainte-Palaye's copy in Moreau 1719, fols.
1–194v.

[55] *Petri Vallium Sarnaii Monachi Hystoria Albegensis*, ed. P. Guebin and E.
Lyon (Paris, 1926–39), vol. 3, pp. lxv *et seq.*

[56] For references to the work before Sainte-Palaye, see Meyer's edition for the
Société de l'Histoire de France (Paris, 1875–79), vol. 2, pp. xxv–xxvi.

[57] *Histoire de la poésie provençale* (Paris, 1846), 3:345–46. Had Fauriel known
of Sainte-Palaye's copy he would have been able to trace the history of the MS
further back than the La Vallière collection. Sainte-Palaye had noted that it was
in the Bombarde collection.

[58] *Lexique Roman*, 1:225–89. It is worth recording that editors who did not
examine Sainte-Palaye's papers with sufficient care often missed important points
of information. Joly for instance would have been able to draw on a wider
range of MSS for his 1870–71 edition of the *Roman de Troie* of Benoît de Sainte
More if he had consulted Sainte-Palaye's *Notices et extraits de MSS*, where there
is a full description of a thirteenth-century MS of this work in the former Royal
Library at Naples (see Alfonso Miola, *Notizie di manoscritti neolatini della Biblioteca Nazionale di Napoli* [Naples, 1895], pp. 1–2). The Naples MS was the object
of a notice by Sainte-Palaye, who examined it in 1739 (Moreau 1658, fol. 267,
notice 2195).

[59] *Political Poems and Songs relating to English History Composed during the
Period from the Accession of Edward III to that of Richard III* (London, 1859),
1:1–25 (Rolls series, 14).

claimed there were errors in Sainte-Palaye's edition and proposed to establish a better text, he never in fact did so, and in 1949 the *Histoire littéraire de la France* was still quoting from the text in the *Mémoires sur l'ancienne chevalerie*.[60]

In 1867–68 J. Brackelmann published Sainte-Palaye's copy of the Berne manuscript (No. 389) of the *Chansons* of Thibaut de Navarre, which he considered so carefully executed that it could take the place of the original in almost all respects.[61] The usefulness of Sainte-Palaye's copies was again demonstrated in 1925, when A. Wallenskold had recourse to his transcripts of Vatican 1490 and 1522 (Arsenal 3101, 3102) and Berne 389 (B.N. Moreau 1687, 1688) for the edition of Thibaut's *Chansons* which he prepared for the *Société des anciens textes français*.

[60] Alfred Coville in *Histoire littéraire de la France* (1949), 38:268 *et seq.*
[61] *Archiv fur das Studium der neueren Sprachen* (1867), 41:339–76; (1868), 42: 241–392; (1869), 43:241–394; cf. Gröber and Lebinski in *Zeitschrift fur romanische Philologie* (1879), 3:39–60.

CHAPTER 8

THE *DICTIONNAIRE DES ANTIQUITÉS*

One of the most ambitious of Sainte-Palaye's projects was a Dictionary of Antiquities, through which he intended to do for the Middle Ages and early modern times what classical scholars had done for ancient Greece and Rome. The Dictionary was ostensibly based on the *Lexicon* of Samuel Pitiscus (1713), but it differed from it in that whereas Pitiscus, on his own admission, had aimed simply to present in a more readily accessible form material which had already been published by other classical scholars, Sainte-Palaye's work involved much original research into document collections and manuscript sources which had not before been exploited or had been only partially exploited.

Even a cursory examination of Sainte-Palaye's sources reveals not only the thoroughness of his investigations, but also his keen sense of the possibilities of historical documentation. Wherever possible he sought out information in contemporary sources, which included not only histories and chronicles, but record sources like the *Ordonnances des rois de France*, the provincial *Coutumiers*, and the collections of early documents compiled by his friends Secousse and Foncemagne. Modern historians such as Fleury, Boulainviller, Montesquieu, and the Benedictines were also frequently consulted, however, as were the great sixteenth and seventeenth century historians and antiquaries—de Thou, Fauchet, Pasquier, Le Laboureur, Du Cange, Favyn, Loysel. A close watch was kept on modern works of scholarship or history, and the articles were continually added to from newly combed sources.[1]

---

[1] Most of the articles in the manuscript are distinctly divisible into two parts, which are the work of different hands, and which can be dated approximately pre- and post-1750. The second part contains references to several works which had been compulsed only at a later stage in the composition of the dictionary— Montesquieu's *Esprit des lois,* Foncemagne's "Extraits," Née de la Rochelle's *Histoire du Nivernois* (1746).

The most interesting feature of the Dictionary is indeed the wealth and variety of the source material. More eagerly than any of his contemporaries, Sainte-Palaye sought to realize for the medieval period what Professor Powicke called "the unity of our knowledge of history at any given time . . . the cross section which we can cut through the whole body of contemporary evidence."[2] The extensive documentation he derived from chroniclers, historians, and record sources was supplemented by an astonishing familiarity with literary and other nonhistorical texts, many of which were as yet available only in manuscript. Romances, *fabliaux*, poems, treatises on hunting, chivalry, deportment, or morals were scoured for information about the laws, customs, manners, outlook, and social conditions of medieval people. Completely disparate works like the histories of Jean de Venette or of Glaber, the Provençal poets, Eustache Deschamps, the two *Gérard de Roussillon*, the Chevalier de la Tour's *Instructions à ses filles*, the *Arbre des batailles*, the medieval versions of Ovid's *Ars amandi*, and Bouteiller's *Somme rurale* were conceived as complementary sources, cutting across distinctions of genre. Once a source had been dated, and its reliability and documentary possibilities determined, there was no reason—in Sainte-Palaye's view—why it should be handled in isolation from other sources of a different type.

As a guide to the history of French society from the thirteenth to the seventeenth centuries, the *Dictionnaire des antiquités* is an impressive achievement even today. Its articles deal with the government, administration, and finances of the realm, with ecclesiastical antiquities and the relations and spheres of influence of Church and State, with the social classes and their changing relationships, with commerce and the national economy, with the laws and their administration, with the ideas and attitudes of different classes of society at different times, with education, the arts and sciences, with medieval customs, royal and ecclesiastical ceremonial, methods of warfare, architecture, clothing and dress, furnishing—in short, with everything from medieval communications or

[2] *Modern Historians and the Study of History* (London, 1953), p. 187. Interestingly enough, Hume showed a lively interest in record sources, account books, household books, etc.; see the intriguing note, based on study of an early sixteenth-century household book of the Dukes of Northumberland in the *History*, ch. 26, note (*o*).

fish merchants to the origins of the monarchy and to the wool trade in the fourteenth century. Some entries are veritable monographs of the type Sainte-Palaye published in his *Mémoires sur l'ancienne chevalerie*. Many others contain sufficient documentation for such monographs.[3] The *Mémoires sur l'ancienne chevalerie* and the *Mémoires sur la chasse* were, indeed, drawn from articles in the Dictionary.

Many articles brought precision to subjects which had been known only imperfectly before. Knowledge of medieval dress, furniture, and armour, for instance, had been sketchy and often anachronistic. Even Montfaucon's *Monumens de la monarchie françoise* left much to be desired. Sainte-Palaye's article "Habillemens," in contrast, which fills three volumes quarto of over 250 pages each, contains a minute examination of the dress of every class of society, of every trade and profession, of every rank on different occasions, and in each successive period of the Middle Ages. Not surprisingly, theatre people anxious to lend an authentic air to plays dealing with medieval subjects sought his advice on costumes and decor.[4] In general, the Dictionary was well known

---

[3] E.g., the articles 'Armes et armoiries' (Arsenal 4280, entire volume), 'Cérémonial' (Arsenal 4285, fols. 61–411), 'Chasses' (Arsenal 4287, fols. 206–341), 'Chevalerie' (Arsenal 4288, entire volume), 'Commerce' (Arsenal 4290, fols. 85–149), 'Diplomatique' (Arsenal 4294, fols. 54–121; the last 17 folios contain notes on medieval palaeography made by Sainte-Palaye himself from his study of manuscripts in France and Italy), 'Droits' (Arsenal 4295, fols. 24–99), 'Duels' (Arsenal 4295, fols. 240–512), 'Fiefs' (Arsenal 4302, entire volume), 'Finances' (Arsenal 4303, fols. 62–321), 'Gouvernement' (Arsenal 4308, fols. 1–254), 'Habillemens' (Arsenal 4315–4317, 3 vol.), 'Justice' (Arsenal 4322, entire volume), 'Monnoies' (Arsenal 4330, fols. 1–291), 'Meubles' (Arsenal 4328, fols. 175 to end of volume), 'Noblesse' (Arsenal 4331, fols. 92–341), 'Parlement' (Arsenal 4335–4336, 2 vols.), 'Rois' (Arsenal 4344, 4345, fols. 1–34), 'Tournois' (Arsenal 4351, fols. 1–149).

[4] Baculard d'Arnaud gives a brief account of chivalry "emprunté sur-tout de l'excellent ouvrage de M. de Sainte-Palaye" in the preface to his *Fayel*. (*Oeuvres* [Paris, 1795], vol. 10, pp. xi–xii, xxv–xxxv.) Baculard quotes almost word for word from the *Mémoires sur l'ancienne chevalerie* here. But the detailed descriptions of the costumes to be worn by the characters (*ibid.*, pp. xxxvi–xxxviii) was probably based on information obtained from the article 'Habillemens' in the *Dictionnaire des antiquités*. De Guibert refers to Sainte-Palaye's *Mémoires* for the costumes of the knights in his play *Le Connétable de Bourbon* (Paris ed., 1786, p. 32), but the investiture scene is described in such detail that it seems likely De Guibert also had access to the *Dictionnaire des antiquités*. Dramatic critics who were advocating stricter costume and décor realism had certainly consulted the relevant articles in the *Dictionnaire;* cf. *Costumes des grands théâtres de Paris*, ed. d'Auberteuil then Le Vacher de Charnois (Paris, 1786–89).

and frequently consulted in the eighteenth century, especially by scholars concerned with legal and institutional procedures.[5] Indeed, in 1788 when Malesherbes consulted Bréquigny about the convocation of the Estates General,[6] the latter found considerable assistance in the one hundred or so pages devoted to this topic in the Dictionary.

The Dictionary of Antiquities was at no time ready for publication. About 1761 Sainte-Palaye may still have hoped to have it finished and made available to the public, for he wrote to the Minister Saint-Florentin in that year for financial assistance in order to "mettre la dernière main à cet ouvrage." But the work was further from completion than Sainte-Palaye allowed.

Despite the rich documentation lavished on every article, very little effort had been made to put it together in a systematic way. No distinction was made between the evidence of literary sources and that of documentary sources; often, there are bare references without even an indication of what is contained in the relevant passages; or again, in matters of controversy, contrasting views are quoted without any attempt to build up the supporting evidence around the main points in the argument of either side, as in the articles *Francs* and *Gaulois*, where Le Laboureur, Boulainviller, Montesquieu, Du Bos, and Foncemagne are drawn upon indiscriminately. Many of the references, moreover, are to unpublished collections—Foncemagne's "Extraits," Secousse's "Mélanges," his own "Notices de manuscrits." These would have had to be considerably expanded and the original sources named if they were to be of any value in a published work. The same holds true of many references to works of imagination, which in the *Antiquités* are to Sainte-Palaye's own copies and not, as in the Glossary, to the original manuscript. In offering to sell the manuscript of his Dictionary to

[5] Dupuy, 'Éloge de Sainte-Palaye,' *MAI** 45:114. Bréquigny prepared a memorandum for De La Rue of London on the 'Notaires du Châtelet' for which he got most of his information in the *Dictionnaire* (Bréquigny 62, fols. 18–29).

[6] Bréquigny 56, fols. 83–298, papers on the "Assemblées des États Généraux" by Bréquigny. An undated letter from Malesherbes to Bréquigny (received by the latter, 7.11.1787) indicates that Bréquigny undertook this research at the behest of Lamoignon. Copies of his memorandum were sent both to Malesherbes himself and to the Archbishop of Paris. The vast majority of Bréquigny's references in these papers were to sources quoted in the *Dictionnaire*, which by that time had been deposited in the library of the Marquis de Paulmy, a close friend of Bréquigny.

the Royal Library, Sainte-Palaye admitted that he had given up hope of preparing it for publication himself.[7]

Though conceived on an ambitious scale the *Dictionnaire des antiquités* was sacrificed to the Glossary, and its influence was limited to those scholars who either had ready access to the Royal Library in Paris, or were intimate friends of Sainte-Palaye himself. Its effect would have been far more deeply felt had it been more widely available, for in design and in documentation it set a new standard in medieval studies.[8] When Chéruel produced his *Dictionnaire des antiquités* in 1865, the need was no longer so pressing. The Middle Ages had been fairly well explored, and Chéruel was summing up what was already known, rather than opening up new horizons. It is a tribute to Sainte-Palaye's forgotten and unfortunate project that Chéruel, even in the nineteenth century, drew on it heavily and found in it a great deal of useful material.

[7] Bréquigny 62, fol. 242, draft of a letter by Bréquigny, probably for Moreau.
[8] According to J. Bauquier, 'Les Provençalistes du XVIIIᵉ siècle,' p. 190, there was a suggestion as late as 1857 that it be published in thirteen volumes in the *Collection des documents inédits*.

CHAPTER 9

THE *MÉMOIRES SUR L'ANCIENNE CHEVALERIE* AND THE *MÉMOIRES HISTORIQUES SUR LA CHASSE*

From the *Dictionnaire des antiquités* Sainte-Palaye extracted material for several papers which he presented to the Académie des Inscriptions. The five *Mémoires sur l'ancienne chevalerie*—read between November, 1746, and August, 1750, and published together in Volume 20 of the Academy's *Mémoires* and again in two small duodecimo volumes in 1751—had an immediate and enormous success, not only in France, but in England, in Germany, and as far afield as Poland.[1] For over a century they remained the principal source from which writers and historians took their information and in some cases their ideas about chivalry.

Sainte-Palaye was by no means the first writer to concern himself with chivalry. Indeed, the study of chivalry had been pursued with such vigor since the end of the Middle Ages that in the Preface to his *Dissertation historique et critique sur la chevalerie*, which appeared in 1716, Honoré de Sainte-Marie could remark that the subject "passe pour épuisé." In England the new merchant class which rose to power and eminence at the end of the fifteenth century had tried to appropriate in the chivalric tradition the only form of worldly sophistication it knew. In France chivalry was studied by the new aristocracy associated with the service of the King and the royal administration. The elaborate etiquette of the court and the inevitable preoccupation of courtiers with questions of rank and precedence also encouraged a lively interest in all the ceremonial forms and honors by which individuals were dis-

---

[1] A recent discussion of them in E. Fueter, *Geschichte der neueren Historiographie* (2d ed.; Munich and Berlin, 1936), pp. 324-25, and in F. Meinecke. *Die Entstehung des Historismus* (Munich, 1936), pp. 202, 275-78.

tinguished. As the orders of chivalry, in appropriately modified forms, were one commonly used means of distinction,[2] interest in the history of the different orders and in their relation to each other came as easily to courtiers as an interest in genealogy. Generally, it was an interest in externals, and many histories of chivalry did not go beyond a purely factual and external account of the orders of chivalry, an account which became more and more charged with learned evidence as time went on and, perhaps, as chivalry itself became more and more alien to the real lives and activities of noblemen. By the time we reach La Roque de La Lontière's *Traité de la noblesse*,[3] each chapter consists of a single brief affirmation, followed by pages of demonstration and example. La Roque has nothing to say that had not already been said by Aubertus Miraeus, for instance, in his *Origines equestrium sive militarium ordinum*, published at Antwerp in 1609; he has only substantiated what he does say with more material than almost all his predecessors put together. Other early eighteenth century studies of chivalry were on similar lines. Honoré de Sainte-Marie's *Dissertation historique et critique* is a less formidable but equally external description, while the essay "Sur la Chevalerie," prefixed to Gueulette's edition of the *Petit Jehan de Saintré* (1725), though written more elegantly and for a wider public, confines itself to an account of ceremonies and of different names and ranks.

In addition to curiosity about the orders themselves, there was in court circles considerable curiosity about the activities of the knights. The tournaments and pageants associated with knighthood survived in an altered form throughout Europe in the fêtes marking royal marriages, the signing of peace treaties, and other important events. A need was thus created for a certain amount of research into and literature on the conduct of these spectacles. Menestrier's *Traité des Tournois* (Lyon, 1669) was one book written to satisfy this need. Menestrier himself, however, considered it a manual for masters of ceremonies responsible for court celebrations and festivities rather than a work of historical interest in the later Enlightenment sense, and in it, quite fittingly, the pro-

---

[2] See *Ordres de chevalerie et récompenses nationales* (catalog of an exhibition held at the Musée Monétaire [Paris, 1956]).

[3] G. A. La Roque de La Lontière, *Traité de la noblesse et de ses différentes espèces* (Rouen, 1735).

cedure of tournaments was touched up to fit the prevailing classical fashion.

While the administrators and the court aristocracy of triumphant absolutism saw chivalry as a development of certain forms of Roman military organization and as an instrument of centralized government (one might call this the "Romanist thesis" in the history of chivalry), the writers who expressed the aims of the still struggling and rebellious nobles of the early seventeenth century and who exhorted them to remain true to their past greatness— André Favyn, Vulson de la Colombière—presented it as an original creation of their Frankish ancestors, an instrument of noble government and a glorious tradition from the golden age of their class (the "Germanist" thesis). In their works chivalry appeared in a less formal light than in the works of La Roque or Honoré de Sainte-Marie; it was always part of a particular social organization —that of the invading and conquering Frankish nobles. At the same time it was idealized, so that it could be seen as a high moral achievement and a justification of noble power. This idealizing tendency was encouraged and exaggerated by the reliance of the apologists on relatively late theoretical treatises like Hugues de Tabarin's thirteenth-century *Ordène de chevalerie* and on romances such as *Perceforest*, which were frequently treatises of chivalry in disguise, being hortative rather than descriptive.[4] The rationale of chivalry worked out in these tracts and romances was taken at face value. Even Fauchet, a man of the robe, wrote that chivalry was instituted "tant pour oster l'oppression (que l'Anarchie avoit engendrée sus les vefves et orphelins) que pour le règlement des moeurs dissolues et des mauvaises coutumes et désordonnées impositions."[5] Fauchet admitted that he learned what he knew of chivalry from his reading of romances, in which, he relates, "les bons Chevalliers qui deffendoient les veufes, pucelles, orfelins et autres misérables personnes . . . sont grandement louez comme au contraire les cruels tirans représentez soubs le corps et nom de géans . . . sont battus, tuez et villenez."[6] In Vulson's view, not un-

---

[4] On *Perceforest* as a didactic work, see Jeanne Lods, *Le roman de Perceforest* (Geneva and Lille, 1951), p. 217 *et passim*.

[5] *Origines de chevalerie* (Geneva, 1611), pp. 77–78. The dedication to Gilles de Souvre in the 1610 Paris ed. of Fauchet's *Oeuvres* (page preceding p. 506) emphasizes Fauchet's idealized view of the knight.

[6] *Ibid.*, p. 81.

expectedly, knights were created "pour la deffense de la justice et des Loix; pour le soulagement des oppressez et la conservation des Royaumes."[7]

The noble view of chivalry was carried into the eighteenth century by Boulainviller. With its emphasis on the social function of the knights, their dedication, their paternal interest in the well-being of all, it fitted Boulainviller's conception of the historic role of the nobility and flattered the ambitions of those who hoped, as he did, to regenerate their caste and restore it to a guiding function in the State. Boulainviller insisted that chivalry was an original creation of the Frankish nobility. It was, he declared, a discipline which the nobles imposed upon themselves for the good of the community as a whole and was instituted in the eleventh century to act as a check on "l'extrême désordre où la multiplicité des Seigneurs particuliers avoit mis toute la France."[8] The weakness of the Royal authority at this time was so great—Boulainviller went on—that it could not put an end to the anarchy which threatened the nation. The nobility itself, therefore, undertook to set its own house in order and to restore peace and security to the realm. Chivalry was thus reaffirmed by Boulainviller as an invention of and an organ of government by the nobility: "Les personnes d'honneur se laissèrent persuader et ils formèrent entr'eux une certaine association, dans laquelle tous ceux qui se piquoient de probité et de gloire effective s'empressèrent d'entrer. L'engagement que l'on y prenoit étoit de défendre les opprimez, les veuves, les orphelins, les Dames et Demoiselles, de procurer la liberté des chemins, la destruction de la tyrannie, la facilité des semences et des moissons, enfin la ruine des Châteaux qui servoient de retraite aux Méchans. Voilà l'origine de ce qu'on appelle depuis la Chevalerie . . ."[9]

Still another interpretation of chivalry—in essence a modification of the "Germanist thesis"—was put forward at the end of the sixteenth century by the scholarly magistrate Étienne Pasquier, whose work was well known to Sainte-Palaye.[10] Like his teacher

---

[7] Vulson de la Colombière, Le vray Théâtre d'honneur et de chevalerie (Paris, 1648), vol. 1, ch. 2, p. 15.

[8] 'Sur l'origine et le droit de la noblesse,' in Continuation des Mémoires de M. Sallengre (1730), 9:63.

[9] Ibid., p. 65.

[10] There was a re-edition of Pasquier's works (Trévoux, 1723), shortly before Sainte-Palaye's study of chivalry appeared.

Hotman, Pasquier underplayed the influence of the Roman invasion of Gaul and of Gallo-Roman civilization on the history of France. The Frankish invasion, on the other hand, had something almost providential about it in Pasquier's scheme. Gaul was not to be pitied for having fallen into the hands of "ces braves Français qui par succession de temps se naturalisèrent en ce pays, comme légitimes Gaulois."[11] Pasquier's purpose in emphasizing indigenous traditions was conservative. He defended local peculiarities, customs, and privileges—writes de Capariis—"in nome di una sistema politico-sociale che all'osservazzione si era rivelata affatto inassimilabile a quello di Roma."[12] He could therefore be expected to support the "Germanist thesis." Pasquier's loyalty was not to the nobility of the sword alone, however. He consistently supported Catherine de' Medicis in her struggle against the feudal lords; and while he regretted the brutal measures of repression she used against the Protestant noblemen, for instance, he recognized with her that these measures were necessary to safeguard the unity of the realm. His deepest allegiance as a man of the robe was to the unified yet corporate state, and it was this, rather than the feudal state, that his *Recherches* celebrated and justified as the historical destiny of France.[13] Pasquier could thus turn a cold eye on the early history of feudal France, and it is in keeping with his general political position—he was a member of the parlement of Paris, *avocat-général* at the *Chambre des Comptes*, and a friend of such notable *parlementaires* as Fauchet and Loysel—that he discovered the origins of chivalry not in an ideal which the nobility itself had formulated but in the political ambitions of the King and the powerful barons, who endeavored to bind their vassals to them with bonds stronger than those of the fief.[14]

Sainte-Palaye's position was close to Pasquier's in many respects. Like Pasquier he was favorably disposed to the "Germanist thesis," and he emphasized, as noblemen and parlementaires were both wont to do, the "Gothic" element in French customs, even in his

---

[11] *Recherches*, quoted by Vittorio de Capariis, *Propaganda e pensiero politica in Francia durante le guerre di religione, 1559–1572* (Naples, 1959), 1:264.

[12] *Ibid.*, pp. 260–61.

[13] *Ibid.*, p. 316.

[14] *Recherches*, (Paris ed., 1596), bk. 2, ch. 13; p. 81v. This realistic view has stood the test of time rather well. (Cf. Charles Petit-Dutaillis, *La Monarchie féodale en France et en Angleterre X⁰—XIII⁰ siècle* [Paris, 1950], p. 337.)

own day.[15] At the same time, however, his view of the nobility was tempered, as Pasquier's had been, by the pre-eminence he accorded to the monarchy and to the authority of the King.[16] Given his robe origins, it would have been surprising if Sainte-Palaye had set himself up as the champion of the old *noblesse de race*. He considered the nobility a class, rather than a caste,[17] and it was not his intention to make of his study of chivalry—as Favyn, Vulson, and Boulainviller had done—an apology for the old nobility. Indeed, he took pains to emphasize his total commitment to the civilization of his own time, that is of the modern monarchy. "Défions-nous des éloges que donne un siècle au siècle qui l'a précédé," he warned. The fifth *Mémoire*, in particular, was designed to dispel any suspicion that he might value past times higher than his own. "En lisant tout ce que nous avons dit à l'honneur de la Chevalerie, on se sera rappelé que les siècles dans lesquels elle étoit la plus florissante, furent des siècles de débauche, de brigandage, de barbarie et d'horreur."[18] Sainte-Palaye's standards and values remained resolutely those of the unheroic nobility of his own time, the new aristocracy of the monarchical state—urbanity, civilized behavior, law and order, comfort, enlightenment and, latterly, the good of humanity. The superstitious piety and the gross sensuality of the knights, as

[15] Cf. for instance, his introduction to the *Mémoires* (1781), vol. 3, p. vi: "À travers les altérations et les déguisemens qu'une longue suite de siècles doit nécessairement apporter dans les moeurs et dans le génie d'un peuple, il est toujours facile d'appercevoir un fonds de ressemblance qui ne change jamais; aussi un esprit attentif retrouve-t-il encore aujourd'hui dans notre Nation tout le caractère des anciens Francs, mélangé de quelques nuances de celui des Gaulois."

[16] Cf. a passage from his introduction to the fifteenth century *Honneurs de la Cour:* "On remarquera avec satisfaction dans tout le cours de ce Traité les prééminences d'honneur attribuées dès-lors sans difficulté aux Enfans de France. Ils jouissoient d'un rang supérieur aux Princes les plus puissants. Sans égard à l'étendue de domination plus ou moins vaste, l'unique mesure de grandeur étoit alors le degré qui approchoit plus ou moins de la souche Royale . . . Etre plus près de la Couronne dans le style de ce temps-là, c'étoit être plus grand." (*Mémoires sur l'ancienne chevalerie*, 2:178).

[17] This was also the view of Montesquieu, *Esprit des lois*, 20:22.

[18] See 2:2. Cf. also what he writes of the religion of the knights: "Ils ne connoissoient que des pratiques extérieures recommandées par des prêtres, la plupart presque aussi ignorans que ceux dont ils gouvernoient les consciences. Astreints scrupuleusement à des obligations journalières dont on ne les vit presque jamais se dispenser, ils croyoient par cette régularité, et par quelques dons faits aux Églises et aux Moines, être en droit de violer dans tout le reste les lois du Christianisme . . . Des Chevaliers souillés de crimes se flattoient d'avoir un moyen facile de les expier à la première occasion qui so'offroit d'aller faire un pélérinage dans les lieux Saints, ou quelque expédition, soit contre les infidèles, soit contre les hérétiques." (*Ibid.*, pp. 12–13.)

he described them in the fifth *Mémoire*, were genuinely repulsive to him. The very style of his book, however—limpid, persuasive, almost weightless—as well the elegant presentation in neat duo-decimos, demonstrated amply his allegiance to his own civilization and to the modern and educated aristocracy of which he was a member. The Introduction to the third volume, which appeared in 1781, stressed once more the contemporary tone of the work, and the author's acceptance of and desire to satisfy the tastes and values of his enlightened eighteenth-century public: "En ménage-ant moins l'érudition, j'aurois sans doute satisfait davantage la curiosité des amateurs de l'antiquité; mais aurois-je également plu à cette partie aimable de la société à laquelle cet ouvrage est prin-cipalement consacré? Puissent les Dames accueillir avec bienveil-lance ce dernier fruit d'une Plume qui s'est toujours exercée de préférence dans un genre de littérature dont elles font leur plus cher amusement."[19] The combination of a completely contempo-rary outlook with curiosity about and sympathy for the Middle Ages is not so much an oddity as the very condition of Sainte-Palaye's work, as it was, in large measure, of Montesquieu's. He was neither a precocious romantic who somehow strayed into the wrong century nor was he a dyed-in-the-wool conservative still dreaming of the vanished glories of the old blood nobility and scornful of the new aristocracy. His description in the final *Mé-moire* of those aspects of chivalry which were unattractive to him and to his readers was thus by no means a concession to con-temporary taste, as has been suggested,[20] it was an integral part of his design and of his highly original interpretation of chivalry. We must now try to determine what that interpretation was and in what ways Sainte-Palaye's *Mémoires* are different in aim and method from earlier histories of chivalry.

The *Mémoires* first appeared before the *Esprit des lois*, but Sainte-Palaye was by then already familiar with other works by Montesquieu, whom, as we have seen, he knew personally. If he was not Montesquieu's disciple, he had been to school with the same masters at Juilly and in Paris. He belonged to the same soci-eties as Montesquieu and shared many of the same interests, intel-

---

[19] *Mémoires sur l'ancienne chevalerie*, vol. 3: Preface, pp. xiii–xiv.
[20] 'De Télémaque à Candide' by Albert Cherel, in *Histoire de la littérature française*, ed. J. Calvet, 6:47.

lectual and political. Montesquieu on his side knew the *Mémoires*, read them carefully, and made notes on them.[21] While very little, probably, would be gained by trying to establish an influence of Montesquieu on Sainte-Palaye or of Sainte-Palaye on Montesquieu, the striking similarity of outlook and approach in the *Mémoires sur l'ancienne chevalerie* and in the far greater and more ambitious work of Montesquieu must be investigated if we are to understand the intellectual and historical significance of the *Mémoires* themselves. In order that we may carry out this investigation we must make an attempt to summarize briefly the methods and achievements of Montesquieu.

Before Montesquieu reality and ideal, incoherency and system were distinct realms in political thought. Men wrote about what was, or about what ought to be, about facts, or about principles. If they dealt with reality, they often became bogged down in descriptions of isolated elements without internal unity and if they achieved unity, they did so at the cost of reality and only by constructing ideal systems. Montesquieu provided a means of discerning the system of the real, the internal unity drawing together all the varied aspects of actual bodies politic—laws, customs, education, property rights, the condition of women, etc. The form of political organization became with him a model or ideal not in the moral sense, but in the experimental sense, a construct enabling the thinker to measure and understand reality. Thus, the actual concrete situation of any given society could be defined by establishing first, what the *nature* of its political organization was (monarchy, republic, tyranny), and second, what the relation of this nature or form was at any given historical moment to the *principle* or content (honor, virtue, fear) which Montesquieu had deduced almost *more geometrico* as inherent in and appropriate to that form. The model, in which the relation of the two is obviously adequate, represents a state of equilibrium. As reality is found, on examination, to correspond to the model and as the relation of nature and principle is found to tend toward harmony, so the political organization can be said to have good survival prospects; as reality is found to diverge from the model and as the relation of nature and principle is found to tend toward opposition, so the state can be

---

[21] These notes are at the end of the 'Spicilège,' *Oeuvres complètes* (Paris, 1964), p. 434.

said to be in decline—or, at least, in process of change from one form to another. In short, Montesquieu establishes a series of model political structures or systems and argues that within any given system, certain relations have to obtain with minimum instability for the structure to operate efficiently and maintain itself in being. In fact, as one would expect, most of Montesquieu's own historical examples are of "impure" states, states which have diverged in some significant degree from the model and in which nature and principle are not in accord. Montesquieu was thus in possession of an intellectual tool which allowed him both to describe formally the nature of societies and to account historically for the dynamics of social change.

Sainte-Palaye's method in the *Mémoires sur l'ancienne chevalerie* corresponds strikingly to Montesquieu's. Instead of the formal and external account of chivalry given by predecessors like La Roque, he tried to explain the internal coherence of the whole system and all its parts and to view chivalry itself as a system of education integral to the monarchy. Sainte-Palaye emphasized the novelty of his procedure. In describing the initiation ceremonies of the knights, he declared, "j'ai seulement voulu montrer quelle idée on attachoit à l'institution d'un chevalier, quels moyens on employoit pour lui faire sentir l'étendue et la sainteté de ses engagemens . . ."[22] Similarly, in his *Mémoires sur la chasse* he later disclaimed any intention of writing a treatise on hunting or a description of the laws and ceremonies concerning it. His aim, here too, was to view hunting only as "un objet relatif aux moeurs." Sainte-Palaye's account of the institution of chivalry thus resembles the construction of a model. It describes what chivalry in its perfect form was intended to be. In fact, Sainte-Palaye tells us in the final *Mémoire*, the *principle* was not maintained, and the nature of the institution entering into contradiction with the principle which must sustain it, chivalry was corrupted almost beyond recognition: "À la vue de tant de désordres, comment se persuader que les loix de la Chevalerie ne respirassent que la religion, la vertu, l'honneur et l'humanité? Néanmoins ces deux vérités, si contraires en apparence, sont également constatées . . . Les hommes sont inconséquens; il y a toujours bien loin de la spéculation à la pratique . . . À mesure que l'on s'éloigne de l'origine, le temps introduit des abus, mais ces abus

---

[22] *Mémoires sur l'ancienne chevalerie*, 1:77.

doivent être imputés aux hommes et non pas à la profession qu'ils ont embrassée. La Chevalerie eut à cet égard le sort de tous les autres instituts."[23] Instead of being animated by honor—which Sainte-Palaye, again like Montesquieu, conceives as a kind of easier substitute for virtue, achieving painlessly what virtue achieves only at great cost[24]—the knights came to be animated by avarice and ambition. The barons, in their desperate need of men to wage their wars, short-sightedly sacrificed the code of chivalry to their immediate selfish interests, "ne songeant point que c'étoit la bonne constitution de la Chevalerie et non la multitude des Chevaliers qui faisoit la force des États, ils cherchèrent à se procurer un grand nombre de créatures, par de fréquentes promotions faites sans discernement."[25] As children, ruffians, and wealthy parvenus were recruited into the ranks of chivalry with little regard for the qualities previously demanded of a knight, discipline collapsed and chivalry fell into disrepute.

On the basis of the growing contradiction he discerned between the *nature* and the *principle* of chivalry, Sainte-Palaye thus described its decline and fall. The "institution" itself, however, was seen to be quite coherent and sensible—"l'ouvrage d'une politique éclairée," as we are told on the first page of the first *Mémoire*.

Sainte-Palaye's entire argument rested on his view of chivalry as a creation of the early monarchy[26] rather than an instrument of government by the nobility, as Boulainviller had considered it. He held that chivalry as an "institution" is appropriate to "monarchical government," in Montesquieu's sense of the term, in the way Montesquieu believed certain laws, institutions, and forms of education were appropriate to this or that form of social and political organization. Thus, it was unfortunate that "dans ces siècles malheureux" the monarch could not yet afford to provide and support from his own resources schools for the training of the young nobility, so that this task fell to the great barons.[27] The decline of chivalry was indeed caused—Sainte-Palaye argued—by the power

---

[23] *Mémoires sur l'ancienne chevalerie*, 2:2–4. Cf. Montesquieu, *EL*, 11:6: "Comme toutes les choses humaines ont une fin, l'État dont nous parlons [England] perdra sa liberté, il périra. Rome, Lacédémone et Carthage ont bien peri. Il périra lorsque la puissance législative sera plus corrompue que l'exécutrice."
[24] *Mémoires sur l'ancienne chevalerie*, 1:4.   [25] *Ibid.*, 2:31.
[26] *Ibid.*, 1:60.   [27] *Ibid.*, 1:3.

and rebelliousness of the lords and the relative weakness of the royal authority, aggravated by rivalries among the princes of the realm themselves during the reign of Charles VI.[28] As there was no proper authority, there was no enforcement of discipline and no way of containing the pride, egotism, and impetuousness of the knights, so that they might work toward the harmony of the state rather than toward its disruption. It is significant that in Sainte-Palaye's view the culture which accompanied the growing ability of the royal authority to control and harmonize the unruly barons did in fact provide lessons more appropriate to chivalry than the knights had been able to find in the literature of the early feudal period: ". . . Leur goût n'étoit cultivé que par la lecture des ouvrages de leurs Trouvères et Jongleurs, gens grossiers et libertins qui sans cesse courant le monde, la plupart pour gagner leur vie, n'avoient pas le temps de puiser dans les sources pures de l'antiquité, les principes raisonnés du bon goût et de la morale. Instruits par de meilleurs maîtres et formés sur des modèles moins imparfaits, nos chevaliers eussent appris que ce ne sont point quelques traits de feu ou de génie, jettés au hasard; mais la justesse des idées et l'heureux accord du tout avec ses parties, qui rendent un ouvrage digne de l'estime des connoisseurs."[29] Properly reconstituted, therefore, chivalry could be adopted, Sainte-Palaye thought, "par les plus sages législateurs et par les plus vertueux philosophes" of his own time.[30] The modern French aristocracy, for its part, would welcome a revival of chivalry because of that "fonds de ressemblance qui ne change jamais," which Sainte-Palaye had discovered in the ancient Franks and in their modern successors. If anything, in short, the times were more suitable to chivalry than they had been in the past.

Sainte-Palaye's *Mémoires* came at a singularly opportune moment, as Professor Ford has pointed out.[31] They provided a kind of sentimental and imaginative rallying point for all those who wished to revitalize and modernize the ancien régime while maintaining, indeed even strengthening its essential character, and they tried to reconcile, as did the *Esprit des lois*, the claims of the royal authority and those of the aristocracy, by pointing out that each required

---

[28] *Ibid.*, 2:4–5, 21–22, 29–30.　　[29] *Ibid.*, 2:43.　　[30] *Ibid.*, 1:78.
[31] Ford, pp. 244–45.

and depended on the other. It was, in fact, about the time the *Mémoires* appeared that Sainte-Palaye's old protector, Pâris-Duverney, who had returned to power under the wing of Madame de Pompadour, set up the École Royale Militaire in order to prepare the sons of impecunious provincial nobles for careers in the army. Sainte-Palaye's view of chivalry was also acceptable, however, to the men of his own class. Following Pasquier he had emphasized that chivalry was a form of service devised to circumvent the shortage of fiefs, and as such, not subject to the hard and fast conditions of the fief-holding vassal. Once the King was recognized as the only leader on whom a man can properly be *directly* dependent, chivalry could fit into that more modern and "enlightened" conception of the monarchy which Bréquigny, among other robins or former robins, opposed to "feudalism." The knights could even be considered a kind of predecessor of the sixteenth and seventeenth century *officier* class.

The appearance of Sainte-Palaye's *Mémoires* also coincided with a great deal of talk about extending and regularizing the award of distinctions to men in the professions, the arts, the army, and above all in commerce and manufacturing, who had served the country well. In an enlightened monarchy, it was felt, the orders of chivalry could be transformed into an élite of distinguished servants of the king and the nation.[32] Sainte-Palaye's contribution lent support to this suggestion. At the same time, however, it implied certain restrictions, which help to define the character of the reforms proposed. In the end, the reforms would have honored the most active and productive elements in the nation, but they would have altered nothing in their favor and given them no power to shape the national destiny; rather, they were intended to create a band or "order" of dedicated servants to guide and supervise the programs

---

[32] Marcel Reinhard, 'Élite et noblesse dans la seconde moitié du XVIIIᵉ siècle,' *Revue d'histoire moderne et contemporaine* (1956), 3:5–37. Reinhard points out that little was actually done to honor citizens active in trade or manufacturing. A similar contrast between the language and the ideology of reform and the prudence of actual practice among the enlightened administrators of eighteenth century Spain is pointed out by Marcelin Desfourneaux, "Tradition et Lumières dans le 'Despotismo ilustrado'," in *Utopie et institutions au XVIIIᵉ siècle; le pragmatisme des Lumières*, ed. Pierre Francastel (Paris and The Hague, 1963), pp. 229–45. Georges Livet, 'Introduction à une sociologie des Lumières,' *ibid.*, pp. 265–73, argues that much remains to be done to define the precise reality to which Enlightenment terms correspond in particular cases.

devised by the monarchy itself. Likewise the argument of the *Mémoires*, while it appeared to envisage a modern application of chivalry, also favored an exclusive policy designed to maintain the integrity of the existing classes and of the existing social structure. It had been the wholesale knighting of aspiring parvenus, the loss of the sense of honor which—in Sainte-Palaye's argument—had brought about the decay of chivalry.[33]

Sainte-Palaye's view of chivalry as a monarchical "institution" can thus be understood in the light of the political and social attitudes of the eighteenth century aristocracy. Like the *Esprit des lois*, it aimed to reconcile the different traditions and prejudices of the groups composing the aristocracy and of the monarchy itself, and in this way to contribute to the building of a composite tradition behind which the dominant—and very mixed—elements of the society of the ancien régime could unite. The reconciliation was achieved at a price, however. Sainte-Palaye was entitled to argue that the chivalric ideal was theoretically appropriate to monarchical government and that its practical failure in the Middle Ages was due to the weakness of the monarchy at the time and the corresponding weakness of the principle of honor which alone could discipline the knights. But he confused this theoretical argument with a factual one, and the theoretical model of chivalry with the actual historical phenomenon. He claimed that chivalry was *in fact* the creation of the monarchy, and this led him into a number of positions which proved untenable. It was not, of course, uncommon to misrepresent or misunderstand the social significance of the institutions, laws, and customs of earlier times. Despite all their warnings against applying modern standards to past ages, Montesquieu and his Swiss disciple Paul-Henri Mallet both glorified the ancient "liberties" of the "Goths." Englishmen of several political persuasions looked back for support to the "ancient constitution" and the old "common law" of the people before the Norman con-

---

[33] The same apparent contradiction is found in Montesquieu, who argues (*EL*, 20:22) for an open-door policy allowing merchants and others to aspire to and to enter the ranks of the nobility, and who, at the same time, insists on maintaining the purity of the nobility—not, indeed, a genealogical purity but a social and functional one. Montesquieu is thus opposed to a *noblesse commerçante* (*EL* 20:21), since the spirit of commerce, as he argues throughout bk. 20 of the *Esprit des lois*, in his notes on England, and elsewhere, is incompatible with nobility and monarchical government.

quest.[34] The trouble with Sainte-Palaye's view of chivalry was not simply that he took the romances and the theoretical manuals literally. He showed in the fifth *Mémoire* that he knew the reality was often very different from the code. To that extent he approached his sources honestly and critically. The trouble was that he took the code as it was elaborated in late manuals and apologies to be the original *goal* of chivalry, and he therefore assumed that the "laws" described in them were intended to govern a real *institution*. It did not occur to him that they might have been devised more or less seriously by later generations to provide a rationale for the social form or title which chivalry had become.

It was thus the whole historical development of chivalry that Sainte-Palaye did not grasp. He did distinguish between the ritual of the Germanic peoples as reported by Tacitus and knighthood as it began to emerge in the eleventh century;[35] but he failed to recognize the social meaning of the ceremony in its early stages in the eleventh century. He never discerned or admitted the pronounced caste nature of chivalry. The case of a knight who obliges a young nobleman disguised as a minstrel to quit his borrowed robes and return to those befitting his station, for example, was taken to illustrate the moral authority of knights in general.[36] Sainte-Palaye did not explain that to a closed caste society any derogation is a serious offense.[37] The herald's cry at the tournaments—"Honneur aux fils des preux"—was not explained in the light of the closed system of chivalry which tended to exclude all but the sons of knights from its ranks,[38] but in a paraphrase of the moral terms used by Monstrelet in the fourteenth century: "On vouloit . . . les avertir que ce n'étoit qu'au bout de la carrière d'une vie illustre et sans tache que le titre de preux les attendoit; que s'ils se relâchoient un instant ce

---

[34] Samuel Kliger, *The Goths in England* (Cambridge, Mass., 1952) and, more precise in many ways, J. G. A. Pocock, *The Ancient Constitution and the Feudal Law* (Cambridge, 1957). Pocock shows that, even more clearly than in France, because at an earlier stage perhaps, the Gothic argument was also used in England in the service of liberal and democratic movements—by the Levellers in particular. There is a fine résumé of the different interpretations of the Norman Conquest and the political causes they served in an article by Christopher Hill, 'The Norman Yoke,' *Democracy and the Labour Movement: Essays in Honour of Dona Torr*, ed. John Saville (London, 1954), pp. 11–66.

[35] See Marc Bloch, *La Société féodale: les classes et le gouvernement des hommes* (Paris, 1948), p. 47; also L. Genicot, 'La Noblesse au moyen âge,' *Comparative Studies in Society and History* (1962), 5:52–59.

[36] *Mémoires sur l'ancienne chevalerie*, 1:87.   [37] Marc Bloch, p. 59.

[38] *Ibid.*, pp. 59, 62–63.

seul instant pouvoit leur faire perdre le fruit de tant de travaux."[39] In this way, the social content of the cry with all the light it sheds on the real nature of chivalry was overlooked in favor of an interpretation based not on study of the historical reality of the times themselves but on the idealizing formulae of a later age. The fiscal privileges of the knights were similarly accounted for.[40] So, too, their various distinguishing marks were held to be so many incentives to virtuous conduct, rather than the outward signs by which a closed caste asserted its identity.[41] Sainte-Palaye was aware that it was often through advantageous marriages that "nos plus grands Seigneurs acquirent les terres qu'ils ont possédées," but instead of seeking the economic conditions determining this "course à l'aventure matrimoniale" in Thalamas' pithy phrase,[42] he described it in terms of the knight's duty to protect defenseless women and widows.[43] It did not occur to him that the poor whom the knight was bound to assist were by no means the poor in general, but only gentlefolk in distress.[44] The contradiction which he himself was to underline in the fifth *Mémoire* between the chivalrous code and the pillaging and spoiling of the countryside perpetrated by the knights did not cause him to modify the ideal picture of chivalry presented in the first four *Mémoires*. He might admit in the fifth *Mémoire* that the cruelty and irresponsibility of the knights provoked revolts among the common people,[45] but this did not prevent him from asserting blandly and without comment in the third *Mémoire* that the rebels "comme pour insulter à la douceur et à l'humanité de la Chevalerie . . . érigèrent en vertu la férocité la plus brutale et la plus barbare inhumanité."[46] He depicted lovingly and at length the courtesy and respect with which the English and French knights treated their prisoners and extolled the spirit of chivalry which "seule auroit pu inspirer des sentimens aussi purs et des procédés aussi généreux que ceux dont on voit les exemples toujours continués dans les deux nations, tandis que les peuples les plus voisins ne cessoient de donner à cet égard des exemples affreux

---

[39] *Mémoires sur l'ancienne chevalerie*, 1:98. [40] *Ibid.*, pp. 300-1.
[41] *Ibid.*, pp. 288 et seq., 325; cf. Bloch, p. 72.
[42] A. Thalamas, *La Société seigneuriale française 1050-1270* (Paris, 1951), p. 109.
[43] *Mémoires sur l'ancienne chevalerie*, 1:315-16.
[44] Cf. Jacques Flach, *Les Origines de l'ancienne France, X^e et XIe siècles* (Paris, 1893), 2:569.
[45] *Mémoires sur l'ancienne chevalerie*, 2:24-25. [46] *Ibid.*, 1:201.

de cruauté et de barbarie."[47] At the same time he knew that the same knights, who showed such consideration for their opposite numbers, showed none at all for their foot-soldiers or for the civilian populations of the territories they overran.[48]

Sainte-Palaye's sources did, admittedly, date from the thirteenth century or later. His documentation was, therefore, made up largely of romances, theoretical manuals, and historical sources, such as Froissart's Chronicles, in which chivalry was painted in the most glowing colors. Yet he did have access to some pre-thirteenth-century texts and documents. He had scoured the *Annales de Saint-Bertin* and *Aimoin* in the Duchesne collection, the *Ordonnances des rois de France* and the Provençal version of *Gérard de Roussillon* for ceremonies of knighting up to the eleventh and twelfth centuries; he had nothing to say, however, about the social significance of those early knightings. His interest in them was confined to externals. Moreover, he had, as we have seen, amassed a considerable amount of evidence that conflicted with the view of chivalry given by the manuals, by most of the romances and by his favorite chronicler Froissart. Indeed, the discrepancy between goal and achievement, between code and conduct, was so great that he felt obliged to concede at one point that there must have been something in the very nature of chivalry that caused its disorders.[49] He never reached the point, however, of questioning whether chivalry had in fact been, as he believed, a perfectly devised institution, which the men of the Middle Ages had failed to live up to. It did not occur to him to inquire whether the "institution" and the "laws" of chivalry—as he thought of them—had actually existed, because he was too concerned to show that chivalry was an organization functioning as part of the monarchy. It seems not entirely fair, therefore, to blame his sources for the faults of his interpretation. There was in this interpretation also an element of choice; as much as the nature of his sources, Sainte-Palaye's interpretation of chivalry reflects a political outlook and a political commitment. No less than Montesquieu, he was reaching, consciously or unconsciously, toward a synthetic ideology acceptable to the main privileged groups in the ancien régime.

---

[47] *Ibid.*, 1:108.   [48] *Ibid.*, 1:301.
[49] *Ibid.*, 2:4: ". . . d'ailleurs, pour ne rien déguiser, sa constitution même étoit inséparable de ses inconvéniens."

The *Mémoires sur l'ancienne chevalerie* expressed in other ways the character of the broadly based and modern aristocratic public for which they were intended. Sainte-Palaye's work confronted the contemporary nobleman with a form of chivalry which was in many respects alien to him and quite different from chivalry as he knew it in his own highly ordered and refined society. But it also suggested that there was an historical continuity between the old and the new and that certain aspects of early chivalry might be taken over in order to revivify modern chivalry, just as some of the more picturesque words could be taken over from the "vieux langage" to regenerate the modern language. In fact, however, no substantial change in modern ways was envisaged, only a little dressing up, and in the end it was the most superficial aspects of ancient chivalry that appealed most strongly to Sainte-Palaye's readers and that most impressed them in his book. This is not surprising. The eighteenth-century aristocrat, Sainte-Palaye's reader, whatever his origin, was an intensely alienated being. More and more cut off socially and intellectually from the "feudal" basis of his existence, he had been free for many decades to inspect coolly and to try out modes of thought and behavior quite unconnected with and even inimical to that basis. He had developed speculative tendencies—financial as well as intellectual—which aggravated his alienation. With his extravagance, his love of pleasure, his marriage deals, he had helped to weaken the moral and social standing of that old established nobility, in the passing of which conservatives often bemoaned the decline of the ancien régime as a whole,[50] he had contributed to the growing domination of money and consequently to the increasing formalization of the social order—indeed, he himself was often a graduate of the world of finance. More and more traveled, enlightened, broadminded and curious, he had learned to recognize other cultures and to see that his own world was but one form of organization, one set of conventions among several that were possible. Sometimes he even came to be critical of his society in the name of a broadly conceived humanity. In gen-

[50] Cf., for instance, Nicolas Chérin, Royal Genealogist, 1787-90: "Cette manie de quitter les provinces et d'abandonner les campagnes qui deviennent désertes, l'attachement aux maximes de Cour, l'envie d'y jouir de quelques distinctions passagères, le goût effréné des plaisirs de la capitale, le luxe, la dissolution des moeurs qu'il entraîne, le célibat, voilà les maux qui détruisent la noblesse et qui altèrent tous les ordres de l'État." (Quoted in Bluche, *Les Honneurs de la Cour*, Les Cahiers Nobles, Nos. 10-11 [Paris, 1957].)

eral, however, he accepted his own social order in practice, not as
something natural or divine, but as one form of human organization which happened to suit him well and which might be adjusted
to fit his humanitarian and enlightened theories better. In most
cases his relativism implied no fundamental critique of his society
but rather the irrelevance of all attempts to justify or give absolute
value to any one form of social organization. Rather than to a
revolutionary questioning of the social structure, it led to a kind of
urbane and playful detachment which often manifested and confirmed itself in theatricality, the playing of parts. There was nothing well-to-do people liked to do better in the eighteenth century
than dress up and play parts, for the theater was one of the best
means they had of expressing their humanity, their cosmopolitanism, their superiority to all prejudices, that is to all unconsciously
accepted historical determination.

Sainte-Palaye and his aristocratic readers of the eighteenth century thus delighted in the external and picturesque aspect of chivalry because it allowed them to enjoy the spectacle of a noble way
of life without being captured by it, to reappropriate and reaffirm
the traditions of the ancien régime without ceasing to be detached
and enlightened men of the world. The spectacle of chivalry—the
costumes, the ceremonies, the rituals—does in fact take up a good
part of the *Mémoires*,[51] and as this aspect of chivalry was at no
time and in no place more gorgeously visible than at the court of
Burgundy in the fifteenth century,[52] it is natural that Sainte-Palaye
showed particular interest in texts describing this court. As we
have already observed, it is a moot question whether his view of
chivalry was determined by the late texts he used, or whether his
choice of texts was guided by his view of chivalry. As early as the
twenties, when he was traveling through France viewing local
antiquities, it had been the later flamboyant Gothic rather than the
Gothic of the twelfth and thirteenth centuries that gave him most

---

[51] Cf. the opinion of Edmond Estève, 'Le moyen Âge dans la littérature du
XVIII° siècle,' *Revue de l'Université de Bruxelles* (1923), p. 368: ". . . sur l'origine
de la chevalerie, sur les causes de sa grandeur et de sa décadence on peut estimer
que la Curne n'émet pas de vues bien profondes, que même il n'en a que de con-
fuses et d'insuffisantes . . . Mais pour tout ce qui regarde la partie descriptive et
pittoresque, il réussit par l'abondance et la précision de détails à nous donner sans
recherche ostentatoire, l'impression de la couleur."

[52] See Sidney Painter, *French Chivalry* (Baltimore, 1940), pp. 26–27.

pleasure. Moreover, at the courts of Philip the Good and Charles the Bold the forms and ceremonies of chivalry were the more splendid, as the inner life had already gone out of them. The jousts and tourneys of the court of Burgundy were in fact paid for with revenues drawn from the trade and industry of the Low Countries.[53] The chivalry that most interested Sainte-Palaye was thus one that was well suited to the conditions of his own age, for the tamed and refined aristocracy which read and enjoyed the *Mémoires sur l'ancienne chevalerie*—men of the robe, ennobled financiers, and high civil servants, as well as the old nobility of the blood—was already foreshadowed at the court of Burgundy.

It was, moreover, to a large extent, the picturesqueness and sentimentality of Sainte-Palaye's account of chivalry that assured the success of his book in the nineteenth century. Among his own contemporaries, Voltaire quickly spotted the political ideal which was implied by the interpretation of chivalry given in the *Mémoires*, and he subjected this interpretation to effective criticism in the *Essai sur les moeurs*: "Les inféodations, les droits de ressort et de mouvance, les héritages, les lois, rien d'essentiel n'avait rapport à cette chevalerie. C'est en quoi se sont trompés tous ceux qui ont écrit de la chevalerie: ils ont écrit sur la foi des romans, que cet honneur était une charge, un emploi; qu'il y avait des lois concernant la chevalerie. Jamais la jurisprudence d'aucun peuple n'a connu ces prétendues lois; ce n'était que des usages . . ."[54] Voltaire's criticism was upheld by other liberal historians, such as Gilbert Stuart and later still Guizot.[55] By the early nineteenth century

---

[53] *Ibid.*

[54] 'Essai sur les moeurs,' ch. 97, *Oeuvres*, 12:131. Voltaire's view was realistic and has stood the test of time; cf. R. W. Southern, *The Making of the Middle Ages* (London, 1953), pp. 111-13 and 242-46. By the eleventh century, according to Southern, blood nobility ceased to have much significance. "Nobility had only two roots: property, by which a man entered into a set of relationships determining his place in society; and knighthood, by which he assumed responsibilities and privileges denied to those outside the ranks of the fraternity. The property relationship was born in the act of homage; the knightly relationship in the act of initiation to knighthood. The man who had many lords by his homage was on an equality with the king by his knighthood. It is not surprising therefore that the first was the practical working bond between men, while the second had almost from the beginning something of romance and idealism and ineffectiveness." (p. 111.)

[55] Gilbert Stuart, *A View of Society in Europe in Its Progress from Rudeness to Refinement* (Edinburgh, 1778), ch. 2, sec. 2, pp. 54-55; Guizot, *Cours d'histoire moderne* (Brussels ed., 1839), pp. 513-14.

Sainte-Palaye's view of chivalry as an "institution" had had to be abandoned. There remained, however, for Fauriel, Mills, James, and other writers on the Middle Ages, chivalry as an "ideal" or "sentiment,"[56] and it was the account of the knightly code together with the picturesque descriptions of initiation ceremonies, tournaments, and so forth that they appreciated in Sainte-Palaye. The early Romantic poets and novelists picked up the same thing from the *Mémoires*. The chapter "Vie et moeurs des chevaliers" in Chateaubriand's *Génie du christianisme*, for instance, is entirely based on the *Mémoires* and, despite claims to the contrary, shows no sign of a real breakthrough in historical understanding.[57] There is not much doubt that it was Sainte-Palaye's vivid descriptions of

---

[56] See, for instance, C. Fauriel, *Histoire de la poésie provençale* (Leipzig and Paris, 1847), 484–85. For a good account of the enormous vogue of this idea of chivalry throughout the nineteenth century, but especially in the countless publications of the Restoration period, and some suggestions concerning its political causes and consequences, see F. J. C. Hearnshaw, 'Chivalry and its place in history,' in *Chivalry: a Series of Studies to Illustrate Its Historical Significance and Civilizing Influence*, ed. E. Prestage (London, 1928).

[57] Chateaubriand's debt to Sainte-Palaye has been studied in detail by M. J. Walter, 'Une Source du *Génie du Christianisme*,' *RHLF* (1922), 29:225–35; and by J. M. Gautier, 'Le *Génie du Christianisme*, est-il un de nos premiers 'digests'?' *ibid.* (1948), 48:211–22. (See also the same writer's 'Quelques aspects de l'archaïsme dans l'oeuvre de Chateaubriand,' *French Studies* [1948], 2:315–23). Their analyses have shown that even where Chateaubriand refers to Du Cange or to medieval chronicles and annals, he is simply pillaging Sainte-Palaye's notes and references. Nevertheless, Walter claims that "il serait aisé de montrer qu'il a transformé les matériaux dont il se sert," while in Gautier's view "l'artiste a su remédier à la sécheresse du récit de l'historien et a mis devant nos yeux un véritable petit tableau." In his *French Studies* article Gautier even claims that thanks to the literary skill of Chateaubriand, "le moyen âge authentique revit." This is, to say the least, doubtful. Chateaubriand's sources were almost invariably secondary ones, eighteenth century works for the most part, his criticism of sources was virtually nonexistent, and his historical thinking was unoriginal (cf. A. Dollinger, *Les Études historiques de Chateaubriand*, Publications de la Faculté des Lettres de Strasbourg, 2ᵉ sér. [Paris, 1932], 8:101–2, 111–61, 175–76, 268–96). His knowledge of the sources of medieval history was, in fact, like that of most of the Romantics, inferior to that of Sainte-Palaye himself (on the slight erudition of Romantic writers, see D. Doolittle, *The Relations between Literature and Medieval Studies in France from 1820 to 1860* [Bryn Mawr, 1933], pp. 52–53). Chateaubriand, it seems, merely popularized for the reading public of the Restoration a work that was in many respects already tailored to their requirements, as Nodier's republication of the *Mémoires sur l'ancienne chevalerie*, in 1826, the high point of nineteenth century Romantic medievalism according to Baldensperger indicates ('La grande Communion Romantique en 1827; sous le signe de Walter Scott,' *Revue de littérature comparée* [1927], 7:47–86). A more realistic assessment of Chateaubriand as historian is found in Pierre Moreau, *Chateaubriand: l'homme et l'oeuvre* (Paris, 1956), p. 64.

the gallantries, sports, and ceremonies of chivalry—the very quality of picturesqueness that distinguishes the *Mémoires* from earlier books on chivalry—which appealed to Chateaubriand. Sir Walter Scott likewise found in Sainte-Palaye the picture of chivalry which he presented to the world both in the *Encyclopaedia Britannica* article of 1814 and in his fictional writings. Scott's view of the Middle Ages was richer in social and human significance than Sainte-Palaye's[58] but, perhaps in reaction to the increasing drabness of early industrial civilization, Scott also delighted in the colorful surface of the past—too much so, in the opinion of Heine and a later generation[59]—and he could indulge this taste to the full in the *Mémoires*. Robert Southey's presentation of chivalry was similarly influenced by his reading of Sainte-Palaye.[60]

Among the first Romantics, it was thus the rich surface and moral idealism of Sainte-Palaye's portrait of chivalry that left its mark rather than his interpretation of it as an "institution" associated with "monarchical government." Gradually, however, this side of the *Mémoires* also came under fire. The early nineteenth-century historians and novelists still accepted that the code of chivalry was an ideal to which the medieval knight genuinely aspired, even after they had abandoned the rest of Sainte-Palaye's interpretation. Probably the popularity and high standing of Froissart, which Sainte-Palaye himself had done so much to further, con-

[58] On Scott as historian, see G. M. Trevelyan, 'The Influence of Sir Walter Scott on History,' in *An Autobiography and other Essays* (London, 1949), pp. 200–5; Edith Baho, 'Scott as a medievalist,' in *Sir Walter Scott Today*, ed. H. J. C. Grierson (London, 1932), pp. 131–57; Max Korn, 'Sir Walter Scott und die Geschichte,' *Anglia* (1937), 61:416–41. The most sympathetic appreciation of Scott's historical vision is that of Lukacs, *Der historische Roman* (Berlin, 1955), pp. 23–60.

[59] Heine, 'Die romantische Schule,' *Sämtliche Werke* (Hamburg ed., 1884), 7:215. Carlyle, Taine, and Ruskin also questioned Scott's sense of history (Duncan Forbes, *The Liberal Anglican Idea of History* [Cambridge, 1952], p. 191).

[60] There are long extracts from the *Mémoires sur l'ancienne chevalerie* in Southey's *Commonplace Book*, 4th ser., ed. John Wood Warter [London, 1851], pp. 151–52. Moreover, Southey considered Sainte-Palaye's work exemplary. The medieval chapters of his proposed *History of Portugal* were to be based on the model of the *Mémoires*. "Of the Gothic period, the Moors, and the various Christian states that grew upon their ruins—a sort of Sainte-Palaye chapter. Their barbarous annals are thus best treated, and the moral features of the people more accurately and *rememberably* painted . . ." (Letter to John May, from Lisbon, 16.12.1800, *Robert Southey: Journals of a Residence in Portugal 1800–1801 and a Visit to France 1838*, ed. Adolfo Cabral [Oxford, 1960]).

tributed to the survival of this belief.[61] By the mid-century, however, Arnold, Freeman, Greene, Buckle, even the conservative
Stubbs, perhaps because they recognized that the Restoration view
of chivalry no longer had much to offer the modern liberal or conservative, felt free to investigate it more closely and began to question whether chivalry had ever been more than a "picturesque
mimicry of high sentiment, heroism, love and courtesy, before
which all depth and reality of nobleness disappeared, to make room
for the coarsest profligacy, the narrowest caste-spirit, and a brutal
indifference to human suffering."[62] As the tawdriness of the later
periods of chivalry became more apparent, there was by the end of
the century a tendency to push back its Golden Age into the epic
period of the twelfth century.[63] Sainte-Palaye continued to receive
generous tribute from the very historians who were shaping this
new idea of chivalry,[64] but the century-long influence of the
Mémoires was on the wane. It would no doubt be possible to find
traces of them lingering in popular and children's literature, and
the great writers who had appropriated the Mémoires for their
own purposes also did much to maintain their influence on many

[61] Thus, for instance, George Beltz, the Lancaster Herald, in his *Memorials of the Order of the Garter* ([London, 1841], p. 113) believed he could rely entirely on the Chronicles of Froissart for his biography of Walter Manny, and leaves no doubt that he was led to do this by Sainte-Palaye's biography of Manny in the *Mémoires sur l'ancienne chevalerie;* similarly Hallam, although he considered Froissart "undeserving to be quoted as an authority" on political history (*View of the State of Europe in the Middle Ages* [London ed., 1868], 3:81, n. b) did not entertain the idea that Froissart's picture of customs and manners might be as colored by his prejudices and by his personality as his account of events, and that in any case it was relevant not to the entire history of chivalry, but only to the history of chivalry in the fourteenth century. Even in 1895 an English editor of the Chronicles declared that "they are a truer picture of the period than any modern historian, with all his researches, or any modern novelist with all his genius and imagination could present to us." (*Chronicles of Froissart,* ed. Macaulay, [London, 1895], Preface, p. vi.) On Sainte-Palaye's role in popularizing Froissart, see above, pt. III, ch. 5, n. 35.

[62] Hearnshaw, p. 30.

[63] For instance, Léon Gautier, *La Chevalerie* (Paris, 1884).

[64] Gautier still invoked Sainte-Palaye. Not only are the *Mémoires* constantly summarized or referred to, Gautier accepts Sainte-Palaye's dictum that the laws of chivalry could be adopted by the philosophers and legislators of all times, remarking that "on ne saurait guère reprocher à cet hommage qu'un léger parfum de XVIIIe siècle. Il est au reste souverainement juste." (p. 51) Gautier even exaggerated the scope of Sainte-Palaye's work, as, for instance, when he asserted that there is hardly a page in the *Mémoires* where the testimony of the medieval epics is not invoked (p. xiv). In fact, Sainte-Palaye knew very few of the great epics in their earliest form, nor does he quote them.

generations of readers; but as an original source of inspiration, they had ceased to be alive. The "heroes" required by the generation of Carlyle and even more by that of Nietszche were tougher and of a different caliber from those whom Chateaubriand and Nodier had found in Sainte-Palaye's *Mémoires*.

Sainte-Palaye's study is both more and less, however, than what it was for the nineteenth century. The demands of the eighteenth-century aristocrat were in some ways more complex than those of his nineteenth-century successor. He enjoyed tales of jousts and tourneys, but he was never completely captured by the play, and the occasional light irony of Sainte-Palaye, the combination of old matter and modern manner, enabled the reader to control his relation to the work at will. It is characteristic of the constantly shifting ground on which the author and the eighteenth century reader of the *Mémoires* both stood that a passage in which Sainte-Palaye condemns the gross sexual mores of the knights is accompanied by a long note in which many examples of these sexual mores from the twelfth, thirteenth, and fourteenth centuries are complaisantly detailed for the curious reader.[65]

Sainte-Palaye's interpretation of chivalry as an "institution" associated with monarchy, his failure to distinguish its historical phases, his concentration on late materials, his emphasis on externals, his acceptance of contemporary values such as tolerance, humanity, and cosmopolitanism are all integral aspects of the total view which the *Mémoires* express, and they cannot be isolated from each other. The final *Mémoire*, for instance, cannot be judged, as some later readers judged it, a "concession" to the taste and ideas of the time. Rather the entire work is a unity which expresses the taste and ideas of the time and, more specifically, of that sophisticated aristocracy of the last century of the ancien régime of which Sainte-Palaye was part and for which he wrote.

This is by no means to underestimate the seriousness or the extent of Sainte-Palaye's research. There is no doubt that as his knowledge of the sources of medieval history was greater than almost any of his contemporaries could lay claim to, so his exploitation of them was on a scale vaster than they could attempt. Later scholars, as we have observed, leaned heavily on him and could do

[65] *Mémoires sur l'ancienne chevalerie*, pt. 5, n. 17, 2:66–70.

so with confidence, at least as far as the material sources of his work were concerned. Nor can it be denied that the *Mémoires* helped to enrich the historical consciousness of an era by illustrating how our understanding of particular aspects of the past—customs, institutions, laws, etc.—can be deepened when we view them not in isolation but in their relation to a whole culture and way of life. There are, in short, connections between different currents of Enlightenment thought and feeling. The playful "medievalism" and "primitivism" of the enlightened aristocrat were not incompatible with a valuable and novel way of considering society, and the politics and prejudices of the robin did not prevent him from presenting the most complete and richly documented study of chivalry that had yet appeared.

Published in 1781 in a companion volume to the two that had already been published on chivalry, the *Mémoires historiques sur la chasse* were read to the Académie des Inscriptions between August, 1752, and January, 1758. Sainte-Palaye declared at the outset that he was not writing a manual or treatise of hunting and that he did not intend to go into technical details: "Ceux que ces détails pourroient intéresser feront bien de consulter ces divers Traités. Pour moi, je me contenterai de faire voir, comme un objet relatif aux moeurs, quel a été le goût de la nation pour la Chasse."[66] The *Mémoires sur la chasse* were thus intended, like the *Mémoires sur l'ancienne chevalerie*, as a contribution to social history.[67]

Since he was not concerned with hunting as an institution 'proper' to the monarchy, Sainte-Palaye could afford, this time, to recognize the caste nature of hunting. As the sport of warriors and as part of their education it rapidly became the distinguishing mark of a social group, he argued, on the evidence of laws, customs, and medieval iconography, and severe punishments were meted out to those who transgressed the rights of the nobility. Among themselves, however, the nobles vied with each other to acquire or usurp traditional hunting rights. A man's position was increasingly measured by the number of his hounds and falcons, and this pre-

---

[66] *Mémoires sur l'ancienne chevalerie*, 3:167.
[67] Hans J. Epstein, 'The Origin and Earliest History of Falconry,' *Isis* (1943), 34:497, draws attention to the value for the historian of the study of such social phenomena as sports and games, but seems not to have known of Sainte-Palaye's work.

occupation with outward show, coupled with frequent sacrifice of all considerations of good husbandry to the pleasures of the hunt, not only led to the oppression and misery of the non-noble classes, but ultimately contributed to the ruin of the nobles themselves. "On avoit la manie des oiseaux et des chiens: c'étoit à qui en auroit un plus grand nombre, et cette rivalité jetoit dans des dépenses ruineuses."[68]

Sainte-Palaye emphasized the significance of hunting for the whole culture of feudalism. It not only provided poetry with its metaphors,[69] its terminology invaded the entire domain of taste and entertainment. As late as the reign of Henri IV, the ballets and spectacles of the court drew on it for their principal themes.[70] Likewise, it was love of hunting that led François I to construct new castles and rebuild old ones in his finest hunting forests. In this way some of the great architectural achievements of the Renaissance itself—Chambord, Villers-Cotterets, La Muette, Fontaine-bleau—owed their existence to the favorite sport of the feudal nobility.

Hunting gradually ceased, however, to be the preserve of the old nobility. While the nobles squandered their wealth, the bourgeois grew prosperous and acquired hunting rights by purchase, so that the well-to-do among them were soon able to adopt the external signs of noble life. By the fifteenth century apologists of the nobility were frequently complaining of the degradation of their caste and of the sport that had once been its exclusive preserve.

Significantly, Sainte-Palaye's realization that the period of the decline of hunting as an exclusively noble sport was at the same time the period of its greatest picturesqueness did not diminish his interest in colorful detail. Quite the contrary was true. Texts from the fourteenth century and later were again predominant among the sources of the *Mémoires sur la chasse,* and while the early and high Middle Ages were treated summarily, the late Middle Ages commanded almost all Sainte-Palaye's attention. "Ce que j'ai dit jusqu'à présent sur la Chasse," he wrote at the end of the first *Mémoire,* "se réduit à quelques fragments que j'ai trouvés épars soit dans les anciens Auteurs, soit dans les anciennes Ordonnances de nos Rois sur la Chasse." The following centuries, however,

[68] *Mémoires sur l'ancienne chevalerie,* 3:226–27.   [69] *Ibid.,* pp. 248–49.
[70] *Ibid.,* p. 351.

"vont me fournir une assez grande abondance de matériaux . . .
Depuis le Roi Jean, il n'est presque aucun règne que ne fournisse
quelque trait capable de piquer la curiosité des Amateurs de la
Chasse."[71] Sainte-Palaye's readers shared his curiosity. Members of
old established noble families read with pleasure of the traditions
by which they had once been distinguished, while new recruits to
the aristocracy were intrigued, as new recruits always are, by the
traditions and signs of the way of life with which they had associated themselves.

[71] *Ibid.*, p. 194.

CHAPTER 10

THE *HISTOIRE LITTÉRAIRE DES TROUBADOURS*

Many factors coincided in the eighteenth century to promote a revival of interest in the troubadours. The civilization of the South of France in the twelfth century was generally held to be the first notable secular culture since classical antiquity. As such it drew the attention of all Enlighteners, and as it had been an aristocratic culture, it appealed particularly to an enlightened aristocracy. Troubadour poetry was usually considered the first modern poetry. The *Modernes* were therefore interested in it from an historical point of view. They also enjoyed what they considered its simplicity and naïveté and tended to read it as pastoral. On the other hand, it is possible that the virtuosity of the Provençal poets—if anyone was capable of recognizing it, and not enough work has been done for us to say whether anyone was—intrigued an aristocratic public which admired any display of expertise, skill, and elegance, whether it occurred in poetry, on the battlefield, or in the boudoir. Most of the *Modernes*, moreover, held that good poetry was distinguished by the poet's originality and inventiveness within fixed conventions; to them, artistic creation consisted largely in "la difficulté vaincue"—as against the view of the *Anciens* that true poetry has an element of divine inspiration. As lyric poetry the work of the troubadours also appealed, perhaps through a misunderstanding, to the new private and individualistic man of the eighteenth century, the inward-looking and self-conscious bourgeois; indeed, the themes of the troubadours found an echo in many contemporary writers. It is no accident that Rousseau's Saint-Preux compares himself to Petrarch. Finally, the provincial pride which over the centuries had continued to sustain a modicum of interest in the poets of the *Midi*, was in a sense justified and given general significance by growing criticism of Paris and of the court. The dignity given by writers such as Rousseau or Gessner to the simpler life of the provinces smoothed the way for a revival of interest in those poets who did not belong to the courtly tradition of absolutism or even to the humanist tradition of the Renaissance. The article "Poète" in the *Encyclopédie*, translated from the German of Sulzer, emphasized what the author considered the *popular* nature of medieval poetry. The medieval poets did not write for a restricted circle of specially privileged readers, it was argued, but for a whole society. On the Provençal poets Jaucourt had as yet little to say, but it is easy to see that the *Encyclopédistes* were ready to welcome any French equivalent of the Middle High German poets as Bodmer and Sulzer presented them. Provençal poetry thus entered into those vast considerations of poetry and its relation to society—of culture, in short—which Rousseau dealt with in the Letter to d'Alembert and which Grimm developed in the article "Poème lyrique" of the *Encyclopédie*.[1]

In the eighteenth century the troubadours were thus no longer a mere antiquarian curiosity. On the contrary, they appealed to the most diverse tastes and for the most diverse and contradictory reasons. They could be all things to all manner of men—aristocratic and popular, courtly and individual, brilliant formally, charmingly naïve and full of authentic passion. This was a substantial change from the previous age, which had shown only perfunctory interest in them.[2] Pasquier, for instance, had devoted three pages of his *Recherches* to the briefest account of the forms of the Provençal lyric.[3] At the end of the seventeenth century, Huet described their poetry with contemptuous irony.[4] As a churchman with important robe connections, Fleury had little sympathy for a secular poetry

---

[1] "Lorsqu'un spectacle ne sert que d'amusement à un peuple oisif," Grimm writes, "c'est-à-dire, à cette élite d'une nation qu'on appelle la *bonne compagnie*, il est impossible qu'il prenne jamais une certaine importance; et quelque génie que vous accordiez au poète, il faudra bien que l'exécution théâtrale, et mille détails de son poëte [poème?] se ressentent de sa destination. Sophocle en faisant des tragédies, travailloit pour la patrie, pour la religion, pour les plus augustes solennités de la république . . . Chez les anciens, le spectacle étoit une affaire d'état; chez nous, si la police s'en occupe, c'est pour lui faire mille chicanes, c'est pour le faire plier à mille convenances bizarres."

[2] Ermanno Mozzati, 'Note sulla protostoria della filologia italiana,' p. 216, in Viscardi, *Preistoria e storia degli studi romanzi*, pp. 171-219. Also, Käte Axhäusen, *Die Theorien über den Ursprung der provenzalischen Lyrik* (Marburg, 1937), p. 10.

[3] *Recherches*, ed. 1621, Livre 7, ch. 3, pp. 606-9.

[4] P. D. Huet, *Origine des romans* (7th ed.; Paris, 1693), pp. 133-37.

that sang only "de combats et d'amours; mais d'amours brutales et sottes, comme celles des gens grossiers." It was, he declared, in no way comparable with the poetry of the Hebrews and the Greeks, but the work of "des débauchés vagabonds."[5] Huet did indeed concede that Homer was a wandering minstrel like the troubadours,[6] and Fleury gave them credit for having been the first to use the vernacular as a literary medium. Nothing in the work of either, however, suggests that they themselves had any direct knowledge of Provençal poetry or that they considered such knowledge desirable or profitable.

This is not to say that all knowledge of the Provençal poets had disappeared from France. With all its faults, its inaccuracies, its crass fabrications, Jean de Nostredame's *Les Vies des plus célèbres et anciennes poètes provensaux* (published at Lyon in 1575) succeeded in preserving the troubadours from oblivion for nearly two hundred years. The Southern magistracy in particular cultivated the troubadours; the works of Catel and Caseneuve bear witness to this interest. Even at the close of the seventeenth century Pierre de Chasteuil had sufficient pride in his literary heritage to take offense at the current denigration of Provençal and of the poets who wrote in it and to recall that Provençal had once been the language of the most civilized courts in Europe, that its poets had perfected the use of rhyme, and that outstanding writers such as Dante and Petrarch had avowed their debt to their Provençal models.[7]

The growth of interest in history which accompanied the early Enlightenment created a new context for the study of the troubadours. Works such as Crescimbeni's *Storia della volgar poesia* (1698) and Mervesin's *Histoire de la poésie françoise* (1706)[8]

---

[5] *Discours sur l'histoire ecclésiastique* (Nîmes ed., 1785), 'Discours sur la Poésie des Hébreux,' pp. 372–73. Fleury's *Discours* were written between 1680 and 1690.

[6] *Origine des romans*, p. 138.

[7] Quoted in *Mercure*, Feb., 1726, pp. 326 *et seq.* Chasteuil in fact wrote a defense of the troubadours, *Apologie des anciens historiens et des troubadours ou poëtes provençaux, servant de réponse aux Dissertations de Pierre Joseph* (Avignon, 1704), but this series of dialogues defending the troubadours against the imputation that they were no more than vagabonds and ruffians, contains no new information. Chasteuil was also the author of an unpublished history of the troubadours, which was for a time in the possession of Mazaugues, so that Sainte-Palaye probably consulted it (Chabaneau, 'Sur quelques manuscrits provençaux perdus ou égarés,' *Revue des langues romanes* [1885], 28:72).

[8] For a list of histories of taste, poetry, the arts, etc., published between 1710 and 1756, see Krauss, 2:208–10.

assured a definite place for Provençal poetry in the history of literature and of civilization.[9] Fontenelle indicated what that place was.
"Ces temps-là," he declared, "furent fort ignorans, et il semble que
la nature les choisit exprès pour faire voir ce qu'elle peut par elle-
même, et pour produire des Poètes qui lui dussent tout . . . La
poésie et les Poètes de ces tems-là etoient bien différens de ce qu'ils
sont aujourd'hui. La Poésie étoit sans art, sans règle, telle enfin
qu'elle doit être dans sa naissance." One cannot therefore expect
perfection. Nevertheless, these early poets are not without a certain
charm which the civilized eighteenth century reader might savor if
he maintained an ironical distance. "Ils ont une simplicité qui se
rend son Lecteur favorable, une naïveté qui vous fait rire sans vous
paroître ridicule et quelquefois des traits de génie imprévus."[10]
Despite its limitations, among them a marked tendency to read
early poetry as pastoral, the historical outlook of the early Enlightenment brought Provençal poetry out of the antiquarian's study.
Everybody who wrote about poetry was now expected to have at
least some awareness of it.[11]

But there was no sign, as yet, in the histories of poetry of original
research or extensive first hand knowledge. Like Pasquier and
Huet, Mervesin and Massieu relied mostly on Italian scholarship
for what they knew of the troubadours. In 1727, therefore, Falconet could truly complain to his colleagues at the Académie des
Inscriptions that the history of French poetry and of the troubadours remained to be written.[12]

[9] Cf. Mervesin's comment in his *Histoire de la poésie françoise* (Paris, 1706),
pp. 62–63: "C'est là (in Provence) qu'au commencement du douzième siècle, on
vit paroître ces agréables génies, qui tirèrent les Muses de l'assoupissement où elles
étoient depuis longtemps en France . . . Ils n'ont pas inventé l'art de rimer . . .
mais on doit leur attribuer la gloire d'avoir les premiers fait sentir à l'oreille le
véritable agrément de la rime." A similar place was assigned to the troubadours by
the Abbé Massieu, one of Sainte-Palaye's early mentors, in his *Histoire de la poésie
françoise* (Paris, 1739), p. 92.
[10] Fontenelle: 'Histoire du Romieu de Provence,' *Mercure*, Jan., 1751, pp. 7–8.
There is a similar account, in almost identical terms, in Formey, *Principes élémen-
taires des belles-lettres* (Amsterdam, 1763), pp. 68–69. Fontenelle's essay was reprinted in his *Oeuvres* (Paris, 1767), 8:355–81.
[11] Cf. a criticism of Juvenal de Carlencas's *Essai sur l'histoire des belles lettres*
(Paris, 1740): "Pourquoi passer sous silence les Troubadours de Provence qui en
sont sans contredit les premiers Auteurs." (Noblet de la Clayette, *L'Origine et les
progrès des arts et des sciences* [Paris,1740], quoted in *Mercure*, April, 1741, pp.
735–36).
[12] 'Essai de bibliothèque françoise,' Bréquigny 61, fols. 10–33.

Sainte-Palaye undertook to write this history. He made it clear that he shared the views of Falconet and considered original research indispensable. "Les Troubadours furent en effet les fondateurs de la littérature chez les deux nations (France and Italy)," he wrote in his 'Projet d'étude sur l'histoire de France,' "et c'est de leurs ouvrages que doit partir quiconque veut se faire une idée juste du progrès de l'esprit en France."[13] Hitherto, however, he went on, there have been only some general statements about the debt of Italian literature to Provençal literature. Bembo and many other Italian men of letters had made this point repeatedly. But few people were familiar with the actual works of the Provençal poets. Histories, like those of Crescimbeni and Bastero,[14] "piquent la curiosité sans la satisfaire." The scholar who would write the literary history of the troubadours cannot consequently be satisfied to repeat a few traditional commonplaces, he must present the works themselves to the public. It was indispensable in Sainte-Palaye's opinion "que quelqu'un se dévouât à la pénible entreprise de les faire connoître."

The final product of Sainte-Palaye's interest in Provençal poetry was the *Histoire littéraire des troubadours*, published by the Abbé Millot in 1774 in three volumes. There were three distinct phases in its preparation. First, Sainte-Palaye collected, collated, and translated as many manuscripts of the Provençal poems as he could find; second, he prepared extracts from his own copies of the manuscripts; and third, he handed over these extracts to Millot, who arranged them for the press.

Sainte-Palaye set to work shortly after Falconet's paper was read to the Académie des Inscriptions, and by 1737 he had already made copies of the Provençal *chansonniers* in the Bibliothèque du Roi and of the d'Urfé *chansonnier*.[15] According to the Marquis de Caumont, he had collected over two thousand poems in all.[16] The work to be done on the troubadours was so vast, however, that he was forced to enter into relations with scholars pursuing similar interests in France and in Italy.

---

[13] 'Projet,' Bréquigny 62, fol. 212.

[14] Antonio Bastero, *La Crusca provenzale* (Rome, 1724).

[15] J. Bauquier, 'Les Provençalistes du XVIIIᵉ siècle', p. 187, La Bastie to Mazaugues, 23.2.1737.

[16] *Ibid.*, p. 181, Caumont to Mazaugues, 25.2.1737.

While Sainte-Palaye and Falconet were busy in the North, Thomassin de Mazaugues, who belonged to one of the foremost families of the South of France, had been collecting copies of *chansonniers* in Provence and Italy for a projected *Bibliothèque des auteurs de Provence*.[17] The leader of a group of Southern French and Italian scholars interested in Provençal literature and history,[18] Mazaugues was abreast of the latest techniques of criticism,[19] and his Northern colleagues soon recognized that his assistance would be invaluable. In 1737 Caumont, who was a friend of both Falconet and Mazaugues, wrote to the latter on Falconet's behalf, suggesting that he and Sainte-Palaye pool the results of their work.[20] The collaboration with Mazaugues which resulted from this letter and which continued until Mazaugues' death in 1743 turned out to be extremely fruitful. From Aix Sainte-Palaye received notices and copies of Provençal manuscripts, even as they were discovered or communicated to Mazaugues himself.[21]

Outside the cities of the South, Italy was the main center of

[17] Achard, *Dictionnaire de la Provence et du Comté-Venaissin* (Marseille, 1787), 4:265–69. According to Achard, d'Aguesseau had tried to persuade Mazaugues to compose a history of Provence, but the latter was prepared to publish only "les pièces originales qui pouvoient servir de preuve à cette histoire. Il auroit effectivement exécuté ce projet, si la mort lui en avoit laissé le temps."

[18] The group included Lami and Muratori, whom Mazaugues had gotten to know in Italy (Carlo Pellegrini, *Tradizione italiana e cultura europea* [Messina, 1947], pp. 109–10).

[19] Chabaneau, who examined his notes and papers commented on "le progrés sensible dans l'espace de quelques années, de Pierre de Chasteuil (1644–1727), qui copiait presque partout Nostredame, à Thomassin de Mazaugues (1684–1743), qui rejetait sans hésiter les fables de ce dernier, même les erreurs d'historiens plus autorisés (tels que Baluze) et ne s'en rapportait qu'aux documents originaux." (*Revue des langues romanes* [1885], 28:79.)

[20] J. Bauquier, 'Les Provençalistes du XVIIIᵉ siècle,' p. 181. Caumont to Mazaugues, 25.2.1737.

[21] Among the items he received through Mazaugues were copies of a *Vie de Saint-Honorat* in verse (Bréquigny 66, fol. 29, Mazaugues to Sainte-Palaye, 4.5.1742, and Bréquigny 65, fols. 150–153, Mazaugues to Sainte-Palaye, 24.9.1742), of the *Livre d'Esdras* (*ibid.*), of a *Vie de Sainte-Marie Madeleine* (*ibid.*), of a *Vie de Saint-Trophime* (Bréquigny 65, fol. 155, Mazaugues to Sainte-Palaye, 19.10.1742), and notices of several Provençal *chansonniers* in Italian libraries: Florence, Riccardiana 2981 (MS *Fᵃ*) (Cf. J. Bauquier, 'Les Provençalistes du XVIIIᵉ siècle,' pp. 209–11); Venice, Marciana App. cod. XI (MS *V*) (cf. Sainte-Palaye's 'Notice' of this MS in Moreau 1658, fol. 65, notice 2063, where Mazaugues is given as the source); Rome, Vaticana 3204 (MS *K*) (*ibid.* fol. 101, notice 2098) and Florence, Laurentiana Plut. XLI, 43 (MS *U*) (*ibid.* fol. 86, notice 2085). It was also thanks to Mazaugues that Sainte-Palaye located the Milan *chansonnier* (Ambrosiana 71, MS *G*), *ibid.*, fol. 86, notice 2085.

Provençal studies. As the teachers and in some ways the models of Dante, Petrarch, and the poets of the *dolce stil nuovo*, the Provençal poets stood at the origins of literary Italian, and they had never ceased to be studied by writers and scholars in the Peninsula.[22] The difference between the Italian and the French attitude toward the troubadours is illuminated by an important difference between the *Vocabolario della Crusca* and the *Dictionnaire de l'Académie*. Both were normative works; but the *Vocabolario* looked back to the fourteenth century for the authority of national writers in Italian, whereas the *Dictionnaire* "ne cite point, parce que plusieurs de nos plus célèbres Orateurs et de nos plus grands Poètes y ont travaillé et qu'on a creu s'en devoir tenir à leurs sentiments."[23] It was not unusual in the Peninsula for a classical scholar, such as the celebrated Hellenist Anton Maria Salvini (1653–1729), to concern himself with the poets of the Trecento, with Dante, and with the Provençal poets.[24] Salvini collaborated with Crescimbeni on the *Giunta al Nostradama*, which the latter appended to the translation of Nostredame's *Vies* in the second volume of his *Commentarî* (Rome, 1710), and in which he supplied information on some poets not mentioned by Nostredame. For the first time, indeed, in Salvini's *Appendix*, a number of Provençal poems and fragments were published together with Italian translations.

Not surprisingly, Italian amateurs had collected and annotated many manuscripts of Provençal poetry. As he wished to base his account of the troubadours on original sources, Sainte-Palaye was obliged, therefore, to visit Italy and to consult the manuscripts in Italian libraries. His two journeys to the Peninsula, in 1739 and in 1749, were undertaken in part with this task in mind. It was not

[22] Santorre Debenedetti, 'Tre Secoli di studi provenzali,' in *Provenza e Italia, studi pubblicati a cura di Vincenzo Crescini* (Firenze, 1930), pp. 143–81. The Renaissance did not interrupt the tradition of Provençal studies. Ficino, for instance, referred gladly to the Provençal poets (see Walter Mönch, *Die italienische Platonrenaissance und ihre Bedeutung fur Frankreichs Literatur-und Geistesgeschichte, 1450–1550*, Romanische Studien [Berlin, 1936], Heft 40, pp. 121–24). Humanists such as Bembo and Varchi, who saw the troubadours as the founders of modern lyric poetry in the vernacular did much to extend knowledge of their works (Axhausen, pp. 6–7). Santorre Debenedetti, *Gli Studi provenzali in Italia nel '500* (Turin, 1911), provides a detailed account of the work of Italian scholars in the sixteenth century.

[23] *Dictionnaire de l'Académie Françoise* (Paris, 1644), Preface. Cf. Mozzati, p. 219.

[24] Natali, *Storia letteraria d'Italia: il Settecento*, 1:542–43.

always easy to fulfill,[25] but Sainte-Palaye was fortunate in having influential contacts. Passionei's intervention secured him access to the manuscripts of the Biblioteca Apostolica, and as a result he was able to examine seven Provençal *chansonniers* in the Vatican Library (*K, g, L, H, O, M,* and *A,* in Jeanroy's classification).[26] The Barberini collection, also in Rome, was easily visited for another *chansonnier* (*b* in Jeanroy), but the Chigi collection "estoit bien plus formidable. Tout le monde m'assuroit qu'il n'y falloit seulement pas songer," he wrote to Mazaugues. "Alexandre Albani avoit répondu que le Prince n'accorderoit jamais la permission d'y entrer; ces difficultés ont picqué Mr. le Card. Tencin; il l'a emporté et je suis maistre de la place."[27] The Chigi Library contained the important manuscript *F.* In Florence the Riccardi and Laurentian collections were made available to him without any ado and yielded further manuscripts of the troubadours (*P, Q, U*). In Venice he consulted the *chansonnier* in the San Marco Library (*V*) and in Milan the Ambrosian Codex (*G*). In Modena, Muratori showed him the celebrated Estense Codex (*D*).

By 1740, on his return from the first journey, Sainte-Palaye felt he had broken the back of his research work. "Pour les Poètes Provençaux," he had already told Bouhier on the last day of 1739, "mon objet est presque rempli."[28] His correspondence with Muratori shows that he had taken ample notices of the manuscripts which concerned the troubadours, and that by 1740 he had received copies of most of the items required to make up his collections.[29]

From the beginning his aim had been to make an exhaustive survey of all the manuscript sources. "Si l'ouvrage est par lui mesme très ingrat," he wrote to Bouhier, "j'espère le rendre si complet que

[25] A report by Sainte-Palaye to Maurepas, recommending that Assemani, the learned librarian of the Vatican, be invited to Paris, is illuminating. "La bibliothèque du Vatican est la plus riche," Sainte-Palaye explained, "mais aussi la plus inaccessible . . . Il seroit fort advantageux pour les gens de lettres d'y avoir quelqu'un qui levât les obstacles qu'on suscite lorsqu'on y veut faire quelque recherche. . . ." (B.N. Nouv. Acq. Fr. 5853, fol. 15, dated "juin, 1740")

[26] Sainte-Palaye to Bouhier, 15.12.1739 (B.N. Français 24418, fol. 360) and to Mazaugues, 15.12.1739 (J. Bauquier, 'Les Provençalistes du XVIIIᵉ siècle', p. 209).

[27] To Mazaugues, 15.12.1739. Even in 1864 the German Provençalist Gruzmacher failed to gain entry to the Chigi collection (*Archiv. f.d. Studium der neueren Sprachen* [1864], 35:98).

[28] B.N. Français 24418, fol. 360.

[29] Modena, Bibl. Estense, Archivio Soli Muratori, Filza 85, fasc. 29, letters from Sainte-Palaye to Muratori, dated Turin, 12.3.1740, and Paris, 30.12.1740.

personne après moi ne sera plus tenté d'y perdre son tems."[30] As a result of his endeavors he had tracked down and obtained copies of over twenty manuscripts containing Provençal poems in the libraries of France and Italy, and he was always on the lookout for additional sources.[31] The thoroughness with which Sainte-Palaye sought out the elements of the written tradition was something quite new in Provençal studies. Colocci had been primarily concerned to annotate his own manuscripts. Bembo had compared a number of manuscripts but haphazardly, using those which he found to hand; his selection of readings from them was arbitrary and often based on the principle of the *lectio facilior*. There is no evidence that Barbieri and Castelvetro planned a complete survey of the manuscripts.[32] Even in the eighteenth century Antonio Bastero, the Catalan author of the *Crusca provenzale* (Rome, 1724), was not more exacting. Although he promised to employ "ogni diligenza per leggere e scoprire dalle tenebre dell'oblivione i componimenti di questi antichi Maestri e Padri della Volgar Poesia,"[33] in fact, a list of Provençal troubadours which he appended to the first and only published volume of his work shows that he took cognizance of only the Vatican manuscripts 3204, 3205 (a copy of 3794 which he appears not to have consulted), 3206, 3207, and 3208 (i.e., *K, g, L, H*, and *O*).[34]

The question how Sainte-Palaye proposed to make use of the extensive material he had gathered together immediately presents itself. The most valuable consequence and probably the primary aim of his immense labors was that he acquired a more complete coverage of Provençal poetry than anyone before him. This was reflected in Millot's publication, which included the lives of and extracts from the works of innumerable troubadours of whom no

[30] B.N. Français 24418, fol. 372, Sainte-Palaye to Bouhier, 12.1.1742.

[31] Bréquigny 165, fol. 47, Sainte-Palaye to Bréquigny 8.6.1764; and again *ibid.*, fol. 66, to Bréquigny, 25.3.1765, where he asks Bréquigny to have a notice made for him of a manuscript supposedly containing Provençal songs in England. He also tried to get a description of this manuscript from Horace Walpole (*Letters of Horace Walpole,* ed. Toynbee, Supplement, [Oxford, 1925], 3:179).

[32] Debenedetti, *Gli Studî provenzali in Italia nel '500,* pp. 87–91.

[33] Pp. 10–11.

[34] *Ibid.,* pp. 71–102. Unlike Sainte-Palaye, Bastero seems to have been interested in Provençal poetry from the point of view of language rather than from that of history. His aim was to illustrate the dependence of literary Italian on Provençal, or, as he would have had it, Catalan. See, on his work, Milá y Fontanals, *Obras completas* (Barcelona, 1892), 4:444.

mention had ever been made in print, and of whom many were unknown to the Italian scholars of the sixteenth century.[35] (Much of this additional material was found in manuscripts *C* and *R* of the Royal Library in Paris, which had not been consulted by the Italians.) Sainte-Palaye also looked into the poems themselves for reference to troubadours not otherwise known.[36] The evidence of the texts thus helped him to judge how far his collection of the poems was complete. "Par le travail que je fais à present," he told Bouhier, "je reconnois avec complaisance qu'il me manque très peu de leurs anciennes Pièces, puisque je retrouve dans mes recueils presque tous les fragments dont il y a un très grand nombre citez dans les Poésies les uns des autres."[37] As Diez pointed out, this use of the internal evidence of the texts themselves was an innovation in Provençal studies, and a further instance of the way Sainte-Palaye was bringing all the techniques of recent scholarship to bear on the study of medieval literature.[38]

When it came to establishing texts, however, Sainte-Palaye was less successful. His collections show that his primary concern was to have a copy of every Provençal poem preserved in the manuscripts. He carefully wrote in variant forms, always with precise reference to the manuscript in which they had been found. If the manuscripts offered widely varying versions of the same poem, he had copies made of all of them, taking care to refer from one to another in his own volumes. But he rarely indicated a preference. In this sense he advanced no further than the most conscientious Italian amateurs of the sixteenth century. What Debenedetti remarked of Piero del Nero's variant notations applies equally well to those of Sainte-Palaye: "Son materiali raccolti, e null'altro: a quel forma egli desse le sue preferenze non risulta."[39]

We have seen that in his study of Froissart, Sainte-Palaye tried to assess the value of the manuscripts, and that in one or two in-

---

[35] See Appendix 5.

[36] He compiled an extensive biographical guide to the Provençal *chansonniers* in which he listed every proper name found in them (Arsenal 3099–3100, another copy in B.N. Moreau 1582, fols. 75–214).

[37] B.N. Français 24418, fol. 372, Sainte-Palaye to Bouhier, 12.1.1742.

[38] Friedrich Diez, *Leben und Werke der Troubadours*, 2te vermehrte Aufl. (Leipzig, 1882), Vorwort, pp. v–vi.

[39] Debenedetti, *Gli studî provenzali*, p. 92. Cf. August von Schlegel, *Observations sur la langue et sur la littérature provençales* (Paris, 1818), p. 82, n. 1.

stances he went so far as to suggest relationships between them. His comments on the Provençal manuscripts reveal similar groping attempts to establish such connections. Thus he drew attention to the "grande conformité" of C and R,[40] two manuscripts which later editors like Appel and Gröber found fairly consistently forming a united block.[41] He was also careful to observe that Florence Ricc. 2981 (F^a) is a copy of Chigi 2348 (F). His attentiveness to the order in which the poems were arranged in the manuscripts—the basis to a large extent of Gröber's abortive attempt to draw up a stemma—is a further indication of his interest in manuscript filiation.[42] But these tentative observations in no way offer the basis of a serious study of manuscript tradition.[43]

The most urgent task, as he saw it, was the immediate one of reading the manuscripts. Many of those he consulted had been used by Italian scholars like Cariteo (M), Colocci (M, g), Piero del Nero (a^1), Bembo (D, E, K, L, O, g), Beccadelli (E), Fulvio Orsini (A, H, K, L, O, g) and Castelvetro (H), and their notes and occasional translations into Italian doubtless proved useful. But the task of mastering the language and the grammar of Provençal was one which Sainte-Palaye had to tackle himself. He set about it in his usual methodical way. By consulting early printed and manuscript glossaries and by carefully combing a number of Provençal texts in manuscript, he was able to compile a four-volume glossary of Provençal,[44] which he supplemented with a further ten volumes drawn from the texts of the troubadours themselves.[45] Neither work was intended for anything other than Sainte-Palaye's own personal use.[46] To the same end he studied the grammar of

---

[40] Arsenal 3091, fol. 1.

[41] C. Appel, *Leben und Lieder des Troubadours Peire Roger* (Berlin, 1882), Einleitung. Gustav Gröber, 'Die Liedersammlungen der Troubadours,' *Romanische Studien* (1875–77), 2:337–670.

[42] Bréquigny 65, fols. 119–48, notes on Florence Ricc. 2814 (MS a^1). Sainte-Palaye remarks on the unusual arrangement of the authors and poems in this MS: "Je ne trouve point de MS qui ressemble à celui pour l'arrangement des autheurs dans touttes les notices que j'ai faites des MSS d'Italie."

[43] The Provençal *chansonniers* do not in fact lend themselves to a simple classification. (Gröber, "Die Liedersammlungen der Troubadours," p. 656.) In his edition of Bernart de Ventadorn ([Halle, 1915], p. 36, n.18) Carl Appel suggests that the originals themselves of some poems might well have contained author variants.

[44] Moreau 1568–71.　　　[45] Moreau 1572–81.

[46] " . . . le Glossaire provençal que nous avons rédigé pour notre usage . . ." ('Projet d'étude', Bréquigny 62, fol. 212).

Old Provençal, consulting all the extant manuscripts of the grammars of Hugues Faidit and Raymond Vidal.[47] Rochegude's criticism of Sainte-Palaye's linguistic competence—"il a plus souvent deviné qu'entendu son texte"[48]—was justly judged excessive by Raynouard, who had good reason to appreciate Sainte-Palaye's research at its true value.[49] Had Sainte-Palaye's knowledge of Provençal been as poor as Rochegude suggested, he would have been unable to detect mistakes in the work of Muratori's copyist, yet it is certain that he did do so. The imperfections of his copies and translations are the imperfections of a pioneer scholar, not of an ignorant one.

At any rate, his project was in itself imaginative enough to excite the curiosity of the reading public and the enthusiasm of the scholarly world. Muratori in particular followed its progress anxiously and continually pressed Sainte-Palaye to publish.[50] Mazaugues was equally enthusiastic and exhorted his friend not to weaken in his resolve. "Je présume que vous suivés constamment votre projet," he wrote in 1742, "et que vous voulés toujours voir au bout de nos Troubadours, et je m'attends que vous nous ferés part du progrès de votre travail et de vos découvertes."[51] Lévesque de la Ravalière judged Sainte-Palaye's work on the troubadours a vital contribution to literary history, and urged him to communicate the results of his research as early as possible.[52] Even Bouhier, who

---

[47] Of these he had used Paris, Bib. Reg. 7700 for his Glossary. He also consulted two MSS in the Laurentian Library in Florence (Plut. XLI, cod. 42 and Fondo Santa Maria dei Fiori 187) as well as a further MS in the Riccardian Library (2814), to which his attention had been drawn by an article in Lami's *Novelle letterarie di Firenze* (no. 7, 7.2.1741, col. 97–102, and no. 8, 24.2.1741, col. 113–15). In his description of the Riccardian MS (Bréquigny 65, fol. 119) he observes that it bears the same title as Santa Maria dei Fiori 187—"Donato Provenzale fatto per raggione di trovare"—and is in other respects similar to it.

[48] *Parnasse occitanien* (Toulouse, 1819), Preface, p. xiv.

[49] *Journal des Savants* (May, 1820), pp. 291–93.

[50] Modena, Bibl. Estense, Arch. Soli Muratori, filza 85, fasc. 29, Sainte-Palaye to Muratori, 30.12.1740; *Epistolario di L.A. Muratori,* ed. Matteo Campori (Modena, 1906), 10:4283, M. to Mazaugues, 24.5.1724; *ibid.,* p. 4342, M. to Mazaugues, 17.10.1742.

[51] Bréquigny 66, fol. 30, Mazaugues to Sainte-Palaye, 4.5.1742.

[52] "Les anciens poètes provençaux vous sont aussi connus et aussi familiers que ceux du beau siècle de Louis XIV. Les six ou sept siècles de vieillesse qu'a leur langage ne vous ont point arrêté; vous avez démêlé leur génie qui subsiste tousjours, à travers des expressions qui sont tombées . . . Occupé dans vos études des autres, autant et plus que de vous, vous n'avez point fait tant de recherches en France et en Italie pour les ensevlir. L'Europe sçavante, la France, la patrie même des poètes, tout le monde curieux enfin espère que vous lui ferez part de vos découvertes. On est

could write unaffectedly of the "ennui" and the "travail fatigant" of reading medieval poetry, assured Sainte-Palaye that "si . . . vous pouvez arriver au but, vous rendrez un grand service à la République des Lettres."[53] In England Horace Walpole waited impatiently for the book to appear.[54]

Encouraged by the interest his work had aroused, Sainte-Palaye threw himself into it with energy and determination. "J'ai plus que jamais la frénésie des Troubadours," he wrote to La Bastie in 1740.[55] But the magnitude of the task he had prescribed for himself soon became apparent. There was no question of actually publishing all the poems in the manuscripts. This had never been Sainte-Palaye's intention, nor was it desired by any of his most ardent supporters. What was expected at the time was not a thesaurus of documents but a reliable history of the Provençal poets and their works, based on firsthand study of the texts, and illustrated by suitable extracts. Like Lévesque, Goujet looked to Sainte-Palaye to clear up the errors and uncertainties in Jean de Nostredame, while Lacombe desired "un choix de leur Poésie."[56] Likewise the *Mercure* reviewer who called on Sainte-Palaye in 1745 to publish the results of his research was thinking of a literary history, not of a collection of texts. Noting that the authors of an *Histoire*

---

dégoûté des fables et des anacronismes . . ." (B.N. Français 9355, 'De l'Ancienneté des chansons françoises, à M. de Sainte-Palaye,' fol. 431. A shortened version of this in *Poësies du Roy de Navarre,* pp. 185–86).

[53] Bréquigny 66, fol. 12, Bouhier to Sainte-Palaye, 30.1.1742; fol. 14, Bouhier to Sainte-Palaye, 5.6.1742; fol. 15, Bouhier to Sainte-Palaye, 27.6.1742.

[54] In the article on Richard Coeur de Lion in his *Royal and Noble Authors of England* (London, 1759), 1:1–8, Walpole complained of inaccuracies in Crescimbeni. A few years later, he observed in a letter to Thomas Warton that de Sade's study of Petrarch was marred by the author's lack of critical judgment. "When you read the notes to the second volume, you will grow very impatient for Mons. de St. Palaye's promised History of the Troubadours" (16.3.1765, *Letters of Horace Walpole,* ed. Toynbee [Oxford, 1904], 6:198–200). Walpole had already heard of Sainte-Palaye in connection with the troubadours. Sir Horace Mann, who had procured him a copy of the Laurentian poem said to be by Richard, had referred to Sainte-Palaye in a covering letter as to a well-known authority on things Provençal. (*Horace Walpole's Correspondence,* Yale ed. by W. S. Lewis; *Correspondence with Sir Horace Mann,* vol. 5 [New Haven, 1960], Mann to Walpole, 25.3.1758.) Among Walpole's friends, Thomas Gray and William Mason, in addition to Warton, were likely to be interested in Sainte-Palaye's work on the troubadours. They were preparing a history of English poetry and had been studying Provençal sources in Nostredame, Fauchet, and Crescimbeni. (William P. Jones, *Thomas Gray Scholar* [Cambridge, Mass., 1937], pp. 89–90.)

[55] Bréquigny 68, fol. 80, Sainte-Palaye to Bimard de La Bastie, 29.9.1740.

[56] Goujet, *Bibliothèque françoise* (Paris, 1740–56), 9:19; Lacombe, 'Coup d'Oeil,' p. 15 in *Supplément au Dictionnaire du vieux langage françois* (Paris, 1768).

du théâtre françois "passent légèrement sur plusieurs Troubadours qu'ils appellent Poètes Comiques sur la foi de Nostradamus, quoique plusieurs d'entre eux n'aient point fait de Comédies," he pointed out that Sainte-Palaye possessed "tous les matériaux nécessaires pour donner une histoire excellente de ces Troubadours."[57]

Realizing that he could not bring his task to a successful and speedy conclusion by his own efforts, Sainte-Palaye decided in 1741 to enlist the help of his friend Foncemagne,[58] and in May of the same year the two men set off for Sainte-Palaye's estate in Burgundy to devote themselves exclusively to the work of sorting and arranging the material. Sainte-Palaye was confident at this time that it would be possible to "expédier les Troubadours en moins de deux ans."[59] With Foncemagne's assistance, he put his material in order and began compiling the Extracts which would form the basis of the future history.[60] These consisted of biographical notices of the troubadours and of summaries or translations of a selection of their works. As an earnest of what was to come two papers on the troubadours were read to the Académie des Inscriptions. The first, by Sainte-Palaye alone, concerned the life and works of Bertran de Born, and was read on March 5, 1740. The second, on Guillaume de Cabestain, was read on March 24 of the following year, and was offered as a joint contribution by Sainte-Palaye and Foncemagne.[61] Both were well received.[62]

The régime to which the two men subjected themselves in the summer of 1741 proved too strenuous, however, and before the end of the season both had succumbed to ill-health.[63] Nevertheless, Sainte-Palaye thought he had gotten over the major hurdles, for in

---

[57] *Mercure*, Oct., 1745, p. 82.

[58] B.N. Français 24418, fol. 362, Sainte-Palaye to Bouhier, 24.4.1741: "M. de Foncemagne mon ami a bien voulu s'associer à ce travail qui en ira beaucoup plus viste et qui en sera bien meilleur."

[59] Bréquigny 68, fol. 84, Sainte-Palaye to La Bastie, 15.5.1741.

[60] The Extracts are in Arsenal 3281–84. A duplicate copy, now B.N. Moreau 1584–87, is listed among 'Manuscrits de M. de Foncemagne,' in an 'Ordre du Cabinet des Chartes et Diplômes de l'histoire de France à la bibliothèque du Roy au 1er janvier 1782' in Moreau 1799, fol. 21, nos. 10–17.

[61] B.N. Français 9428, 107, 189 (Procès-Verbaux de l'Ac. Insc.) and *Registres* 1740, p. 108; 1741, pp. 46–48.

[62] Bréquigny 68, fol. 82, Sainte-Palaye to La Bastie, 31.12.1740. 'Le succès qu'a eu mon premier Mémoire sur les Troubadours m'encourage à en donner la suitte." The two papers were selected to be read at the Academy's *assemblées publiques* of 15.11.1740 and 11.4.1741. (*Registres* 1740, p. 125, and 1741, p. 48.)

[63] B.N. Français 24418, fol. 364, Sainte-Palaye to Bouhier, 27.8.1741.

1742 he told Mazaugues that, though he would have to renounce "ces excez de travail dont j'ai esté si rudement corrigé," he was confident that by continuing "doucement et paisiblement la petite tâche que je me suis imposée . . . à l'entrée de l'hiver j'aurai fini tous les extraits ou sommaires des pièces de chaque troubadour."[64] The reduction of his material into a few volumes of extracts could not be left to others, since it demanded an ability to read the texts which few besides himself possessed. For this reason, he was determined to go through with this part at least of the future history himself. "Je ne veux point quitter mes Troubadours que je n'aie fini ce qui est du moins nécessaire pour que les peines que j'y ai prises ne soient pas entièrement perdues"—he wrote to Bouhier in May, 1742—"quoique je me modère beaucoup sur le travail j'ai la satisfaction de voir que mon assiduité me mettra bientost en estat de finir ce que d'autres auroient de la peine à faire sans moi."[65]

It is obvious, however, that he was already thinking of inviting someone else to mold the extracts into a form suitable for publication, for two weeks later he declared that "l'ouvrage qui doit résulter de tous ces matériaux (the Extracts) ne pourra pas être fait de longtemps."[66] With Foncemagne's assistance the Extracts were probably completed according to plan. The long awaited *Histoire littéraire des troubadours* could now pass into the third and final phase. But even at this point, with the material ready and prepared for a willing editor, difficulties were encountered which held up publication until 1774.

It was not easy to find an editor for the Extracts. In 1767 Sainte-Palaye invited the Abbé Rive, a Provençal who had been recommended to him by Barthélémy, to undertake the work, but Rive imposed conditions which could not be met, and this plan fell through.[67] Of a number of scholars who subsequently tried their hand at putting the work together, among them Meusnier de Querlon, only the Abbé Laugier completed the task, according to Le Grand d'Aussy.[68] Laugier's version of the *Histoire littéraire des*

[64] Sainte-Palaye to Mazaugues, 2.7.1742, in J. Bauquier, 'Les Provençalistes du XVIIIe siècle,' p. 215.

[65] B.N. Français 24418, fol. 374, Sainte-Palaye to Bouhier, 18.5.1742.

[66] To Mazaugues, 2.7.1742.

[67] Rive's account of his negotiations with Sainte-Palaye is in a letter to David of Aix, dated 11.3.1767, Arsenal 6392, fol. 23.

[68] *Fabliaux ou contes du XIIe et du XIIIe siècles* (nouvelle édition; Paris, 1781), 2:4.

troubadours is an honest one, consisting of straightforward biographies of the principal troubadours with extracts from their works usually in translation, but sometimes also in the original Provençal. Copious notes explained literary and historical allusions or pointed out how the poems illustrate the social and intellectual conditions of the age.[69] There is no indication that Sainte-Palaye himself was dissatisfied with what Laugier had done, but it may have been too sober for the publishers. At any rate Le Grand recounts that his compilation "fut jugé ne pas mériter l'honneur de l'impression."

Sainte-Palaye looked around for another editor, and this time he found his man in Millot. The Abbé Millot had published histories of France and of England which had been sufficiently well received to win him an appointment to a chair of history at Parma, and which were still being reprinted in the early years of the nineteenth century. Intellectually he was drawn to the *philosophes* and they liked him. "M. l'abbé Millot est philosophe et vrai autant que son habit peut le permettre," Grimm observed. His *Eléments de l'histoire de France depuis Clovis jusqu'à fin du règne de Louis XIV* won Grimm's unqualified approval: "Voilà donc encore un abrégé! Peu s'en faut cependant que je ne fasse grâce à celui-là . . . Il faut savoir gré à un grand vicaire d'avoir en général des principes de droit public sains, et de préférer la cause du genre humain à l'intérêt et à l'ambition de l'Eglise. Je me sens du faible pour ce prêtre. On peut au moins mettre ce livre entre les mains de la jeunesse sans craindre de lui empoisonner l'esprit."[70] Millot's reputation with the *philosophes* was made when he was condemned to be burned in effigy in Spain, whether for his *Mémoires du Maréchal de Noailles,* or for his *Catéchisme d'histoire,* is not clear.[71] When, toward the end of his life, Voltaire was brought to a sitting of the Académie Française, Millot, together with the Abbé de Boismont, was alone present of the churchmen who were members

---

[69] Laugier's version is probably B.N. Français 9409, "Brouillon de la main de Mr. L.," consisting of three packets, fols. 2–161, 162–227, 228–307. There is a concordance in Sainte-Palaye's hand with the pagination of another copy of the same text. References to the MSS are to Sainte-Palaye's classification. A reference in Moreau 1582, fol. 6, to a copy of the *Vies des Troubadours* by "Mr. le Grand" may throw doubt on my attribution of Français 9409 to Laugier, but Le Grand himself does not admit to authorship of it. Herrmann's contention that Laugier died before he could complete the work seems unfounded (Herrmann, p. 12).

[70] *Corr. litt.,* 7:442. See likewise Diderot, 'Plan d'une Université pour le gouvernement de Russie,' *Oeuvres,* 3:494, and Voltaire, *Oeuvres,* ed. Moland, 30:392.

[71] Grimm, *Corr. litt.,* 12:330 (Oct., 1779).

of the Academy.[72] The work which Millot published in 1774 from the material Sainte-Palaye placed at his disposal bears all the marks of a serious but unimaginative manufacturer of *abrégés* with a sincere attachment to *philosophie*.[73]

As Millot has frequently been held responsible for the shortcomings of the *Histoire littéraire des troubadours*,[74] it is worth considering briefly how far this is true and how much of the responsibility must be borne by Sainte-Palaye himself.

When he invited Millot to edit his material, Sainte-Palaye knew that, lacking any knowledge of Provençal, the Abbé would have to rely entirely on the extracts, notes, and translations placed at his disposal. Millot himself makes it plain that Sainte-Palaye is the real author of the *Histoire* and that his own role in its composition was a minor one: "Le mérite de cet ouvrage appartient spécialement à M. de Sainte-Palaie. Je n'ai fait que mettre en oeuvre avec plaisir les matériaux qu'il a rassemblez avec tant de peines . . . Ses remarques et celles de ses premiers cooperateurs m'ont épargné l'ennui des recherches."[75]

Contemporary readers usually ascribed the work to Sainte-Palaye as much as to Millot.[76] The mistake of later critics has been

[72] *Mémoires de Bachaumont*, 1er avril, 1778.

[73] This was more or less Grimm's view of him; cf. *Corr. litt.*, 8:241: "M. l'abbé Millot n'est pas un homme profond, ni un homme lumineux, ni un homme d'un grand sens, mais simplement un homme de bon sens, un esprit droit et juste . . . Son style n'a rien de distingué, ni en bien, ni en mal." Similarly Nodier, *Mélanges* (Paris, 1820), 2:120—"L'abbé Millot ne sera pas cité parmi les historiens remarquables, mais il est digne de l'être parmi les écrivains bien intentionnés qui ont appliqué les notions d'une philosophie tolérante à l'étude de l'histoire, dans l'éducation des jeunes gens."

[74] E.g., Paul Meyer, review of Mahn's *Geschichte der Troubadours*, *Romania* (1874), 3:303; Chabanneau in *Revue des langues romanes* (1879), 15:157. But the same view was expressed by some contemporaries. In an article in the *Deutsches Museum* of Nov., 1777, Herder compared the success of Millot's history with the relative failure of Bodmer: "Wäre Bodmer ein Abt Millot, der den Säklenfleiss seines Curne de St Palaye in eine histoire littéraire des Troubadours nach gefälligstem Auszuge hat verwandeln wollen, vielleicht wäre er weiter umher gekommen als itzt, da er den Schatz selbst gab, und uns zutraute, dass wir noch dem Bissen schwäbischer Sprache leicht hinauf bemühen würden." (*Werke*, ed. Suphan, 9:528.)

[75] *Hist. litt. troub.*, vol. 1, Avertissement, p. x.

[76] E.g., a note by William Cole inserted into Bodley copy of Horace Walpole, *A Catalogue of the Royal and Noble Authors of England* (Strawberry Hill, 1758) 1:2—"See an undoubted account of Richard and his poetical Abilities in an ingenious work . . . by Monsieur de Sainte-Palaye, entitled *Histoire littéraire des troubadours*." So too Burney, *History of Music* (London, 1776–89), 2:222: "M. de Lacurne de Sainte-Palaye and his faithful squire, M. Millot . . ." Likewise Grimm, *Corr. litt.*, 10:490–91 (Oct., 1774).

to overlook that Millot was compiling the work from Sainte-
Palaye's extracts and to assume that he was working from the
Provençal texts themselves.[77] In fact, a comparison of Millot's text
with that of the extracts reveals that Millot followed Sainte-Palaye
fairly closely, both in his literary appreciations of the poems and in
his historical comments. If a few minor alterations to the language
of Sainte-Palaye's translations hardly gave his style the "tournure
plus libre et plus variée" which Millot intended,[78] they did not
harm it much either. Sainte-Palaye himself failed completely to
convey any idea of the poetry, the humor, or the technical bril-
liancy of the originals, and Grimm was fully justified in holding
him as responsible as Millot for this important weakness in the
Histoire littéraire.

Nevertheless, the work produced by Millot was inferior in several respects even to the extracts. Sainte-Palaye had written to
Muratori in the forties that his object was to "faire connoistre
l'histoire de nos Troubadours et le goust de leurs compositions,"[79]
and this was also Millot's professed purpose as he expounded it in
his *Discours préliminaire*. Drawing attention to the inadequacy of
eighteenth-century ideas of Provençal poetry, he wrote that "la
plupart des gens de Lettres eux-mêmes ne s'en forment qu'une idée
fort imparfaite. On se contente de savoir que ces anciens poètes
provençaux fleurirent dès le XII siècle lorsque la barbarie et l'ignorance dominoient encore en Europe . . . qu'ils furent dans nos cli-
mats les pères de la poésie moderne. Mais on se les figure d'ailleurs
comme des aventuriers sans état; comme des écrivains sans lumière
et sans goût, dont les fades galanteries méritent un oubli éternel, et
dont les ouvrages n'ont rien d'intéressant que pour ces amateurs
d'antiquités qui passent inutilement leur vie à dérouiller de misérables monumens gothiques."[80]

The *Histoire littéraire des troubadours* was to correct and refine
these crude notions. It was to give readers a real and firsthand
knowledge of troubadour poetry, Millot declared, and to suggest
that this poetry might be related in some ways to that of other

---

[77] Herrmann, p. 12, makes the same mistake concerning Laugier.
[78] *Hist. litt. troub.*, vol. 1, p. x.
[79] Modena, Bibl. Estense, Archivio Soli Muratori, Filza 85, fasc. 29, Sainte-Palaye
to Muratori, 30.12.1740.
[80] *Hist. litt. troub.*, vol. 1, pp. xiii–xv.

peoples at a similar stage of their development. The questions to be studied were listed: "Quelle étoit la poésie avant que les peuples sortissent de leur premier état de simplicité? Quels progrès fit-elle à l'epoque des troubadours? quelle idée doit-on avoir des moeurs de leur tems, et sur-tout de cette galanterie célèbre qui les inspira sans cesse, parce qu'elle étoit comme l'âme de la société? quels grands événemens excitèrent leur génie, et fournirent matière à leurs compositions? quels sont les principaux caractères de leurs différens ouvrages? quelle influence ont-ils eue, ainsi que leur langue, sur la littérature moderne? enfin, quelles sont les sources dont nous avons tiré leur histoire?"[81] Had Millot done what he said he would do here, his book would probably have been less severely criticized than it was, for it would have fitted well into the incipient inquiry into the relation of the arts and society which was occupying some of the most thoughtful men of the age. "Quand on voit les barbares, les sauvages mêmes chanter leurs dieux, ou leurs amours ou leurs exploits," we read in the *Discours préliminaire*, "on se persuade aisément que la poésie est presque aussi naturelle à l'homme que le langage, le chant et les passions," and Millot goes on to compare the cultures of "les forêts de l'Amérique, les montagnes incultes de l'Écosse, les déserts glacés de l'Islande," arguing that in all primitive peoples, poetry acts as a kind of communal memory and is intimately tied to the life of the community.[82]

Millot's preliminary considerations and statement of aims were thus promising. But the promise was not fulfilled. In the articles themselves almost nothing remains of the good intentions of the *Discours préliminaire*. Having no firsthand knowledge of the Provençal texts himself and judging them from Sainte-Palaye's translations, Millot formed an even poorer opinion of them than Sainte-Palaye had had. Few of the poems, in his view, deserved to be remembered for their literary merit, and he did not hesitate to consign all the anonymous works to eternal oblivion. "La plupart ne renferment rien d'intéressant et doivent rester dans l'oubli," he declared.[83] The principal and almost the only justification for the history of the troubadours came to reside in the light it would throw on the institutions and manners of the Middle Ages. "Le but de notre ouvrage," he announced at one point, in flat contradiction

[81] *Ibid.*, pp. xvi–xvii.   [82] *Ibid.*, pp. xvii–xviii.   [83] *Ibid.*, 3:439.

to what he had said in his *Discours préliminaire,* "est de faire connoître les idées plutot que le style des Troubadours."[84] In the end,
the *Histoire littéraire* presented the poetry mostly as documentary
material. Sainte-Palaye himself had emphasized this use of the
manuscripts: he had carefully annotated his copies with historical
observations, he had begun a *Dictionnaire des antiquités des troubadours* from the information he found in the poems,[85] and he had
composed an historical introduction, a *Tableau historique des
siècles où régna la poésie provençale,* in which he tried to outline
the political and intellectual background of Provençal poetry, and
the "étrange confusion d'idées qui en étoit résultée dans les
esprits."[86] Millot, finally, despite his promises, discerned no more
than this in the voluminous extracts and notes Sainte-Palaye put at
his disposal, no more than a mass of data on the political and social
history of the Middle Ages—the decline of the nobility at the close
of the period, the religious fanaticism of the Crusades, the abuses
of the clergy, and the political struggles of feudal powers in medieval France.[87] His choice of poems was largely determined by
this predominantly political and historical interest. The works
which he judged worthy of reproduction in full or at length were
those which threw light not so much on the literature of the troubadours as on the religious and political controversies and on the
social conditions of their age.[88]

Even in this aspect of his work, however, Millot was disappoint-
ingly heavy-handed, imparting to his compilation a serious moral
tone quite foreign to the worldly and aristocratic Sainte-Palaye.
Once again, moreover, he promised more than he produced. The
Discours préliminaire outlined what was to be found by studying
the lives and times of the troubadours: "On y voit cette bravoure
ardente et emportée, qui caractérisoit encore la nation ... on y voit
cette prodigalité des seigneurs, érigée en vertu essentielle de leur

---

[84] *Ibid.,* 2:309.   [85] Moreau 1582, fols. 34-57.
[86] Bréquigny 154, fols. 193-214.
[87] E.g. *Hist. litt. troub.,* 3:238 *sub* Peire Cardinal.
[88] Thus, Izarn's *tenson* on the Albigensian heresy was printed in full, in translation of course; a long poem by Arnaut Guillem de Marsan was presented as "une
espèce d'introduction de chevalerie," which "peint les moeurs antiques et la
manière de vivre des seigneurs, qu'on estimoit la plus honorable." (*Ibid.,* 3:62.)
Passages from Amanieu de Sescas were justified by what they told of the manners
and deportment of ladies in the earliest age of gallantry; and Peire de Corbiac's
works were described on account of the information they contained on the state
of learning in Provence in the Middle Ages.

rang, aussi peu délicate sur les moyens d'acquérir que sur la manière de dissiper . . . On y voit cet esprit d'indépendance qui entretenoit les désordres de l'anarchie, quelquefois se pliant par intérêt aux humbles démarches du courtisan . . . On y voit cette franchise mâle et agreste, que rien n'empêche de s'exprimer librement et sur les personnes et sur les choses . . . sans paroître se douter des égards de la bienséance, encore moins de la politesse moderne. On y voit l'aveugle superstition, se repaissant d'absurdités et de folies . . . On y voit l'ignorance et le fanatisme d'un clergé vicieux; la pétulance d'une noblesse inquiète et indomptable; l'activité et la hardiesse d'une bourgeoisie à peine délivrée de la servitude."[89] As he presents Provençal society here, Millot recognizes in it, as Sainte-Palaye had done in the *Mémoires sur l'ancienne chevalerie* and as the Enlighteners did generally, the interdependence of apparently opposed characteristics—simplicity, frankness, loyalty, high-spirited independence, and at the same time anarchy, brutality, and ignorance. But in the body of the work he was constantly proving that far from damaging the quality of life or of morality, as its enemies charged, Enlightenment was essential to decent behavior: "Les aventures et même les pièces galantes des troubadours, épurées de tout ce que la pudeur doit proscrire, peuvent servir sans pédantisme, soit à caractériser l'esprit et les moeurs des siècles de la chevalerie, soit à peindre le vice haïssable quand il trouble l'harmonie et les devoirs de la société . . . Aussi l'histoire et la morale sont-elles étroitement liées l'une à l'autre. La première offre les faits, la seconde en tire les conséquences. Jusqu'aux satires indécentes de quelques troubadours contre le clergé ou contre la cour de Rome, tout devient matière d'instruction. Elles tiennent aux faits historiques et aux moeurs du tems: elles prouvent que les siècles d'ignorance furent des siècles de désordres; que les ministres de l'église nuisoient beaucoup à la religion même . . . que leur ministère n'auroit point été en butte de la haine, si les lumières et la vertu en avoient garanti leur personne."[90]

As a *Moderne*, Sainte-Palaye himself would have agreed with Millot that progress had been made in all areas since the time of the troubadours, but he would have been less vehement in his condemnation of what Millot judged the gross immorality of the trouba-

---

[89] *Hist. litt. troub.*, vol. 1, pp. xxx–xxxi.
[90] *Ibid.*, vol. 1, Avertissement, p. ix.

dours. "En vérité," Millot observed, "la morale de ces temps-là ne se conçoit point: mille exemples en découvrent les faux principes . . . Si nous ne valons pas mieux au fond, qu'on ne nous conteste pas au moins l'avantage de connoître les devoirs." The frequent comparison of divine and profane love was a monstrous impiety in his eyes: "Il n'est pas possible de s'accoutumer à des profanations si fréquentes." As for the troubadours themselves they were usually, for all their noble birth, ignorant reprobates. "Qu'il est ridicule," he wrote of Marcabru, "à des âmes de boue, qui démasquent leur propre honte, de s'ériger en censeurs de l'univers." Such were the reflections with which Millot hoped to "remédier autant qu'il est possible à une ennuyeuse uniformité."[91] He had in fact turned the *Histoire littéraire des troubadours* into a rather clumsy *machine de guerre* against the enemies of Enlightenment.

It was in the matter of accuracy that Millot permitted himself the greatest divergence from his source. On this point at least Sainte-Palaye had been uncompromising. He had carefully indicated where he felt he could not vouch for his translations, he had noted with scrupulous attention poems which different manuscripts attributed to different authors, and he had invariably given detailed reference to the manuscript sources where the originals of his translations and his summaries were to be found. Millot professed his care for accuracy by attacking Nostredame in the *Discours préliminaire* and at several points subsequently in the text of the history.[92] He himself, however, did not hesitate to publish translations on the validity of which Sainte-Palaye had explicitly cast doubt,[93] he never mentioned the frequent alternative attributions recorded in the Extracts, and he omitted all reference to manuscript sources. Even the bare list of sources he printed at the end of the *Discours préliminaire*, a list which gave only a summary indication of the libraries in which the manuscripts were deposited, contains errors.[94]

---

[91] *Ibid.*, vol. 1, p. 441, *sub* Gui; p. 75, *sub* Arnaud de Marveil; 2:261, *sub* Marcabrus.

[92] *Ibid.*, vol. 1, p. xiv.

[93] E.g., *sub* Albert, marquis, Arsenal 3281, fols. 44–48, *Hist. litt. troub.*, 1:337–39. There are many such cases.

[94] In addition to "5 du Vatican," Millot lists "5 de Saibante ou Vatican." This is an error. The only MS to which this can refer is Vat. 5232, of which there was in fact a copy at Verona, Saibante 410, now lost, but which Sainte-Palaye had consulted.

Yet there can be no doubt that for most of these defects in the *Histoire littéraire des troubadours*, Sainte-Palaye must bear some of the responsibility. The dull, monotonous translations were substantially his, as were too the literary judgments and comments. He himself had shown his lack of feeling for the literary value of the poems and had pointed the way to an external exploitation of them as source material for the historian, or, at best, elements of a picturesque décor. Moreover, he expressed himself completely satisfied with Millot's work. "Je vous ai entretenu il y a longtems," he wrote to Sinner, "du projet que j'avois de donner l'histoire de nos anciens Troubadours; j'en suis enfin venu à bout avec l'aide d'un excellent rédacteur."[95]

Sainte-Palaye may have been content. The public was disappointed. This was not the revelation that had been so long expected. After forty years of waiting for it, Tiraboschi complained, the *Histoire littéraire des troubadours* should have been a definitive work. "Ma l'espettazione degli eruditi è stata delusa."[96] Speaking for the scholarly community, Tiraboschi regretted not that Sainte-Palaye's book did so little to make the poetry of the troubadours better known, but that it left the biographies, in his view, still uncertain.[97] Even Sainte-Palaye's friends on the *Mercure* were apologetic: "On doit s'attendre qu'un ouvrage de ce genre est plus utile à consulter qu'agréable à lire de suite."[98] The *Journal littéraire* of

---

[95] Berne, Bürgerbibliothek, MS Hist. Helv. X, 106 (4), Sainte-Palaye to Sinner, 19.1.1775.

[96] G. Tiraboschi, *Storia della letteratura italiana* (Modena, 1787–93), 3:366, note.

[97] He charged (1) that Sainte-Palaye had not made sufficient use of the Estense MS (MS D); and (2) that the lives of the troubadours could be established only by comparing the Provençal biographies with external evidence, and that Sainte-Palaye had never gone outside the manuscripts themselves. Tiraboschi's reproach was not entirely justified. Sainte-Palaye did sometimes try to use historical and even monumental evidence conjointly with the internal evidence of the texts and the Provençal biographies, in order to rewrite the lives of the troubadours. Moreau, fols. 6–8, for instance, contains a letter to Raimondo Niccoli, secretary of the Tuscan legation at Paris, with details of a tomb of Aimeri de Narbonne in the Church of the Annunziata in Florence. There is also a detailed drawing (fol. 8) of the tomb, on which the inscription is clearly legible. The correspondent also refers to a number of Italian historical sources on the death of Aimeri de Narbonne. There is no doubt that Sainte-Palaye asked his friends at the Tuscan legation to procure this information for him. Diez paid tribute to Sainte-Palaye's pioneer work. (*Leben und Werke der Troubadours* [2d ed.; Leipzig, 1882], pp. v–vi.) It is true, however, that his efforts in this direction were sporadic, and he appears to have had no idea that the *Vidas* were in many cases put together by later writers from tales told in the poems.

[98] December, 1774, p. 132.

Berlin was more outspoken: "Nous observerons que l'histoire que nous annonçons ne suffit pas pour satisfaire les gens de lettres: ils regretteront de n'avoir pas le texte même des poètes dont on a traduit quelques morceaux."[99]

From the camp of the gentlemen scholars and amateurs came another complaint. "Have you got the *History of the Troubadours?*" Horace Walpole asked Lady Ossory. "I have longed for it several years, and yet am cruelly disappointed. Sainte-Palaye was too old to put his materials together—his friends called, Odd man! and nothing was ever so dully executed. You will say of the chapters, as I did of the houses at Paris; there is such a sameness, that one does not know whether one is in That one is in, or in That one came out of."[100] It is in Grimm's *Correspondance littéraire*, however, that we can see most clearly how far Sainte-Palaye's work had fallen behind current interests in France in the second half of the century. Not deficiencies of scholarship, but an inadequate conception of the subject matter was what Sainte-Palaye was reproached with by the reviewer (in all likelihood, Meister). The difficulties Sainte-Palaye had had to contend with were fully appreciated and he received generous credit for what was considered a major piece of research.[101] But both Millot and Sainte-Palaye, the critic charged, had forgotten that their history was in the first instance a history of literature. Works of art are not interesting because of the ideas in them: "Otez aux Homère, aux Virgile, aux Racine leur ramage, vous comblerez presque l'abîme immense qui les sépare des Ronsard, des Chapelain, des Pradon." Millot's mistake was to have imagined that he could write a history of the troubadours without giving any idea of their poetry. "Avec quel soin le traducteur des Poésies Erses [i.e., Macpherson] et même celui de la mythologie des Scandinaves [i.e., Mallet] n'ont-ils pas tâché de

---

[99] May–June (1775), 7:89. Millot was urged to rewrite the work in this sense. Cf. also Herder's comments, cited n. 74 above.

[100] *Horace Walpole's Correspondence*, Yale ed. by W. S. Lewis; *Correspondence with the Countess of Upper Ossory* (New Haven, 1965), pp. 217–19, letter of 23.11.1774.

[101] "M. de Sainte Palaye, si célèbre par ses Mémoires sur l'ancienne Chevalerie, a fait aussi les recherches les plus savantes sur l'Histoire des troubadours. Il y a employé plusieurs années d'une vie infiniment active et laborieuse. Il a voyagé exprès en Italie et en Provence et s'y est donné des soins et des peines incroyables pour ramasser tout ce qui pouvait répandre quelque lumière sur une partie si intéressante et si peu connue de notre littérature. Le travail qu'il a fait sur cet objet est immense." (*Corr. litt.*, 10:488, October, 1774.)

conserver à leurs copies l'oeil original, le tour antique, et ce qu'on appelle le goût du terroir. On ne pardonnera jamais ni à M. de Sainte-Palaye, ni à M. l'abbé Millot d'avoir négligé à ce point une partie si intéressante de leur travail." The trouble with the *Histoire littéraire des troubadours* is that the author "dans un ouvrage de ce genre ne soit jamais qu'historien." His own admission that he had determined to describe the ideas rather than the literary style of the troubadours is most damning: "Rien ne prouve mieux assurément qu'avec tout le mérite possible ailleurs, il n'était guère propre à faire l'ouvrage qu'il a entrepris."

Judged severely by contemporaries and later scholars alike, the *Histoire littéraire des troubadours* was nevertheless an important literary event. It contributed considerably to existing knowledge of the medieval Provençal lyric, and through it and the works which derive from it—until Raynouard's *Choix* it was the principal source for historians in France, England, and Germany[102]— the troubadours were popularized and incorporated securely into the pattern of modern cultural history. Even its defects, and the criticisms to which they gave rise, had in the end a salutary effect in that they led scholars to pay more attention to the literary qualities of the poems of the troubadours. When Le Grand d'Aussy, a disciple of Sainte-Palaye, used the *Histoire littéraire des troubadours* to question the international reputation of the troubadours,[103]

---

[102] In Papon's *Histoire de Provence* 4 vols. (Paris, 1777–86), which included a "Dissertation sur l'origine et les progrès de la poésie provençale," originally read to the Académie de Marseille in 1773, in the same author's *Voyage littéraire de Provence* (1780) and in Achard's *Dictionnaire de la Provence et du Comté Venaissin* (Marseille, 1785–87), there are clear echoes of Sainte-Palaye–Millot. In the course he taught at Geneva and which was published as *Histoire de la littérature du midi de l'Europe*, the great liberal historian Sismondi deplored the lack of good sources for the study of the early literature of the South. He knew of Sainte-Palaye's work, he wrote, but "son immense collection qui se compose de 25 volumes in-folio n'a pas été imprimée et ne saurait l'être." For lack of anything better, therefore, he said, historians will continue to have recourse to Millot.

[103] "Leur histoire existe; ouvrez-la, qu'y trouverez-vous? Des Sirventes, des Tensons, d'éternelles et ennuyeuses Chansons d'amour, sans couleur, sans images, sans aucun intérêt; en un mot, une assoupissante monotonie, à laquelle tout l'art de l'Éditeur et l'élégance de son style n'ont pu remédier." (*Fabliaux ou contes*, Préface, p. li.) The publication by the Académie des Inscriptions of Zurlauben's paper on the Swabian Minnesänger was likewise opposed by certain members on the ground that "les chansons des trouvères allemands qui se ressemblent presque touttes, ne diffèrent en rien de celles des Trouvères françois dont M. de Ste Palaie nous a donné une compilation déjà trop longue. Les beautés tecniques qu'elles pourroient renfermer disparoissent absolument sous la plume du traducteur." (B.N. Nouv. Acq. Fr. 6196, fol. 283.)

the young Provençal poet L. P. Bérenger replied that the Northern French *contes* published in translation by Le Grand appeared superior to the Provençal poems only because as a genre the *conte* survives translation more easily than the lyric poem. The qualities of the Provençal poems, he said, "tiennent du génie d'un idiome délicat et poli. On ne doit pas en juger par les traductions qu'on nous en a données."[104]

Above all, the *Histoire littéraire des troubadours* set a new standard in literary scholarship. Sainte-Palaye's work had made readers aware that medieval poetry was not really known and could not be properly discussed until the extensive manuscript sources in which it lay buried had been explored. By the end of the century Le Grand d'Aussy could dismiss Mervesin's *Histoire de la poésie françoise* as "une production d'écolier," while of a similar work by Massieu—who at the beginning of the century had been one of Sainte-Palaye's masters—he wrote: "Ce qui est inconcevable, cet homme qui entreprenoit de nous faire connoître nos vieux Poètes n'en avoit pas lû un seul en manuscrit."[105] Sainte-Palaye was largely responsible for this change in outlook, and his work was a source of inspiration not only to his immediate disciples but to later generations of Provençalists in the nineteenth century.[106]

[104] L. P. Bérenger, *Porte-feuille d'un troubadour, ou Essais poétiques, suivis d'une lettre à M. Grosley* (Marseille, 1782), pp. 91–92, 94.

[105] B.N. Nouv. Acq. Fr. 6628, fol. 50. In similar vein, B. de Roquefort-Flamericourt, *De l'État de la poésie française dans les XIIe et XIIIe siècles* (Paris, 1815), pp. 4–6.

[106] A century after the publication of the *Histoire littéraire des troubadours*, Paul Meyer still recalled Sainte-Palaye's work with admiration and compared it favorably with that of later scholars. (*Romania* [1874], 3:303.) Cf. also Émile Ripert, *La Renaissance provençale, 1800–60* (Paris, 1918), p. 25, where Sainte-Palaye is hailed as the "Columbus" of Provençal studies.

PART IV

CONCLUSION:
MEDIEVALISM AND ENLIGHTENMENT

CHAPTER I

THE CONTRIBUTION OF SAINTE-PALAYE TO THE THOUGHT OF THE EIGHTEENTH AND EARLY NINETEENTH CENTURIES: A DISCUSSION OF MEDIEVALISM IN THE ENLIGHTENMENT

Sainte-Palaye's work stands at the center of a vast literature of European proportions through which a certain image of the Middle Ages was propagated in the eighteenth century and passed to the early Romantics of the succeeding century. This literature included histories, more or less scholarly editions of medieval works, and plays, novels, and romances on medieval themes or in "medieval style."[1]

In France Sainte-Palaye made his advice and his extensive collection of manuscripts available to a large number of writers engaged in the most varied literary enterprises. The elegant adaptations of medieval romances published by his friends Tressan and Paulmy d'Argenson,[2] the novels of Mlle de Lubert, authoress of a successful

[1] On medievalism in eighteenth-century French literature see in particular F. Baldensperger, 'Le Genre troubadour,' *Études d'histoire littéraire*, 1ère série (Paris, 1907), pp. 110–46; E. Estève, 'Le Moyen Âge dans la littérature du XVIIIᵉ siècle,' *Revue de l'Université de Bruxelles* (1923), 28:353–82; T. Gerold, 'Zum Genre Troubadour um 1780,' *Archiv f. d. Studium d. neueren Sprachen* (1911), 126:168–74; René Lanson, *Le Goût du moyen âge en France au XVIIIᵉ siècle* (Paris and Brussels, 1926); Paul van Tieghem, *Le Préromantisme*, 3 vols. (Paris, 1924–48). A number of studies deal particularly with medievalism in the theatre: Max Aghion, *Le Théâtre à Paris au XVIIIᵉ siècle* (Paris, n.d. [1926]); C. D. Brenner, *L'Histoire nationale dans la tragédie française au dix-huitième siècle*, University of California Publications in Modern Philology (1929), vol. 14, no. 3, pp. 195–329; Georges Cucuel, 'Le Moyen Âge dans les opéras comiques du XVIIIᵉ siècle,' *Revue du Dix-huitième Siècle* (1914), 2:56–71; Nicole Decugis and Suzanne Reymond, *Le Décor de théâtre en France* (Paris, 1954); Alexis Pithou, 'Les origines du mélodrame français à la fin du XVIIIᵉ siècle,' *RHLF* (1911), 18:256–96.

[2] See H. Jacoubet, *Le Comte de Tressan et le genre troubadour* (Paris, 1923), p. 190 *et passim*. In Paulmy's *Bibliothèque universelle des romans* (1777), 14:45–46, we read: "Monsieur de Sainte-Palaye, à qui l'Histoire de la Chevalerie et même celle de la langue françoise ont de si grandes obligations, a voulu que nous lui en eussions de particulières. Il nous a ouvert les trésors de son cabinet, et nous a procuré le moyen d'en tirer parti." The extracts published by Tressan and Paulmy

version of the *Amadis de Gaule*,[3] Lévesque's edition of Thibaut de Navarre,[4] Belloy's *Chansons du Chatelain de Coucy*,[5] the excerpts from the troubadours published by Lacombe,[6] Querlon's introduction to Monnet's *Anthologie françoise*,[7] La Borde's *Essai sur la*

---

were not identical with those which Sainte-Palaye had prepared for his own proposed collection. A comparison of the extracts from *Erec et Enide* or the *Roman de la Charette* of Chrétien de Troyes in the *Bibl. des romans* (Feb., 1777, pp. 49–86; April, 1777, pp. 67–94), with those in Sainte-Palaye's papers (Moreau 1724, fols. 302–20; *ibid.*, fols. 276–98) reveals several differences. The extracts in the *Bibl. des romans* are shorter, and the copious quotations in O.F. verse, which are characteristic of Sainte-Palaye's extracts, have been drastically reduced and translated into modern French prose. There seems no doubt that the extracts in the *Bibl. des romans* were specifically prepared by Le Grand d'Aussy from those of Sainte-Palaye (Le Grand's collection is in B.N. Nouv. Acq. Fr. 6226–27). But Tressan and Paulmy were capable of adding gratuitously even to Le Grand's text (e.g., the advice of Érec to his sons and the 'Lay d'armes et d'amours, composé en l'honneur du Prince Erec et de la belle Enide' which concludes the extract in the *Bibl. des romans* and which figures neither in Sainte-Palaye's text nor in Le Grand's).

Sainte-Palaye made extracts of the following romances: *Saint-Graal* (Moreau 1724, fols. 209–75), *Chevalier au Lyon* (*ibid.*, fols. 321–43), *Erec et Enide* (*ibid.*, fols. 302–20), *Roman de la Charette* (*ibid.*, 276–301), *Athys et Porfilas* (Moreau 1722, fols. 110–21). An extract of *Partenopeus de Blois* (Arsenal 5871, fols. 13–18) may be by him, though more probably it is by Le Grand who used it in the fourth volume of his *Fabliaux ou contes*.

[3] On her work, see *Mercure*, Feb., 1752, p. 156. In a letter to Bréquigny (Bréquigny 161, fol. 172, 28.5.1781) shortly after Sainte-Palaye's death, she refers with gratitude to the encouragement she had always received from the old scholar.

[4] Lévesque de la Ravalière, *Poësies du Roy de Navarre* (Paris, 1742), vol. 1, pp. xiv–xv.

[5] In his *Mémoires historiques sur la Maison de Coucy* (Paris, 1770), p. 61, Belloy reproduced extracts from Sainte-Palaye's copy of the *Roman de Raoul de Coucy* (this copy, preceded by an introduction establishing the identity of Raoul and the date and circumstances of composition of the work, is now in Moreau 1725, fols. 134–43). Sainte-Palaye had augmented the text available hitherto and published by Fauchet in his *Recueil* of 1581. The success of the Coucy theme was enormous in the pre-Romantic and early Romantic periods (see Maurice Delbouille's edition of the *Roman du Castelain de Couci et de la Dame de Fayel* [Paris, 1936], p. lxxviii, *et passim*). Sainte-Palaye played an important part in this work of popularization. His copy was used not only by Belloy, but by Burney (*General History of Music* [London, 1782], 2:281–88) and by Forkel (*Allgemeine Geschichte der Musik* [Leipzig, 1801], 2:757–58), both of whom reproduced a selection of the songs with music.

[6] In his 'Coup d'oeil,' prefixed to *Supplément au Dictionnaire du vieux langage françois* (Paris, 1768), pp. xviii–xxv. In the 'Avis' (1767) he had already acknowledged that Sainte-Palaye had lent him his immense collection of copies of Provençal poems, while in the 'Avis' to the *Supplément* (1768) he promised a history of French poetry for the following year: "On ose se flatter qu'avec le secours de M. Lacurne de Sainte-Palaye, on rendra cette Histoire intéressante et neuve." The history never appeared, but it is clear that Sainte-Palaye was the man to whom anyone working on Old French or Provençal literature naturally turned.

[7] Moreau 1650, fols. 1–2, letter from Querlon to Sainte-Palaye thanking him for his assistance in composing his study of the *chanson*.

musique,[8] and the selection of Froissart's poems published in the *Almanach des muses*[9] all owe a great deal to him and would have been inconceivable without him. The writers of *drames nationaux* on heroic themes from medieval history, as well as those responsible for staging and costuming them, received advice and encouragement from him, and it was the account of chivalry given in the *Mémoires* which inspired many of these writers to turn to medieval themes in the first place.[10] He himself suggested to Grétry and Sedaine that they take his text of the *Aucassin* as the basis of an opera.[11] After a poor start, this work became a resounding success and led the way for many other operas on medieval themes. It was also Sainte-Palaye who prepared the material which his pupil Le Grand d'Aussy published in his *Fabliaux ou contes*.[12] Sainte-Palaye's central role in the medievalizing movement in France was recognized by Nodier when he republished the *Mémoires sur l'ancienne chevalerie* in a fine Romantic edition in 1826.

In other countries Sainte-Palaye's role in encouraging interest in the Middle Ages was almost as great as in France. This is particularly true of England and Scotland. The *Mémoires* appeared in English translation in 1784, the *Literary History of the Troubadours* came out in 1779 and in a second edition in 1807, and the papers on Froissart were translated and several times published by Thomas Johnes. But these translations only reinforced Sainte-Palaye's position among English amateurs of the Middle Ages. It

[8] La Borde's list of twelfth and thirteenth century *chansons* in his *Essai sur la musique ancienne et moderne* (Paris, 1780), 2:309-52, includes 452 items from the manuscripts of Sainte-Palaye. It was also through Sainte-Palaye's copies of manuscripts that La Borde knew the Vatican manuscripts, on the basis of which he established the authorship of a number of *chansons*.

[9] *Almanach des muses* (1778), 1:53-72.

[10] According to Sabathier de Castres, *Les trois siècles de la littérature* (The Hague, 1779), 4:47, it was Sainte-Palaye's *Mémoires* that inspired Baculard d'Arnaud to "ressusciter parmi nous les heureuses étincelles de cet enthousiasme d'honneur qui produisit tant de Héros et tant de Sages dans des siècles si amèrement taxés d'ignorance et de barbarie."

[11] Ladislas Günther, *L'Oeuvre dramatique de Sedaine* (Paris, 1908), p. 87; also Th. Gerold, p. 172; and Grétry, *Mémoires, ou Essais sur la musique* (Paris, an V), 1:336-37.

[12] Le Grand declared that he had been introduced to the *fabliaux* by Sainte-Palaye (*Fabliaux ou contes* [nouvelle édition; Paris, 1781], 2:7) and that almost everything he published had been drawn from the collations which Sainte-Palaye had placed at his disposal and of which he gives a brief description (vol. 1, pp. xcv-xcvi).

had already been established by British historians and men of letters who had access to the French texts. The account of chivalry in Gibbon's *Decline and Fall* is entirely based on the *Mémoires*,[13] as is that provided by Robertson in the influential *View of the Progress of Society in Europe from the Subversion of the Roman Empire to the Sixteenth Century*, which he prefixed to his *History of Charles V*.[14] In the circle of Richard Hurd, William Mason, Thomas Warton, and Thomas Gray, who had been friends since their Cambridge days, Sainte-Palaye was a familiar name. The *Mémoires*, the *Histoire littéraire des troubadours*, and the papers on Froissart were eagerly read, copied, and annotated by these amateurs of the Middle Ages and of medieval poetry, and the letters which passed among them, and between them and their correspondents in various parts of England, contained numerous allusions to Sainte-Palaye.[15] For their own work they were deeply indebted to the French scholar, and Hurd's *Letters on Chivalry and Romance*,[16] Percy's *Reliques of Ancient English Poetry*,[17] Warton's *History of English Poetry*[18] popularized the picture of chivalry given by Sainte-Palaye and carried forward his work on medieval poetry.

---

[13] *Decline and Fall*, ch. 58.

[14] *Works* (London ed., 1878), pp. 66–69. Cf. p. 250, n. 27: "Almost every fact which I have mentioned in the text, together with many other curious and instructive particulars concerning this singular institution, may be found in Mémoires sur l'ancienne Chevalerie . . . par M. de La Curne de St. Palaye."

[15] For example, a letter from Gray to his young friend Nicholls in 1777, in which there is an account of the different ranks and dignities of "men at arms," entirely taken from the *Mémoires sur l'ancienne chevalerie*, to which Gray specifically refers his correspondent (*Correspondence of Thomas Gray*, ed. Toynbee and Whibley, 3 vols. [Oxford, 1935], letter 543).

[16] Sainte-Palaye's work lies behind Hurd's argument. A suggestion by V. M. Hamm ('A seventeenth century French source for Hurd's Letters on Chivalry,' *PMLA* [1937], 52:821, 824) that Hurd was relying on Chapelain is farfetched. Hurd may have found the reference to Chapelain in Sainte-Palaye's paper, but the Dialogue was not an easy work to obtain, and Hurd does not refer to it, although he admits his debt to Sainte-Palaye on several occasions (notably *Letters on Chivalry and Romance*, 4th letter, [London ed., 1911], pp. 93–94). There is a more conventional and convincing study by A. L. Smith, 'Richard Hurd's Letters on Chivalry and Romance,' *ELH* (1939), 6:58–82.

[17] Percy recognized in Sainte-Palaye "the industrious French collector to whom (Hurd) is indebted for all his materials." (Letter to Shenstone, 17.6.1762, *The Percy Letters*, ed. Cleanth Brooks; *Correspondence of Thomas Percy and Richard Farmer* [Baton Rouge, 1946], p. 5, n. 11) and he instructed his publisher to procure the *Mémoires* for him (*ibid.*, pp. 10–11). See also Percy's *Reliques* (London, 1765), 'Essay on the Ancient Metrical Romances,' vol. 3, p. iii.

[18] Ed. Hazlitt (London, 1871; 1st ed., 1774–81), 1:147–49 *et passim*.

It would be a considerable task to catalogue all the books in English which appropriated Sainte-Palaye's work and transmitted it to an entire generation of readers. In addition to the eighteenth-century works which we have mentioned and to those early nineteenth-century productions which are still remembered—the essays and romances of Scott and Southey, Hallam's often republished *View of the State of Europe in the Middle Ages* (1819)—we should have to include many works which have been forgotten: erudite ones such as Daines Barrington's *Observations on the Statutes* (1766)[19] or Joseph Sterling's *Dissertation on Chivalry* (1781),[20] and works of vulgarization like Thomson's *Spirit of General History* (1792), Adams' *Universal History* (1795), or Richmal Magnall's *Historical Questions for Young People* (1815). As a result of this extensive literature Sainte-Palaye maintained his position as a leading authority on chivalry during a large part of the nineteenth century in England. Charles Mills, who published a two volume *History of Chivalry* in 1825, declared that the *Mémoires* were still standard,[21] and even at the beginning of the twentieth century the author of another popular work on chivalry, F. Warre Cornish, still felt able to affirm that "little can be added to the conception of chivalry as it was evolved from medieval records by Curne de Ste Palaye, and set forth by Scott, Southey, and their followers, whose obligation to Ste Palaye cannot be exaggerated."[22]

Sainte-Palaye's work must have come early to the attention of German students of the *Minnesänger*. Schoepflin, for instance, was a friend both of Sainte-Palaye and of Bodmer and Breitinger, and he was active in procuring copies of German medieval poetry in manuscript in the Paris libraries for his Zürich friends.[23] Herder, on the other hand, seems to have known of Sainte-Palaye's work at first only through Hurd's *Letters on Chivalry*. In the *Philosophie der Geschichte zur Bildung der Menschheit* of 1774 it is Hurd, not Sainte-Palaye, who is mentioned in the section dealing with the Middle Ages and chivalry. By 1791, however, when he published

[19] (London, 1766), esp. pp. 257, 314, 152 (n. 5).
[20] 'Dissertation on Chivalry,' prefixed to *History of the Chevalier Bayard* (Dublin, 1781), p. 3.
[21] Charles Mills, *History of Chivalry* (London, 1825), vol. 1, Introduction.
[22] *Chivalry* (London, 1908), pp. 9–10.
[23] On Bodmer's treatment of medieval chivalry, which was similar in some ways to Sainte-Palaye's, see Max Wehrli, *Johann Jakob Bodmer und die Geschichte der Literatur* (Leipzig, 1936), pp. 92–95.

his *Ideen zur Philosophie der Geschichte der Menschheit,* Herder had read Sainte-Palaye's *Mémoires* in Klüber's translation (1786–91), and he refers in a number of places both to them and to the *Histoire littéraire des troubadours.* Indeed, on his own admission, the entire chapter on "Rittergeist in Europa" was based on Sainte-Palaye.[24] Through Herder, through the English writers, and directly through Klüber's translation, Sainte-Palaye's picture of chivalry and his account of the troubadours reached the first generation of German Romantic poets and scholars—Wackenroder, the Schlegels, Tieck, and Novalis.

The mere list of these names—and there must be many others that might have been added—is enough to indicate the diversity of uses to which Sainte-Palaye's work was put, and the diversity of intellectual currents into which it flowed. The nineteenth-century interest in Sainte-Palaye and in the Middle Ages in general, however, cannot be dealt with on the same level as that of the eighteenth century, complex as the latter might be in itself. Eighteenth-century medievalism was often associated with political conservatism, as we shall see; and it sometimes implied a questioning of the values of "civilized" society, as the eighteenth century understood it; it also offered a colorful distraction from the routine of everyday life with its strict rules and conventions. But all of these tendencies took on different proportions and new meaning in the nineteenth century. The conservatism of the post-Revolutionary generation was quite different from that of the eighteenth century, since it no longer attempted to reconcile social order and Enlightenment, but overtly rejected Enlightenment. At the same time, moreover, as the Middle Ages were brought closer in desire than they had been to the eighteenth century writers, they became, through the twin revolutions—the political and the industrial—in fact more remote. The nineteenth century thinker or poet, whatever the class of society or the nation for which he spoke, was inevitably in a quite different relation to the Middle Ages from that of the thinker or poet of the Enlightenment.

Similarly, the doubts about civilization and the self-examination which eighteenth-century accounts of medieval life and literature inspired in some Enlighteners bear little resemblance to the protests

[24] Pt. IV, bk. 20, sec. 2, *Werke,* ed. Suphan, 14:457n.

of the nineteenth century at the dehumanizing and socially damaging effects of industrialism. The eighteenth century sometimes prettified chivalry to make it more acceptable, but it did so on the whole with remarkably little pathos. The writers and poets of industrial society—Cobbett, Coleridge, Southey—idealized the Middle Ages so that they might hold them up, in contrast to the egoism, the ugliness, and the materialism of their own world, as a period of community and high aspiration, when relations among men were more direct and more human than those of the cash nexus, and when the goal of human endeavor was something more than the production of goods for the market—a moral ideal, a way of life, the realization of a human value.

Even as a world in which to escape, the Middle Ages acquired a different coloring in the nineteenth century. The eighteenth century had seen the advantages of escaping from the difficulties and the rules of social life, but Fontenelle at the beginning of the century and Schiller at the end, however differently they envisaged the function of the escape, never saw it as more than a momentary respite. By the nineteenth century the desire to escape into a different world and a different way of life had become charged with all the oppressiveness of the conditions of life in industrialized society.

At the same time the very remoteness of the industrial and post-Revolutionary world of the nineteenth century from the past, its sense of its own newness and difference, heightened its awareness of the individuality of other cultures and led thinkers and artists to make a far greater effort than had been envisaged in the eighteenth century to re-establish contact with them. Nineteenth-century medievalism was not only more full of pathos and significance than eighteenth century medievalism, it was also more ready to look for and to grasp the peculiar character of medieval life and literature. Above all, the popular element in the culture of the Middle Ages, from which the eighteenth-century scholars had held themselves somewhat aloof, was at last recognized and made an object of study.[25]

---

[25] This change is notable among scholars and among literary men alike. Mérimée, for instance, who was both, is indebted to Sainte-Palaye for some of the external details of his play *La Jacquerie*, but he does not share either Sainte-Palaye's view of chivalry or his unsympathetic judgment of the revolt of the *Jacques* or peasants; cf. P. Trahard, *La Jeunesse de Prosper Mérimée* (Paris, 1924), pp. 303–20, 737 *et seq.*

Sainte-Palaye's work must therefore have been read by nineteenth-century readers in a spirit quite different from that in which he wrote himself, and the medievalism to which, through them, he contributed would have been quite foreign to him, as it would have been to others—Percy, Hurd, Warton, Mallet, Herder—whose works were likewise put to use by the men of the nineteenth-century. There are, in short, external filiations between his work and that of nineteenth-century medievalists, but the framework of ideas and feelings in which it was carried out was entirely different from that in which it was later put to use. Sainte-Palaye's activity and the specific character of his achievement as a medievalist—and, indeed, eighteenth-century medievalism as a whole—cannot, therefore, be understood in nineteenth century terms; they have to be seen in relation to the world of which they were part and, in particular, to the framework of ideas and feelings in the latter half of the eighteenth century.

Eighteenth-century medievalism was part of a wider movement of curiosity about and sympathy for earlier and more "primitive" cultures. The appearance of Sainte-Palaye's major works coincided, indeed, with that of Mallet's *Histoire du Danemarck* (1758), Gessner's *Idylls* (first French translation 1756), Macpherson's Ossianic fragments (1760), Wood's *Essay on Homer* (1769), Percy's *Reliques* (1765), Rousseau's *Discourses* (1750, 1755), and throughout the latter part of the century this "primitivist" tendency gathered strength in countless productions of history and literature. Its significance, however, was never unambiguous.

Enlightenment men and women in the early eighteenth century had freed themselves, in idea at least, from the "prejudices" of their own time and their own society, and they were not tempted to give themselves up to the "prejudices" of other times or other societies. The glorification of "primitive" man and "primitive" society was alien to them, since in their view primitive society was not "natural" but simply unaware of its own conventions. From the superior vantage point of enlightenment and emancipation they enjoyed surveying, like Gibbon amid the ruins of Rome, the infinitely varied spectacle of human activity and human history, for by this vision their sense of freedom was enhanced. Tourists in Rome eagerly bought up those astonishing Paninis in which the monuments of all the ages of the city's history offer themselves to view in fantastic juxtaposition. Wealthy Englishmen strewed their gracious parklands with the bric-à-brac of centuries. At Stowe and Stourhead the masks of nature and culture—Greek and Roman temples, Gothic ruins, grottos, and waterfalls—led the reflective stroller to muse on the passing show of man and his history.[26] What appealed in other cultures, as in nature herself, was not their otherness—this was believed to be as inscrutable and in the end as terrifying as that brute matter which so frequently distressed Voltaire—but those external and picturesque aspects of them which could be appropriated into the existing culture and which would lend color and variety to it without disturbing its fundamental patterns. In the return to the antique, it was Pompeii and Spalato not the strange and "barbaric" Doric of Paestum that first triumphed in the eighteenth century.[27] The latter was relegated to the garden as at Hagley or Drottningholm, where, characteristically, Desprez found no difficulty in substituting a Gothic fabric for the "temple paëstique" he originally planned.[28] For Gothic was likewise used for variety, rather than to undermine classical-humanist principles of construction. French architects, Krafft recounts, employed it "à des constructions peu importantes où la sévérité des principes peut être modifiée et se prêter sans conséquence aux élans de l'imagination."[29] The men of the Enlightenment, in short, transformed the elements they borrowed from other cultures and adapted them to established and familiar forms which perfectly expressed their own personality. In those *veduti* to which artists of the caliber of Desprez and Fragonard did not disdain to devote their talents, the most varied scenes and objects—deserted landscapes, medieval fortresses, Gothic churches in the moonlight, frightening natural phenomena like the eruptions of Vesuvius— were indifferently appropriated to and informed by the vision of the artist.[30]

[26] Cf. H. F. Clark, 'Eighteenth Century Elysiums,' *Journal of the Warburg and Courtauld Institutes* (1943), 6:165.

[27] S. Lang, 'Early Publications of the Temples at Paestum,' *Journal of the Warburg and Courtauld Institutes* (1950), 13:48–64.

[28] J. Summerson, *Architecture in Britain, 1530–1830* (Pelican History of Art. 2d ed.; 1955), p. 342, n. 5; Nils Wollin, *Desprez en Suède* (Stockholm, 1939), p. 92.

[29] J. C. Krafft, *Recueil d'architecture* (Paris, 1829), p. 15.

[30] See notably the sketches done by Châtelet, Desprez, and Fragonard during their journey to Italy with the wealthy Abbé de Saint-Non and published as *Voyage pittoresque dans le royaume de Naples et Sicile*, 5 vols. (Paris, 1781–86).

To many people throughout the eighteenth century, therefore, "primitive" societies and forms of expression continued to be viewed in the perspective defined at the beginning of the century by Fontenelle in his essay on the pastoral. In this perspective the state of nature was a charming myth that relaxed momentarily the tensions of a highly refined and formalized social life; it was not a model to be followed or even seriously studied. Fontenelle and those who shared this view with him neither believed nor wished to believe in the reality of the state of nature, nor did they wish to transform their own society in order to make it more "natural." To them, the literature and the life of the Middle Ages offered an entertaining spectacle in which naïve actors unreflectingly spoke their simple and charming lines like the children of "nature" in Marivaux's comedy *La Dispute*. Horace Walpole gives us some idea of the way in which many people must have read Sainte-Palaye's study of chivalry when he explained to Madame du Deffand why he so enjoyed Vertot's *Histoire des chevaliers hospitaliers de Saint-Jean de Jérusalem:* "La Terre Sainte ne valait-elle pas le quiétisme et la bulle Unigenitus? Et les folies des jésuites et des jansénistes, qu'en diriez-vous, si ce n'étaient des absurdités inintelligibles et plus tristes et moins amusantes que la Conquête de Jérusalem?"[31] Walpole was himself an amateur of medievalia and a friend of Warton and Gray, but he grew caustic when he thought he detected in Warton's *History* a real preference for medieval over contemporary literature, a genuine cultural comparison, in short, in which modern civilization was implicitly judged and found wanting. "I am sorry Mr. Warton has contracted such an affection for his materials that he seems to think that not only Pope but Dryden himself have added few beauties to Chaucer." Warton's comparison of the original *Nut Brown Maid* with Prior's adaptation and avowed preference for the original outraged Walpole altogether. "I believe it is the certain fate of an antiquary to become an old fool," he declared in a letter to Mason.[32]

Increasingly, however, in the second half of the century, primitivism was coming to assume a new significance. The very nature

[31] *Correspondance de Madame du Deffand,* ed. Lescure, 2 vols. (Paris, 1865), I:122n.

[32] Quoted by Clarissa Rinaker, *Thomas Warton* (University of Illinois Studies, 1916), pp. 114–15.

of the pastoral changed. From being a playful relaxation, it became with Gessner and Rousseau at once a more intensely longed for escape and a serious model of what ought to be.[33] Even Schiller, when he warned against the potentially debilitating effects of the pastoral, held that in the state of civilization men need to be reminded of and to seek guidance from the laws of nature, whether these be discovered in the infancy of mankind or in the memory of their own childhood.[34] The new attitude to the primitive was clearly part of a more vigorously critical attitude to the society and civilization of the ancien régime as a whole. "I detest every species of aristocracy and would be tout à fait *sans culottes*," the ardently radical scholar and folklorist Joseph Ritson declared.[35] Not surprisingly, he was strongly critical of Percy's *Reliques* because they were not primitive enough and bore too many marks of contemporary refinement. In France, Diderot's *Deux Amis de Bourbonne* (1770) was in effect a critique of the artificial pastoral tone of Saint-Lambert's *Les Amis iroquois* and aimed to give a picture of true passion, true fidelity, true simplicity, true generosity as they were preserved among simple people who were held outwith the bounds of "society." The manners of primitive peoples were similarly used by Herder to criticize the culture of the petty, feudal-absolutist German states of his own time. The Middle Ages in particular became for him, as one critic has put it, a poetic and cultural myth directed against both the absolutism of the French and the enlightened despotism of Frederick II.[36] In the formation of this myth the work of Sainte-Palaye and of Mallet played a significant part. But it is worth noting that the revolutionary

[33] The change can be observed in Rousseau's work itself. The idea of the simple life found in the writings that date from the Lyons period or from the early years in Paris, during which time Rousseau was trying to play according to the rules of his society, reflects a conventional attitude of literary people in the late seventeenth and early eighteenth centuries, now playful in the manner of Fontenelle or Gresset, now tinged with bitterness as in some of Boileau's later works, but in either case remote from the later tone of the *Discourses*.

[34] 'Über naive und sentimentale Poesie,' *Werke*, Säkular-Aufgabe in 16 Bänden (Stuttgart and Berlin), 12:224–25. Lichtenberg expressed a view which Herder and even Goethe would have seconded when he declared that Gessner presents an unspoiled image of "die reine menschliche Natur." (G. Chr. Lichtenberg, *Gesammelte Werke* [Baden-Baden, n.d.—1950?] 2:167.)

[35] Quoted by Bertrand H. Bronson, *Joseph Ritson, Scholar at Arms*, 2 vols. (Berkeley, 1938), 1:155.

[36] Max Rouché, *La Philosophie de l'histoire de Herder* (Paris, 1940), pp. 52–53.

Herder rejected the prettified Middle Ages which amateurs "von etwas abentheuerlichem Gehirne" had presented in their writings.[37] His Age of Chivalry was not one of colorful and gallant episodes, but one whose harshness he accepted alongside its nobility—in principle no better than any other age of history but superior in Herder's feeling and imagination, because of its energy and high ideals, to the corrupt, sophisticated, and external culture of the Germany of his own time.

In the conditions of eighteenth century Germany it was easier to make a radical critique of existing "civilization" than in England or France, since in the German lands "civilization" was readily identified not only with a particular social order but with a foreign tradition. Even among moderate spirits in England and France, however, reflection on early societies sometimes led beyond historical relativism and gave rise to a genuine self-questioning. Hume sincerely admired the virtues of the Scottish Highlanders, who at that time were considered little better than savages. "There is not any people in Europe," he said, "not even excepting the Swiss, who have more plain honesty and fidelity, are more capable of gratitude and attachment than that race of men."[38] Similarly Joseph Sterling argued on behalf of the "Goths" that "their sentiments, though tinctured with ferocity, were liberal and generous, their language, though inferior to the Greek and Latin, was nervous and expressive."[39] Like views were expressed by the Swiss Mallet concerning the old Norsemen. In France Grimm's collaborator, Meister, was led by his reading of Sainte-Palaye's history of the troubadours to wonder not only if human affairs can ever be entirely ruled by reason, but if, indeed, civilization as commonly envisaged, that is the comfortable and urbane way of life of an intelligent and leisured aristocracy, was altogether desirable: "C'est à l'expédition de Troie et à ses suites que la Grèce dut ses premiers poètes. C'est aux Croisades que la France et l'Italie doivent les leurs . . . Je ne sais pourquoi l'on est convenu de nous représenter les Muses comme amies de la paix. Leur enthousiasme ne se réveille et ne s'enflamme qu'au milieu des orages de la guerre ou de l'amour . . . Les siècles

---

[37] 'Auch eine Philosophie der Geschichte' (1774), *Werke,* ed. Suphan, 5:523.
[38] 'Of the poems of Ossian,' in *David Hume, Philosophical Historian,* ed. Norton and Popkin (New York, 1965), p. 400.
[39] 'Dissertation on the Icelandic Odes,' pp. 30–31, in *Poems* (Dublin, 1782).

paisibles sont ceux de la philosophie; mais il est rare que le génie et les actes n'y dépérissent pas, ou du moins n'y dégénèrent . . ."[40]

Of the various forms of primitivism, which research and imagination had popularized, the severest critics of contemporary society in France usually preferred classical antiquity, Polynesia, or the simpler inhabitants of Europe itself—Rousseau's *Haut Valaisiens* and *Montagnons* or Diderot's smugglers. The Middle Ages were too closely associated with the nobility and with the social order they rejected to be easily adapted to the ends of social criticism. Grimm and Diderot did on occasion express their admiration for medieval chivalry and for the energetic and passionate actions it had inspired. But they seem to have been principally attracted by the colorful, pictorial qualities of chivalry—the striking gesture, the memorable tableau. Grimm found the manners of the Christian knights "singulièrement théâtrales,"[41] while of Christianity in general, he declared that, though it was less favorable to poetry than Greek mythology, it was "plus pittoresque."[42]

On the whole, therefore, the Middle Ages seem to have played a more significant role in conservative versions of the primitivist myth in France. Self-criticism in the light of ever more numerous studies of earlier societies was not confined to what might be referred to somewhat loosely as the left wing of the Enlightenment. Men whose interests and goals were fundamentally conservative participated, as our previous chapters have already suggested, in all phases of the Enlightenment. One need only think of the so-called enlightened despots to be reminded that Enlightenment was by no means the prerogative of the revolutionaries of '89 or of those who

---

[40] *Corr. litt.* (Oct., 1774), 10:491–92. One of the most famous statements of the "paradox" of civilization is, of course, that of Diderot: "C'est lorsque la fureur de la guerre civile ou du fanatisme arme les hommes de poignards, et que le sang coule à grands flots sur la terre, que le laurier d'Apollon s'agite et verdit . . . Le siècle d'or eût produit une chanson, peut-être ou une élégie. La poésie épique et la poésie dramatique demandent d'autres moeurs" (*Oeuvres*, 7:371–72). Even minor writers raised the question—thus Jacques de Chambry in his *Contes et proverbes suivis d'une notice sur les troubadours* (Amsterdam, 1784), p. 124: "L'esprit philosophique produit une incertitude, une nonchalance, une indifférence absolue. Quel est donc le bon temps?" Cf. likewise Galiani, *Correspondance*, ed. Perey and Maugras (Paris, 1890), 1:53–54.

[41] *Corr. litt.*, 4:292.

[42] Unpublished note in MS of *Corr. litt.*, printed by J. J. Seznec, 'Diderot and *Le Génie du Christianisme*,' *Journal of the Warburg and Courtauld Institutes* (1952), 15:230–31.

are still widely held to have prepared the way for them. We have already seen that conservative-minded men were in the van of the attack on the rococo and that they instigated the academicism and supported the return to "nature" and to antiquity that marks the second half of the century. The Crown itself tried to encourage artists to become more serious and to devote their talents to depicting the heroic past of the nation.[43] The Middle Ages came more and more to be considered the heroic age of French society, the primitive origin and the "natural" model, as it were, to which contemporaries could look for guidance. At the end of the *Mémoires* Sainte-Palaye himself took up a suggestion of Frederick the Great that the heroic age of chivalry was comparable with the heroic age of Greece, and in Bougainville's introduction to the 1759 edition the point was driven home. Bougainville observed that "les moeurs à la fois grossières et respectables" of the French knights were "comparables en bien des points, et même supérieures en quelques-uns, à celles des temps héroiques chantés par Homère." After the *Mémoires* it became more and more fashionable, especially in conservative circles in France, to put the Middle Ages on a par with classical antiquity and to answer the admirers of Republican Rome and Sparta with heroic episodes from the medieval past.[44] Many contemporaries recognized, moreover, that Sainte-Palaye's work offered excellent material for a conservative political myth with which to counter the radicals' glorification of nature and antiquity. In 1779, for instance, Sabathier de Castres, a well-known journalist who had turned against the *philosophes*, took the trouble to praise Sainte-Palaye's work highly: "Cet académicien aimable s'est attaché à une partie de notre Littérature, aussi intéressante qu'utile: l'Histoire du bon vieux temps de notre Monarchie a décidé son goût et fixé ses études. Rien de plus détaillé, de plus instructif, et de mieux présenté que ses Mémoires sur l'Ancienne Chevalerie. Toute âme Françoise ne peut y voir qu'avec le plus grand intérêt le

---

[43] See Loquin, *La Peinture d'histoire en France* (Paris, 1912); James A. Leith, *The Idea of Art as Propaganda in France, 1750-99* (Toronto, 1965).

[44] E.g., *Année littéraire* (1760), vol. vii, p. 97, review of Berville, *Histoire de Pierre de Terrail, dit le Chevalier Bayard,* in which the chivalric notion of honor is compared with Roman patriotism; Belloy, *Siège de Calais* (Paris, 1765), Preface, p. vi; and somewhat later, Geoffroy in *Journal de Monsieur* (1781), 4:33. After the Revolution Nodier resumed this tradition; see his *Mélanges de littérature et de critique* (Paris, 1820), 1:402, 2:322, 327 (reviews of Marchangy and Madame de Staël).

touchant tableau des moeurs, des usages, de la bravoure, de la pieuse et noble simplicité de ces anciens Chevaliers, qui furent la gloire de la Nation par leurs faits d'armes."[45] The Polish translator of the *Mémoires* was even more outspoken in drawing political conclusions from Sainte-Palaye's work. "Why should it not be possible to unite the virtues of chivalry over the past three centuries with the refinements of our present civilization," he asked, and warned the Polish nobility to put its house in order or suffer the same decline as its counterpart in France.[46]

The meaning of eighteenth-century medievalism was thus different in different countries and for different social groups. In almost no case, moreover, can it be defined unequivocally, for the most radical *philosophes* never completely freed themselves even from those aspects of their civilization that they rejected, while the conservatives, on their side, were often filled with genuine desire for a more richly human existence than contemporary society seemed to allow, and eager for a reform of the state. Diderot and Rousseau sometimes mistook rhetoric and pathos for real sentiment and "expressiveness"; the bourgeois pastoral of Clarens and the bourgeois drama of *Le Père de famille* are as forced and false as the patriotic gesturing of de Belloy's heroes in *Le Siège de Calais*. On the other hand, when the Abbé Papon found life in medieval Provence characterized by "beaucoup de vraie grandeur et peu d'étiquette"[47] or when L. P. Bérenger recalled the former glories of the impoverished Southern nobility, their invocation of the past went beyond mere political conservatism; there was in it something of that aspiration, which the Enlightenment itself had nourished, toward a renewal of the quality of human life itself. Bérenger's Letter to Grosley, in which the echo of Sainte-Palaye is clearly audible, offers a notable example of the way in which troubadourism and the ideal of chivalry came to express a mixture of humane principles, feudal prejudices, conservative politics, and poetic melancholy, which is characteristic of a good part of the educated public

[45] *Les trois siècles de la littérature* (The Hague, 1779), 4:47.
[46] *Wiadomosci Historyczne o dawnym Rycerstwie zwazanym iako Ustanowienie polityczne y zolnierskie* (Warsaw, 1772), p. 159. See also G. de Bertier de Savigny, *Le Comte Ferdinand de Bertier (1782–1864) et l'énigme de la Congrégation* (Paris, 1948), on a plan by this nobleman to unite all the Royalist elements in France in "un ordre religieux, politique et chevaleresque." The plan, drawn up in 1801, was apparently based on Sainte-Palaye's *Mémoires* among other sources.
[47] *Voyage littéraire de Provence* (Paris, 1780), p. 27.

in the later eighteenth century. "C'est sur les bords enchanteurs de la Sargue et du Rhône," Bérenger writes, "dans ces vallées consacrées par la pure tendresse de deux coeurs sensibles et constans, aimables lieux, où leur âme attachée semble respirer encore, et d'où je n'approchai jamais sans ressentir la plus vive émotion, sans tomber dans la plus douce mélancolie, sans éprouver le doux besoin de chanter sur la lyre de Pétrarque les sentimens qui pénétroient mon âme . . . c'est dans les délicieuses plaines du Comtat . . . que se formèrent ces Académies de femmes aimables, et de jeunes beautés aussi célèbres par leur esprit, que par leur sensibilité et les charmes de leur figure. Là, les Mabile de Villeneuve, les Huguette de Sabran, les Dagoult, et vous, ô belle de Sade, avec qui l'Élève des Troubadours a partagé son immortalité; là, Blanchefleur de Ponteves, Estephenette de Gantelme, Garsende de Sabran, Comtesse de Provence, et mère de Raymond-Bérenger [whom the writer claims as an ancestor], toutes accompagnées de leur Troubadour en titre, tenoient ces charmantes Cours d'amour . . . Là, se traitoient toutes les questions que peuvent fournir, ou les sentimens ou les aventures des amans; questions si ingénieuses, dit Fontenelle, que celles de nos Romans modernes ne sont souvent que les mêmes . . . Ô tems heureux! Ô jours à jamais regrettables! Nation brillante et fortunée! tu ne connoissois encore ni l'audace effrénée de raisonner sur tout, sans principes certains, ni l'inquiète curiosité qui se jette au-devant des erreurs, et qui semble la maladie de notre siècle. L'égoisme, ce poison destructeur de toute sensibilité, n'avoit pas encore attaqué la Patrie, la société, la nature même, et brisé les derniers ressorts de la vertu; la triste émulation d'un luxe scandaleux, le faste insolent et superbe d'un vil Publicain, n'insultoit pas à la vertueuse pauvreté du Citoyen indignement dépouillé; alors la franche et loyale courtoisie de nos pères ne savoit pas se couvrir du masque d'une politesse perfide . . . à cette époque enfin, la Nation avoit un caractère simple, et, si j'osois le dire, poétique et plein de grandeur . . ."[48]

[48] L. P. Bérenger, *Porte-feuille d'un troubadour*, pp. 102–4. In a recent popular edition of Stendhal's *De l'Amour*, put out by Garnier, Michel Crouzat points out that an intermingling of 'conservative' and 'radical' motifs continues well into the nineteenth century: "Ce conflit du progrès et des mythes du coeur, 'De l'Amour' l'exprime en opposant l'émancipation de la femme et sa puissance affective; l'univers romanesque de Stendhal l'exprime bien plus encore. La femme élue par le désir y est toujours la moins libre, la plus prisonnière des traditions, de celles-là même que l'idéologue refuse: noblesse, dévotion, honneur. Toute héroïne est d'Ancien Régime . . ."

Eighteenth century primitivism and eighteenth century medievalism were thus open to numerous interpretations and subject to many adaptations. They could be taken seriously or playfully, they could be construed as lending support to the established order or as offering various kinds of criticism of it. Yet, it would be inappropriate in most cases to consider the interpretation of any particular work a misinterpretation, both because eighteenth century medievalists were themselves ambiguous in their attitude to the Middle Ages, and because it was of the very essence of their works to be open to whatever interpretations their contemporary readers might wish to put upon them.

The attitude of medievalists on both sides of the Channel was strikingly similar. Walpole may have judged that Thomas Warton had gone overboard in his admiration for medieval poetry. Warton himself usually professed a conventional enough attitude to his material, and it is not obvious that his taste differed fundamentally from the neoclassical taste of the time.[49] Bishop Percy disavowed any serious literary consideration of the old English and Scottish ballads. "I only considered these things pardonable, at best, among the levities (I had almost said follies) of my youth," he wrote to John Pinkerton. "However, as I must confess that I have always had a relish for the poetic effusions . . . of our ancestors, I have commonly taken up these trifles, as other grave men have done cards, to unbend and amuse the mind when fatigued with graver studies."[50] There is no need to assume that Percy was speaking anything but the truth. He certainly did not have to apologize to Pinkerton for his love of the old ballads.

The French antiquaries expressed similar views. "Ce seroit abuser de la presse," La Bastie wrote to Mazaugues, "que de la faire rouler sur les morceaux grossiers de nos ancêtres."[51] Lévesque

---

[49] Thus: "We look back on the savage conditions of our ancestors with the triumph of superiority, we are pleased to mark the steps by which we have been raised from rudeness to elegance; and our reflections on the subject are accompanied by a conscious pride, arising in great measure from a tacit comparison of the infinite disproportion between the feeble efforts of remote ages and our present improvements in knowledge." (*History of English Poetry* [London ed., 1871], 1:3.)

[50] J. Pinkerton, *Literary Correspondence*, ed. Dawson Turner 2 vols. (London, 1830), 1:10, Percy to Pinkerton, 20.7.1778. The preface to the *Reliques* is largely an attempt to justify the book by an appeal to the elegant critics "eminent for their genius and taste" who had assisted and encouraged him—Johnson, Shenstone, Warton, Farmer, Garrick, etc. (ed. of 1765, vol. 1, p. xiv).

[51] J. Bauquier, 'Les provençalistes du XVIII⁰ siècle,' p. 193.

de la Ravalière, having admired the "tendresse," "délicatesse" and
"naïveté" of Thibaut de Navarre, declared that "il mériteroit une
estime sans réserve, si . . . son siècle avoit eu la retenue et la sagesse
de celui dans lequel nous vivons."[52] In the Preface to his edition of
the *fabliaux*, Le Grand d'Aussy disclaimed in no uncertain terms
any intention of apologizing for the "siècles d'ignorance." "Je ne
crois pas mériter assez de mépris pour être soupçonné d'une
démence pareille," he declared.[53] Le Grand does request a limited
indulgence for the early French poets, but he does not envisage
putting them on the same level as works of polite literature. Papon,
who wrote understandingly of medieval Provence, did not hide his
contempt for the efforts of the medieval poets—"choses basses,
triviales et méprisables."[54] Mallet disavowed any intention of drawing his picture of the early Norsemen in order to criticize his own
society or its fundamentally bourgeois values. "What evidently
proves the unhappiness of those nations who live in such a state as
this," he observed at the end of one chapter, "is the facility with
which they throw their lives away. The pleasure arising from
property, from sentiment and knowledge, the fruits of industry,
laws and arts, by softening life and endearing it to us, can alone
give us a relish for peace and justice."[55] La Borde avoided Warton's
mistake of preferring the originals of medieval or folk poems to the
versions subsequently made of them by the poets of the Age of
Elegance. Discussing the authenticity of an alleged fragment of a
Chanson de Roland "discovered" by Paulmy, he declared that "si
les débris sur lesquels M. le Marquis de Paulmy a composé sa chanson ne sont pas les véritables, nous sommes tentés de lui en savoir
gré; car il n'est guères possible de croire que l'ancienne chanson
fut aussi agréable et aussi expressive que la nouvelle."[56] In view of
all this, there is no cause for surprise at Le Grand's decision to exclude from his collection of *fabliaux* pieces whose grossness might
not contribute to the decorative effect of "grâce" and "naïveté"
which, according to the *Almanach des muses*,[57] was what readers
liked in the old poems. "Ce n'est point là dépouiller un Auteur,"

[52] *Poësies du Roy de Navarre*, Preface, pp. xviii–xix.
[53] *Fabliaux ou contes*, vol. 5, p. xxxii.
[54] *Voyage littéraire de Provence*, p. 390.
[55] Quoted from Percy's English translation, *Northern Antiquities* (London, 1770),
1:123. Cf. also pp. 231–33, 347, 352–53, 375–76.
[56] *Essai sur la musique* (Paris, 1780), 2:143.
[57] *Almanach des muses* (1778), Avertissement, vol. 1, p. lvii.

this disciple of Sainte-Palaye exclaimed; "c'est le mettre en état d'entrer chez les honnêtes gens."[58]

If the medievalists themselves did not commit themselves to taking medieval literature and medieval life seriously, it is equally difficult to find in their work an unequivocal indication of the general political significance they wished to give to their medievalism, supposing it were taken seriously. This uncertainty, as we have already suggested, is due in large measure to the fact that conservative thinking was as marked by Enlightenment as radical or revolutionary thinking. Mallet, for instance, was an arch-conservative in the politics of his native city of Geneva, and the praise he gives in his history of Denmark to the States General or Alting of Iceland, which he himself associated with other similar bodies—"the Als-heriarting of the other Scandinavian nations . . . the Wittena-Gomot or Parliament of the Anglo-Saxons . . . the Champ de Mars or de May of the French, . . . the Cortes of the Spaniards, etc."[59]— would not have been displeasing to noblemen or members of the parlements in France. His hatred of "despotism" which he shared with his master, Montesquieu, was of the same ilk as theirs. Yet Mallet's work, like Montesquieu's, could be integrated without much difficulty into a total context of ideas and intentions different from his own. His glowing picture of the ancient Danes with their "spirit of independence and equality" and their "elevation of soul" and the Rousseauist accents he borrowed as he associated the liberty of these early Norsemen with their rudeness, their rustic pursuits, their ignorance of the arts, and the extreme simplicity of their relations with each other,[60] were given a rousing and revolutionary significance by Herder when he reviewed Mallet's book in the first of his *Kritische Wälder* in 1769.[61] The fundamentally conservative meaning of Mallet's "republicanism" and "primitivism" and the radical difference between his thought and that of Rousseau can be detected now by the alert reader. (Mallet held, for instance, that even after the early Danes had been civilized, their freedom continued to find expression in their institutions, and he saw in the earliest of their laws not an instrument of domination by the rich,

---

[58] *Fabliaux ou contes*, vol. 1, Preface, p. lxxviii.
[59] *Northern Antiquities*, 1:178.   [60] *Ibid.*, pp. lii, 183.
[61] *Werke*, ed. Suphan, 3:24ü. Cf. also 'Uber die Wirkung der Dichtkunst auf die Sitten der Völker in alten und neuen Zeiten,' delivered before the Bavarian Academy in 1778 and published in its *Abhandlungen* (1781), *Werke* 8:389.

as Rousseau had done, but the achievement of wise men truly anxious to institute justice.)[62] But they do not impose themselves, and they were not obvious to contemporaries or even, perhaps, to Mallet himself.

There is nothing in Sainte-Palaye's work that distinguishes its tone from that of Mallet or Le Grand. His opinions of Old French poetry—of the poetry of Froissart in particular—have been alluded to in previous chapters, and we have seen how limited his appreciation of the Provençal poets was. The very fact that he willingly made his advice and his manuscripts available to writers of the stamp of La Borde, Tressan, and Paulmy indicates that he had as little respect or, indeed, feeling for the particular quality and merit of medieval literature as any of his contemporaries. As literature it was for him, as for them, an entertaining diversion, and he had no objection to anybody's shaping his materials into an eighteenth-century mold.

At the same time he did not object to the attribution of political and moral significance to his representation of the Middle Ages. "L'affoiblissement des moeurs anciennes, des moeurs généreuses et franches," he observed in a manuscript note, "nous a successivement enlevé non seulement un très grand nombre de termes énergiques, lumineux, nécessaires même, et remplacés par de foibles équivalens; mais un très grand nombre aussi de tournures naturelles, naives, simples comme la vérité et fortes comme elle. Dans ce tems de vertu et de bonheur, ou selon l'expression de Montaigne la vérité avoit sa 'franche allure,' dans ces jours où l'on osoit avoir un coeur et ne pas rougir de le prouver, on peignoit toute idée comme elle venoit d'être conçue, on rendoit tout sentiment comme il venoit d'être éprouvé. La nature ne risquait rien à paroistre. Ce n'est qu'avec les anciennes moeurs que renaîtront la *simplesse*, la *loyauté*, termes vénérables et propres au style du siècle de ces vertus. Régénérer en partie la langue de Montaigne, d'Amyot et de Sully, ce seroit peut-être régénérer les moeurs naïves de leurs siècles, car si les moeurs influent sur le langage, le langage influe à son tour sur les moeurs. Si les idées agissent sur les termes, les termes agissent sur les idées."[63]

We ourselves have tried to show that the view of chivalry and of the Middle Ages given in Sainte-Palaye's work was funda-

[62] *Northern Antiquities*, 1:165, 184.   [63] Moreau 1722, fol. 343.

mentally conservative in its import—while always bearing in mind that eighteenth-century conservatism is itself associated with Enlightenment and reform—but the reader of the *Mémoires* or the essays on Froissart was by no means obliged to come to this conclusion. He was perfectly free to entertain or not to entertain the thought that Sainte-Palaye's work seriously advocated moral, social, and political reform, and he was equally free to specify himself the kind of reform which he thought it supported. The very limitations of Sainte-Palaye's medievalism and primitivism—his disgust at the excesses, the brutality, and the grossness of knightly behavior, for instance—could be construed to mean that he was opposed to glorification of the old nobility and committed to modern civilization, that is, to the civilization of the ancien régime in its final phase; but this very commitment could also be read as one of the most important signs of his underlying conservatism.

This quality of openness to many interpretations is characteristic of a large body of literature in the eighteenth century. One of its most concrete manifestations is the literary mystification, by which the reader was made to take responsibility for ascribing the authorship or determining the authenticity, indeed the meaning, of a given work. One of Hume's main objections to the Ossian poems was the fact that their "editor" and "translator" insisted on their authenticity, instead of allowing the public to exercise its wit upon them and to play the game of belief and disbelief at its pleasure. The value of ambiguity, which would have been incomprehensible to nineteenth-century scholars (Mérimée is one of the rare nineteenth-century writers who continued the tradition of mystifications), was accepted as naturally by most eighteenth-century primitivists and medievalists as by other eighteenth-century writers, and the exceptional case of Macpherson serves only to prove the rule. We have already come across the *Chanson de Roland* allegedly "discovered" by Paulmy. On the other side of the Channel, the Scotsman Pinkerton argued openly for the right of medievalists to practice some innocent and pleasure-giving mystifications.[64]

Sainte-Palaye's work falls wholly into this characteristically eighteenth century tradition. The *Mémoires*, the *Histoire littéraire*

---

[64] *Ancient Scottish Poems* (1786), Preface. Pinkerton was, after all, only claiming for literature what was readily allowed in architecture, where the construction of "ruins" was by no means unusual.

des troubadours, the essays on Froissart convey the Enlightenment antiquarian's delight in the color and pageantry of the medieval past. There is also in them a note of nostalgia for an age of greater expressiveness and independence of spirit than the contemporary one. But this nostalgia was by no means unambiguous. It received its meaning and its emphasis not from the author but from the reader. If the latter chose to abandon himself to it, it easily became sentimental; if he chose to maintain or to resume his self-awareness, it became tinged with irony; the most agile reader, however, knew how to adopt both these attitudes at the same time, so that he experienced the ambiguity of Sainte-Palaye's medievalism not in successive and alternating moments but simultaneously and directly, as its very essence. In so doing he was able to reconcile in thought and feeling, if not in practice, several conflicting tendencies in the Enlightenment itself: acceptance of the values of modern civilization and longing for spontaneity and renewal, eagerness for reform and apprehension of change, allegiance to law and order and desire for freedom.

CHAPTER 2

THE PLACE OF SAINTE-PALAYE'S WORK IN THE HISTORY OF HISTORIOGRAPHY AND OF HISTORICAL SCHOLARSHIP

During the heyday of positivism, eighteenth century historiography came under a cloud. Even its actual scholarly achievements were not widely recognized and its propagandist tone was frowned upon. More recently, there has been a revival of interest in Enlightenment historiography and since Dilthey's essay on *Das achzehnte Jahrhundert und die geschichtliche Welt*[1] it has been the object of several reappraisals. The most influential of these, after Dilthey's own, was probably Friedrich Meinecke's *Die Entstehung des Historismus*. The lasting effect of this work has been to have shifted the emphasis in the history of historiography from the Romantic movement to a wider current of ideas, which has its source much further back than Romanticism and within which, as Herbert Butterfield suggested in a recent book, the Romantic attitude to the past might even have been something of an aberration.[2] It now appears that the roots of nineteenth-century historicism are in the intellectual world of the Enlightenment. In particular, the elaboration by the thinkers of the Enlightenment of a naturalist, historical view and their growing consciousness, within this framework, of the historicity of all things, human as well as natural, prepared the way—according to both Dilthey and Meinecke—for the rise of historicism.

While there is much to learn from this *rapprochement* of eighteenth-century historiography and nineteenth-century histori-

---

[1] *Gesammelte Schriften* (Leipzig and Berlin, 1901), 3:207–75.

[2] H. Butterfield, *Man on His Past* (Cambridge, 1955). Among other recent reappraisals of eighteenth-century historiography, see R. Stadelmann, 'Die Romantik und die Geschichte,' in *Romantik, ein Zyklus Tübinger Vorlesungen*, ed. T. Steinbüchel (Tübingen and Stuttgart, 1948), pp. 151–76; G. Giarizzo, 'Cultura illuministica e mondo settecentesco,' *Itinerari* (1956), 4:514–33; U. Marcelli, 'L'antistorico secolo decimottavo,' *Convivium* (1956), 24:385–93.

cism, and while it has served to correct some crude notions concerning the Enlightenment conception of history, there may also be much in it that is misleading. Significant differences remain between the goals and methods of Enlightenment historiography on the one hand and historicism on the other. Although the Enlightenment scholars and historians were among the first to see the whole culture of an age as a unity, they seem not, in general, to have had the idea of the uniqueness of historical cultures that was so essential a part of historicist thought. Their aim was not to understand particular cultures, but to discern the general laws of human behavior and of social organization: "the uniform steps of civilization in all ancient and modern nations."[3] These laws were conceived of as themselves not subject to historical determination or change, but fixed and unvarying, like the laws of physics or, indeed, of thought. Understanding them, it was hoped, man could limit the tyranny they had exercised on him heretofore. If it was important that the people be enlightened—as Montesquieu claimed in the Preface to the *Esprit des lois*—this was because it was expected that man would do better for himself when he acted in full knowledge of the laws and determinations of the social world, when, consequently, he understood what the limited choices open to him were and what would be the consequences of these choices, than he had done when he acted blindly and, as it were, instinctively.

Together with all the members of his school—and Sainte-Palaye must be included in it, even though the *Mémoires* antedate the *Esprit des lois* by a few years—Montesquieu believed that reason could mediate between the present and the past. It was widely realized that man's thought itself was part of history and subject to its determinations, but few eighteenth-century historians can have imagined that their own thought was in turn determined and limited by their historical situation. It was only mythical thinking that was historically determined, and reason, which revealed myth for what it was and freed men from it, was by that very power and activity independent of history. Montesquieu believed himself free of "prejudice," having understood its workings, and Marat, when he pointed to the unconscious prejudices of Montesquieu—"Montesquieu," he said, "possessed a great fortune in

[3] Pinkerton, *History of Scotland* (London, 1797), 1:340. Similarly Robertson, 'View of the State of Europe,' *Works*, p. 14.

landed property; he came from a family of notables; he had a wife and children; what a lot of ties!"[4]—believed doubtless that *he* had none.[5] The eighteenth-century historians thought they could write the laws of history and even the historical laws of thought, but not of their own thought, which for them, precisely because they recognized "prejudice," remained rational, impartial, philosophical, and thus free from historical determination. They did not, therefore, doubt their own categories or that their goal should be to master the social and historical world as effectively as the natural scientists had mastered the physical one. Far from emphasizing the distinction between the human and the natural sciences, Montesquieu and all his followers—Mallet, Sainte-Palaye, Robertson, Millar, Smith—sought to reduce it and to model the study of man on the successful sciences of nature. It is entirely appropriate that Montesquieu was widely referred to as the Newton of the social and historical world.

Both the object and the method of the eighteenth-century historians were thus different from those of nineteenth-century historicism. The general rather than the particular interested them, and their model was a mechanism of functionally interrelated parts, each of which could, in principle, be detached and studied on its own rather than an organism, all of whose parts are bound inseparably together, so that they cannot even be conceived properly apart from the whole. Thus, Sainte-Palaye saw that medieval chivalry bore the stamp of the culture of which it was part and that it could be understood only in relation to other aspects of medieval life and society, but he did not think that chivalry as such was unique to the Middle Ages and an inseparable part of medieval life. The same type of organization, according to his way of thinking, could appear at different moments in history, in different guises, as part of similarly structured societies and to fulfill similar needs—and he was interested in the *type* as much as in the

---

[4] Quoted by J. Dedieu, *Montesquieu* (1913), p. 323.

[5] It has been pointed out that early forms of a sociology of knowledge can be found in the thought of the Enlightenment (where the figure of Fontenelle springs to mind) and indeed earlier still; see Robert Merton, 'Karl Mannheim and the Sociology of Knowledge,' *Journal of Liberal Religion* (1941), 2:124-47. Merton also clarifies, however, that a sociology of knowledge, properly speaking, emerged only when the 'special' formulation of the concept of ideology was extended to a 'general' formulation—that is, one which regards not simply the thought of adversaries as a function of social or historical situation, but all thought, including the critic's own.

particular manifestation. It is quite consistent with this way of thinking that he believed the "institution" of chivalry, suitably modified, could be made part of a reformed monarchy in his own time and that it could in fact be made to "work" better there than in the imperfect monarchical state of the Middle Ages.

Since the members of the historicist school viewed each culture as a unique and entirely integrated whole, on an organic rather than a mechanical model, they could not approach their object in the same way as their eighteenth-century predecessors. Indeed, they came more and more to emphasize the difference between the humanities and the sciences and to demand for the former methods and a mode of understanding appropriate to them. Often the historical understanding was found to be closer to the artistic than to the scientific understanding, and the aim of history seemed more to achieve a contemplation of the past than a grasp of the means required to control the present. In extreme cases, since the aim was to get at the historical object from the inside, to mimic it in a way, the historical understanding came close to a kind of communication of consciousnesses, similar to that established by the poet or the artist "carrying everywhere with him relationship and love," as Wordsworth said, and binding together "by passion and knowledge the vast empire of human society, as it is spread over the whole earth, and over all time."[6] In the imaginative Verstehen of the past, as Dilthey described it, for instance, "kann der von innen determinierte Mensch in der Imagination viele andere Existenzen erleben. Vor dem durch die Umstände Beschränkten tun sich fremde Schönheiten der Welt auf und Gegenden des Lebens, die er nie erreichen kann. Ganz allgemein gesprochen: der durch die Realität des Lebens gebundene und bestimmte Mensch wird nicht nur durch die Kunst—was öfter entwickelt ist —sondern auch durch das Verstehen des Geschichtlichen in Freiheit versetzt."[7]

In this passage, it is already apparent that history and the understanding of other cultures is coming to assume a new role. History here opens the doors to that realm of truly human values, which increasingly in the nineteenth century was set over against the

[6] Quoted in Raymond Williams, Culture and Society 1780–1950 (Penguin Books, 1966; first ed., 1958), p. 58.
[7] 'Plan der Fortsetzung zum Aufbau der geschichtlichen Welt in den Geisteswissenschaften,' Gesammelte Schriften, 7:216.

realm of actual social living. Culture, organic unity, is opposed to "civilization," the mere assemblage of atomic elements smoothed and refined so that they will "work" together with minimum friction like a good machine invented by Utilitarians. Through this opposition, the living spiritual and human aspects of social life—the culture properly so called—come to act as a superior court of appeal before which all particular social arrangements can be judged, but at the same time they are more and more idealized and divorced from the reified, "outward" forms of social life—the family, the clan, the state. This opposition has been studied with great understanding for England by Raymond Williams (*Culture and Society, 1780-1950* [London, 1958]), but it is found in all European thought from Herder and Humboldt through Dilthey to Scheler and beyond. While it is incipient in the eighteenth century, it does not play the role in eighteenth-century historiography that it plays in that of the nineteenth century.

The Enlightenment did indeed begin that expansion of the field of cultural history and of the very notion of culture which is one of the distinguishing marks of the modern as opposed to the humanist vision of the world, and Sainte-Palaye's contribution to this movement was an important one. But the notion of culture which developed in the nineteenth century could only have developed, in all probability, dialectically, in opposition to the immediate reality of "non-culture," the soulless, mechanical society of industrial capitalism. There is, in short, a line that leads from the cultural history of the eighteenth century to nineteenth-century historicism, but it does not lead there directly or inevitably. The men of the Enlightenment would have found themselves at least as much at home with certain of the Utilitarians or even with the "structuralist" thinkers of the mid-twentieth century as with the historicists of the nineteenth century. When Paul Landsberg referred to historicism as a "Radikalisierung der Aufklärung,"[8] he may thus have been partly right, but it was a radicalization that expressed a different outlook and different preoccupations from those of the Enlightenment and that significantly altered its character.

Two aspects of Enlightenment historiography which have been rather neglected in popular accounts of it are its prodigious achievement of research and its contribution to critical methods.

---

[8] 'Zur Soziologie der Erkenntnistheorie,' *Schmollers Jahrbuch* (1931), 55:769-808.

As both of them are rather well illustrated by Sainte-Palaye's career, a final word about them might not be out of place here. It is simply not true, for instance, as Gooch claimed, that it was Ranke who "founded the science of evidence by the analysis of authority, contemporary or otherwise, in the light of the author's temperament, affiliations, and opportunity of knowledge and by comparison with the testimony of other writers."[9] Butterfield corrected Gooch's view but only to attribute the development of the critical method to the Göttingen school.[10] In fact, as we have seen, a large part of the program which Butterfield ascribes to the Göttingen scholars—the idea of universal history, concerted plans of research, expansion of the range of historical sources, systematic criticism of these sources—had been at least adumbrated and had been in part executed at the French Académie des Inscriptions between 1726 and the outbreak of the Revolution. What Butterfield calls "the greatest achievement of the historical understanding— the recovery and exposition of the medieval world" was, likewise, deliberately planned by the medievalists at the Académie des Inscriptions—Falconet, Sainte-Palaye, Secousse, Foncemagne, and Bréquigny—some decades before the school of Göttingen came into existence. Scholars like Foncemagne and Sainte-Palaye had also anticipated Gatterer and Schlözer to some degree in the idea which they formed of the place of scholarship and research in the wider framework of general history. Both had a vision of history which enabled them to see further than the mere document or fact, and both were aware that the sources of history are not limited to written accounts or even to documents; hence, their efforts to bring new materials within the scope of historical scholarship and to work out methods for exploiting them.[11]

The scholars and historians of the nineteenth century continued

---

[9] *History and Historians in the Nineteenth Century* (2d ed.; London, 1952), p. 97.
[10] Butterfield, p. 61.
[11] See, for instance, a memorandum by Foncemagne concerning the publication of the sources of French history: "On a reconnu depuis longtemps combien il seroit important d'avoir une histoire de notre monarchie dans laquelle, outre les faits militaires, on fît connoitre l'esprit et les principes du gouvernement, la politique à l'égard des puissances voisines, les moeurs, les usages, les coutumes de la nation, son agriculture, son commerce, ses droits, ses privilèges, les changemens qu'ont éprouvés ces différens objets et les causes qui les ont opérés. On a reconnu pareillement que l'unique moyen de parvenir à executer cette entreprise étoit de commencer par recueillir les actes, les chroniques, les chartes et autres pièces de toute espèce qui doivent servir de base à l'immense édifice qu'on veut élever." (B.N. Nouv. Acq. Fr. 3294, fol. 212.)

their work. The *Table chronologique* and the *Notices et extraits des manuscrits* were resumed after the Revolution, as were two similar enterprises which had been begun by the Benedictines and in which Sainte-Palaye had played a part—the *Histoire littéraire de la France* and the *Recueil des historiens*. Guizot drew up a plan for the publication of the chronicle sources of medieval French history—a plan which had already been worked out and put forward in the eighteenth century by members of the Académie des Inscriptions and of which Dacier's edition of Froissart was to have been the first fruit.[12] Other institutions were founded—the École des Chartes, the Société de l'Histoire de France—and other collections begun, such as the series put out by the Société des Anciens Textes Français, which carried forward the exploration of the Middle Ages begun by Sainte-Palaye and his colleagues a century before.

Sainte-Palaye's own labors won generous recognition from later scholars aware of the history of their discipline. Paul Meyer invariably paid tribute to a great predecessor and regretted that so much of his work had remained unpublished in his lifetime.[13] Baldensperger described Sainte-Palaye's contribution to medieval literary and historical studies as "le plus colossal effort qui soit tenté par un travailleur de cette époque."[14] Sainte-Palaye had in fact done a great deal for medieval studies. If he actually published little, he brought the weight of his enthusiasm and of his experience to bear on the limited circle of the scholars of his age. At the Académie des Inscriptions he fought for and won a place for medieval studies which put them on a par with classical studies. By building around himself a nucleus of medievalists, by encouraging and training a number of younger men to carry on his work (Bréquigny, Mouchet, Le Grand d'Aussy),[15] by drawing the at-

[12] The plan is outlined twice in Foncemagne's papers: in the memorandum quoted above, note 11, and in a letter requesting government support for it. (Nouv. Acq. Fr. 5853, fols. 18–23, dated 25.1.1777.) It was in fact approved, and Dacier was awarded a pension of 4,000 livres, according to a marginal note in the letter.

[13] Paul Meyer, 'Études sur la Chanson de Gérard de Roussillon,' *Bibl. Éc. des Chartes* (5ᵉ série, 1861), 2:48.

[14] 'Le Genre Troubadour,' *Études d'histoire littéraire*, 1ère série (Paris, 1907), p. 116.

[15] Le Grand's ambiguous attitude to medieval literature should not obscure the value of his scholarly contribution. His analyses of manuscripts in the Academy's *Notices et extraits* and his own researches in the libraries of Belgium (his collection of 'Extraits et notices des MSS de Belgique' is in B.N. Nouv. Acq. Fr. 6228) show that he was a conscientious pupil of Sainte-Palaye.

tention of his colleagues to some of the main problems of medieval scholarship, and by his efforts to bring the study of the Middle Ages into the mainstream of contemporary historiography, he enriched and modernized medieval scholarship in France.

Yet, he does not fit the image of the scholar created by the nineteenth century. Hostile as they were to the new—and sometimes dangerous—philosophical movements of their day, suspicious of any questioning of the bourgeois order of which they were part, many academic historians and scholars of the nineteenth century made an absolute of the fact and of the scholarly labor of finding it. They wished not to question, judge, or interpret their facts in the framework of a general philosophy of history but simply to collect them. They thought that "science" could do without philosophy and that history was a science, not realizing that their very rejection of the philosophy of history was itself a philosophical and methodological position which philosophy was entitled to examine. In their eyes scholarship was free of all partisan bias, the result of a kind of ascesis on the part of those who practiced it. The virtues they recognized and admired in Sainte-Palaye were those of the scholar as they saw him—self-abnegation, tireless labor, utter dedication to the task, whatever it might be.

The eighteenth-century scholar, however, bore only slight resemblance to this ideal of the saintly servant of erudition. He was not without a kind of antiquarian curiosity—indeed, without a dose of this curiosity he would not, possibly, have been what he was—but it was not the same thing as the nineteenth-century positivist's devotion to fact, for the eighteenth-century scholar himself accepted the need to transform his antiquarianism and to put it at the service of the new thought of the Enlightenment. He pursued "facts" eagerly, but so that they would serve as "foundations for reasonings" in Pinkerton's phrase.[16] However guarded their attitude to the *philosophes* might have been, the scholars of the Enlightenment were deeply affected by the Enlightenment passion

---

[16] The early archaeologist Thomas Pownall likewise pleaded that minute study of particulars without any view to the wider framework of history is as sterile as general systems of history which are not grounded in knowledge and understanding of the particulars. "The upstart fungus of system is poison to the mind" but "to make cumbrous collections of numberless particulars . . . and to admire them merely as they are antique . . . is not a true religious study of antiquities, but a devotion for relicks." (*A Treatise on the Study of Antiquities* [London, 1782], pp. 3, 53–55.)

for ideas, indeed they felt *obliged* by it. They believed it was ideas men had to appropriate—not things or objects. Their facts thus had to be revealed to the public as ideas; they had to be interpreted, made significant, and transformed into *thought*. Whatever disagreements the eighteenth-century scholars may have had with the *philosophes* occurred, in short, within the broad context of a single, shared ideology; the positivism of the nineteenth-century scholars, on the other hand, however much it might present itself as a refusal of ideology, was itself an ideology which competed for men's minds with other leading ideologies of the day, notably Hegelianism and Marxism.

The history of scholarship, as indeed of civilization, rests on the assumption that there is a real continuity in human effort and that the achievements of one generation can be passed on to the next, but it also requires us to recognize the particular nature of each generation's work and its relation to the total context in which it was carried out. Sainte-Palaye's orientation toward medieval studies was due in part to the traditions and interests of the social group to which he belonged, while his approach was determined in large measure by the special place which that group occupied in the development of the bourgeoisie and of bourgeois values and ways of thinking in France. The results of his work could be and were put to use by later medievalists, but it would be a mistake to see his interest in the Middle Ages simply as an anticipation of the interest which nineteenth-century scholars had in the Middle Ages. Hating what they saw around them—the atomization of society, the spiritual and physical domination of men by machines, the degradation of human values by the fetishism of the market—nineteenth-century writers from Cobbett, Nodier, and Southey, to Ruskin and William Morris came to see in the Middle Ages a historically real embodiment, not perhaps of the perfect culture, but at least of a culture, as opposed to the mere organization of humanity for the production of material goods which their own society seemed to them to be. In the mind and experience of Sainte-Palaye and his associates the Middle Ages did not, and could not, have this meaning. Nor in the eighteenth century did it have the other, subsidiary though not unrelated meanings, that it acquired in the nineteenth. It did not represent a golden past to which the aristocracy looked back nostalgically—the eighteenth century aristocracy did not make the mistake of confusing itself with the feudal nobility; and it did not serve as a remote world of purely technical historical and scholarly—"scientific"—problems in which escape could be sought from the pressing and difficult choices and commitments demanded by contemporary life. Sainte-Palaye and his fellow medievalists of the eighteenth century were more active and achieved more than is generally known; their work should be understood, however, as part of the civilization of the Enlightenment and in the light of their own experience as a particular group of men living through a particular period in history.

WORKS BY LA CURNE DE SAINTE-PALAYE

Manuscript

Agathocle, tyran de Syracuse, Registres de l'Académie des Inscriptions, 1724, pp. 545–65.

Notices de divers manuscrits de France et d'Italie, Moreau 1654–61, 8 vols. in-folio (first version), Moreau 1662–76, 15 vols. in-quarto (second version).

Dictionnaire des antiquités françoises, Moreau 1511–23, 13 vols. in-folio (first version), Arsenal 4277–4353, 77 vols. in-quarto (second version).

Supplément au Dictionnaire des antiquités françoises, Arsenal 4354–70, 17 vols. in-quarto.

Printed

'Remarques sur la vie de Romulus par Plutarque,' *MAI** 7:114–26.

'Notice d'un manuscrit intitulé Vita Karoli Magni,' *MAI** 7:280–86.

'Observations sur quelques chapitres du deuxième livre de la première décade de Tite-Live comparés au texte de Denys d'Halicarnasse,' *MAI* 7:363–71.

'Mémoire concernant la vie et les ouvrages de Glaber, historien du temps de Hugues Capet,' *MAI* 8:549–59.

'Mémoire concernant la vie et les ouvrages de Rigord et de Guillaume le Breton,' *MAI* 8:528–48.

'Mémoire sur la vie et les ouvrages de Guillaume de Nangis et ses continuateurs,' *MAI* 8:560–78.

'Mémoire sur la Chronique de Morigny et sur les auteurs qui l'ont composée,' *MAI* 10:541–52.

'Mémoire sur la vie du moine Helgaud, sur l'Épitome de la vie du roi Robert, et sur trois fragments qui sont imprimés à la suite de cette Épitome dans la collection des Historiens de France,' *MAI* 10:553–62.

'Mémoire sur deux ouvrages historiques concernant Louis VII, intitulés, l'un Gesta Ludovici VII regis filii Ludovici grossi, et l'autre Historia gloriosi regis Ludovici grossi ab anno 1137 usque ad annum 1165, et sur les auteurs anonymes de ces ouvrages,' *MAI* 10:563–70.

'Mémoire concernant la vie de Froissart,' *MAI* 10:664–90.

'Mémoire concernant les ouvrages de Froissart,' *MAI* 13:534–54.

'Jugement de l'Histoire de Froissart,' *MAI* 13:555–79.

> The above papers on Froissart republished by Buchon, *Collection des chroniques nationales françaises* (Paris, 1824–28), 10:1–97.
>
> English translation: *Memoirs of the Life of Froissart with an Essay on His Works and a Criticism of His History*, translated from the French of Mr de la Curne de St. Palaye by Thomas Johnes. London, 1801. 2d edition, London, 1810.
>
> Reprinted in Johnes' edition of the *Chronicles*, vol. 1 (London, 1802–5), and once more in the 2d ed. (London, 1805–6).

'Mémoire concernant la vie de Jean de Venette, avec la notice de l'histoire en vers des Trois Maries, dont il est l'auteur,' *MAI* 13:520–23.

'Notice des poésies de Froissart,' *MAI* * 14:219–26.

'Mémoire concernant les principaux monumens de l'histoire de France, avec la notice et l'histoire des Chroniques de Saint-Denys,' *MAI* 15:580–616.

'Mémoire concernant la lecture des anciens romans de chevalerie,' *MAI* 17:787–99.

'Mémoires sur l'ancienne chevalerie considérée comme un établissement politique et militaire,' *MAI* 20:597–847.

> Published separately, Paris, 1759. 2 vols.
>
> 2d edition, with 'Mémoires historiques sur la chasse.' 3 vols. Paris, 1781.
>
> New edition, by Charles Nodier. Paris, 1826.
>
> Extracts printed in *Extraits des mémoires de Commines.* Geneva, 1829.
>
> Adaptation by Armand de Solignac. Limoges, 1877.
>
> English translation: *Memoirs of Ancient Chivalry.* London, 1784.
>
> German translation: *Das Ritterwesen des Mittelalters nach seiner politischen und militärischen Verfassung.* 3 vols. Nurnberg, 1789–91.
>
> Polish translation: *Wiadomosci historyczne o dawnym Rycerstwie zwazanym iako Ustanowienie polityczne y zolnierskie.* Warsaw, 1772.

'Lettre à M. de la Bruère sur le projet d'une place pour la statue du Roy.' *Mercure*, July, 1748, pp. 147–53.

> Reprinted in *Lettres de divers auteurs sur le projet d'une place devant la colonnade du Louvre pour y mettre la statue équestre du Roy,* Paris, 1749. (Copies rare; one in Paris, B.N. 8° lk^7 7283.)

Lettre de M. de S. P. à M. de B. sur le bon goût dans les arts et dans les lettres, Paris, 1751. (Copies rare; one in Paris, B.N. ZP 2118.)

'Remarques sur la langue françoise des XIIe et XIIIe siècles comparée avec les langues provençale, italienne et espagnole dans les mêmes siècles,' *MAI* 24:671–86.

> Reprinted by J. M. C. Leber, *Collection des meilleures dissertations*, Paris, 1826–38, 14:278–300.

'Histoire ou romance d'Aucassin et Nicolette, tirée d'un ancien manuscrit,' *Mercure*, February, 1752, pp. 10–64.

> Reprinted with 'La Châtelaine de Saint Gilles' as *Les Amours du bon vieux temps*, Vaucluse and Paris, 1756. 2d edition, Vaucluse and Paris, 1760.
> Republished by Mario Roques, *C'est d'Aucassin et de Nicolete . . . Chantefable du XIIIe siècle*, Paris, 1936.

'Notice de deux manuscrits du livre intitulé Le Jouvencel conférés avec l'exemplaire imprimé,' *MAI* 26:700–27.

Projet d'un glossaire françois, Paris, 1756. (Copies rare; one in Paris, B.N. Rés. X–4826.)

Glossaire de l'ancienne langue françoise, one volume printed, without title page, shortly before the Revolution. (Three copies in Paris, B.N. X–504, Rés. X–231, Rés. X–232.)

Dictionnaire historique de l'ancien langage français, ou glossaire de la langue française depuis son origine jusqu'au siècle de Louis XIV. 10 vols. Niort, 1875–82. (This work was edited by Lucien Favre from the manuscript of Sainte-Palaye's Glossary, Moreau 1524–54 [31 vols. in-folio] and Moreau 1588–1648 [a later version of 61 vols. in-quarto].)

Histoire littéraire des troubadours. 3 vols. Paris, 1774.

> English translation: *The Literary History of the Troubadours*, London, 1779. 2d ed., London, 1807.

Table chronologique des diplômes, chartes, titres et actes imprimés concernant l'histoire de France. 8 vols. Paris, 1769–1876. (This work, begun by Secousse and Sainte-Palaye, was continued by Bréquigny and Pardessus in the later eighteenth century and by La Boulaye in the nineteenth.)

Catalogue des tableaux du cabinet de M. Crozat, baron de Thiers. Paris, 1755. (This work is attributed to Sainte-Palaye in the catalogue of the Bibliothèque Nationale, probably on the basis of a pencil note in the Réserve copy, V–2438. While Sainte-Palaye was certainly collecting antiquities for Crozat in Italy, according to his letters to Bachaumont and Madame Doublet in 1749, I have come across no evidence that this catalogue is by him. The attribution seems to me uncertain.)

SAINTE-PALAYE'S EXAMINATION OF THE MANUSCRIPTS OF FROISSART

Book 1

	Sainte-Palaye			Luce
Bib. Reg.	6760	(B.N. Français	86)	A–20
Bib. Reg.	8317	(B.N. Français	2640)	A–11
Bib. Reg.	8318	(B.N. Français	2641)	A– 8
Bib. Reg.	8319	(B.N. Français	2642)	A– 9
Bib. Reg.	8320	(B.N. Français	2643)	A–23
Bib. Reg.	8324	(B.N. Français	2649)	A– 2
Bib. Reg.	8331^2	(B.N. Français	2662)	A–18
Bib. Reg.	8332	(B.N. Français	2663)	A– 3
Bib. Reg.	8334–6	(B.N. Français	2665–7)	A–24
Bib. Reg.	8343	(B.N. Français	2674)	A– 4
Séguier-Coislin	169	(B.N. Français	15486–9)	A–25
Colbert	15	(B.N. Français	2675)	A–12
Colbert	85	(B.N. Français	2657)	A–13
Colbert	231	(B.N. Français	2655)	A– 7

Book 2

				Raynaud
Bib. Reg.	8321	(B.N. Français	2644)	B–13
Bib. Reg.	8330	(B.N. Français	2660)	B– 4
Bib. Reg.	8333	(B.N. Français	2664)	A– 7
Bib. Reg.	8337–8	(B.N. Français	2668–9)	B– 9
Colbert	16	(B.N. Français	2676)	B– 7
Colbert	86	(B.N. Français	2658)	A– 8

Book 3

Bib. Reg.	8325	(B.N. Français	2650)
Bib. Reg.	8328	(B.N. Français	2653)
Bib. Reg.	8337–8	(B.N. Français	2668–9)
Colbert	87	(B.N. Français	2659)
Colbert	232	(B.N. Français	2656)

Book 4

Bib. Reg.	8329	(B.N. Français	2654)
Bib. Reg.	8331	(B.N. Français	2661)
Bib. Reg.	8341–2	(B.N. Français	2672–3)
Colbert	17	(B.N. Français	2648)

SAINTE-PALAYE'S COLLATIONS OF MANUSCRIPTS OF *FABLIAUX*

Gaignat	1750	(Arsenal	3142)
Bib. Reg.	7218	(B.N. Français	837)
Bib. Reg.	$7534^{3.3}$	(B.N. Français	1446)
Bib. Reg.	7989^2	(B.N. Français	1593)
Bib. Reg.	7935^6	(B.N. Français	2043)
Saint-Germain	1830	(B.N. Français	19152)
Notre-Dame	N2	(B.N. Français	25545)
Berne, Bibl.	354	(no change)	

Turin, Bib. Reg. $G.1.19^1$ (Turin, Bib. Univ. L.v.32)

Sainte-Palaye's collated transcripts are preserved in B.N. Moreau 1680–83 and in Arsenal 2763–67.

APPENDIX 4

SAINTE-PALAYE'S COPIES OF PROVENÇAL *CHANSONNIERS*

1. Sainte-Palaye's copy	2. Sainte-Palaye's classification		3. Old description	4. Present day description	5. Jeanroy's classification [1]
Arsenal	3091	*A*	Bib. Reg. 7226	B.N. 856	*C*
Arsenal	3092	*B*	Copy by Lancelot of a MS of Peiresc	Oxford, Bodley Douce 269[2]	*S*
Arsenal	3092	*C*	Bib. Reg. 7614	B.N. 1592	*B*
Arsenal	3093	*D*	Bib. Reg. 7225	B.N. 854	*I*
Arsenal	3094	*E*	Bib. Reg. 7698	B.N. 1749	*E*
Arsenal	3094–95	*G*[3]	Bib. d'Urfé	B.N. 22543	*R*
Arsenal	3096	*H*	Vatican 3794	B.N. 12474	*M*
Arsenal	3096	*I*	Vatican 3204	B.N. 12473	*K*
Arsenal	3096	*K*	Modena, Estense IV.163	Modena, Estense R.4.4	*D*
Arsenal	3097	*L*	Florence, Laur. Plut.XLI.42	unchanged	*P*
Arsenal	3097	*M*	Florence, Laur. Plut.XLI.43	unchanged	*U*
Arsenal	3097	*N*	Florence, Ricc. 2909	unchanged	*Q*
Arsenal	3097	*O*	Rome, Chig. 2348	Rome, Chig. L.iv.106	*F*
Arsenal	3097	*P*	Vatican 3208	unchanged	*O*
Arsenal	3097	*Q*	Vatican 3206	unchanged	*l*
Arsenal	3097	*R*	Vatican 3207	unchanged	*H*
Arsenal	3098	*S*	MS of Caumont	B.N. 15211	*T*
Arsenal	3098	*T*	Vatican 5232	unchanged	*A*
Arsenal	3098	*V*	Rome, Barberini XLVI.29. n.a. 2777	Vatican, Barb. 4087	*b*
Arsenal	3098	*X*	Milan, Ambros. R.71 supp.	unchanged	*G*
Arsenal	3309[4]	—	Big. Reg. 7227, 7619	B.N. 858, 1601	∝

Sainte-Palaye made notices of the following manuscripts containing Provençal poetry:

Moreau 1658, fol. 65			Venice, Bib. Marc. App. cod. XI	unchanged	*V*

| Moreau 1658, fol. 102 | Vatican 3205 | unchanged | g |
| Arsenal 3098, fol. 119 | "Copie des premiers feuillets" of Verona Saibante 410, a copy of Vatican 5232 | now lost | — |

Other manuscripts containing Provençal poems consulted by Sainte-Palaye:

| Florence, Ricc. 2981[5] | description unchanged | F^a |
| Florence, Ricc. 2814[6] | description unchanged | a |

Notes

[1] Jeanroy's classification (*Bibliographie des chansonniers provençaux*) is substantially the same as that of Bartsch. The more recent *Bibliographie des troubadours* of Pillet and Carstens (Halle, 1933) makes only slight changes.

[2] The Bodleian manuscript is the original manuscript of Peiresc.

[3] Chabaneau emits conjectures about Sainte-Palaye's copy F (*Revue des langues romanes* [1881], 19:76; [1885], 26:45). There is in fact no manuscript F among Sainte-Palaye's papers. The simplest explanation is that Sainte-Palaye avoided F for fear of confusion with E, just as he avoided J, U, and W.

[4] This is a collated text of Matfre Ermengau's *Breviari d'amor*. Although he did not group it with the other *chansonniers*, Sainte-Palaye refers to it frequently in the *Extraits* (Arsenal 3281–84).

[5] At the head of his copy of Chigi 2348 (Arsenal 3097) Sainte-Palaye refers to this Riccardiana manuscript as a copy of the Chigi one.

[6] A brief account of this manuscript is given in Bréquigny 65, fols. 119–48.

TROUBADOURS MENTIONED OR DISCUSSED FOR THE FIRST TIME IN THE *HISTOIRE LITTÉRAIRE DES TROUBADOURS*[1]

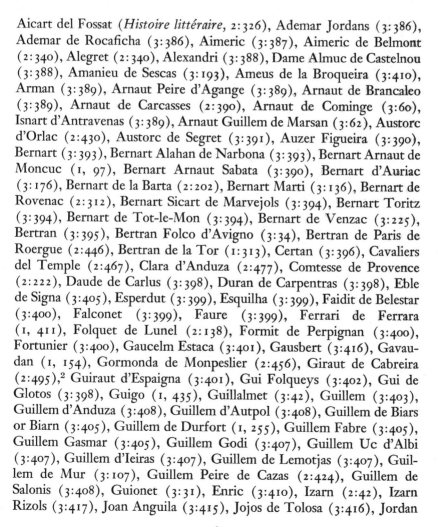

Aicart del Fossat (*Histoire littéraire*, 2:326), Ademar Jordans (3:386), Ademar de Rocaficha (3:386), Aimeric (3:387), Aimeric de Belmont (2:340), Alegret (2:340), Alexandri (3:388), Dame Almuc de Castelnou (3:388), Amanieu de Sescas (3:193), Ameus de la Broqueira (3:410), Arman (3:389), Arnaut Peire d'Agange (3:389), Arnaut de Brancaleo (3:389), Arnaut de Carcasses (2:390), Arnaut de Cominge (3:60), Isnart d'Antravenas (3:389), Arnaut Guillem de Marsan (3:62), Austorc d'Orlac (2:430), Austorc de Segret (3:391), Auzer Figueira (3:390), Bernart (3:393), Bernart Alahan de Narbona (3:393), Bernart Arnaut de Moncuc (1, 97), Bernart Arnaut Sabata (3:390), Bernart d'Auriac (3:176), Bernart de la Barta (2:202), Bernart Marti (3:136), Bernart de Rovenac (2:312), Bernart Sicart de Marvejols (3:394), Bernart Toritz (3:394), Bernart de Tot-le-Mon (3:394), Bernart de Venzac (3:225), Bertran (3:395), Bertran Folco d'Avigno (3:34), Bertran de Paris de Roergue (2:446), Bertran de la Tor (1:313), Certan (3:396), Cavaliers del Temple (2:467), Clara d'Anduza (2:477), Comtesse de Provence (2:222), Daude de Carlus (3:398), Duran de Carpentras (3:398), Eble de Signa (3:405), Esperdut (3:399), Esquilha (3:399), Faidit de Belestar (3:400), Falconet (3:399), Faure (3:399), Ferrari de Ferrara (1, 411), Folquet de Lunel (2:138), Formit de Perpignan (3:400), Fortunier (3:400), Gaucelm Estaca (3:401), Gausbert (3:416), Gavaudan (1, 154), Gormonda de Monpeslier (2:456), Giraut de Cabreira (2:495),[2] Guiraut d'Espaigna (3:401), Gui Folqueys (3:402), Gui de Glotos (3:398), Guigo (1, 435), Guillalmet (3:42), Guillem (3:403), Guillem d'Anduza (3:408), Guillem d'Autpol (3:408), Guillem de Biars or Biarn (3:405), Guillem de Durfort (1, 255), Guillem Fabre (3:405), Guillem Gasmar (3:405), Guillem Godi (3:407), Guillem Uc d'Albi (3:407), Guillem d'Ieiras (3:407), Guillem de Lemotjas (3:407), Guillem de Mur (3:107), Guillem Peire de Cazas (2:424), Guillem de Salonis (3:408), Guionet (3:31), Enric (3:410), Izarn (2:42), Izarn Rizols (3:417), Joan Anguila (3:415), Jojos de Tolosa (3:416), Jordan

de l'Isla de Venessi (3:398), Lamberti de Bonanel (3:417), Lantelm
(3:417), Lemozi (3:418), Marques (3:419), Matfre Ermengau (3:418),
Matieus de Caerci (2:262), Le Moine de Foissan (2:224), Montan Sartre
(3:419), Olivier del Temple (3:421), Ozil de Cadarz (3:421), Palais
(3:421), Pauldt de Marseilla (3:138), Peire Basc (3:422), Peire de Cols
d'Aorlac (3:425), Peire Duran (3:419), Peire de Durban (3:425), Peire
Espaignol (3:427), Peire de Gavaret (3:425), Peire Guillem de Luzerna
(3:428), Peire Imbert (3:428), Peire Salvatge (3:152), Peire Torat
(3:428), Peire de Valeira (3:426), Pons de la Garda (2:311), Pons de
Montlaur (3:326), Pons d'Ortafas (3:431), Pons Santolh de Tholoza
(3:105, 431), Raimon (3:431),[3] Raimon Bistortz de Rusillon (3:396),
Raimon Escriva (3:431), Raimon Gaucelm de Beziers (3:187), Raimon
de Las Salas (3:394), Raimon Menudet (3:432), Raimon Rigaut (3:434),
Raimon Vidal de Bezaudu (3:277), Rodrigo (3:431), Rofin (3:434),
Rostaing de Mergas (3:435), Serveri de Girona (3:316), Sifre (3:435),
Taurel (3:436), Tomas (3:436), Uc (3:411), Uc Catola (3:414), Uc de
l'Escura (2:205), Uc de Murel (3:415).

Notes

[1] The orthography of Pillet and Carstens has been adopted. Millot gives all the
names in a French form. Many of the names on this list are drawn from C and R.
Sainte-Palaye relied heavily on these, possibly because the originals were easily
accessible. When the manuscripts record varying versions of a name, he in every
case adopted the reading of C and R. Thus, Jordan de l'Isla de Venessi in A and D
appears as Escudier de la Ylha in H and R, and as Ecuyer de l'Isle in the *Histoire
littéraire*. Similarly the name Joan Anguila appears only in C and R, which attribute
to this troubadour a poem attributed in all the other manuscripts to Berenguier
de Palazol. A poem attributed by D^a, I and K to Cadenet, but by C and R to
Tibaut de Blizon, is attributed in the *Histoire littéraire* to the latter.

[2] Millot also lists a Guiraut. This troubadour has been identified as Giraut
Riquier. (Cf. Pillet and Carstens, p. 93, *sub* Bofill.)

[3] Cf. Bartsch, *Grundriss* (1872), no. 393.

INDEX

Designed by Edward D. King.

Composed in 11/13 Janson with Janson display
by William J. Keller Inc.

Printed offset by William J. Keller Inc. on P & S, R.

Bound by The Haddon Craftsmen, Inc. in Riverside Linen.

Jacket printed in two colors on Kilmory Text
by John D. Lucas Printing Company.